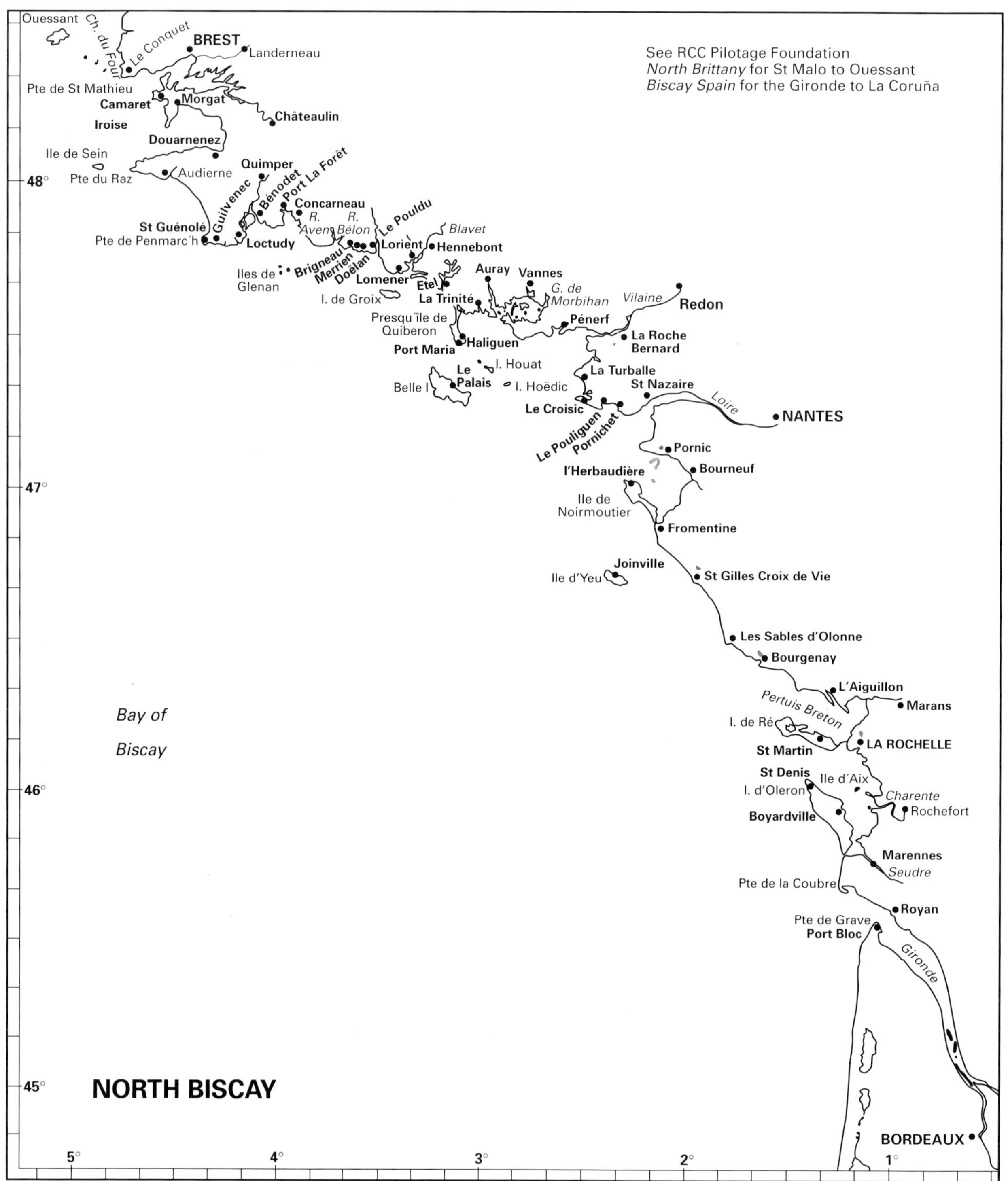

See RCC Pilotage Foundation
North Brittany for St Malo to Ouessant
Biscay Spain for the Gironde to La Coruña
Ouessant
Ch. du Four
Le Conquet
BREST
Landerneau
Pte de St Mathieu
Camaret
Morgat
Châteaulin
Iroise
Douarnenez
Ile de Sein
Pte du Raz
Audierne
Quimper
Bénodet
Port La Forêt
Guilvenec
Concarneau
R. Aven
R. Bélon
Le Pouldu
St Guénolé
Pte de Penmarc'h
Loctudy
Blavet
Lorient
Hennebont
Iles de Glenan
Brigneau
Merrien
Doëlan
Lomener
Etel
Auray
Vannes
G. de Morbihan
Vilaine
Redon
I. de Groix
La Trinité
Presqu'île de Quiberon
Pénerf
La Roche Bernard
Port Maria
Haliguen
I. Houat
La Turballe
Le Palais
Belle I
I. Hoëdic
St Nazaire
Le Croisic
Loire
NANTES
Le Pouliguen
Pornichet
Pornic
l'Herbaudière
Bourneuf
Ile de Noirmoutier
Fromentine
Joinville
Ile d'Yeu
St Gilles Croix de Vie
Les Sables d'Olonne
Bourgenay
L'Aiguillon
Marans
Pertuis Breton
I. de Ré
St Martin
LA ROCHELLE
St Denis
Ile d'Aix
I. d'Oleron
Charente
Rochefort
Boyardville
Marennes
Seudre
Pte de la Coubre
Royan
Pte de Grave
Port Bloc
Gironde
Bay of Biscay
NORTH BISCAY
BORDEAUX
48°
47°
46°
45°
5°
4°
3°
2°
1°

North Biscay

Ouessant to La Gironde

ROYAL CRUISING CLUB
PILOTAGE FOUNDATION

K. Adlard Coles
Revised by Gavin McLaren

Imray Laurie Norie & Wilson Ltd
St Ives Cambridgeshire England

Published by
Imray Laurie Norie & Wilson Ltd
Wych House St Ives Huntingdon
Cambridgeshire PE17 4BT, England
☎ +44 (0)1480 462114 *Fax* +44 (0)1480 496109
E-mail ilnw@imray.com
Web http://www.imray.com

Partly based on *Harbours and Anchorages Vols I and II* by K Adlard Coles, first published in 1959 and 1960.

As *North Biscay Pilot* published by Adlard Coles Ltd
Revised by Professor A N Black
Second edition 1977
Reprinted with amendments 1978
Third edition 1982
Revised by the RCC Pilotage Foundation
Reprinted with amendments 1985
Reprinted with amendments 1987
Fourth edition 1990
Fifth edition 1994
Sixth edition 2000

ISBN 0 85288 416 8

British Library Cataloguing in Publication Data.
A catalogue record for this book is available from the British Library.

CAUTION
Every effort has been made to ensure the accuracy of this book. It contains selected information and thus is not definitive and does not include all known information on the subject in hand; this is particularly relevant to the plans, which should not be used for navigation. The Pilotage Foundation believes that its selection is a useful aid to prudent navigation, but the safety of a vessel depends ultimately on the judgement of the navigator, who should assess all information, published or unpublished.

CORRECTIONS
The editor would be glad to receive any corrections, information or suggestions which would improve the book. Letters should be addressed to the Editor, *North Biscay*, care of the publishers. The more precise the information the better, but even partial or doubtful information is helpful, if it is made clear what the doubts are.

CORRECTIONAL SUPPLEMENTS
This pilot book will be amended at intervals by the issue of correctional supplements. These are published on the internet at our web site www.imray.com and may be downloaded free of charge. Printed copies are also available on request from the publishers at the above address.

PLANS
The plans in this guide are not to be used for navigation – they are designed to support the text and should always be used together with navigational charts. Even so, every effort has been made to locate harbour and anchorage plans adjacent to the relevant text. They are not suitable for the plotting of positions from electronic navigation systems such as GPS.

It should be borne in mind that the characteristics of lights may be changed during the life of the book, and that in any case notification of such changes is unlikely to be reported immediately. When the book is no longer new, light characteristics, both in the text and on the plans, may be updated from the current edition of the *Admiralty List of Lights*.

All bearings are given from seaward and refer to true north. Scales may be taken from the scales of latitude. Symbols are based on those used by the British Admiralty – users are referred to *Symbols and Abbreviations (Chart 5011)*.

Printed in Great Britain by Butler & Tanner Ltd, Frome, Somerset

Contents

Foreword

The Royal Cruising Club Pilotage Foundation was created by members of the RCC to enable them and others to bring their experience of sailing and cruising to a wider public and to encourage the aspiring sailor to cruise further afield with confidence. It was established in 1977 as a registered charity whose object is 'to advance the education of the public in the science and practice of navigation'. Initial funding was provided by a very generous gift by an American member, Dr Fred Ellis, and the gift of the copyrights of several books from other RCC members has allowed the Foundation to fulfil its remit by producing and maintaining pilot books and cruising guides. It now manages the production and updating of over 20 such books.

Adlard Coles' original book – *Biscay Harbours and Anchorages* – was first published in 1959 and the 6th Edition marks 40 years of regular updating. The work of preparing this edition of North Biscay was undertaken by Gavin McLaren who researched the area most thoroughly by land and sea. He was helped by other members of the RCC and many others interested in the project, noted elsewhere. The Pilotage Foundation is most grateful to Gavin McLaren and to all other contributors.

In order to keep this book up-to-date during its lifetime, supplements are produced by the Foundation and published by Imray. To assist us in doing this we need feedback from users and we ask that you send us (through Imray) updated information and any comments that you feel would benefit others. Contributions – large or small – are carefully considered and collated in annual amendments which may be obtained free of charge from Imray.

Francis Walker
Director
RCC Pilotage Foundation
October 1999

ACKNOWLEDGEMENTS

In preparing the present edition, I was able to visit and photograph the many harbours and anchorages in North Biscay by sea. It would however, have been impossible to complete the work without the valuable assistance of harbourmasters, members of the RCC and of other British yachtsmen and women.

I am particularly grateful to Peter Carnegie (RCC) who generously gave his time and expertise to take the majority of the aerial photographs which form such an important part of this pilot, and to John Lawson (RCC) the editor of *Biscay Spain*, for permission to make use of his research material in the chapter on the Gironde.

Many others provided information and assistance. Amongst those to whom thanks are due are: Eve Bonham-Cozens (RCC), Anna Brunyee (RCC), Peter and Clare Bishton, John Davys, Michael Forster (RCC), Mike Grubb (RCC), Nick Heath (RCC), Alan Hopton and the staff of Marine Instruments Falmouth, Claire James, John Power (RCC), Andrew Pool (RCC).

Those who sailed with me aboard *Margaret Wroughton* during the research certainly had no holiday. I am grateful to Tim Bolton, Chris Haughton, Morag Johnson, Georgie McLaren, Eon Reyneke and Stuart Wilson for their hard work, companionship and assistance.

Gavin McLaren
Falmouth
October 1999

Also by the RCC Pilotage Foundation

Published by Imray Laurie Norie & Wilson Ltd
Islas Baleares
Mediterranean Spain – Costas del Sol & Blanca – Costas del Azahar, Dorada & Brava
The Baltic Sea
Atlantic Spain and Portugal
Atlantic Islands
North Biscay
Biscay Spain
North Brittany
Channel Islands
Lesser Antilles
North Africa
Faroe, Iceland & Greenland
Chile

Published by A & C Black Ltd
Atlantic Crossing Guide
Pacific Crossing Guide

Published by RCC Desktop Publishing Unit
Cruising Guide to West Africa
The Falkland Islands Shores
The South Atlantic Coast of South America

Introduction

Cruising in South Brittany and Biscay

A small yacht heading for the Bay of Biscay will pass Ouessant, often passing inside through the Chenal du Four. After she has rounded Pointe de St Mathieu, the Rade de Brest lies to the east, providing a magnificent cruising ground. Next comes the Baie de Douarnenez, a fine big bay, having however only two secure harbours.

Bound south, a vessel will next pass through the Raz de Sein. Here, as in the Chenal du Four, the tidal streams are strong and in bad weather the seas are dangerous, but once through the channel the Bay of Biscay is entered. The tidal streams are weaker and the weather becomes progressively warmer the further south one sails. Between Penmarc'h and La Rochelle there are three granite islands, Ile de Groix, Belle Ile and Ile d'Yeu, each of which has a harbour and minor anchorages. To the north and east of these islands, the mainland coast offers the variety of harbours and anchorages which makes it so attractive to the cruiser. There are anchorages in deep water and shallow, fishing harbours, busy ports, sophisticated holiday resorts, yachting centres, estuaries and peaceful rivers.

The first busy sailing area to be reached is the large bay from Loctudy to Concarneau, sheltered by the Iles de Glénan with their famous sailing school. Thence some passage-making leads to the Baie de Quiberon, another sheltered area, very popular with French yachtsmen. Here, between the yachting centres of La Trinité and Le Croisic, there lie all the anchorages in the Morbihan ('the little sea'), Pénerf and the beautiful Vilaine river. To seaward there are the little islands of Houat and Hoëdic, and to the W Belle Ile with the crowded harbour of Le Palais and another, at Sauzon. In this area one could spend a month exploring and sailing in shelter even in bad weather.

Beyond Le Croisic is the Loire, the southern boundary of Brittany. The coastal scene changes, rock reluctantly, but never entirely, giving place to sandy shores. The character of the harbours changes too; there are not so many harbours in which a yacht can lie afloat and come and go freely at any state of the tide. On this part of the coast there are two large islands, Noirmoutier and Ile d'Yeu. Noirmoutier offers interesting anchorages, and one marina. Port Joinville is the only good harbour on Ile d'Yeu.

Another passage leads to the area around Ile de Ré and La Rochelle. La Rochelle is an historic city with two fine old towers guarding the entrance to the harbour and with a vast marina. Equally historic, Ile de Ré is low and sandy. St Martin, the capital, has a secure harbour with a wet dock and there is a new marina at the north end of the island.

Beyond La Rochelle lies Pertuis d'Antioche between Ile d'Oléron and the mainland. Traditionally this area was little visited by cruising yachtsmen due to its lack of harbours, but this has changed. There are now three harbours on Ile d'Oléron where a yacht will remain afloat and at Rochefort, up the Charente river the basins in the 17th century town have been converted into an attractive marina. With its generally fine summer weather, sheltered water and sandy beaches this area, together with the Ile de Ré, is becoming increasingly popular. This marks the end of the cruising grounds described in this book, but a brief description of the Gironde estuary and river is included for those yachtsmen bound to the Canal du Midi, which connects with the Mediterranean.

Getting there

The cruising area which this book covers is a fascinating and varied one. For many British yachtsmen, the difficulty lies in the time taken to get there and return within the span of a summer holiday. A good plan is to work the yacht down Channel in weekends before the real cruise begins, setting off across the channel from one of the West Country ports to the South Brittany coast. The English Channel is fairly wide here; it is about 110 miles from Falmouth to Ouessant.

The choice of destination on the French coast will depend on the time available for a cruise, the area to be visited and the weather. If it is intended to cruise south of the Raz de Sein there is much to be said for passing outside Ouessant. The wind during the summer is most likely to be from between southwest and northwest and with a little luck Ouessant can be weathered without a tack. From there it is best for a yacht to head for the most southerly port on her itinerary. She can then cruise back up the coast – which is likely to involve more windward work – in shorter stages, visiting a selection of the harbours en route.

The distances involved are not great – from Falmouth direct to Belle Ile is 210 miles, which would probably involve a modern yacht in only a single night at sea. La Rochelle is only another 110 miles further on and can usually be reached in 48 hours. If taking this course, in fine weather the shipping lanes can be crossed north of Ouessant, and the inshore traffic zone taken passing close to the island. In thick or heavy weather it is best to pass outside the shipping lanes and to cross them south of Ouessant when turning in towards the coast.

Those passing inside Ouessant should aim to reach the entrance to the Chenal du Four when the tide will be fair. The Chenal is much easier than it looks from a casual glance at the chart and in fine weather presents no difficulties. Yachts passing through the Four usually stop at Camaret and then make their way further south in stages. The tidal streams in the Raz de Sein and off Pte de Penmarc'h will be significant factors when planning the cruise.

Because of time constraints, many British yachts are left in Brittany either before or after a cruise. There are many suitable ports. The following are particularly recommended: Brest, Port La Forêt, Vannes, Pornic, La Rochelle (Minimes), Rochefort. At all of these places security appears good, the staff are helpful and there is likely to be space away from the visitors pontoons for a yacht to remain undisturbed. From them, it is comparatively easy to reach Roscoff or St Malo for ferries, or Paris for Eurostar.

Shallow-draught yachts which do not wish to make the passage down Channel and through the rough waters of Four and Sein can use the Breton Canals. The usual exit from these is to La Vilaine, but it is also possible to go on to Nantes and travel down the Loire. The real canal enthusiast, if his draught is small enough, can turn aside at Redon, where he is almost at sea, and after another hundred locks, emerge at Lorient.

Winds

Winds in the north of Biscay are variable, but westerly winds (SW to NW) are most frequent in the summer months, especially in July and August. In spring, early summer and late autumn, winds between N and E are also common. The Bay of Biscay has a reputation for gales, but from May to September winds of force 7 and over are recorded only about once in 25 days. Most summer gales are associated with depressions passing to the northward, with backing winds followed by a veer to the W or NW. At intervals of several years, very severe short storms may occur. Beware of a sudden fall in the barometer in muggy, thundery weather, with poor visibility.

Land and sea breezes near the coast are common in settled summer weather. Especially in the southern part of the area they result in the *vent solaire*. After a noonday calm a westerly sea breeze sets in. This goes round to NW and by evening to N and finally about midnight, or a little later, it settles in the NE, when it sometimes blows very freshly, causing quite a rough sea, and continues until about eight in the morning.

Visibility

Fog, mist or haze is quite frequent during the summer. There is visibility of under 5 miles on about one day in five, but real fog, reducing visibility to less than ½ mile, averages only one day in twenty. The coast is so well marked by beacons and towers that navigation in poor visibility is possible, but thick fog is very unpleasant if it occurs when one is sailing in narrow tidal waters.

Swell

Swell is a factor which sometimes has to be reckoned with on the northwest and west coasts of France. It appears to run higher in some parts than others, and is notable in the vicinity of Ouessant and northeast of Le Four. In the Bay of Biscay itself swell seems to be less frequent as the weather is better, and the swell is rarely as uncomfortable as between Ile Vierge and Ouessant.

A large swell will break heavily on bars and in shallow water, with the result that the approaches to some of the harbours, such as Bélon, Le Pouldu and Etel, are dangerous even in fine weather if there is a swell. Swell can break intermittently and dangerously on rocks rising from deep water, even when there is apparently a safe depth over them.

Another characteristic of swell is that when it enters a narrowing inlet it tends to increase in height and steepness. It funnels up the entrance and will surge into anchorages which one would expect to be sheltered from the direction of the swell. For this reason, anchorages open to the Atlantic, such as those on the W side of Ile de Groix, Belle Ile and Ile d'Yeu, should be used only with caution, in settled weather, with an offshore wind and in the absence of swell. Furthermore, if ground swell manifests itself in calm weather (and it can arrive with little warning, originating in disturbances far out in the ocean), a vessel should leave the open anchorage before it builds up. French fishermen take swell seriously, and none should know better. The French weather forecasts for shipping include forecasts of swell (*la houle*).

Type of yacht – draught and drying out

The North Biscay coast suits all types of yacht, large or small, deep-keeled or shallow-draught.

For large yachts there are plenty of deep-water harbours; most of the shallower harbours can be entered near high water, and the yacht can dry out against a quay. Before doing so it is best to make local enquiries, as the bottom in parts of some harbours is rough or rocky. Good fenders are needed, as quay walls are often very rough; they should be hard and not squashy or they will be squeezed flat and the yacht will lean heavily inwards.

French fishing vessels and many French yachts are equipped with legs. Not only can they dry out against a quay more safely, but they can dry out anywhere in any sheltered anchorage if the bottom is smooth and hard. Legs are a great asset to cruising on the Biscay coast. Best of all is a bilge-keel yacht that can take the ground. She can often find a snug berth inside the local moorings while her deep-keeled sister is rolling farther out.

Where reference is made in the text to a 'yacht which can take the ground', it is implied that she does not need the outside support of a quay wall.

A very large number of French yachtsmen sail dinghies or small yachts that are launched from trailers and the launching facilities are good nearly everywhere. It is quite easy, therefore, to trail a boat out and spend a happy holiday on this coast exploring its nooks and crannies, rocks and sands.

Navigating among rocks

The coast of Brittany and North Biscay is famous for its rocks which, to a stranger, may cause some apprehension. This will especially be the case if he is accustomed to mud pilotage, as on the east coast of England. He will soon come to realise that, although it is much more important to avoid hitting the bottom, the many landmarks, natural and man-made, make it easy to know exactly where he is.

Beacons and towers are permanent, although occasionally damaged by gales. It is often said that less reliance should be placed on buoys, which may drag their moorings during gales, though in 30 years I have never found one out of position. Many of the rocks and shoals shown on the charts are not dangerous to moderate-draught yachts, except in bad weather, when they may cause the seas to break. Much depends upon the state of the tide.

It is useful to estimate the height of tide at the time when a harbour is to be approached, and then to mark on the chart each rock or shoal which will not have a safe depth of water over it. It is often surprising to find how few they are, so that pilotage is simplified by concentrating on the rocks which may be dangerous.

A common feature of a rocky coast is the extension of a pronounced headland in the form of a reef continuing seaward under water. For this reason, when approaching an inlet between two promontories, never cut across one of the promontories to the entrance, unless the chart indicates clear water. Approach from seaward with the middle of the inlet well open, allowing for the probable extension of the promontory under water.

If there is a big swell the seas will probably break over sunken rocks which are dangerous, and it may be necessary to avoid rocks which are covered by water of a depth equal to several times the yacht's draught. In strong streams the presence of rocks may be indicated by rips, or in smooth water by circles of oily-looking water. Even in deep water an uneven bottom causes a disturbance on the surface if the current is strong, so the oily circles do not always denote danger. In parts of Brittany the water is very clear, and if a member of the crew stands forward he can often see underwater rocks.

Some harbours, such as the Ile de Sein and St Guénolé, have many rocks in the approaches. These present no great difficulty to the experienced cruiser, but a newcomer to these coasts may prefer to limit his explorations on the first occasion to the better known and more easily accessible harbours. The more difficult anchorages should only be attempted in settled weather with clear visibility and preferably at neaps. The transits and landmarks should be identified with certainty before the yacht enters the danger area of rocks.

It is a good idea to check the yacht's position regularly by reference to natural features. New beacons can be built, or one mistaken for another, the large white building can be rendered inconspicuous by a larger whiter building, but nobody replaces or removes headlands or islands.

The advent of GPS has had a very marked influence on navigation, both when on passage and when inshore. On passage it enables the coast to be approached more closely at night or in poor visibility. Inshore a yachts position can be plotted quickly and with certainty. Having done so the navigator can immediately tell where he must look to find a particular buoy, headland or other object. In pilotage this should be the main use of GPS. It should not be used in narrow passages as a substitute for the navigational marks.

There are places where GPS might enable passages to be made which would not be possible without its use. These should only be attempted by the experienced and even then only after careful consideration of all the factors including GPS accuracy, chart and receiver datums and equipment reliability.

When navigating using waypoints it is very important to be continuously aware of the cross track error – the distance the yacht has strayed from the direct line between two waypoints. On this coast one is continually passing close to rocks and the fact that the yacht is heading for a safe waypoint is no guarantee that she is not in danger. Waypoints should always be taken from the chart; although lists of waypoint positions are published, by selecting and plotting his own the navigator becomes immediately aware of the dangers which may be close to them. *Positions given at the start of each chapter in this book are not for GPS use.* They are rather intended to assist the stranger in locating a particular harbour or anchorage on the chart.

British Admiralty charts of the Biscay coast are all referenced to the European Datum. This can differ from the WGS84 datum, on which most GPS sets operate by default, by as much as 150m, a significant distance in many places.

Harbours

In artificial harbours formed by breakwaters, it is inadvisable to cross close off the end of a breakwater, as these are often built on rocks or have rocks at their bases. When entering a strange harbour it is best to approach about midway between the jetties.

Mooring

It may be worth mentioning some methods of mooring which are more common in France than in Britain. The first is lying closely packed, side by side, with a mooring or anchor ahead and the stern pulled in to a quay or pontoon. If it is necessary to lay out an anchor ahead, one must note the direction in which the chains of those already berthed lead, and lay the anchor accordingly. Sometimes there is a line of buoys to which to secure the bow. Sometimes the pick-up rope for the bow mooring is led back to the pontoon; this can be tricky, as one has to back into the pontoon before getting the mooring on board, unless one sends out a dinghy.

Another method of mooring uses a large metal buoy. Each new arrival takes a bow rope to the buoy and a cluster forms. When this is full a second circle is sometimes formed, by anchoring and taking a line to the buoy.

All of these methods call for a good supply of fenders.

Anchoring and moorings

It is a sad fact that the Biscay coast is now so crowded with yachts that many of the traditional anchorages are occupied by moorings. Sometimes it is possible to anchor outside them, but often they occupy all of the available space. Even where room to anchor can be found, a yacht is likely to be in a less sheltered position or to be in the stream. Because of the congestion, the use of anchor buoys, which result in a yacht taking up a great deal more space than she need, should be avoided unless the bottom is known to be foul.

Often a mooring must be hired or borrowed. A mooring marked *V* or *Visiteur* should be chosen if available. If one must lie on a private mooring then it should be chosen with care. If it has a maximum weight or length on the buoy, do not exceed this. If, as is more likely, it does not then the size of boat for which it is intended can be judged to some degree by the size of the tackle and the dimensions of the other boats on moorings nearby. One should take great care not to chafe the gear. A yacht should never be left unattended on a private mooring unless it is certain that the owner will not require it.

On any mooring the state of the buoy and the riser may give an indication of the condition of the mooring, but this is no guarantee. Many a bright shiny chain is secured to the ground tackle by an ancient, corroded shackle.

Provisions

Ordinary provisions can be bought in all towns, most of which have a supermarket, and even in small villages there are shops which supply necessities and are open long hours. Very small communities sometimes rely on a travelling shop, which is less convenient. Groceries and meat are similarly priced to the UK. Seafood such as mussels, crabs and prawns is good and reasonably priced when bought in the market, though lobsters, alas, command their price anywhere. French bread is delicious, but does not keep. A *baguette* can sometimes be given a second life after 24 hours if placed in a hot oven for a short time. If bread is required to remain edible for several days, buy *pain complet*, which is similar to a wholemeal loaf. Where there is a baker, bread will be available early, but there may be a delay where it comes by van.

In the text, under *Facilities*, 'all shops' implies at least bread, grocer, butcher, cooked meats and usually ironmonger as well.

Telephones

Most public telephones now require cards and few accept coins. Cards can be bought in tobacconists, bars and post offices as well as other shops. There is good GSM mobile phone coverage of most of the coast, but it is more patchy on the islands.

Water

If there is a marina or pontoon berths it may be assumed that water is available on them and it is not mentioned in the text under facilities. At other places, water may only be available in cans. If lying on a harbour wall the water supply may be of a size more suitable for a large fishing boat than for a yacht.

French marinas' water taps rarely have hoses so a yacht should carry her own, with a set of threaded adapters. These are obtainable from some British garden centres. If piped water is available it can be assumed that it is safe to drink, but it should be left to run for a while as there may be stagnant water in the pipes. As dogs often frequent French marinas it is as well to give the tap a good wash before use.

Fuel

Diesel and petrol are available at the waterside in many places. Duty-free diesel is not permitted for yachts and occasionally there will only be an untaxed pump for fishermen.

It is now common for pumps to be card operated. At present UK cards do not contain the necessary microchip and will not work. (This situation also arises at '24 hour' roadside petrol stations.) A marina attendant, or even a friendly local yachtsman, can usually be persuaded to operate the pump for cash.

Formalities

EU countries, including the UK but not the Channel Islands, no longer require yachts travelling from one EU country to another to report their departure or arrival, unless dutiable or prohibited goods are carried, or non-EU nationals are on board. Yachts arriving from non-EU countries should fly a Q flag and report to customs on arrival.

It is essential to carry on board evidence that VAT has been paid on the vessel, and all yachts visiting France must carry a Certificate of Registry. Either full or small ships registration is acceptable. Documents must be originals and not photocopies. Heavy, on the spot, fines are imposed on defaulters.

Personal passports should be carried by all members of the ship's company. In practice they are likely to be required only for cashing cheques, for independent return to the UK by public transport and, in the case of the owner, for dealing with the Customs.

During its stay in French waters a yacht may be boarded on several occasions by Customs – including when underway. During the first visit ask for *une fiche*; if the officers are satisfied, you will be given one to show that the vessel has been cleared. Should you be approached at a later date, it may only be necessary to show *la fiche* to satisfy the officials.

It is no longer forbidden for one skipper to hand over to another in French waters, but owners must be aware of, and abide by, European VAT regulations and the French regulations for chartering.

Fishing boats and yachts share most Biscay harbours

Search and rescue

The French search and rescue organisations (CROSS CORSEN north of Pointe du Raz; CROSS ETEL, south of Pointe du Raz) operate an excellent passage-surveillance service. Some harbourmasters require a form to be completed showing 'where from' and 'where to'. This information is passed on to CROSS CORSEN/CROSS ETEL. It is important that, if a yacht does not go to where she has said she is going, the information should be reported quickly. Otherwise a futile search may be instituted.

Yacht clubs

There are yacht clubs and sailing schools in most French harbours; they are invariably hospitable to visitors. Assistance or advice is always given readily, and showers are often available.

Laying up

In order to spend more time on the Biscay coast, it may be convenient to leave the yacht in France for the winter. The cruise can be continued the following year. There are many ports where this is possible, those mentioned under *Getting there* above are particularly suitable, but are by no means the only ones for a longer stay. Considerable savings are usually made compared with an English south coast marina – these savings generally become more noticeable the further south in Biscay one lays up.

Radio

The times given under the *Radio* heading for marinas refer to the times that watch is kept during the sailing season. In the winter, more limited hours may apply. MF and HF radio frequencies are not covered.

Facilities

Not all facilities can be listed for every harbour and some common sense must be used. For example, in a large town it may be assumed that there are café-bars and they are therefore not mentioned; likewise it is unreasonable to expect a small village to have a large department store, even if the text reads 'all shops'. If there is a marina it may be assumed that there is water and electricity available on the pontoons, that there are showers and toilets and that the weather forecast is displayed. Only the absence of these facilities is mentioned in such harbours. The numbers of visitors berths are not generally given as in the season permanent berths are often made available for visitors.

Colourful Breton fishing boats crowd together in many harbours

The average size of French yachts seems to be somewhat smaller than those from Britain. There are comparatively few berths in most harbours for yachts over 12m LOA and proportionately few visitors' berths for yachts above that size. That being said, most harbourmasters will manage to squeeze a larger yacht in somehow if they possibly can, but it may not be a very easy berth.

Fishermen

There are many fishermen's dan buoys round the coast and sometimes well out to sea. They present a hazard, especially at night when under power, and a constant lookout is necessary. The buoys are usually in pairs, flying the owner's particular flag. If the pair can be identified, it is advisable not to pass between them.

South from Lorient a line of very small floats may be seen running between the larger dans. Do not pass between these pairs of dans!

Charts, tides and navigation

In this pilot metres (m) are used to measure short distances and depths. Larger distances remain in nautical miles (M).

Chart datum

Datum in this pilot, both in the text and in the plans is the same as British Admiralty charts; soundings are reduced to the level of the lowest predicted tides, referred to as LAT (lowest astronomical tide). This level is very seldom reached. In exceptional meteorological conditions, tides can fall below the datum, but this is extremely rare, as for it to happen such conditions would have to combine with very big spring tides.

This datum is of the utmost importance when navigating in the Bay of Biscay for it means that at an average LW springs there will be up to 1m more water than is shown on the chart, and at mean LW neaps up to 2·6m more.

Heights

Heights of land or rocks that never cover is given above MHWS. Drying heights of rocks or shoals that cover and uncover are given above chart datum. On the plans such soundings are underlined. This is a changed practice from previous editions, but is that used on British Admiralty charts.

Lighthouses

The elevation of the lights (not the actual heights of the structures) is given above MHWS.

Traditional boats are popular in France and are frequently seen in Biscay

Directions

The description of each port is set out in the same form, so that the reader will come to know where to look for the information he wants. It is written from the point of view of the skipper of a sailing yacht of normal size. Depths of more than 3m are described as deep, on the assumption that users of this book will not have a greater draught than this. Low bridges are treated as blocking navigation; although many motor yachts will be able to pass them unhindered, the upper reaches beyond them have not been inspected.

It is assumed that yachts are fitted with auxiliary power and are equipped with GPS. Although neither of these are essential for cruising this coast, both are now so widespread that a yacht without them must be considered unusual. In particular, the use of GPS makes the identification of harbours generally easy. No longer must the yachtsman, from a doubtful position, try to identify particular natural features or buildings to find his destination. From a known safe position in the offing, provided by GPS, the bearing of the harbour can be measured from the chart and the entrance identified.

Beacons

The offshore marks on this coast are subject to damage in bad weather which may not be repaired for some months. Beacons and beacon towers can lose their topmarks or even be totally destroyed. In this case a small buoy with the appropriate marking may be positioned close by until a repair is effected.

Beacons are commonly painted to conform with the buoyage systems (cardinal or lateral) and have the appropriate topmarks. The heads of breakwaters, forming a harbour entrance, are often marked with white paint, with a green triangle or red square indicating the side on which to pass them. When passing under a bridge there may be similar marks to indicate the appropriate arch for the channel.

Key to plans

The plans follow, where possible, normal British Admiralty chart conventions

Most plans have been subdivided along the left-hand and bottom margins into tenths of a minute of latitude and longitude. The use of identical units in each plan should give an immediate indication of the scale. Alternatively, in some large-scale plans, a scale of metres is shown on the plan.

Dry land is tinted grey, drying areas are blue/grey. Areas where the depth is less than 2 metres are shown blue and deep water is left white. On some charts the blue tinting is extended to the 5-metre contour, giving an extra margin of safety. When first entering an area, for safety, keep in the white if possible.

Symbols used on plans

- ⚓ harbourmaster/port office
- ⛽ fuel
- ⊖ customs
- ✉ post office
- ◣ slipway
- ⚓ anchorage
- ⚓ anchoring prohibited
- Ⓥ visitor's berths

See Admiralty chart 5011 for the full list of hydrographic symbols and abbreviations

Bearings

Bearings are expressed in degrees true, but in the text magnetic bearings in points are occasionally given to indicate the approximate direction of a course or object. Variation is at present approximately 5°W in the north and 2°W in the south of the area.

Lights

The descriptions of all the lights to be used in entering a port are collected into one tabulation to assist in identification. The heights are given in metres (m), and the range of visibility is given in miles (M). Where a light has sectors the limits of the sectors are usually shown on the plan. Details of the lights on buoys with a height of over 7m are given, but smaller buoys are only included if they are particularly important to the yachtsman.

The distance at which a light may be seen depends on two things, its brightness and its height. Although its loom may be visible from a very long way off, a light itself cannot be seen when it is below the observer's horizon. Tables at which lights of various heights can be seen from different heights of eye are given in most almanacs.

The distance at which a light is visible depends also on the clarity of the atmosphere at the time. A 'nominal' range can be calculated for each light; this is the range its rays will reach if the meteorological visibility is 10M. It is this nominal range (given in Admiralty light lists) which is quoted in this book. Before accepting it at face value, the yachtsman should look up the range at which the light will come above his particular horizon as this may be less than the range quoted. On a clear day the light may shine further than the nominal range. Conversely on a hazy day its light may not reach the observer, even if it is above his horizon. Lights with a nominal range of 10M or less are relatively weak and may be difficult to identify among other lights on the shore.

The characteristics referred to in the text are for 1999, and are liable to alterations which will be shown on chart corrections and in the current *Admiralty List of Lights Volumes A and D.*

Although the general practice is for coloured sectors to indicate dangers and white sectors the clear passages, this is not universal and it should not be assumed that the white sectors indicate deep water over the whole sector at all distances from the light. Generally, if a light shows a white safe sector with red and green sectors on each side, the green sector is to starboard and the red to port, at least in the principal channel. This rule is not universal and should be checked for each light. Narrow intensified sectors usually, but not always, fall within the safe width of the channel.

Lights are often 'directional'; that is, they show brightly over a very narrow sector and sometimes faintly outside the sector.

Tides

Tidal streams

The tidal streams are of great significance on the coast, both when passage-making and when cruising, particularly in light weather and fog. The *Admiralty Tidal Stream Atlas for France, West Coast (NP 265)*, is recommended. It shows the main streams, and at a glance the overall picture can be grasped. Inshore, there are local variations and numerous eddies. Sometimes these can be estimated from the pot buoys, which are numerous on the coast.

Compared to, say, the English Channel the tidal stream in open waters is not strong. But in the narrow harbour entrances, amongst rocks and shoals and in some of the constricted passages it runs fast. If the wind is against the stream, particularly if it is a strong wind and a spring stream, overfalls will develop and sometimes these can be dangerous. Places where particular attention needs to be paid to the stream include: Chenal du Four, Goulet de Brest, Raz de Sein, Quiberon bay, the Morbihan entrance, La Gironde.

Tidal heights

The corrections to be applied to the times and heights of HW and LW Brest or Pointe de Grave (the standard ports for this coast, used in *Admiralty Tide Tables*) are given in each chapter. By applying them, with appropriate interpolation, to the published times at the standard ports the times and heights of local HW and LW are calculated. Heights at intermediate times can be determined using the tidal graph for the appropriate standard port – these graphs are reproduced in Appendix A. Such precision is not often needed and more usually the 'rule of 12ths' described in many navigation textbooks will suffice.

French tide tables give a coefficient for each tide. The coefficient is a measure of the rise and fall; large coefficients equate to spring tides and smaller ones to neaps. They are significant to the yachtsmen as the times at which a harbour is accessible or at which a lock gate opens are often given in harbour offices relative to the coefficient. Appendix B gives a table to convert the coefficient to the approximate heights of HW and LW at Brest or Pointe de Grave or vice versa.

It is worth noting that on the coast – as opposed to up rivers or within the Morbihan – the times of HW and LW only occasionally differ from those of the standard port by more than 30 minutes.

It should not be forgotten that *Admiralty Tide Tables* give predictions in French standard time and that the local corrections given in the chapters of this book apply to those times. Only after the corrections have been applied should an hour be added to convert the result to French summer time (if appropriate).

Weather forecasts

Forecasts broadcast by the French coastal stations are more detailed than those broadcast by the BBC and the English coastal stations. The form of the forecast is: the general situation, followed by, for each area, firstly for the next 12 hours general weather type, wind direction and speed in knots, state of sea (*calme* to 0·1m, *belle* to 0·5m, *peu agitée* to 1·25m, *agitée* to 2·5m, *forte* to 4m, *très forte* to 6m = 20ft, *grosse* to 9m, *très grosse* to 14m, *énorme* the rest), swell (if necessary) and visibility in M; secondly for the following 12 hours similar information in rather less detail; finally, the outlook. The forecasts are read slowly and repeated, so they are not hard to follow with even limited French.

Some less familiar words: *brume* = mist, *coup de vent* = gale, *averses* = showers, *houle* = swell, *syroit* = southwest, *noroit* = northwest, *sudé* = southeast, *nordé* = northeast.

There are also forecasts broadcast by the national stations, including a special one for yachtsmen, during the summer only, on long wave.

The sea areas covered by this book are Ouest Bretagne (Brest to Quiberon), Nord Gascogne (Quiberon to Les Sables d'Olonne) and Sud Gascogne (south of Les Sables d'Olonne). The broadcasts are detailed below. The times change occasionally but up-to-date information can be obtained from harbourmasters and marinas, or from a commercial almanac. For those of us with less than fluent French a tape recorder is useful for the forecast.

Les Centres Régionaux Opérationnels de Surveillance et de Sauvetage (CROSS) Forecasts

Broadcasts weather information from stations as shown.

Times UT+1; add one hour for French summer time.

Stiff Ch 79 – 0715, 1115, 1545, 1915
Raz Ch 79 – 0445, 0703, 1103, 1533, 1903
Penmarc'h Ch 80 – 0703, 1533, 1903
Groix Ch 80 – 0715, 1545, 1915
Belle Ile Ch 80 – 0733, 1603, 1933
St Nazaire Ch 80 – 0745, 1615, 1945
Ile d'Yeu Ch 80 – 0803, 1633, 2003
Sables d'Olonne Ch 80 – 0815, 1645, 2015
Chassiron Ch 79 – 0703, 1533, 1903

Yachtsmen's forecasts

France-Inter 162kHz (1852m LW) 2003 LT

Port signals

The French authorities use two systems of signals to control the traffic into harbours. These are best explained by means of the following diagrams.

By day and night three green lights one above the other signify that the port is open but that there are obstructions in the channel and vessels must navigate with caution. The traffic signals are not usually hoisted for yachts, and they should therefore be regarded more as a signal to keep out of the way of large vessels.

Fig. i International port symbols

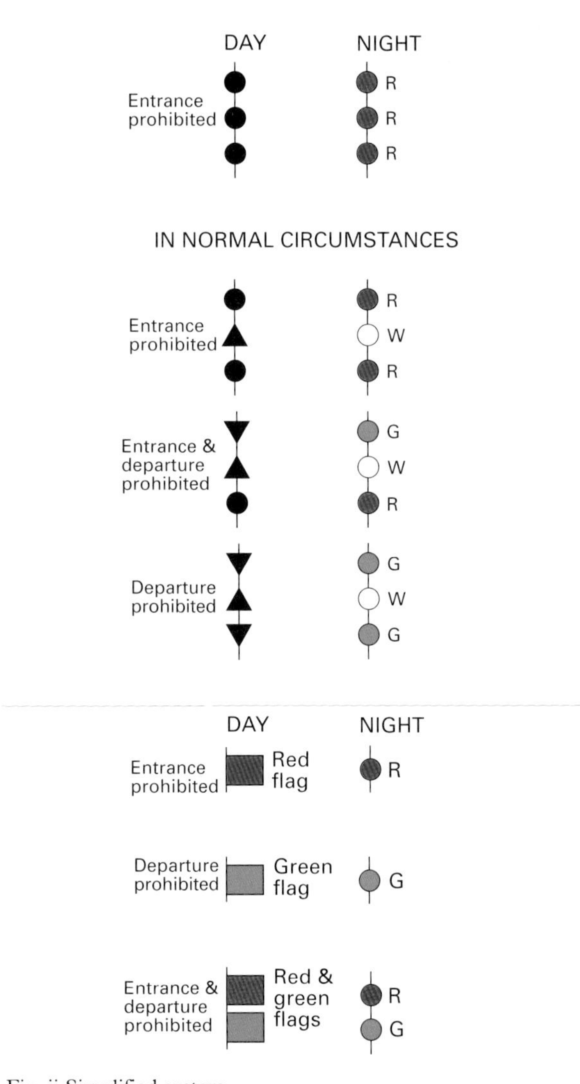

Fig. ii Simplified system

Charts

For the British yachtsman cruising in the Bay of Biscay Admiralty charts are recommended. They give excellent cover of the area and use familiar conventions, abbreviations and symbology. They are obtainable from Admiralty chart agents, which means, in effect that they must be obtained before leaving English waters. They can be kept corrected from Admiralty *Notices to Mariners*, published weekly and obtainable from chart agents, or from the quarterly small craft summaries. Imray, Laurie, Norie & Wilson Ltd, Wych House, The Broadway, St Ives, Huntingdon, Cambridgeshire PE17 4BT ☎ 01480 462114 *Fax* 01480 496109 *E-mail* ilnw@imray.com, will supply Admiralty charts and publications.

Imray, Laurie, Norie & Wilson Ltd publish eight charts, Nos C35 to C42, covering the coast from L'Aberwrac'h to the Pointe de Grave. They include large-scale insets of harbours. Bulletins of corrections may be obtained from the publishers. These charts are adequate for passage-making and for entering the harbours for which plans are included, but are not sufficiently detailed for work close inshore or some of the more intricate channels

Only in a very few places will it be necessary for the yachtsman to use French charts, although these naturally provide the most comprehensive cover of the coast. Increasingly British Admiralty charts are replicas of their French equivalents, only the symbols and appearance being changed to reflect British practice.

British Admiralty charts

Chart	*Title*	*Scale*
20	Ile d'Ouessant to Pte de la Coubre	500,000
304	Lorient Harbour	10,000
	Blavet river	12,500
798	Goulet de Brest to Chausée de Sein including Bai de Douarnenez	60,000
	Douarnenez; Morgat	15,000
1104	Bay of Biscay	1,000,000
2351	Chausée de Sein to Anse de Bénodet	75,000
2352	Anse de Bénodet to Presqu'ile de Quiberon	75,000
2353	Presqu'ile de Quiberon to Le Croisic	75,000
	Le Croisic	20,000
2357	Baie de Quiberon	20,000
2358	Golfe du Morbihan	25,000
2641	Pertuis Breton	50,000
2643	Ile d'Ouessant to Pointe de Penmarc'h	200,000
2646	Pointe de Penmarc'h to Ile d'Yeu	200,000
2663	Ile d'Yeu to Pointe de la Coubre	200,000
2664	Pointe d'Arcachon to Pointe de la	200,000
	Coubre Le Four to Goulet de Brest including Ile d'Ouessant	50,000
2743	La Rochelle and La Pallice	15,000
2746	Pertuis d'Antioche, with the Approaches to La Rochelle and Rochefort	50,000
2748	La Charente, Fouras to Rochefort	20,000
2910	Entrance to La Gironde	50,000
2916	La Gironde	various
2981	Pointe de Saint Gildas to Goulet de Fromentine	50,000
	Pornic, l'Herbaudière and Noirmoutier	15,000

British Admiralty and Imray chart coverage

2985	La Loire, St Nazaire to Nantes	various
2986	Approaches to La Loire	50,000
2989	Entrance to La Loire	15,000
3345	Chenal du Four	25,000
3427	Approaches to Brest	22,500
	Camaret-sur-Mer	10,000
3428	Brest	7,500
3429	Rade de Brest	22,500
3640	Harbours and anchorages on the west coast of France	
	Point Joinville	10,000
	Le Guilvinec	15,000
	Saint-Giles-Croix-de-Vie	15,000
	Les Sables d'Olonne	15,000
	Audierne	24,000
	Iles de Glenan	30,000
3641	Loctudy to Concarneau	20,000

IMRAY CHARTS

C17 Bay of Biscay Passage Chart
Ouessant to La Gironde & Bilbao
Plans Approaches to Brest, Entrance to La Gironde, Santander 1:686,000

C35 Baie de Morlaix to L'Aberildut
Plans Ile de Batz, Approaches to L'Abervrac'h and L'Aberbenoit, Argenton, Portusval, Moguериec, Port-Sall, L'Aberildut 1:76,600

C36 Ile d'Ouessant to Raz de Sein
Plans Le Conquet, Port de Brest, Morgat, Camaret-sur-Mer, Douarnenez, Baie de Lampaul (Ouessant), Marina du Moulin Blanc, Brest 1:77,300

C37 Raz de Sein to Bénodet
Plans Lesconil, Guilvinec, Bénodet, Audierne, Loctudy, S. Guénole, L'Odet Fleuve, Ile de Sein 1:77,800

C38 Anse de Bénodet to Presqu'île de Quiberon
Plans Le Poldu, Port de Fôret, Concarneau, Port Maria, Lorient Yacht Harbour, Port Tudy, Etel, Brigneau & Merrien, Port Manech, Loc Maria, Lomener, Doëlan 1:78,500

C39 Lorient to Le Croisic
Plans La Trinité-sur-Mer, Le Croisic, La Turballe, Port de Crouesty, Port Haliguen, Le Pouliguen, Pornichet, La Palais 1:78,500

C40 Le Croisic to Les Sables d'Olonne
Plans Joinville, Pornic, St-Nazaire, Goulet de Fromentine, St-Gilles-Croix de Vie, Les Sables d'Olonne, Le Croisic, L'Herbaudière 1:109,000

C41 Les Sables d'Olonne to La Gironde
Plans Jard-sur-Mer, Bourgenay, Ars-en-Ré, St-Martin-de-Ré, La Flotte-en-Ré, Rochefort, Douhet, St-Denis d'Oléron, Rade de Pallice, Boyardville, La Rochelle and Port des Minimes, Royan 1:109,400

C42 Embouchure de la Gironde to Bordeaux and Arcachon
Plans Royan, Pauillac, Port Bloc, Bordeaux, Arcachon, La Garonne to Bordeaux, La Dordogne to Libourne 1:127,000

The Breton language

It is of interest, and sometimes actually of value to the navigator, to know the meanings of some of the more common Breton words which appear in place names. Those who have cruised on the Celtic fringes of Britain will recognise some of them; the Irish *inish* corresponds to the Breton *inis*, and those who have cruised in West Highland waters will know the meanings of *glas* and *du*. I have no pretensions to a knowledge of Breton, but set down here the results of a few investigations.

The pronunciation is, or should be, more like English than French, with the final consonants sounded. The letters *c'h* represent the final sound of Scottish *loch* or Irish *lough* (but not English lock); there is indeed a word *loc'h*, meaning a lake or pool; *ch* is pronounced as in shall. The French books and charts do not always distinguish between these, and there may be some errors in this book in consequence. In France, as in England, mobility and the radio/TV are killing regional differences and Raz is now usually pronounced Rah; Penmarc'h, pronounced Penmargh a generation ago, is now often Painmar, and Bénodet has gone from Benodette to Bainoday and collected an accent in the process. The most misleading example of this process is *porz*, which means an anchorage, possibly quite exposed and/or lacking in all shore facilities, not a port. This gets frenchified into *port*, and the French word *port* does mean a port, and not an anchorage, which is *anse* or *rade*.

A Breton glossary is hard to use because initial letters are often mutated into others, following complicated rules, depending on the preceding word. I have tried to meet this by suggesting, after the relevant letters, other(s) from which the initial might have come. Suppose that one wants to find the meaning of *I. er Gazek* (which is quite likely since The Mare seems to be the commonest name given to an islet). There is no word *gazek* in the glossary, but after G it says 'try K'; *kazek* means a mare; it mutates into *gazek* after *er*. Mutations of final letters also occur, but these do not usually cause difficulty in finding a word.

Breton	*English*
aber	estuary
anaon	the dead
al, an, ar	the
arvor	seaside
aven	river
B (try P)	
balan, banal	broom
bann, benn	hilltop
barr	summit, top
baz	shoal
beg	point, cape
beniget	cut, slit
benven, bosven	above-water rock
bian, bihan	small
bili, vili	shingle
bir, vir	needle, point
bran	crow
bras, braz	large

bre, brenn	small hill
breiz	Brittany
bri, brienn	cliff
C (try K)	
D (try T)	
daou	two
don, doun	deep
dour	water
du	blac k
ell	rock, shallow
enez	island
er a, an	the
fank	mud
froud, fred	strong current
freu	river
G (try K)	
garo, garv	rough
gavr	goat
glas	green
goban	shallow
gromell, gromilli	roaring
gwenn	white, pure
hir	long
hoc'h, houc'h	pig
iliz	church
izel	shallow
inis	island
kan(iou), kanal	channel
karn	cairn
kareg	rock
kastel	castle
kazek	mare
kein	shoal
kel(ou)	large rock
ker	house, hamlet
kern	summit, sharp peak
kleuz(iou)	hollow, deep
koad, goad	wood
kornog	shoal
koz	old
kreiz	middle
kriben	crest
lan, lann	monastery
marc'h	horse
melen	yellow
men	rock
mor, vor	sea, seawater
nevez	new
penn	head, point
plou, plo	parish
porz, porzig	anchorage
poul	pool, anchorage
raz	strait, tide race
roc'h	rock
ros	wooded knoll
ruz	red
ster	river, inlet
stiv, stiff	fountain, spring
teven, tevenneg	cliff, dune
toull	hole, deep place
trez, treaz	sand, beach
V (try B, M)	
W (try Gw)	
yoc'h	group of rocks

Ports of registration

The ports of registration of fishing vessels may be identified by the letters on their bows, as follows:

AD	Audierne
AY	Auray
BR	Brest
BX	Bordeaux
CC	Concarneau
CM	Camaret
DZ	Douarnenez
GV	Le Guilvinec
IO	Ile d'Oléron
LO	Lorient
LS	Les Sables d'Olonne
MN	Marennes
NA	Nantes
NO	Noirmoutier
SN	Saint Nazaire
VA	Vannes
YE	Ile d'Yeu

Pilotage

1. Chenal du Four

Passage notes

GENERAL

The Chenal du Four is the normal inshore route used by vessels travelling between the English Channel and the Biscay ports; it saves distance and avoids the larger seas and heavy traffic outside Ouessant. Those unfamiliar with it may think that the passage presents special difficulties in navigation, but it is wide and well marked and anyone who has piloted his boat along the north coast of France as far as Ouessant will find the Chenal du Four rather easier than some of the coastline that he has already passed. The difficulties are rather that the strong tides and exposure to the Atlantic swell often result in steep seas, and the visibility is frequently poor. There are two other channels, the Chenal de la Helle, which is farther west and is also described here, and the Passage du Fromveur, southeast of Ouessant, noted for the strength of its tidal streams, which attain 9kts at extreme springs. In rough weather the Chenal de la Helle is to be preferred to the Chenal du Four.

The roughest seas do not occur in the Chenal du Four itself, but in the approaches. Eastward, between Ile Vierge and the Four lighthouse, north winds often bring a considerable swell, and a strong weather-going stream over an irregular bottom produces steep seas. With westerly winds, some shelter is found as the Chenal du Four is approached and the vessel first comes under the lee of Ouessant and then of the inner islands and shoals. The seas drop as soon as the tide turns.

With a fair wind the passage should be taken when the tide is favourable, but if the wind is ahead it is best to go through the narrow part, where the tides run hard, at slack water. Coming from the north it is unfortunate that the tide turns in the Four channel before it does in the English Channel, so that starting from, for example, l'Aberwrac'h on the first of the SW tide, most of the stream in the Four channel will have run to waste before one gets there. But one can cross the Iroise on the foul tide without difficulty, and reach the Raz de Sein as the stream turns fair again.

In fog or thick weather navigation in the Chenal du Four requires special care. Once the narrows are reached a yacht with the wind and tide behind her will be committed to the passage; if she is depending largely on electronic aids she will be at considerable risk should they fail. The bottom is too uneven and the reefs too steep-to for the echo sounder to give adequate warning of danger. Speed over the ground is likely to be high, making the buoys themselves a considerable hazard and their lights cannot be entirely relied upon.

If the outer marks have been sighted, and the visibility is sufficient to enable the towers and buoys to be seen at a reasonable distance, pilotage is possible even if the distant landmarks and lighthouses are hidden in the mist. In very poor visibility however, it is better to remain either in harbour or well out at sea. A yacht can be talked through on VHF even in nil visibility by the English-speaking radar station on Pointe St Mathieu, but this should be considered an emergency procedure only.

Charts

BA *3345, 2694, 2643*
Imray *C36*

TIDAL DATA

Times and heights

	Time differences			Height differences			
	HW		LW	MHWS	MHWN	MLWN	MLWS
BREST							
	0000 and 1200	0600 and 1800	0000 and 1200	0600 and 1800	6·9	5·4	2·6	1·0
Le Conquet							
	–0005	+0000	+0007	+0007	–0·1	–0·1	–0·1	0·0

Tidal streams

The N-going stream begins about −0600 Brest, spring rates: 1kt at 1M N of Les Plâtresses, 2¼kts at St Pierre buoy (SW of Corsen), 5¼kts at La Vinotière. The S-going stream begins about HW Brest, spring rates: 1kt at 1M N of Les Plâtresses, 2½kts at St Pierre buoy, 5kts at La Vinotière. At Les Vieux Moines the stream runs as follows (spring rates): at −0100 Brest, N 1¼kts; at +0200 Brest, SSE 3½kts; at +0500 Brest, SW 1kt; at −0600 Brest, WNW 1½kts. The streams are considerably affected by the wind.

Depths

The main channels are deep.

LIGHTS

1. **Le Four** 48°31'·4N 4°48'·3W Fl(5)15s28m18M Horn(3+2)60s Grey tower

Chenal du Four Ldg Lts 158·5°

2. *Front* **Kermorvan** 48°21'·7N 4°47'·4W Fl.5s20m22M Horn 60s White square tower
3. *Rear* **Saint Mathieu** 48°19'·8N 4°46'·3W Fl.15s56m29M & DirF.54m28M 157·5°-intens-159·5° White tower, red top

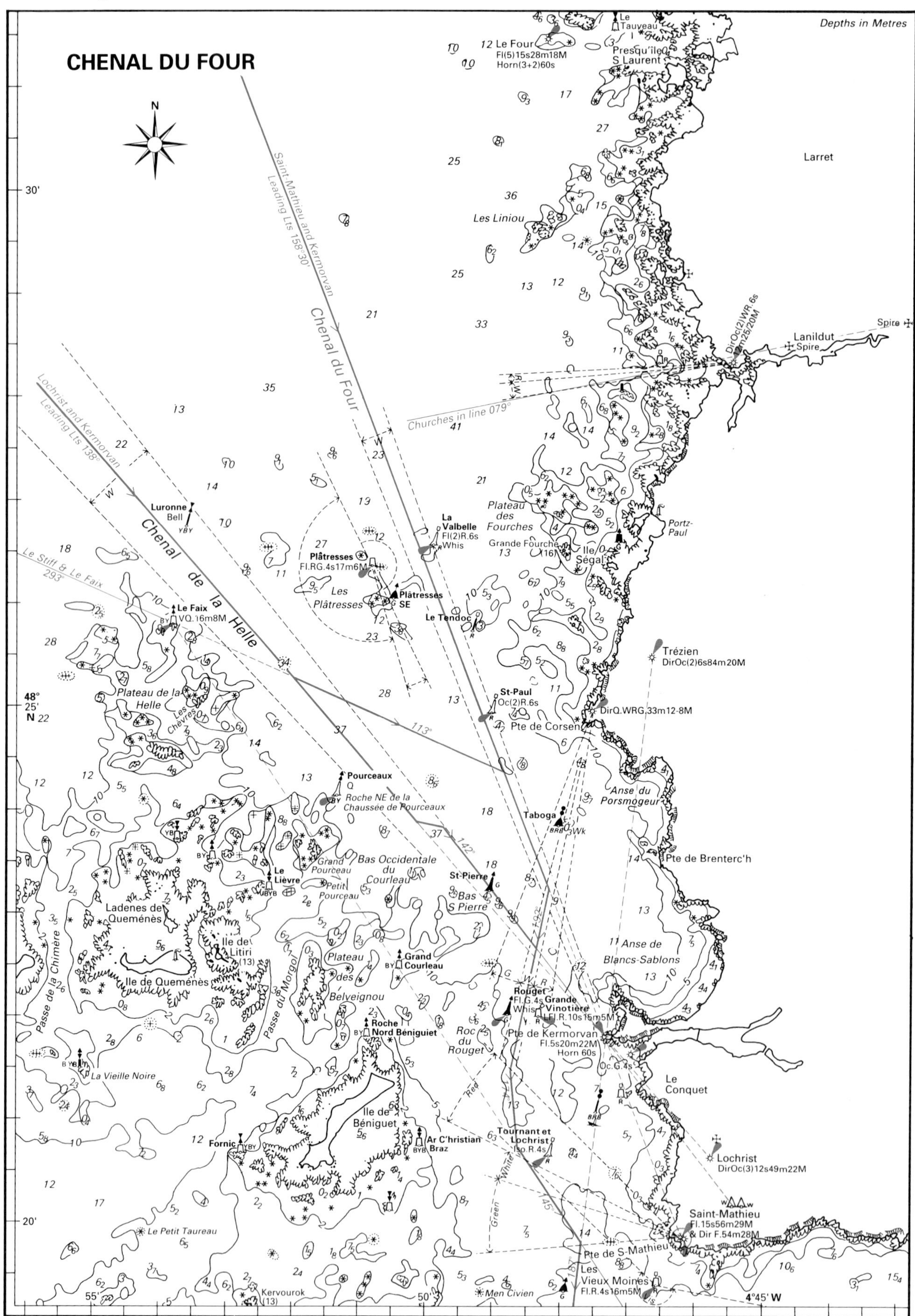
CHENAL DU FOUR
Depths in Metres
Le Four
Fl(5)15s28m18M
Horn(3+2)60s
Presqu'île
S Laurent
Larret
Les Liniou
Saint-Mathieu and Kermorvan
Leading Lts 158°30'
Chenal du Four
Lanildut
Spire
DirOc(2)WR.6s
Churches in line 079°
Lochrist and Kermorvan
Leading Lts 138°
Chenal de la Helle
Lurónne
Bell
La Valbelle
Fl(2)R.6s
Whis
Plateau des Fourches
Grande Fourche
Ile Ségal
Portz-Paul
Plâtresses
Fl.RG.4s17m6M
Les Plâtresses
Plâtresses SE
Le Tendoc
Le Stiff & Le Faix 293°
Le Faix
VQ.16m8M
Plateau de la Helle
Les Chèvres
Trézien
DirOc(2)6s84m20M
St-Paul
Oc(2)R.6s
Pte de Corsen
DirQ.WRG.33m12-8M
113°
Pourceaux
Q
Roche NE de la Chaussée de Pourceaux
Taboga
Anse du Porsmogeur
142°
Pte de Brenterc'h
Grand Pourceau
Bas Occidentale du Courleau
Le Lièvre
Petit Pourceau
St-Pierre
Bas S Pierre
Ladenes de Queménès
Ile de Litiri
Ile de Quemènès
Passe de la Chimère
Passe du Morgol
Plateau des Belveignou
Grand Courleau
Anse de Blancs-Sablons
Rouget
Fl.G.4s
Whis
Grande Vinotière
LFl.R.10s15m5M
Roche Nord Béniguet
Roc du Rouget
Pte de Kermorvan
Fl.5s20m22M
Horn 60s
Oc.G.4s
Le Conquet
La Vieille Noire
Ile de Béniguet
Fornic
Ar C'hristian Braz
Tournant et Lochrist
Iso.R.4s
Lochrist
DirOc(3)12s49m22M
Red
White
Green
Saint-Mathieu
Fl.15s56m29M
& Dir F.54m28M
Pte de S-Mathieu
Le Petit Taureau
Les Vieux Moines
Fl.R.4s16m5M
Kervourok
Men Civien
30'
48° 25' N
20'
55'
50'
4°45' W

Plan 1

4. **Les Plâtresses** 48°26'·3N 4°50'·9W
   Fl.RG.4s17m6M 343°-R-153°-G-333°
   White octagonal tower
5. **Valbelle buoy** (port) 48°26'·5N 4°50'·0W
   Fl(2)R.6s8m5M Whis
6. **Basse St Paul buoy** (port) 48°24'·9N 4°49'·1W
   Oc(2)R.6s
   Chenal de la Helle leading lights 138°
2. *Front* **Kermorvan** 48°21'·7N 4°47'·3W
   Fl.5s20m22M Horn 60s White square tower
7. *Rear* **Lochrist** 48°20'·6N 4°45'·7W
   DirOc(3)12s49m22M 135°-intens-140°
   Octagonal white tower, red top
8. **Le Faix** 48°25'·8N 4°53'·9W VQ.16m8M
   Tower (N card)
9. **Le Stiff** 48°28'·5N 5°03'·4W Fl(2)R.20s85m24M
   Two white towers, side by side
10. **Pourceaux buoy (N card)** 48°24'·1N 4°51'·5W Q
    Both channels
11. **Corsen** 48°24'·9N 4°47'·7W
    DirQ.WRG.33m12-8M
    008°-R-012°-W-015°-G-021°
    White hut
12. **La Grande Vinotière** 48°22'·0N 4°48'·5W
    LFl.R.10s15m5M Octagonal red tower
13. **Le Rouget buoy (starboard)** 48°22'·0N 4°48'·9W
    Iso.G.4s Whis
14. **St Mathieu auxiliary** 54m at 291° from main
    tower Q.WRG.26m14-11M
    085°-G-107°-W-116°-R-134° White tower
15. **Tournant et Lochrist buoy (port)**
    48°20'·6N 4°48'·3W Iso.R.4s
16. **Les Vieux Moines** 48°19'·4N 4°46'·5W
    Fl.R.4s16m5M 280°-vis-133° Octagonal red tower
    Leading lights 007°
2. *Front* **Kermorvan** 48°21'·7N 4°47'·3W
   Fl.5s20m22M Horn 60s White square tower
17. *Rear* **Trézien** 48°25'·4N 4°46'·8W
    DirOc(2)6s84m20M 003°-intens-011°
    Grey tower, white towards south

RADIO

Le Conquet Port Radio VHF Ch 16, 08 0830–1200 and 1330–1800 LT
Ouessant Traffic VHF Ch 13, 79 24hr
St Mathieu radar station VHF Ch 16, 12 24hr

Directions – bound south

Chenal du Four

By day

Coasting southward from Le Four lighthouse a fair offing should be given to Les Linioux and the Plateau des Fourches. The Chenal du Four may then be entered NE of Les Plâtresses tower (white), with the lighthouses of St Mathieu (white circular tower, red top) and Kermorvan (white square tower) in transit, bearing 158°. The remaining transits and marks are shown on the plan on page 14.

Except in certain parts, the area free from danger in normal weather is considerable; when it is rough the orthodox channel should be adhered to, as the overfalls are worse over an irregular bottom, such as the 3·7m patch SE of the Grande Vinotière.

If a vessel bound south is late on the tide she can avoid the worst of a foul stream by standing into the bay towards the Anse des Blancs Sablons, and again into the bay south of Le Conquet, but care must be taken to avoid the dangers.

By night

The transits and sectored lights are shown on the plan. The channel is excellently lit and in good weather the navigation is easy. Bound south, steer with Kermorvan[2] and St Mathieu[3] in transit, bearing 158°. Note that in a narrow sector each side of this transit, St Mathieu shows a fixed white directional light as well as the flashing light that shows all round.

When Corsen light[11] turns white steer in this sector, with the light astern, until the auxiliary light on St Mathieu[14] becomes red. Then steer 174°, entering the red sector of Corsen until the Tournant et Lochrist buoy[15] is abeam, when the auxiliary light on St Mathieu will turn white and the light on Les Vieux Moines[16] will open. Then steer 145°, making sure that Kermorvan is brought in transit with Trézien[17], bearing 007° astern, before the green sector of St Mathieu auxiliary is left.

Chenal du Four, steering south past Les Vieux Moines beacon tower and Pte de St Mathieu lighthouse

Chenal du Four, looking SE. Grande Vinotière centre, Kermorvan and Le Conquet far left, Pte de St Mathieu far right

If proceeding south, steer nothing west of the 007° alignment until clear of the area of the plan as the unlit La Fourmi buoy lies close to the transit; if going east or SE steer to leave Les Vieux Moines[16] to port.

Chenal de La Helle

By day

Bring Kermorvan lighthouse to bear 138°, between the first and second houses from the right of five similar houses forming Le Conquet radio station. In good weather steer on this transit until Corsen lighthouse bears 012°, then steer 192° on this stern bearing. This transit leads across the Basse St Pierre (4·5m), marked by a buoy (starboard), which the transit leaves to port. In bad weather the shoal can be avoided, either by bringing the two white-painted gables, resembling pyramids, of Keravel (near St Mathieu lighthouse) in transit with Kermorvan, bearing 142° or, more simply, by leaving the buoy to starboard.

By night

Steer with Kermorvan[2] in transit with Lochrist[7], bearing 138°. To avoid the Basse St Pierre, if necessary, leave this alignment when Le Stiff light[9] on Ouessant comes in transit with Le Faix[8], bearing 293°, and steer 113° on this stern transit to join the Four channel alignment and thence follow the directions given above for the Chenal du Four.

Directions – bound north

Put the reciprocal courses on the plan and this will enable the above directions to be followed in reverse. If using Chenal de La Helle by night make sure that the unlit Luronne bell buoy has definitely been passed before leaving the Lochrist/Kermorvan transit.

ANCHORAGES

For those who like intricate navigation, the islands between Ouessant and the mainland are an interesting area to explore in settled weather and with the aid of the large-scale chart and *North Brittany*, published by Imray, several anchorages can be found.

In addition, the following temporary anchorages on the mainland are available under suitable conditions:

Anse de Porsmoguer Good holding ground in sand in this pretty bay, with depths shoaling from 6m. It is sheltered from N and E and popular for bathing. The village is about ½M to the north, but there are no shops there.

Anse des Blancs Sablons This wide sandy bay is free from dangers except off the headlands on each side. The anchorage is anywhere, in from 9m to 1m on a sandy shelving bottom which dries out nearly ¼M from the shore, except on the W side, where there is 3m close to the rocks off Kermorvan.

The peninsula protects the anchorage from the SW, and the land shelters it from the E and S. Yachts can work into this bay inshore against a foul tide, anchor there and slip round L'Ilette (the small islet just N of Kermorvan) when the stream becomes fair; note that there is a rock 200m E of this islet which is awash at chart datum. There is little stream in the bay, but often some swell. No facilities.

Le Conquet is a good anchorage in the inlet south of Pointe de Kermorvan, but it is often crowded. Leave the red La Louvre tower to port and go in as far as draught and tide permit. For a full description see *North Brittany*.

Anse de Bertheaume (see plan page 18) This is a convenient bay, about 3M east of Pointe de St Mathieu, in which to wait before making the passage of Chenal du Four. It is sheltered from N and W, but exposed to the S and E. The Fort de Bertheaume, on the SW corner of the bay, should be given a good berth as 250m to the NE is Le Chat, an area of rocks nearly 200m across, with heads drying 6·6m and 7·2m. These are a particular hazard when they are covered near HW springs. Anchor in one of the two bays immediately north of Le Chat, going in as far as possible for shelter. There are some visitors moorings. Farther north and east the bottom of the bay is foul, with rocks. Village and simple shop one mile.

2. Brest

Marina du Moulin Blanc

48°23'N 4°26'W

GENERAL

Many yachts bound south stop the night at Camaret but comparatively few make the detour eastward to visit the Rade de Brest. This is a pity as the Rade is an excellent cruising ground in its own right, somewhat reminiscent of the Clyde.

Brest itself is a commercial port and major naval base with local bus services, good railway connections and a twice-daily air service to Paris. Yachts are not normally very welcome in the commercial port, but the Marina du Moulin Blanc makes a good starting point for an exploratory cruise of the area. It is a pleasant place with all facilities and is convenient for changing crews.

Charts

BA *3428, 3427, 3429, 2694, 798*
Imray *C36*

TIDAL DATA

Times and heights

Time differences				Height differences			
HW		LW		MHWS	MHWN	MLWN	MLWS
BREST							
0000 and 1200	0600 and 1800	0000 and 1200	0600 and 1800	6·9	5·4	2·6	1·0
Standard Port							

Tidal streams

The streams run strongly in the Goulet de Brest. On the northern side the flood begins at −0535 Brest and runs E. On the southern side the flood begins at −0605 Brest, attaining 4kts NE off Pointe des Espagnols, and continues in direction ENE towards the Elorn river. The ebb begins on the northern side at −0030 Brest, on the southern side at HW Brest. Within about 100m of the southern shore there are ENE and E eddies, which begin about +0100 Brest and continue until the flood begins. These eddies cause tide rips where they meet the main ebb from the Rade off Pointe des Espagnols.

Depths

Entrance channel dredged to 2m. 2m at visitors' berths. South basin dredged to 4m.

LIGHTS

Only the lights and buoys essential for Moulin Blanc are listed.

1. **Pointe du Petit Minou** 48°20'·2N 4°36'·9W Fl(2)WR.6s32m19/15M Horn 60s shore-R-252°-W-260°-R-307°-W(unintens)-015°-W-065·5° 070·5°-W-shore
   Grey round tower, W on SW side, red top
   Ldg Lts 068° *Front* DirQ.30m23M
   067·3°-intens-068·8° Same structure
   Fog det lt F.G 036·5°-intens-039·5° 420m NE
2. **Pointe du Portzic** 48°21'·6N 4°32'·0W Oc(2)WR.12s56m19/15M
   219°-R-259°-W-338°-R-000°-W-065·5°
   070·5°-W-219° 041°-vis-069° when W of Goulet
   Grey 8-sided tower
   Ldg Lts 068° *Rear* DirQ.54m22M 065°-intens-071°
   Same structure
   For Passe Sud DirQ(6)+LFl.15s54m24M
   045°-intens-050° Same structure
3. **Basse du Charles Martel buoy (port)** 48°18'·9N 4°42'·2W Fl(4)R.15s Whis
4. **Fillettes W card buoy** VQ(9)10s Whis
5. **Roche Mengam** 48°20'·4N 4°34'·5W Fl(3)WR.12s10m11/8M
   034°-R-054°-W-034° RBR beacon tower
6. **Pénoupèle buoy (port)** Fl(3)R.12s
7. **R2 buoy (port)** Fl(2)R.6s
8. **R1 buoy (starboard)** Fl.G.4s
9. **R4 buoy (port)** LFl.R.10s
10. **R6 buoy (port)** Fl.R.4s (well N of course)
11. **R3 buoy (N card)** Q(6)+LFl.15s (to be left to port)
12. **Beacon** 48°22'·7N 4°26·5W Fl(4)R.15s2M red pile
13. **Moulin Blanc buoy (port)** Fl(3)R.12s
14. **Buoyed channel to Moulin Blanc**
    Starboard and port buoys
    MB1 Fl.G.2s
    MB2 Fl.R.2s
    Marina entrance beacons Fl.G.2s & Fl.R.2s
    MBA Beacon 48°23'·6N 4°25'·7W Q(3)10s
    E card beacon

RADIO

Commercial Port – c/s *Capitainerie Brest* VHF Ch 16, 12 24hr
Military Port – c/s *D.P. Brest* VHF Ch 74 24hr
Marina VHF Ch 9 0800–2000 LT

APPROACH

By day

The outer approach to Brest (Avant Goulet de Brest) is made with the twin lighthouses of Le Petit Minou (two adjacent white towers) in transit with the grey octagonal tower of Pointe du Portzic, bearing 068°. These lighthouses are on the north side of the Goulet de Brest. In poor visibility they may not be seen at first on rounding the Pointe de St Mathieu from Le Chenal du Four. However, if Les Vieux Moines tower and Le Coq port can buoy are left to port, the Charles Martel buoy will be discovered close to the transit of 086° and the lighthouses should be in sight.

The outer approach from the SW, through the Chenal du Toulinguet, is described in Chapter 5.

On approaching Le Petit Minou, bear to starboard and pass up the Goulet on the northern side of the midchannel shoals of Plateau des Fillettes. A W cardinal buoy marks the outer end and the BRB Roche Mengam beacon tower the inner end, with two port-hand buoys marking the northern limit of the southern channel.

When entering the Goulet from the SW, or on the ebb, the north coast of Presqu'île de Quélern is steep-to, with a useful eddy inshore. The central plateau is then left to port and La Cormoranderie

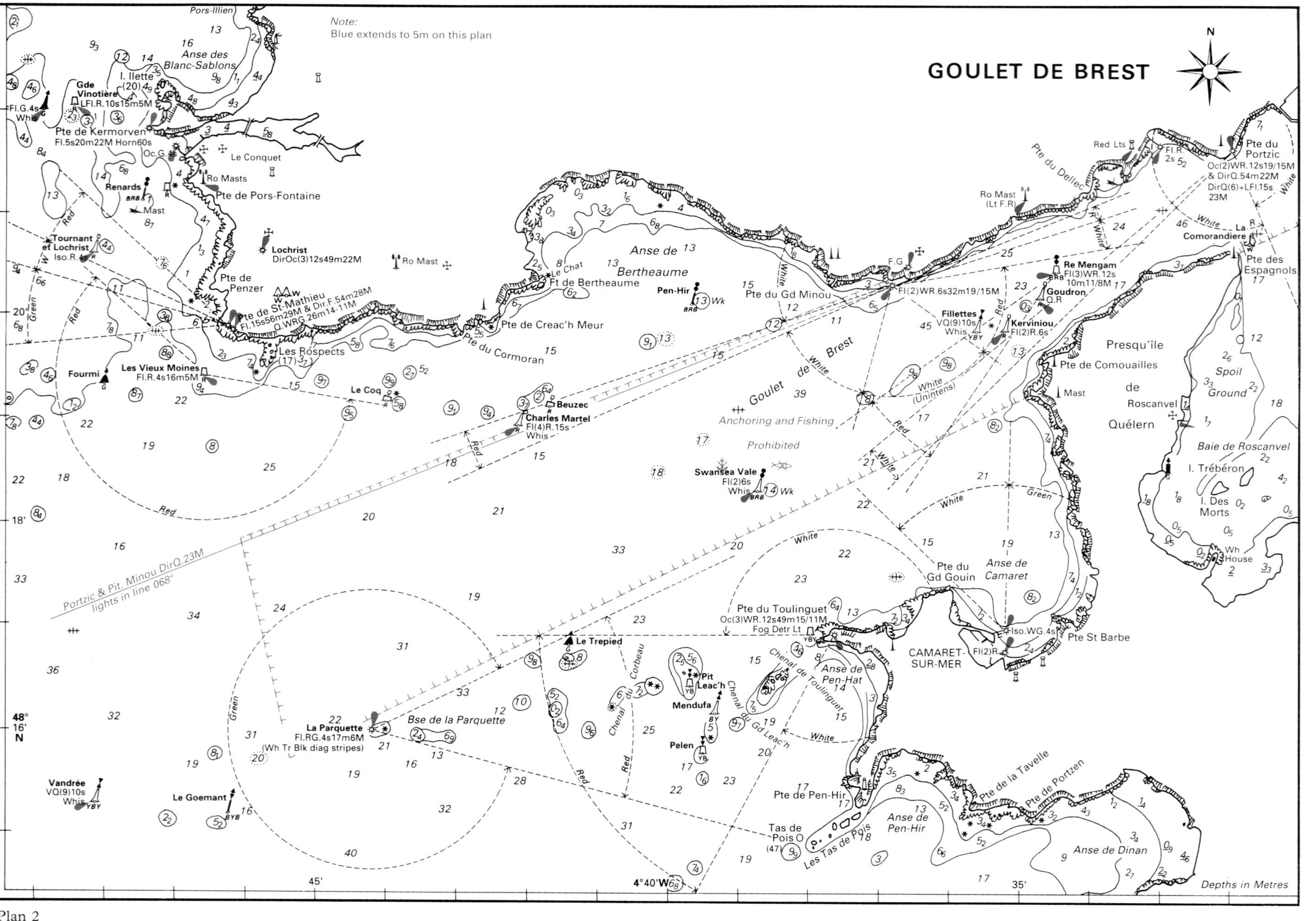
GOULET DE BREST
N
Note:
Blue extends to 5m on this plan
Depths in Metres
Pte du Portzic
Oc(2)WR.12s19/15M
& DirQ.54m22M
DirQ(6)+LFl.15s
23M
Pte des Espagnols
La Comorandiere
Spoil Ground
Baie de Roscanvel
I. Trébéron
I. Des Morts
Wh House
Presqu'ile de Roscanvel
Pte de Comouailles
Quélern
Pte du Dellec
Ro Mast (Lt F.R)
Red Lts
Re Mengam
Fl(3)WR.12s
10m11/8M
Goudron
Q.R
Kerviniou
Fl(2)R.6s
Fillettes
VQ(9)10s
Whis
Fl(2)WR.6s32m19/15M
Pte St Barbe
Iso.WG.4s
Anse de Camaret
Fl(2)R
CAMARET-SUR-MER
Pte du Gd Gouin
White (Unintens)
Goulet de Brest
Pte du Gd Minou
Anchoring and Fishing Prohibited
Swansea Vale
Fl(2)6s
Whis
Wk
Pte du Toulinguet
Oc(3)WR.12s49m15/11M
Fog Detr Lt
Anse de Pen-Hat
Chenal de Toulinguet
Chenal du Gd Leac'h
Pit Leac'h
Mendufa
Pelen
Pte de Pen-Hir
Tas de Pois
Les Tas de Pois
Anse de Pen-Hir
Anse de Dinan
Pte de la Tavelle
Pte de Portzen
Anse de Bertheaume
Pen-Hir
Ft de Bertheaume
Le Chat
Pte de Creac'h Meur
Pte du Cormoran
Beuzec
Charles Martel
Fl(4)R.15s
Whis
Le Trepied
Chenal du Corbeau
Bse de la Parquette
La Parquette
Fl.RG.4s17m6M
(Wh Tr Blk diag stripes)
Le Goemant
Vandrée
VQ(9)10s
Whis
Ro Mast
Lochrist
DirOc(3)12s49m22M
Pte de St-Mathieu
Fl.15s56m29M & Dir.F.54m28M
Q.WRG.26m14-11M
Les Rospects
Le Coq
Pte de Penzer
Pte de Pors-Fontaine
Le Conquet
Ro Masts
Anse des Blanc-Sablons
Pors-Illien
I. Ilette
Pte de Kermorven
Fl.5s20m22M Horn60s
Gde Vinotière
LFl.R.10s15m5M
Oc.G
Renards
Mast
Tournant et Lochrist
Iso.R.4s
Les Vieux Moines
Fl.R.4s16m5M
Fourmi
Fl.G.4s
Whis
Portzic & Pit. Minou DirQ.23M
lights in line 068°
48° 16' N
4°40'W
45'
35'
18'
20'
White
Red
Green

Plan 2

Pte du Portzic lighthouse, with Brest Jetée Sud behind it

Moulin Blanc marina, looking N. Moulin Blanc buoy right centre, conspicuous marine-museum roof left centre

The channel to Moulin Blanc marina at Brest is buoyed

(white beacon) on the northeast tip of the peninsula left well to starboard.

With the Pte du Portzic abeam, a line of port-hand channel buoys will be seen leading past the breakwaters of the naval base and the commercial port towards the bridge over the mouth of the Elorn river. The conspicuous white roof of the marine museum, on reclaimed land at the inner end of the harbour, makes a good landmark for the marina (see plan page 20).

By night

After rounding Pointe de St Mathieu from the Chenal du Four, or from the west, identify the leading lights (068°) of Le Petit Minou[1] and Portzic[2] and steer on this transit. Once past the Charles Martel buoy[3] bear to starboard to pass between Pte du Petit Minou light[1] and Fillettes buoy[4].

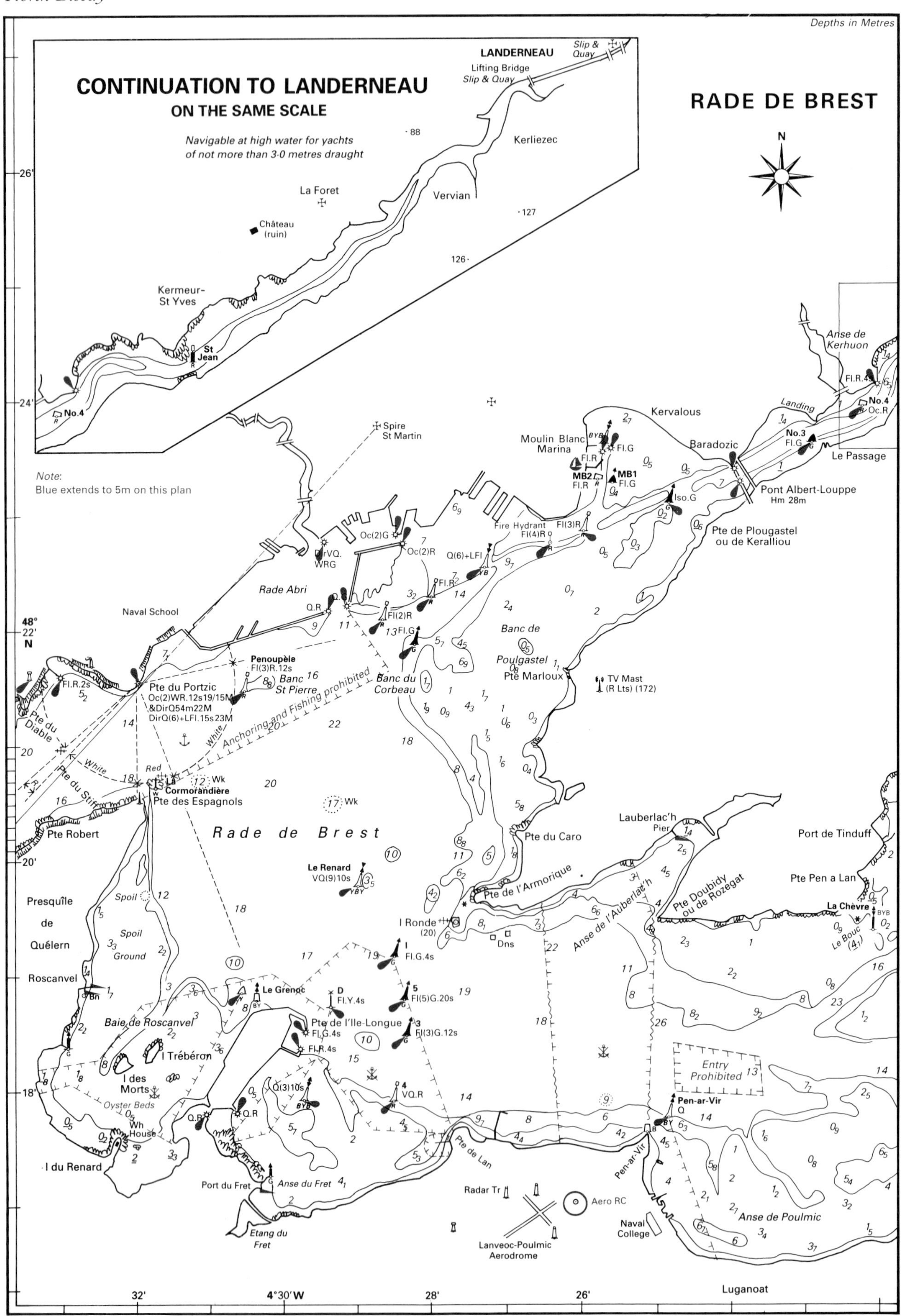

Depths in Metres
CONTINUATION TO LANDERNEAU
ON THE SAME SCALE
Navigable at high water for yachts of not more than 3·0 metres draught
LANDERNEAU
Lifting Bridge
Slip & Quay
Kerliezec
Vervian
La Foret
Château (ruin)
Kermeur-St Yves
St Jean
No.4
RADE DE BREST
Note:
Blue extends to 5m on this plan
Spire St Martin
Kervalous
Moulin Blanc Marina
Baradozic
Anse de Kerhuon
Landing
Le Passage
Pont Albert-Louppe
Hm 28m
Pte de Plougastel ou de Keralliou
Rade Abri
Naval School
Penoupèle
Fl(3)R.12s
Banc St Pierre
Banc du Corbeau
Banc de Poulgastel
Pte Marloux
TV Mast (R Lts) (172)
Pte du Portzic
Oc(2)WR.12s19/15M
&DirQ54m22M
DirQ(6)+LFl.15s23M
Anchoring and Fishing prohibited
Pte du Diable
Pte du Stiff
Cormorandière
Pte des Espagnols
Pte Robert
Rade de Brest
Le Renard
VQ(9)10s
Pte du Caro
Lauberlac'h
Pier
Port de Tinduff
Pte Pen a Lan
La Chèvre
Pte Doubidy ou de Rozegat
Anse de l'Auberlac'h
Pte de l'Armorique
I Ronde
Dns
Presquîle de Quélern
Spoil Ground
Roscanvel
Baie de Roscanvel
I Trébéron
I des Morts
Oyster Beds
Wh House
I du Renard
Le Grenoc
Pte de l'Ile-Longue
Fl.G.4s
Fl.R.4s
Entry Prohibited
Pen-ar-Vir
Port du Fret
Anse du Fret
Etang du Fret
Pte de Lan
Radar Tr
Aero RC
Lanveoc-Poulmic Aerodrome
Naval College
Anse de Poulmic
Luganoat
32'
4°30'W
28'
26'
48° 22' N

Identify Roche Mengam tower light[5] and, leaving it to starboard, steer about 070° towards Pénoupèle buoy[6]. Leaving Pénoupèle close to port, steer 065° to follow the buoyed channel to Moulin Blanc buoy[13]. Leaving it to port, continue for about 200m before steering about 005° to locate the lights marking the narrow dredged channel. When MB1 and MB2[14] (see plan opposite) have been identified, steer between them on 007° to enter the marina.

Coming from Camaret, steer north to enter the intense white sector of Portzic[2] (Q(6)+LFl.6s). Alter to starboard and keep in this sector on about 047° until Roche Mengam tower[5] is abaft the beam to port, then turn onto 065° towards Pénoupèle buoy[6] and continue as above.

ENTRANCE
The Marina du Moulin Blanc is on the eastern side of the reclaimed land; on passing the port-hand buoy (Moulin Blanc) on the point, the small lateral buoys of the dredged channel into the marina will appear. Deep-draught vessels should leave the Moulin Blanc buoy 200m astern before turning in.

There is a central pier that divides the marina into two halves. The *capitainerie* is at the root of this pier and visitors' berths are in the northern basin (see plan).

FACILITIES
The staff in the *capitainerie* are most helpful and the marina is well equipped. There is a fuel berth by the *capitainerie*, two wide slipways, a 35-tonne travel-lift, 12-tonne mobile crane and a large haul-out area. Almost all repairs can be carried out. There are several chandlers on site.

There is a launderette in the marina, together with bars and restaurants.

Outside the marina, a short walk to the north, is a small food store. The bus service into Brest is frequent and passes a large supermarket. Brest has all the usual facilities of a large town and there are chandlers, sailmakers and a shipyard with marine engineer close to the *port de commerce*.

3. Rade de Brest

GENERAL
The Rade de Brest provides an excellent cruising ground, with many anchorages, beautiful creeks and two rivers that present no problems to bilge-keelers and can, with care, be enjoyed by owners of deep-draught yachts. In bad weather it can be choppy, especially with wind against tide, for there can be a fetch of as much as five miles, but as it is sheltered on all sides it is free from the swell of the open sea. It makes an ideal place for a family cruise, or for filling in if caught by bad weather between the Four and the Raz. The river Aulne, which is navigable as far as Châteaulin, is particularly attractive.

Several naval establishments are situated on the shores of the Rade and around some of them are restricted or prohibited areas, marked on the charts. There are a few other areas, also marked on the charts, where navigation is occasionally restricted. The Rade is entered by the Goulet de Brest as described in the previous chapter.

Charts
BA *3427, 3429*

TIDAL DATA
Times and heights

Time differences				Height differences			
HW		LW		MHWS	MHWN	MLWN	MLWS
BREST							
0000 and 1200	0600 and 1800	0000 and 1200	0600 and 1800	6·9	5·4	2·6	1·0
Standard Port							

Tidal streams
For the Goulet de Brest, see Chapter 2. The flood, beginning at −0605 Brest, in the south of the Goulet continues ENE to the Elorn and E towards Pointe Marloux. For the first half-hour the ebb is still running out of the estuary of the Aulne and there are tide rips where the two streams meet off Pointe des Espagnols. Half an hour later, at −0530 Brest, the flood stream divides off Pointe des Espagnols, one branch setting E and ENE as before, with an eddy setting towards Pointe Marloux. The other branch sets S into the Baie de Roscanvel and SE towards the Aulne at 2¾kts springs. The ebb stream from the Elorn begins at HW Brest and from the Aulne about ten minutes earlier.

Depths
Given under the individual headings for the anchorages.

L'Elorn river
This pleasant river leads to the attractive old town of Landernau. It offers an interesting run, particularly for bilge-keelers and if the passage is made near high water well over 2m will be found in the channel. Arrangements must be made in advance for the bridge, about a mile below the town, to be opened and this probably means that a night will be spent in Landernau, which should not be regretted. The river is now seldom used by commercial traffic other than the occasional barge and although it is lit as far as St Jean beacon, night passage is not recommended.

The Moulin Blanc port-hand buoy is one of the buoys marking the channel, which leads under the conspicuous Pont Albert-Louppe and higher Pont de l'Iroise just beyond it and thence into the river L'Elorn. From the bridges the river is navigable at all states of tide to deep-draught yachts for some 2½M, up to the port-hand beacon St Jean.

Above this point the river shallows, but the channel, marked by rather small and widely spaced buoys, is navigable near high water to yachts drawing 2m for another four miles to Landerneau, where a yacht can dry out against the quays. Half a mile below Landerneau is a lifting bridge. This can be opened on request by telephoning in advance (☎ 06 11 03 31 20).

The south bank of the river is thickly wooded, with interesting rocky outcrops on the ridge. There are many houses and the town of Kerhuon on the north bank, with deep-water moorings inside the channel buoys. It should be possible to anchor in this stretch, or to pick up a vacant mooring on either side of the river up as far as St Jean. A dinghy landing can be made for supplies at Kerhuon on a slip, marked by a beacon with an orange top. At the eastern end of Kerhuon there is a wharf where the river curves north and then east again.

The yacht moorings in this stretch give a better indication of the channel than the small green buoys that mark it. Follow the curve round until the St Jean port-hand beacon is passed. After this there is a straight unmarked stretch of river. Keep in the middle and search with binoculars for the next of a succession of small green and red buoys marking the channel to the Landerneau bridge. The channel winds in the river and it is important to follow the buoys closely in order to find a depth of 3m at high water neaps.

When the bridge opens, follow the straight channel into Landerneau. Passing the large sand-barge wharf to port, yachts may dry out against a short length of wall with a slipway on the port-hand side just below the road bridge marking the end of the channel or alongside one of the four ladders just below the bridge on the starboard side. Along the wall the bottom is hard and flat and there is 3m at high water neaps. Below the fourth ladder the bottom is foul.

Facilities

Water and electricity on the quay on the northern side.

Landerneau is attractive, with all the facilities of a fair-sized market town and is on the Morlaix-Brest railway line.

Rade de Brest – southern section

There is a substantial area where navigation is restricted and anchoring prohibited around Ile Longue, the French naval base. Entry is prohibited within about 500m of the shore in this area. Entry is also prohibited to an area east of the Naval College inside a line 160° from the Pen-ar-Vir N cardinal buoy to the shore. Except for a visit to Roscanvel on the west side of Ile Longue or Le Fret on the east, it is best to keep out of this section of the Rade.

Roscanvel

An important feature of the Baie de Roscanvel is the tidal stream. The flood stream begins to run S into the bay at −0530 Brest, but one hour later the stream, running S down the E side of the bay, sweeps along the S shore and causes an eddy up the west side towards Pointe des Espagnols. By −0200 Brest the stream is weak in the inner part of the bay, but the north-going eddy on the west side attains 1kt at springs. The ebb stream is simpler. It runs from Pointe de L'Ile Longue towards Roscanvel and Pointe des Espagnols, leaving only a weak stream in the south of the bay.

The east coast of Presqu'île de Quelern offers good protection from winds from the north through west to the southeast. Between Pte des Espagnols and the village of Roscanvel there are several small coves with yacht moorings, and there is a welcoming yacht club at Roscanvel itself which may loan a mooring on request.

Roscanvel, a small holiday village, has a double slipway, one running out east and the other south. Anchor off the slips clear of the moorings. The eastern slip dries at LW and there are obstructions outside it. If landing at the southern slip towards LW approach from the south and use the inside only.

At Landernau the best place for a deep keeled yacht is on the left bank below the bridge

Facilities
There is a small but well-stocked shop, a PO, café-bars, and an hotel/restaurant grouped round the village green.

Rade de Brest – SE section and L'Aulne river

The southeastern portion of the Rade has much to offer for the explorer. There are many bays and inlets along the north shore as the river L'Aulne is approached. Navigation is restricted along the south shore, but there is a regular ferry service from Brest to the Port du Fret SE of Ile Longue, with a bus connection to Camaret.

The number of yacht moorings along the north shore suggests that the area is generally sheltered in the summer, although a strong southwesterly could cause trouble.

To avoid shallows north of Pointe de l'Amorique make for Le Renard E cardinal buoy and then, if proceeding up L'Aulne, lay a course to leave the conspicuous islet Ile Ronde and two rectangular concrete dolphins 300m to port. A course of 104° will then lead to the outer port-hand river-channel buoy (numbered 4), which lies 1M east of the Grande Ile du Bindy. The remaining channel buoys can then be located. Both port and starboard-hand buoys are conical but are brightly painted in the correct lateral colours.

Anse de l'Auberlach

The picturesque hamlet of L'Auberlach lies at the head of a bay running NE to the east of Ile Ronde. It has a short stone pier with a drying slip behind. There are many moorings, but it is possible to find a space to anchor clear of them. One should not go much beyond the pier as the bay shoals rapidly.

Facility
There is a bar.

Le Fret

The Anse du Fret provides a pleasant, sheltered anchorage SE of Ile Longue. Close east of the ferry pier are a number of moorings and although some may be vacant they are reportedly unreliable. There is, in any case, plenty of space to anchor with good holding on sand/mud A course of 215° from Ile Ronde will lead through the prohibited anchorage area, well clear of the prohibited entry area close to the naval docks, and into the anchorage.

Facilities
A landing slip on the ferry pier (regular service to and from Brest). Active sailing school, bars, restaurants, hotel. There is a small food shop at the south end of the village, close to the main road. Bus service to Camaret.

Tinduff

This is in an inlet on the west side of the shallow Baie de Daoulas, half a mile to the north of Pointe Pen a Lan. In the approach this point must be given a berth of over a ¼M as there are shoals and La Chèvre rock (dries 4·7m), marked by an E cardinal beacon off it, with another rock (drying 4·2m) closer inshore. A third unmarked isolated rock, drying 0·7m, lies 300m WSW of the beacon

The bay may be entered with sufficient rise of tide and there is 2m off the end of the pier, sheltered from W and N. There are many moorings but there is room to anchor, with good holding. Keep clear of the experimental fish farm in the bay, marked by small, unlit yellow buoys.

Facilities
There are no facilities ashore save for two café-bars and a telephone kiosk.

Rivière de Daoulas

This runs into the NE corner of the Baie de Daoulas. The bay is shallow and can only be entered at sufficient rise of tide. There is a bar at the

Le Fret is one of the small villages on the southern shore of the Rade du Brest

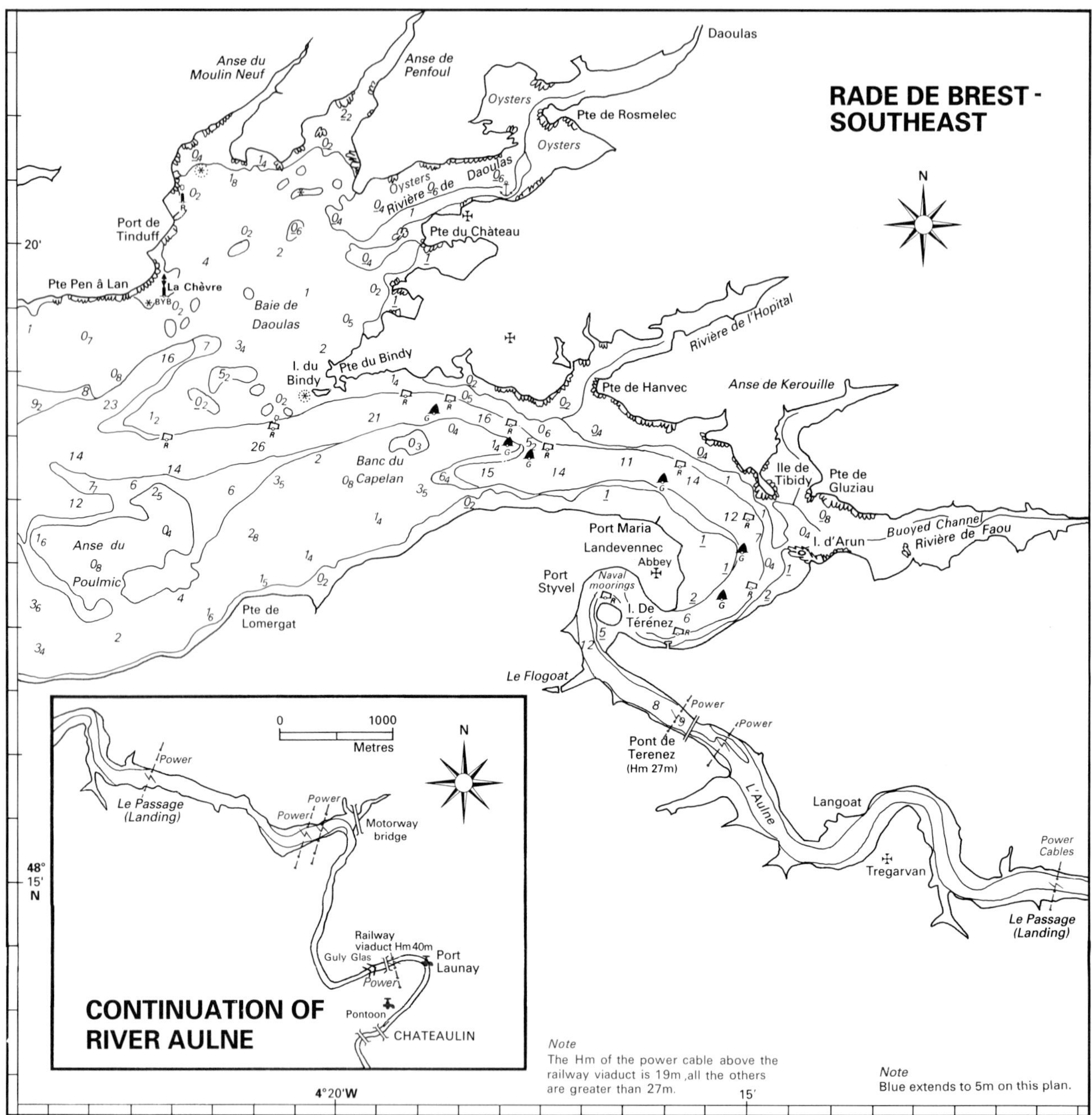

Plan 4

entrance to the river, but once inside there is perfect shelter. The deepest water will be found by keeping Pte de Château on a bearing of about 070°. The Pointe is not easy to distinguish against the land behind it but can be identified by the conspicuous large grey shed with houses above and to the right of it. Once inside there is a deeper pool. Almost all of the river is now taken up with moorings, one of which might be borrowed, and there is hardly any space left to anchor. The best chance of finding room is about ¾M upriver off the second slip, in 1·8m (mud).

It is reportedly possible to proceed upriver to Daoulas, but as the river dries 4·5m this would only be possible (other than by dinghy) at springs.

Facility

There is a small food shop at St Jean, 1km up the hill

Rivière de l'Hôpital

The pretty entrance of this small river lies to the north of the entrance to L'Aulne. As the river dries it can only be visited around HW.

Rivière du Faou

Upstream of the entrance to la Rivière de l'Hôpital, L'Aulne turns south into a large S bend. The mouth of la Rivière du Faou is on the east bank of the

The entrance to Rivière de Daoulas an be identified by the buildings on the Pte du Chateau

curve. The bar dries 0·6m and lies between the Ile de Tibidy and the charming little islet of Arun. North of this islet is a pool with 0·4m (and more in places), but further in the river dries. It is possible to go up to the substantial village of Le Faou at springs, but it is not very attractive and the river is said to be silting.

Rivière de L'Aulne

GENERAL

This is a very beautiful river which winds some 20M inland and is navigable to the market town of Châteaulin. Near the entrance the river runs between steeply-wooded hills. As one goes inland these gradually give way to a lower landscape where fields are interspersed with reed beds and there is little sign of human habitation. The river abounds with bird life and, in the lower reaches, there are several anchorages.

At Guily Glas, some 2½M below Châteaulin there is a lock which operates between 0600 and 2200 LT from 2½ before to 2½ hours after HW Brest. Beyond it there is perfect shelter, and peaceful berths on the river bank are available at the village of Port Launay, a mile further on. Châteaulin is a pleasant and convenient market town, with visitors berths in its centre.

The lock at Guily Glas

Although it is much less visited and is not as sophisticated as the Odet, the Aulne is equally charming and considerably more peaceful. It is worth going out of the way to explore it.

Charts

There is no published chart of the river above Pont de Térénez shown on BA chart *3429*. The plan on page opposite gives sufficient detail for the passage. Alternatively road and tourist maps can be obtained which will show greater detail. Sheet *0518* in the *TOP 25* series of maps published by the Institut Géographique National gives some indication of where the deepest water may lie.

Depths

Apart from the 6m patch at Traverse de l'Hôpital there is 10m as far as Pont de Térénez. From there to within about a mile of the lock 4m, and in places much more, can be found at half tide, after which the depth is reduced in some places to 2·5m at HW neaps. In the upper reaches the bottom is generally very soft mud. Beyond the lock there is between 2·7 and 3m.

DIRECTIONS

Keeping to the buoyed channel, described earlier, the river can be entered at any time. With sufficient rise of tide a yacht may cut across the Banc du Capelan.

On the south bank, inside starboard-hand buoy No. 7, at the start of the large S bend, is the drying jetty of Port Maria, off which one can anchor beside the moorings at neaps, and the attractive-looking village of Landévennec, with the abbey of Penform on the promontory behind. There are mud banks on both sides of the river and it is best to keep in the buoyed channel which curves S, W and NW behind the headland, avoiding the shallows round Ile de Térénez.

In the middle of the S bend there are some large mooring buoys, with a group of retired naval vessels attached, behind which it is possible to land at Port Styvel (not a port; see *The Breton Language*, page 11)

The grass covered quays at Port Launay provide a peaceful mooring

The small visitors pontoon at Châteaulin has room for three or four visiting yachts

and walk up a path through the woods to Landévennec, where there are shops, an hotel and the famous abbey, now restored.

From here to the Pont de Térénez (clearance 27m) the bottom is rock but there are several inlets where one can anchor out of the current on mud. Three are on the starboard bank before the bridge, with a good restaurant on the opposite bank. Channel buoys cease at the naval moorings, but there is enough water for deep-draught yachts to go up with the tide, keeping to the outside of bends and to the middle where the river narrows. It is twelve miles from the bridge to the lock at Guily Glas.

Several power cables cross the river and measurements show that all but one give headroom of 27m or more. This lowest is just upstream of the Guily Glas rail bridge (headroom 40m). The exact height of this cable is not known, but it is over 23m and reported to be over 27m. The cables are shown on the plan on page 24.

Trégarvan, on the south bank about two miles above Pont de Térénez, is a reasonable anchorage; there are several moorings and a slip. There is also a landing at Le Passage, 2M further up. After that the banks become lower and reedy on one and then on both sides and there are no landings until the lock is reached. On rounding the last curve it will be seen on the port-hand side of the river.

One mile above the flower-bedecked lock is Port Launay, a long curve of grass-covered quays, backed by old houses under high tree-covered hills. Many visiting yachts stop at this charming spot where there is plenty of room for visitors. Alternatively it is possible to carry on up to Châteaulin leaving the two green buoys just above Port Launay, which mark a shallow and rocky patch, to starboard. (In 1998 one of these buoys was in a sinking condition. They are opposite the hotel *De Bon Accueil*). Generally, the deepest water from this point right up to Châteaulin is on the left-hand side of the river. At the town there is a pontoon with room for four or five visitors on the starboard bank.

FACILITIES

Port Launay Water and electricity. Showers (key can be obtained from the town hall). Small food shops. Hotel, restaurant. Café/bars.

Châteaulin Water and electricity. Toilets and showers at N end of quay, key obtainable on deposit from tourist office by road bridge, where very modest berthing fees are payable. All facilities of a medium-sized market town. Railway station. Large supermarket some 200m downstream which may be reached by road or dinghy.

4. Camaret-sur-Mer

48°17'N 4°35'W

GENERAL

For yachts bound south after passing through Le Four channel, Camaret is the most convenient port of call in the Brest area. It once supported a considerable shell-fishing fleet, but that activity has declined and today the town is increasingly a yachting and holiday centre. It has good facilities for the visitor with pontoon berths, adequate shopping and many café-bars and restaurants.

The town is built along the edge of the harbour and because of its strategic position has figured in many wars. The old fort on Le Sillon, on the north side of the harbour, and La Tour Dorée near the marina were designed by Vauban and date from 1689. Five years after their construction the defences repelled a combined Dutch and English attack and in 1791 they won a victory against five English frigates.

Much of the inner harbour dries out, but there is a dredged area with pontoon berths. There are 80 places for visitors on the pontoons behind the outer breakwater, though it is a fair walk into the town. In the inner harbour there are also marina berths some of which are available for visitors.

Charts

BA *3427, 798*
Imray *C36*

TIDAL DATA

Times and heights

Time differences				Height differences			
HW		LW		MHWS	MHWN	MLWN	MLWS
BREST							
0000 and 1200	0600 and 1800	0000 and 1200	0600 and 1800	6·9	5·4	2·6	1·0
Camaret							
–0010	–0010	–0013	–0013	–0·3	–0·3	–0·1	0·0

Tidal streams

Within the bay, the tidal streams are weak.

Depths

There are depths of 3m in the outer harbour and its marina. The inner harbour has depths of 2m at the entrance, shoaling as one goes further in. In the inner marina the depths vary from 1·8 to 0·4m.

LIGHTS

1. **North mole head** 48°16'·9N 4°35'·2W
   Iso.WG.4s7m12/9M
   135°-W-182°-G-027° White pylon, green top
2. **South mole head** 48°16'·7N 4°35'·2W
   Fl(2)R.6s9m5M Red pylon

RADIO

VHF Ch 9 0730–2000 LT

APPROACH AND ENTRANCE

By day

The Anse de Camaret is entered between the Pointe de Grand Gouin on the west and Presqu'île de

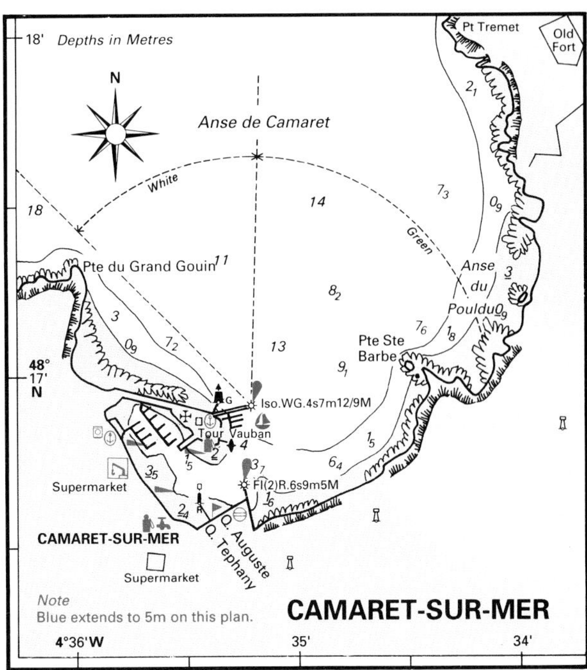

Plan 5

Quélern on the east; the bay is clear of dangers. To the west the high cliffy coast between Pointe de Toulinguet and Pointe de Grand Gouin has no dangers more than 0·1M from the line of the shore and the above-water rocks. Southeast of Pointe de Grand Gouin there is shallow water in the rocky corner of the bay SW of a line from the point to the harbour entrance.

The long breakwater with a green beacon tower on its western end will be seen as soon as it is opened up to the SSE of Pointe de Grand Gouin. Leave the breakwater to starboard to enter the harbour or to find a berth at the outer marina.

By night

Approach in the white sector of the light on the northern breakwater[1] and round it at a reasonable distance. There is an unlit fish farm, and many buoys in the bay to the southeast of the outer marina, but the shore lights usually provide enough illumination to avoid them.

BERTHS AND ANCHORAGE

There are many moorings, including some 30 white ones for visitors, in the bay southeast of the N mole in 3m or more. There might be room to anchor here, clear of the moorings, but much of the space is taken up by the fish farm and the bottom is reported to be foul.

Visitors who wish to berth alongside may do so in the outer marina which has pontoons connected to the south side of the N mole. However, they are exposed to the east and damage may be suffered in strong winds. In these conditions it may be preferable to use one of the buoys mentioned above, or to go into the inner harbour.

In the inner harbour, some of the marina berths are reserved for visitors. Anchoring is forbidden

Rounding Pte du Grand Grouin for Camaret. The breakwater head (arrowed) is left centre with masts behind. Do not be misled into steering for the green tower off the western root of the breakwater

Visitors may use the marina in the outer harbour

The town is at the head of the inner harbour where there are visitors' berths on the pontoons

here, but a yacht which can take the ground may be permitted to do so after consulting the harbourmaster. There is good hard standing off the quays in the middle of the SW side of the harbour which might be used, with an anchor out astern and a bow line to the quay.

FACILITIES

Showers and toilets at both marinas.

Diesel is available from the pontoon connecting the pontoons to the north mole. It is difficult to access, particularly in strong winds.

Ship chandler, shipbuilder and sailmaker.

All shops, supermarkets, launderettes, restaurants and bars.

There is a bus service to Le Fret, where one can take the ferry to Brest.

5. Chenal du Toulinguet

48°16'N 4°38'W

Passage notes

GENERAL

The Chenal de Toulinguet lies immediately west of the Pointe du Toulinguet and gives a convenient passage for vessels bound south from Brest or Camaret, as it saves a long detour round the rocks and shoals outside.

Charts

BA *3427, 798*
Imray *C3*

TIDAL DATA

Times and heights

Time differences				Height differences			
HW		LW		MHWS	MHWN	MLWN	MLWS
BREST							
0000 and 1200	0600 and 1800	0000 and 1200	0600 and 1800	6·9	5·4	2·6	1·0
Camaret							
–0010	–0010	–0013	–0013	–0·3	–0·3	–0·1	0·0

Tidal streams

The S stream begins at +0015 Brest, the N at –0550 Brest, spring rates 3kts. There is a cross tide at the northern end, the flood running to the E and the ebb to the W. To the S, between Les Tas de Pois and Cap de la Chèvre, the stream is weak, 1kt springs, and runs almost continuously southwards.

Depths

As described here the channel has a least depth of 4·9m, though with care a greater depth can be carried

LIGHTS

1. **Pointe du Toulinguet** 48°16'·8N 4°37'·8W
   Oc(3)WR.12s49m15/11M
   shore-W-028°-R-090°-W-shore
   White square tower on building
2. **Pointe du Petit Minou** 48°20'·2N 4°36'·9W
   Fl(2)WR.6s32m19/15M
   shore-R-252°-W-260°-R-307°-W(unintens)-015°-W-065·5°, 070·5°-W-shore
   Grey round tower white on SW side, red top
3. **Pointe du Portzic** 48°21'·6N 4°32'·0W
   Oc(2)WR.12s56m19/15M
   219°-R-259°-W-338°-R-000°-W-065·5°, 070·5°-W-219° Grey 8-sided tower

DIRECTIONS

By day

On the E side of the channel is La Louve tower (W cardinal) on the rocks off the headland, and on the west side are the Roches du Toulinguet, with a rock named Le Pohen, which is steep-to and 11m high, nearest to the channel. The channel is over ¼M wide and carries a least depth of 4·9m. No directions are necessary other than to keep near the middle of the fairway between Le Pohen rock and La Louve tower. If proceeding SSE towards Cap de la Chèvre, note that the beacon on Le Chevreau is partially destroyed; a small unlit W cardinal buoy is situated close W of the rock.

By night

The passage is possible by night if there is enough light to see the rocks and La Louve tower at 100m. There are no lights for the narrows itself and use must be made of two safe sectors. In the southern sector, Le Toulinguet light[1] shows white, bearing less than 028°, and the Pointe de Petit Minou light[2] shows open of Pointe du Toulinguet, bearing more than 010°.

In the northern sector Le Toulinguet light[1] shows white, bearing more than 090°, and the Pointe du Portzic light[3] shows open of the Presqu'île de Quélern, bearing more than 040°. This line passes within a cable of the rocks NNE of La Louve tower and it is therefore desirable to keep Le Portzic light well open of Quélern.

Les Tas de Pois, looking N. The yacht is sailing between La Dentelé and Le Grand Tas de Pois

From the S, enter in the southern safe sector and sail to its apex with Le Toulinguet light just turning red and Le Petit Minou light just shutting in behind Pointe du Toulinguet. From this point La Louve tower bears about 350° and Le Pohen about 270°. Steer to make about 310° to pass between them and into the northern safe sector.

From the N, enter in the northern safe sector, keeping Le Portzic light well open of Quélern as La Louve tower is approached. Once the tower has been seen, course can be shaped to pass through the channel, leaving the tower at least 200m to port, and out by the southern safe sector. From the apex of the northern safe sector, the course to steer is SW for 400m, thence SSE.

Chenal du Petit Leac'h

From the S at night this channel may be preferred, as Le Portzic light[3] can be held on a constant bearing of 043° to lead, with due allowance for tidal streams, between Pelen S cardinal beacon and Basse Mendufa N cardinal buoy (both unlit) to starboard and Petit Leac'h S cardinal beacon (unlit) to port. The channel is 600m wide with a depth of more than 10m.

Les Tas de Pois

48°15'N 4°38'W

There is no need to pass between these rocks, but as some may be interested in doing so (in good weather only) the following notes may be helpful. There are five rocks, which may conveniently be numbered from seaward as follows:

1. Tas de Pois Ouest, 47m high.
2. La Fourche, 10m high.
3. La Dentelé, 35m high.
4. Le Grand Tas de Pois, 64m high.
5. Le Tas de Pois de Terre, 58m high.

Between 1 and 2 is the widest channel. A mid-channel course is clean. A rock dries 0·5m about 50m NE of 1 and there is a drying rock close to 2. Near LW it is therefore necessary to keep midchannel, if anything closer to 2.

Between 2 and 3 the channel is narrow but clean.

Between 3 and 4 keep closer to 3; there is a rock drying 0·6m close NW of 4.

Between 4 and 5 passage is only possible near HW as the channel dries almost right across.

Between 5 and the land there is no passage.

Anchorage

There is a snug anchorage in the sandy Anse de Pen Hir, just inside Les Tas de Pois, in all winds but S or SE. In the centre of the bay, there is a rocky patch just within the 5m line. There are no facilities ashore.

6. Morgat

48°13'N 4°32'W

GENERAL

Morgat is situated in the northwest corner of the Baie de Douarnenez. It is a pretty, sandy bay, sheltered from the N and W by the land, and by the Pointe de Morgat on the SW, almost round to S. The village is a pleasant holiday resort with good beaches and the marina makes it a popular port of call. It is more conveniently situated than Douarnenez as it is not so far east, and is nearer the Four channel and the Raz. Although yachts greater than 12m LOA are not permitted in the harbour this rule does not appear to be enforced.

Charts

BA *798*
Imray *C36*

TIDAL DATA

Times and heights

	Time differences HW		LW		Height differences MHWS	MHWN	MLWN	MLWS
BREST	0000 and 1200	0600 and 1800	0000 and 1200	0600 and 1800	6·9	5·4	2·6	1·0
Morgat	−0008	−0008	−0020	−0010	−0·4	−0·4	−0·2	0·0

Tidal streams

Inside the Baie de Douarnenez the streams are very weak.

Depths

The depths in the marina are 0·6 to 1·8m.

LIGHTS

1. **Basse Vieille buoy** (isolated danger) 48°08'·3N 4°35'·7W Fl(2)6s8m7M Whis
2. **Pointe du Millier** 48°05'·9N 4°27'·9W Oc(2)WRG.6s34m16-11M 080°-G-087°-W-113°-R-120°-W-129°-G-148°-W-251°-R-258° White house

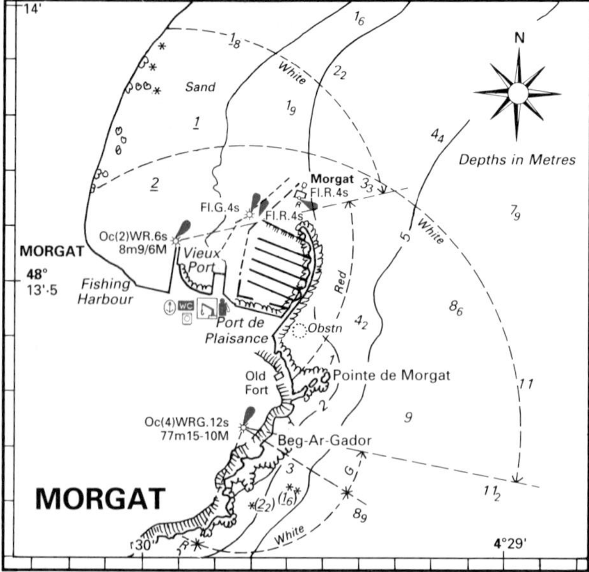

Plan 6

Pte de Morgat lighthouse nestles amongst the trees

3. **Pointe de Morgat** 48°13'·2N 4°29'·9W
   Oc(4)WRG.12s77m15-10M
   shore-W-281°-G-301°-W-021°-R-043°
   White square tower, red top, white house
4. **Morgat buoy (port)** 48°13'·7N 4°29'·6W Fl.R.4s
5. **Morgat old breakwater head** 48°13'·6N 4°29'·9W
   Oc(2)WR.6s8m9/6M 007°-W-257°-R-007°
   White and red metal framework tower

Entrance between wave-breakers (pontoons *brise-lames*)

6. Port Fl.R.4s
7. Starboard Fl.G.4s

RADIO

VHF Ch 9 0800–1200 and 1400–2000 LT

APPROACH AND ENTRANCE

By day

Cap de la Chèvre, 3½M to the south of Morgat, has fangs of rock extending seawards on all sides, especially to the SW, where the bottom is irregular as far as the Basse Vieille whistle buoy. In westerly winds the approach from Cap de la Chèvre provides pleasant sailing, completely sheltered by the land. The cliffs are bold and their tops are covered with grass and heather; many sandy beaches lie at their feet.

Pointe de Morgat, a bold headland with a lighthouse on top, hides the village and anchorage until it has been rounded. Two conspicuous above-water rocks at its foot are steep-to and can be passed within 50m. The breakwater of the new harbour lies just to the north of them, but there is a concrete obstruction in the intervening bay.

Approaching from the southeast, the only outlying dangers are the group of rocks, Les Verrès and La Pierre Profonde, which lie about 2M ESE of Pointe de Morgat. They are not marked, but they can be seen in daylight as they are respectively 9m and 4m high. There is a drying wreck close NE of Les Verrès, and Le Taureau, which dries 1·8m, is situated 400m N of La Pierre Profonde. Approaching Morgat from this direction, leave La Pierre Profonde at least 200m to starboard.

By night

The dangers south of Cap de la Chèvre can be cleared by keeping in one of the two white sectors of Pointe du Millier light[2] until Pointe de Morgat light[3] turns from red to white. Steer towards the light, keeping in the white sector until the 10m line is reached. Turn to parallel the coast on a course of about 035° crossing the green sector of Pointe de Morgat light. Keep a lookout for unlit mooring buoys. The light on the old harbour breakwater[5] will

The entrance to Morgat marina

The rock formations off Pte de Morgat are distinctive

open red, seen over the new breakwater; when it turns from red to white, alter course to leave the harbour entrance buoy[4] to port. There are green and red lights Fl.4s[6,7] marking the entrance between the wavebreakers.

BERTHS AND ANCHORAGE

Yachts may anchor in 2m north and northeast of the wavebreakers. Anchoring is not permitted in the area enclosed by the breakwater and floating concrete wavebreakers. Visitors berth alongside the pontoon under the cranes or on finger pontoons in the main part of the marina.

FACILITIES

Drying slip, travel-lift, 6-tonne crane, large haul-out area. Engineers and sailmakers available from Camaret or Douarnenez. Launderette. Ice.

¼M walk to modest shops, bars and restaurants on the *plage*. More extensive shops at Crozon, the nearest large town (1½M). Good bathing beaches nearby.

In calm weather a dinghy trip to the caves (Les Grandes Grottes de Morgat) is great fun. They lie along the cliff below the lighthouse.

7. Douarnenez

48°06'N 4°20'W

GENERAL

Douarnenez is an important fishing harbour situated in the southeast corner of the bay of the same name. It is off the beaten track of yachts bound south or north, as it lies 17M to the east of Pointe du Raz, but the detour is worth while. The town and harbour are interesting, with a superb museum of old craft; periodically a festival of traditional sailing boats takes place. The town provides all facilities and the harbour offers protection in all weathers.

Charts

BA *798*
Imray *C36*

TIDAL DATA

Times and heights

Time differences				Height differences			
HW		LW		MHWS	MHWN	MLWN	MLWS
BREST							
0000 and 1200	0600 and 1800	0000 and 1200	0600 and 1800	6·9	5·4	2·6	1·0
Douarnenez							
–0010	–0015	–0018	–0008	–0·5	–0·5	–0·3	–0·1

Tidal streams

The tidal streams within the Baie de Douarnenez are very weak.

Depths

In Rosmeur the depths vary, but there is a considerable area with 3–5·5m. In the Rade du Guet the depths shoal from 4m to 0·4m. In the marina at Tréboul the dredged depth is 1·5m and the visitors pontoon berths in Grande Passe have about 1·5m. In the wet basin of Port Rhu the depth is 3m or more.

LIGHTS

1. **Ile Tristan** 48°06'·2N 4°20'·3W
   Oc(3)WR.12s35m13/10M
   shore-W-138°-R-153°-W-shore
   Grey tower, white band, black top
2. **Pointe Biron head** 48°06'·1N 4°20'·4W
   Q.G.7m6M White column, green top
3. **Port-Rhu Directional Light** 48°05'·5N 4°19·9W
   DirFl(5)WRG.20s16m5-4M
   154°-G-156°-W-158°-160° Lantern on bridge
4. **Barrage Lights** 48°05'·7N 4°20·1W
   Fl.G.5s & Fl.R.5s either side of gate.

   Fishing Harbour
5. **E/W mole, E head** 48°06'·0N 4°19'·3W
   Iso.G.4s9m4M White and green pylon
6. **N/S mole, N head** Oc(2)R.6s6m6M
   White and red pylon
7. **Elbow Rosmeur mole head** 48°05'·8N 4°19'·2W
   Oc.G.4s6m6M 170°-vis-097°
   White pylon, green top

RADIO

Fishing harbour, c/s *Douarnenez Port* VHF Ch 16, 12 0800–1200 and 1330–1730 24hr LT

Tréboul Marina VHF Ch 09 0700–1200, 1330–2100 LT

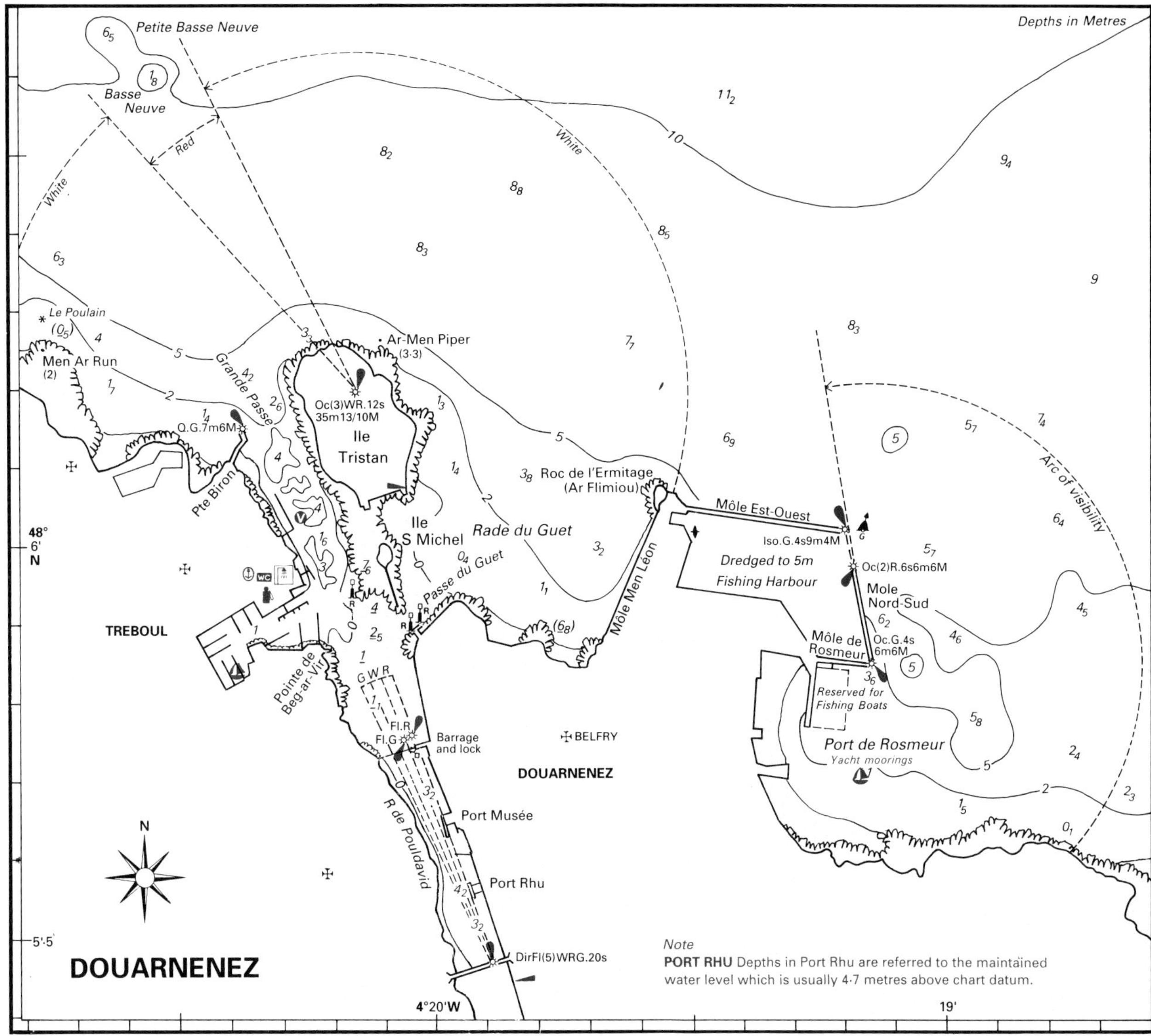

Plan 7

APPROACH AND ENTRANCE

By day

The only considerations in the approach are Basse Veur, with 4·7m over it, and Basse Neuve with 1·8m. Except near LW or when a sea is running these can be ignored. To clear them keep Pointe du Millier lighthouse (5M W of Douarnenez) open of Pointe de la Jument (3M W) until Ploaré church, at the back of the town, comes well open to the left of Douarnenez church and Ile Tristan lighthouse bearing 150°; the two churches and lighthouse are almost in one line. The town is easy to locate from seaward, with Ile Tristan in the foreground, the two churches, and the harbour mole to eastward.

By night

Navigate on Ile Tristan light[1], which has a red sector covering Basse Veur and Basse Neuve, until the inner lights are picked up. For the anchorage at Port de Rosmeur round the breakwaters a reasonable distance off, keeping a good lookout for the numerous unlit mooring buoys. For the visitors pontoon in the Grande Passe, or Tréboul Marina, leave Pointe Biron head light[2] close to starboard. The sectored light[3] at the head of the basin at Port Rhu leads into the Grande Passe and up to the gate in the barrage.

BERTHS AND ANCHORAGE

There are several anchorages or harbours at Douarnenez. As the vessel approaches, the first to be seen is the Rivière de Pouldavid, entered through Grande Passe on the W side between the land and Ile Tristan. There is a pontoon for visitors in the Grande Passe and a yacht harbour at Tréboul, also on the west side. A barrage, with gate, has been built across the river to provide a large wet basin for the museum at Port Rhu.

Next there is the Rade de Guet, an anchorage not much used, in the bay between the east side of Ile Tristan and the main fishing harbour. To the SE of the fishing harbour is the Port de Rosmeur.

Douarnenez approaching the Grand Passe. The visitors pontoons for Tréboul are on the right

Rivière de Pouldavid This is entered through the Grande Passe, west of Ile Tristan. There are rocks close under the island shore, and the best water is nearer the breakwater head on the W side. The river can also be entered through the Passe du Guet (dries 3·5m). There is a long pontoon on which visitors can berth alongside in the Passe on the W side

Tréboul A second, smaller, visitors' pontoon with finger berths on the outside is in the channel just before the turn to starboard into the marina. Passing this pontoon, turn into Tréboul basin, dredged to 1·5m. The marina is crowded and there is not much room to manoeuvre; it is advisable to call by radio or visit the port office to be allocated a berth before entering.

Rivière de Pouldavid/Port Rhu This was once the commercial port. Above the barrage, the wet basin forms part of the remarkable Maritime Museum, with some vessels in the museum building and others afloat in the basin. In front of the barrage the bottom dries 3m (mud and sand) for the most part. It is possible that visiting yachts of sufficient age and appropriate rig may, by prior arrangement, be permitted to berth in the basin.

Rade de Guet This lies between Ile Tristan and the mole leading to Roche d'Ermitage (Ar Flimmou). It is sheltered except from winds from NW to NE, to which it is completely exposed, and is subject to swell from the west. In offshore winds it is a good anchorage, with a convenient dinghy landing at the slip in Passe du Guet. It is quieter than Port de Rosmeur. The depths decrease steadily towards the SW from 3m. Go in as far as draught and tide permit to get as much shelter as possible.

Douarnenez, looking SSW over Ile Tristan into the Rivière de Pouldavid. Tréboul fish and yacht harbour to the right

The maritime museum basin at Douarnenez

The Passe du Guet, leading from the anchorage into the river, dries 3·5m, the best water being on the S side near the port beacons marking the slip. When the base of the first beacon is just covered there should be 1·5m in the Passe.

Fishing harbour Yachts may not use this harbour.

Port de Rosmeur This lies to the E of the town; it is protected by land on the W and S and by the breakwater on the N. Though it is open to the E, the land there is only 1 or 2M distant. The northwestern half of the harbour is for fishing boats and there are many yacht moorings and a fish farm in the remainder of the bay. Anchor in around 5m outside the moorings. There is good holding in mud. Inshore the depths vary rather irregularly and once the 3m line is crossed they shoal quickly in places.

FACILITIES

At Tréboul there is a fuel berth, 6-tonne crane, launderette, cafés, restaurants and shops. Market day Wednesday.

There is a shipyard in the fishing port. Marine engineers, repairs.

At Rosmeur water tap near the dinghy slip and restaurants near the quays.

Douarnenez has all the usual facilities of a substantial town.

8. Ile de Sein

48°02'N 4°51'W

GENERAL

The Ile de Sein is sufficiently detached from the busy world to remain largely unspoilt. Its inhabitants exist largely by catering for tourists, fishing, and farming small plots of soil won from hard rock, which is always so near the surface that it is difficult even to find sufficient depth for burying the dead. The entire male population left the island during the war to join the Free French forces in Britain. It is said that when de Gaulle reviewed the troops he remarked, 'Where is this Ile de Sein? It seems to be half France.'

Though there is considerable tripper traffic with the mainland, the island is a strange, out-of-the-way place. It is worth visiting, if only to see the curious rock formations, but it also has a practical use, as the harbour is convenient if late on the tide, especially when bound south. The facilities are adequate and the anchorage is secure in southerly and westerly winds. It is exposed to the N and NE; if there is a threat of winds from this quarter it is best to leave the Ile de Sein to visit another time, for if the winds are moderate there will be a swell in the harbour, and if they are strong it may be dangerous to remain.

Although the local fishing boats are mostly small, the harbour is a base for larger vessels from Audierne and Douarnęnez, which fish by day and anchor at Sein sufficiently early in the evening to patronise the numerous bars. When the fishing fleet is in the harbour is crowded, but there is still room for a few yachts.

Charts

BA *798, 2351*
Imray *C37, C36*

TIDAL DATA

Times and heights

	Time differences			Height differences			
	HW		LW	MHWS	MHWN	MLWN	MLWS
BREST							
	0000 0600 and and 1200 1800		0000 0600 and and 1200 1800	6·9	5·4	2·6	1·0
Ile de Sein							
	–0005 –0005		–0010 –0005	–0·7	–0·6	–0·2	–0·1

Tidal streams

Between Ile de Sein and Tévennec the NW stream begins +0535 Brest, SE stream begins –0045 Brest, spring rates 3kts. To the north of Nerroth the flood begins NNW at –0600 Brest, turning steadily to W by HW Brest. The ebb begins at +0200, running S.

Depths

The approach is deep until Nerroth is reached; thence the channel has 0·8m. In the anchorage there is 1·8m.

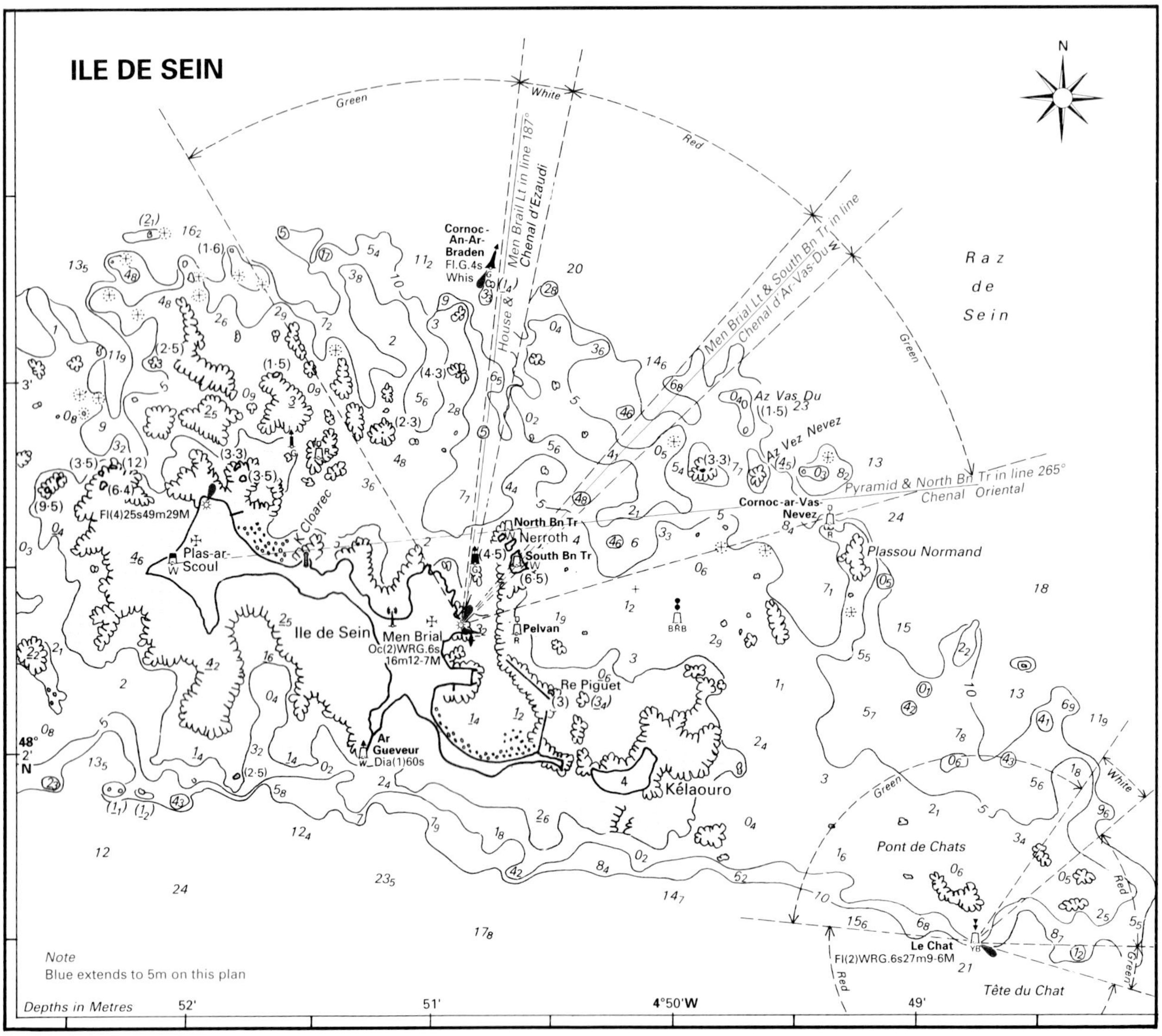

ILE DE SEIN

Green
White
Red
Men Brail Lt in line 187°
House & Chenal d'Ezaudi
Men Brial Lt & South Bn Tr in line
Chenal d'Ar-Vas-Du W
Raz de Sein
Cornoc-An-Ar-Braden
Fl.G.4s
Whis
Az Vas Du
Az Vez Nevez
Pyramid & North Bn Tr in line 265°
Chenal Oriental
Cornoc-ar-Vas-Nevez
Plassou Normand
North Bn Tr
Nerroth
South Bn Tr
Pelvan
Fl(4)25s49m29M
Plas-ar-Scoul
Cloarec
Ile de Sein
Men Brial
Oc(2)WRG.6s
16m12-7M
Re Piguet
Ar Gueveur
Dia(1)60s
Kélaouro
Pont de Chats
Le Chat
Fl(2)WRG.6s27m9-6M
Tête du Chat
48° 2' N
3'
Note
Blue extends to 5m on this plan
Depths in Metres
52'
51'
4°50'W
49'

Plan 8

Ile de Sein from the east

LIGHTS

1. **Ile de Sein, main light** 48°02'·6N 4°52'·1W
   Fl(4)25s49m29M White tower, black top
2. **Ar Guéveur** 48°02'·0N 4°51'·4W Dia 60s
   White tower
3. **Men Brial** 48°02'·3N 4°51'·0W
   Oc(2)WRG.6s16m12-7M
   149°-G-186°-W-192°-R-221°-W-227°-G-254°
   Green and white tower
4. **Cornoc an Ar Braden buoy (starboard)**
   48°03'·3N 4°50'·7W Fl.G.4s Whis
5. **Tévennec** 48°04'·3N 4°47'·6W
   Q.WR.28m9/6M 090°-W-345°-R-090°
   White tower and dwelling
   DirFl.4s24m12M 324°-intens-332° same structure
6. **Le Chat** 48°01'·5N 4°48'·8W
   Fl(2)WRG.6s27m 9-6M
   096°-G-215°-W-230°-R-271°-G-286°-R-096°
   S card tower

APPROACH AND ENTRANCE

On even the largest-scale British Admiralty chart, *798*, the Ile de Sein appears to be so surrounded by reefs and rocks that it looks unapproachable, especially when it is associated in one's mind with the fierce tides of the Raz. But, except in bad visibility or heavy weather, navigation in the area with a chart on a sufficiently large scale is not difficult because:

a. The plateau is compact on the NE and E sides and the fringes are indicated by the whistle buoy on the N, the above-water rock Ar Vas Du to the NNE, the Cornoc ar Vas Nevez tower to the E and Le Chat tower to the ESE. There are no dangers if a vessel is over ½M seaward of these visible marks.
b. The tidal streams on the Sein side of the Raz are not so strong as they are on the E side.
c. The entrance channels are clearly marked. However, when visiting the island for the first time it is best to wait for settled weather, with clear visibility and neap tides.

Nerroth (called An Iarod on some charts) is the key to pilotage in the Ile de Sein. Situated in the approach to the harbour, it looks like a small island. In fact it is composed of three very large rocks; only at low water does it form a continuous island, with a finger of rocks extending from its southern end to the eastern breakwater. There are two white masonry beacons, at its northern and southern ends, which are important leading marks.

North channel

This is the principal channel and the easiest for a stranger. The channel is deep until abreast of Nerroth, after which the depth is 1·4m to the jetties.

By day

Having given a wide berth to all beacons and visible rocks (not less than ½M if approaching from the Raz), approach the Cornoc an Ar Braden pillar whistle buoy (starboard) from the north. Bring Men Brial lighthouse into transit, at 188°, with the third house from the left by the quay; this house is painted white, with a black vertical stripe which should be kept just open to the left of the lighthouse if the latter tends to hide it.

This transit leaves both the buoy and the rock which it marks very close to starboard. It is advisable, therefore, to borrow say 50m to port until the rock is passed, as the tides set very strongly across the channel. Thence follow the alignment; there are drying rocks on either side, but no dangers for 50m on either side of the line. When Nerroth is abeam, if the tide is high, Pelvan concrete beacon (port, R) will come into transit with the eastern end of the E breakwater, bearing 155° (at LW the breakwater is obscured). Follow this transit (or steer 155° for Pelvan), leaving Guernic concrete beacon (starboard) to starboard.

When Guernic is well abaft the beam borrow a little to starboard of the transit, and when Men Brial lighthouse bears 220° the shoal is passed and course can be altered to SW for the anchorage.

By night

There must be enough light to make out Nerroth and Guernic concrete beacon on near approach. As it may not be easy to find the best water, it is desirable also that the tide should be high enough to allow some margin, preferably above half tide.

Enter in the white sector of Men Brial light[3], bearing from 187° to 190°, leaving Cornoc an Ar Braden buoy[4] to starboard. When Nerroth northern beacon is abeam, alter course to 160° and enter the red sector of Men Brial, leaving Guernic tower 60m to starboard. When the other white sector of Men Brial is entered it is safe to steer for the anchorage.

Northeast channel

This channel carries 3·6m until it joins the north channel by Nerroth; thence depths are as for the north channel.

By day

Make a position 300m NW of Ar Vas-du, a rock 1·5m (above MHWS). Here the white masonry beacon S of Nerroth will be in transit with Men Brial lighthouse bearing 224°; follow this transit. When the white masonry beacon at the north end of Nerroth bears 265° turn to starboard and, leaving the northern white beacon 100m to port, join the north channel.

By night

There is a white sector of Men Brial light[2] covering this channel, but sufficient light is needed for the deviation round Nerroth and into harbour.

East channel

This channel carries 2·3m until it joins the north channel by Nerroth; thence depths are as for the north channel. It is only useable by day.

The channel is entered 100m N of Cornoc ar Vas

Men Brial on Ile de Sein. The green beacon is Guernic, left to starboard on entering

Men Brial. Entering from the N, the lighthouse and the black stripe on the wall to left of lighthouse form the leading line on 188°

Nevez tower (R). When coming up through the Raz be careful to avoid the shoals E and N of Le Chat tower (S cardinal), and Plassou Normand (drying 2·4m) to the SE of Cornoc ar Vas Nevez tower. These shoals will be avoided if the tower is kept bearing less than 290°.

The leading marks for this channel are the white masonry beacon on the north end of Nerroth in transit at 264° with a pyramid, with fluorescent orange top, 300m S of the Ile de Sein main lighthouse. Also on the transit is Karek Cloarec, a rock which never covers, and behind it and just south of the transit is a monument (a cross of Lorraine) on Men Dai, a promontory rising to 18m above datum.

The anchorage at Men Brial on a quiet evening with the fishing fleet at sea. The harbour should only be visited in settled weather

If the pyramid cannot be identified either of the above could be used instead, and they will in any case serve to confirm the identification. The marks must be held very closely, as Ar Vas Nevez, drying 5m, is close to the N of the transit, while shortly after there is a rock drying 1m close to the S.

On close approach to Nerroth, bear to starboard and round it to join the north channel, leaving the white masonry beacon 100m to port.

Near high water it is possible to make a short cut east of Nerroth by steering to leave Pelvan concrete beacon (port) close to port, then steering for 200m towards the southern quay to avoid rocks to starboard before rounding into the anchorage. This passage is a difficult one which cannot be recommended to strangers.

BERTHS AND ANCHORAGE

The anchorage is immediately off the lifeboat slip, near the Men Brial lighthouse and SE of it. Off the slip there is 1·8m, and there is 1m further to the SE. Near and S of the quays the whole harbour dries out. The fishing fleet enters the harbour in the evening, and is often there by day. Its position indicates the best water. The round red buoys belong to the fishermen and do not leave much room to anchor between them and the slip; it may be necessary to anchor to the east of them. Permission can sometimes be obtained to use one.

The anchorage is sheltered from S to NW, and from E below half tide. Swell enters if the wind goes into the S and the anchorage would be dangerous in strong winds from any northerly direction. It is also exposed to the E when the rocks are covered. Yachts should not remain in the anchorage if fresh northerly or easterly winds are expected. The bottom is a layer of mud over rock. The stream in the anchorage is weak.

Yachts that can take the ground can do so in the bay S of the slips and can find 1·5m in places at LW neaps. Inspect the bottom first as, although it is mainly sand, there are some weed-covered stony patches.

Facilities

Several small shops, café-bars and restaurants. Ship and engine repairs can be arranged, basic chandlery at the fishermen's cooperative shop. Water is scarce and yachts should bring enough with them.

The village has a considerable population; the houses are clustered together in a small area, providing shelter from the winds in narrow alleyways. Bread comes on first *vedette* from the mainland and should be ordered the night before.

9. Raz de Sein

48°03'N 4°46'W

Passage notes

GENERAL

The Raz de Sein is the area between the Pointe du Raz on the mainland and the Ile de Sein. The scene viewed from the Pointe du Raz during gales, with the wind against a spring tide, is so impressive that it forms an inspiration to artists and photographers. Taken under reasonable conditions, however, the passage through the Raz presents no great difficulties and it is often smoother in the passage than out at sea. It is largely a matter of timing. A yacht leaving the Four channel on the last of the fair tide can usually cross the Iroise, where the tides are less strong and chiefly set across the course, during the foul tide, so as to arrive at the Raz at the correct time, when the tide is just starting to turn fair.

The channel between La Plate tower and the rocks on the Ile de Sein is 2M wide. In the northern approach lies the island of Tévennec, surrounded by rocks; to the SW of Tévennec a rock, Basse Plate, narrows the western passage to 1½M.

Charts
BA *798, 2351*
Imray *C37, 36*

TIDAL STREAMS

South-going, ebb stream

Position	*Begins Brest*	*Direction*	*Spring rate, knots*
Off Pte du Van	−0130	SW	1½
Between Sein and Tévennec	−0045	SE	2¾
Off La Vieille	−0045	SSE	5½
In centre of Raz	−0030	SW	5½
In southern part of Raz	−0045	SE	5½

There is a north-going eddy between La Vieille and a position near La Plate.

North-going, flood stream

Position	*Begins Brest*	*Direction*	*Spring rate, knots*
In southern part of Raz	+0535	NW	6½
In centre of Raz	+0550	NE	6½
Off La Vieille	+0535	NNW	6½
Between Sein and Tévennec	+0535	NW	2¾
Off Pte du Van	+0605	NE	2¾

There is a south-going eddy for ½M N of La Vieille. In the inshore Passe du Trouz Yar the streams are much stronger and in the approaches to the pass they do not run true with the channel. They turn earlier, the S stream beginning about −0120 Brest; the time at which the N stream begins is not known, probably about +0445 Brest.

LIGHTS

1. **Tévennec** 48°04'·3N 4°47'·6W Q.WR.28m9/6M 090°-W-345°-R-090°
   White square tower and dwelling
   DirFl.4s24m12M 324°-intens-332° same structure
2. **La Vieille** 48°02'·5N 4°45'·4W
   Oc(2+1)WRG.12s33m18-13M Horn(2+1)60s
   290°-W-298°-R-325°-W-355°-G-017°-W-035°-G-105°-W-123°-R-158°-W-205°
   Grey square tower, black top
3. **La Plate** 48°02'·4N 4°45'·5W
   VQ(9)10s19m8M W card tower
4. **Le Chat** 48°01'·5N 4°48'·8W
   Fl(2)WRG.6s27m9-6M
   096°-G-215°-W-230°-R-271°-G-286°-R-096°
   s card tower
5. **Men Brial** 48°02'·3N 4°51'·0W
   Oc(2)WRG.6s16m12-7M
   149°-G-186°-W-192°-R-221°-W-227°-G-254°
   Green and white tower
6. **Ile de Sein main light** 48°02'·6N 4°52'·1W
   Fl(4)25s49m29M White tower, black top
7. **Ar Guéveur** 48°02'·0N 4°51'·4W Dia 60s White tower

APPROACH AND PASSAGE

The Raz de Sein can be rough, especially in the overfalls off La Vieille, even in moderate winds if they are contrary to the stream. When wind and tide are together the passage is smoother than outside. In light weather, at neap tides and in the absence of swell, the passage can be made at any time under power, but the seas caused by the irregular bottom knock the way off a boat very quickly. Except when wind and tide are together, slack water for the passage is always to be preferred. The Raz is

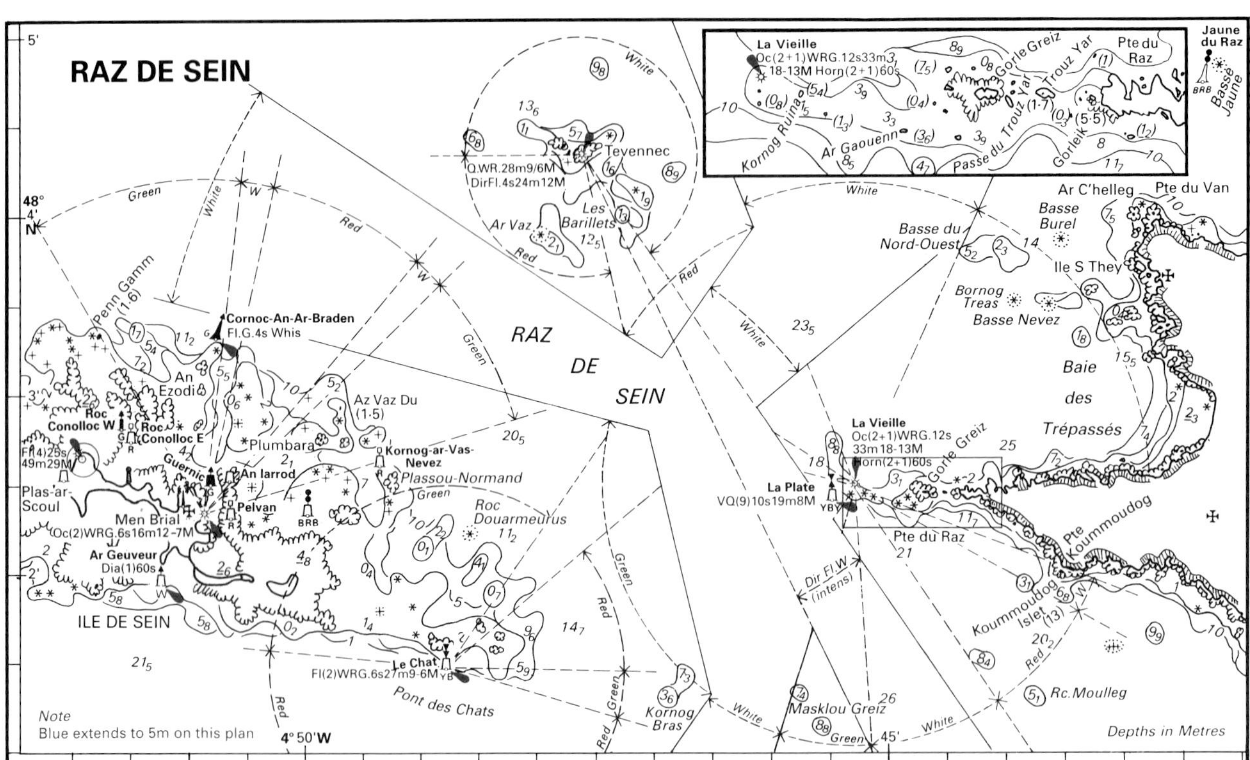

Plan 9

Looking east across the Raz de Sein with a big spring tide running north. La Platte and La Vieille are in the foreground with the Baie des Trépassés at the top right

temperamental and the seas met there vary considerably, but in strong winds contrary to the stream the overfalls are dangerous.

FROM THE NORTH

By day

Steer for La Vieille lighthouse, bearing 180°, about midway between Pointe du Van and Tévennec. When ½M off La Vieille, bear to starboard to pass W of La Plate tower (W cardinal), allowing for any tidal set. There are overfalls W of La Vieille and La Plate.

After passing La Plate the sea soon begins to moderate, but in rough weather the Masklou Greiz (9m) and Kornog Bras (3·6m) must be avoided as the seas break heavily over them. If proceeding seawards, the Pointe du Van in transit at 041° with Gorle Greiz, the large rock between Pointe du Raz and La Vieille, leads between the shoals. If bound for Penmarc'h, steer with Tévennec bearing 324° astern open to the left of La Plate.

By night

Steer for La Vieille light[2] at 180° in the white sector. When Le Chat[4] turns from green to white, steer in that white sector until the directional flashing light on Tévennec[1] opens; thence steer about 150° in that sector. Bound seaward, steer out in the first white sector of La Vieille, about 205°; bound for Penmarc'h, continue in the directional sector of Tévennec until clear. When Le Chat turns from green to red, bearing 286° the vessel is clear of the southern dangers.

La Platte and La Vieille on a calm day at slack water

FROM THE NORTHWEST

By day

The approach is between Tévennec and Ile de Sein. There is the Basse Plate ½M SW of Tévennec to be avoided; keep Koummoudog islet open to the right of Gorle Greiz, bearing 118°. The dangers off Ile de Sein are fairly well defined by the whistle buoy, Ar Vas Du rock (which never covers) and a R tower. Follow these dangers on the Ile de Sein side, leaving them ½M to starboard, and Le Chat tower (S cardinal) ¾M to starboard. Or steer for La Vieille in transit with the southern limit of the cliffs SE of the Pointe du Raz, bearing 112°. When ½M off La Vieille alter course to round La Plate as before.

The ebb stream SW of Tévennec is weaker than in the Raz, and the race itself appears weaker on the Ile de Sein side, though there is no official confirmation of this. In W or SW winds most of the passage is under the lee of the Ile de Sein plateau, and not so rough as E of Tévennec; care must be taken not to get onto Kornog Bras.

By night

Steer for Men Brial light[5] on Ile de Sein, in the white sector (186° to 192°). When La Vieille[2] turns from red to white, steer in this white sector until the directional isophase light on Tévennec[1] opens; thence proceed as described for the northern channel.

FROM THE SOUTH

By day

In good visibility keep Tévennec open to west of La Plate on a bearing of 327°. When ½M from La Plate, bear to port, avoiding overfalls.

If heading north, round the tower about ½M distant to steer 020° until, with due attention to tide, Jaune du Raz (BRB) isolated danger buoy is abeam to starboard.

At spring tides, counter the set of the flood stream towards the Tévennec dangers by holding La Vieille tower on a bearing of 180° when clear north of La Plate. If going west of Tévennec steer well to port to make good a course of 295° from La Plate until the NE-going stream is entered.

The south coast of Pointe du Raz is steep-to, so that with visibility of ½M and otherwise favourable conditions it is possible to steer to sight the cliffs well to the east of the point and follow the coast west, keeping ½M off until La Plate tower has been identified.

By night

Passage at slack water is preferable. Keep in the directional isophase sector of Tévennec light[1] until, with Tévennec bearing 330°, La Plate[3] bears 110°. A course of 020° will then lead northwards clear of the Raz, while a course of 295° leads northwest between Tévennec and Ile de Sein.

PASSE DU TROUZ YAR

This interesting passage is hazardous. It should only be taken by those with experience of these waters, and then only under ideal conditions i.e. in daylight, in calm weather, at slack water, with good visibility and with reliable auxiliary power.

Identify Gorle Greiz, which is the largest rock off the Pointe du Raz. At high water it appears as two large, slightly separated rocks with E Gorle Greiz, a smaller rock, close by to the ESE. Trouz Yar is the small rock midway between them and the shore. The passage lies between Gorle Greiz and Trouz Yar and is deep and clean, except for a 0·5m outlier to the north of the eastern end of Gorle Greiz. Approach on a N or SSW course, allowing for any cross set of the tide in the approach, and go through the centre of the channel, steering NNW (avoiding the outlier) if coming from the south or SSE when coming from the north.

Soon after slack water, even at neaps, the tide runs so hard that the yacht goes out of control, and any sea makes the passage highly dangerous. Note that the tide turns early in the pass; see page 40.

ANCHORAGE

There is a fair-weather anchorage in which to wait for the tide in the Baie des Trépassés – the Bay of Corpses, so called as it is here that the bodies of those shipwrecked on the Raz often come ashore. The bay, sheltered between NE and SE, is sandy and shelving so anchor in the most suitable depth; the best position is in the centre, facing the valley. There is likely to be some swell.

10. Audierne

48°00'N 4°33'W

GENERAL

Situated at the mouth of the Goyen river, the port of Audierne, like all French fishing centres, is interesting and the harbour is picturesque. The outside anchorage at Ste Evette is well protected except from the E and SE, and is suitable for a short stay when on passage. The harbour can be entered around mid tide, but the approach channel is dangerous in heavy onshore weather. Pontoons have been established in the inner harbour to cater for between 25 and 35 visitors, but there are only a very few berths for boats over 9m.

Charts

BA *3640, 2351*
Imray *C37*

TIDAL DATA

Times and heights

	Time differences				Height differences			
	HW		LW		MHWS	MHWN	MLWN	MLWS
BREST	0000 and 1200	0600 and 1800	0000 and 1200	0600 and 1800	6·9	5·4	2·6	1·0
Audierne	–0035	–0030	–0035	–0030	–1·7	–1·3	–0·6	–0·2

Tidal streams

In the approach the NW stream begins at −0515 Brest, the SE at +0025 Brest. Streams in the approach are weak, but strong in the harbour itself.

Depths

The approach is deep until ESE of Ste Evette mole, where there is a depth of 2·2m. The anchorage (with moorings) at Ste Evette has depths of from 1·0 to 3·0m. The entrance channel is dredged but is very subject to silting and it should be considered as drying 1m. There is about 0·5m in the marina.

LIGHTS

1. **Pointe de Lervilly** 48°00'·1N 4°34'·0W
   Fl(3)WR.12s20m14/11M
   211°-W-269°-R-294°-W-087°-R-121°
   White round tower, red top
2. **Jetée de Ste Evette head** 48°00'·3N 4°33'·1W
   Oc(2)R.6s2m7M Red lantern
   Passe de l'Est. Ldg Lts 331°
3. *Front* **Jetée de Raoulic head** 48°00'·6N 4°32'·5W
   Oc(2+1)WG.12s11m14/9M
   shore-W-034°-G-shore, but may show W 037°-055°
   White tower

4. *Rear* **Kergadec** 48°01'·0N 4°32'·8W
   DirF.R.44m9M 321°-intens-341°
   White 8-sided tower, red lantern
   DirQ.WRG.43m12-9M
   000°-G-005·3°-W-006·7°-R-017° same structure
5. **Coz Fornic groyne** 48°01'·0N 4°32'·4W
   Oc.R.4s6m Grey mast
6. **Vieux môle groyne** 48°01'·1N 4°32'·1W
   Iso.R.4s7m Mast
7. **Pors Poulhan 3M ESE of entrance**
   47°59'·1N 4°28'·0W Q.R.14m9M
   White square tower, red top

RADIO

Ste Evette VHF Ch 9 0700–1100 and 1600–2200 LT
Audierne VHF Ch 16, 9 HW±2hr

APPROACH AND ENTRANCE

Audierne is situated in the NE corner of the bay of the same name. The white slate-roofed houses will be seen from a distance clustered on the hillsides, with another group above the village of Pors-Poulhan, 4M to the SE.

The entrance to the harbour can be dangerous in strong onshore winds and swell, but the Ste Evette anchorage is protected by the land and a breakwater, except from the E and SE.

FROM THE WEST AND SOUTH

By day

There are no dangers until the vessel approaches within one mile of Pte Raoulic, on which stands the harbour jetty. The channel, ½M wide, lies between Le Sillon and adjacent rocks on the W side and a group of rocks named La Gamelle, which only dry at springs, on the E side. If there is a swell the seas break on La Gamelle. There is a whistle buoy (W cardinal) ¼M SW and a bell buoy (S cardinal) ¼M SE of La Gamelle.

The approach may be made with the two lighthouses (white with red tops), one disused, to the west of Pte Raoulic in transit, bearing 006°. The rear lighthouse, Kergadec, is on the skyline, but the old front lighthouse, Trescadec, is on the foreshore in a gap between some houses and is not easy to locate.

This line leaves the whistle buoy (W cardinal) about 200m to starboard and passes over a 2·2m patch E of the Ste Evette mole. If bound for the anchorage, steer for the mole head when it bears NW and round it, but not very closely. If making for the inner harbour, leave the transit of the lighthouses steer for the end of the Raoulic jetty when it bears 034° and is in transit with the rather small steeple of Poulgoazec church (St Julien), which stands on a grassy knoll on the eastern side of the river.

The outer harbour (Ste Evette) at Audierne with the yacht moorings beyond the breakwater and ferry jetty

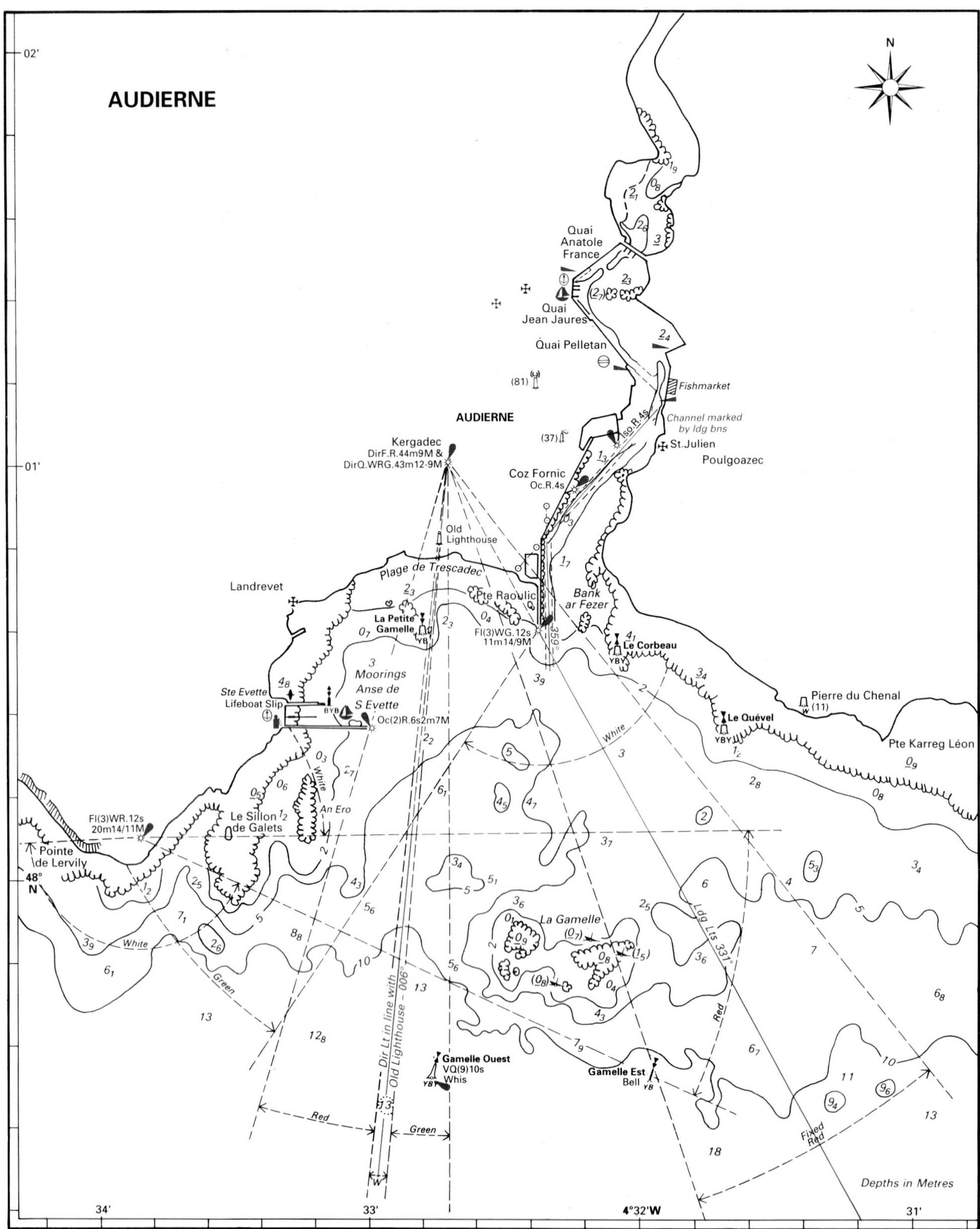
AUDIERNE
N
02'
01'
Quai Anatole France
Quai Jean Jaures
Quai Pelletan
Fishmarket
Channel marked by ldg bns
(81)
AUDIERNE
(37)
Iso.R.4s
St.Julien
Poulgoazec
Kergadec
DirF.R.44m9M &
DirQ.WRG.43m12-9M
Coz Fornic
Oc.R.4s
Old Lighthouse
Plage de Trescadec
Landrevet
Pte Raoulic
Bank ar Fezer
La Petite Gamelle
YB
Fl(3)WG.12s
11m14/9M
359°
Le Corbeau
YBY
Moorings
Anse de
S Evette
Ste Evette
Lifeboat Slip
BYB
Oc(2)R.6s2m7M
Pierre du Chenal
(11)
Le Quével
YBY
Pte Karreg Léon
White
An Ero
Le Sillon de Galets
Fl(3)WR.12s
20m14/11M
Pointe de Lervily
48° N
White
Green
La Gamelle
Ldg Lts 331°
Red
Dir Lt in line with Old Lighthouse - 006°
Gamelle Ouest
VQ(9)10s
Whis
Gamelle Est
Bell
Red
Green
W
Fixed Red
Depths in Metres
34'
33'
4°32'W
31'

Plan 10

By night

Enter the narrow white sector of Kergadec[4] quick flashing light (006°). When the light on the Ste Evette mole head[2] bears NW alter course for the Ste Evette anchorage. If proceeding to the inner harbour, alter course for the head of the Raoulic jetty when the light on it[3] turns from white to green, bearing 034°. Then keep just in the white sector to approach the jetty for entry. However, entry by night is not advised.

FROM THE SOUTHEAST

By day

There is no difficulty in the southeastern approach as the channel between La Gamelle to the W and the land to the E is wide and carries a least depth of 2·5m on the leading line.

Identify Kergadec light tower (white with a red lantern) and keep it on a bearing of 331° in transit with the Raoulic jetty head light tower, leaving La Gamelle well to port.

By night

Approach with Raoulic light[3] and Kergadec light[4] in line on 331°. Pte de Lervilly light[1] has a red sector covering La Gamelle. When this light turns from red to white the way is open to steer for the Ste Evette anchorage.

Ste Evette anchorage

The Ste Evette anchorage half a mile SW of the harbour is good. It is sheltered from W and N by the land and from the S by the mole, though some swell enters if there is S in the wind and this may be considerable if the wind is strong. The depths are 2·5 to 3·1m north of the end of the mole, decreasing steadily towards the shore. There are tightly packed moorings in the anchorage, with a charge collected for their use. There may be room to anchor east of them, with less shelter from the S. The holding ground is not very good and there are a few rocky patches. It is best to tuck in behind the mole as far as depths allow, so as to get out of the swell. The more northerly of the two slips, used by the ferries, extends a long way; the end is marked by an inconspicuous (E cardinal) beacon. A small tower (S cardinal) marks a rock, called La Petite Gamelle, in the northern part of the anchorage; Wt and N of this the bay is shallow.

Land at the ferry slip or, above half tide, at the little pier in the NW corner of the bay. It is also possible to land at Raoulic jetty but this dries out towards LW.

Audierne

Only small visiting yachts will find room at Audierne marina

The harbour

Much of the harbour or river mouth dries out at LW, and there is a bank which dries outside the entrance nearly one cable to the SE of Raoulic jetty head. The channel is dredged to 0·5m above LAT, but shifts and is subject to silting, so that it is best to enter within an hour and a half of high water. As a general rule, keep about 60m off the jetty as far as the bend in the wall some 2 cables from the entrance. The channel is indicated by a pair of panels with red and white chevrons, points uppermost, on the bank beyond the jetty. Thence the channel passes near the ends (marked by lit red beacons) of the two spurs, Coz Fornic and Vieux môle, projecting from the west side, after which it crosses over to run along the quay at Poulgoazec. Finally the channel swings back to the west bank along the Audierne quays and ends at the small marina.

Strangers should not attempt this channel at night.

FACILITIES

Ste Evette

There are café-bars, a launderette and tourist shops at the ferry pier. A restaurant faces the bay at Trescadec and a there is small store at Kergadec, but most of the shops are in the town over a mile away. Fuel is available close to the pier.

Audierne

Audierne is a substantial town with a pleasant atmosphere and is busy with tourists during the season. The harbourmaster is most helpful and the mayor is keen for yachtsmen to enjoy their stay.

There is a shipyard and repairs can be undertaken.

There is a supermarket a short walk upstream past the bridge.

All shops, banks, restaurants and hotels in the town close to the pontoons.

Bus service to Douarnenez and Quimper.

11. Saint-Guénolé

47°49'N 4°23'W

GENERAL

The small town of St-Guénolé is situated about 1M north of Pointe de Penmarc'h. It has a long and interesting history. Before the Second World War the harbour, open to the westward, was untenable in bad weather sweeping in from the Atlantic. Then a sea wall was built, enclosing this entry, and a channel blasted through the rocks to the south; the quays were extended and the harbour was dredged. Although the entrance is exposed and dangerous in bad weather, the harbour now offers good shelter in all winds. A considerable fishing fleet is based here, but there is no yachting activity and yachts may only enter in an emergency.

No attempt should be made to approach the harbour except in settled weather, with no swell. A first entry should be made with the tide more than half up, in daylight; a night entry should not be attempted unless the channel is known. There is very little room for error. The harbour is not attractive.

Charts

BA *2351, 2646*
Imray *C37*

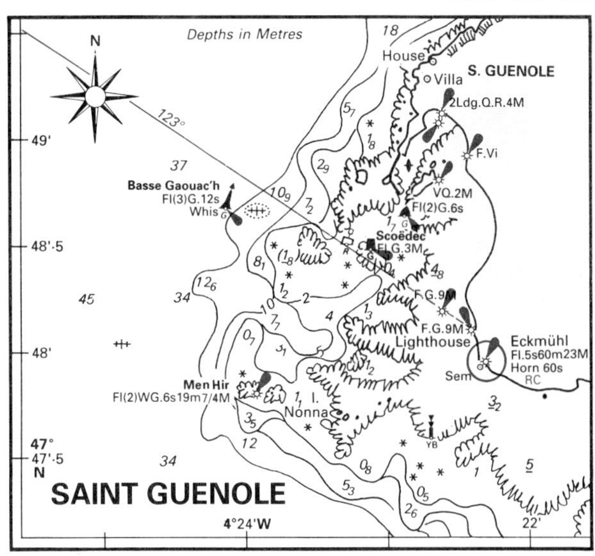

Plan 11

TIDAL DATA

Times and heights

	Time differences				Height differences			
	HW		LW		MHWS	MHWN	MLWN	MLWS
BREST								
	0000 and 1200	0600 and 1800	0000 and 1200	0600 and 1800	6·9	5·4	2·6	1·0
Saint Guénolé								
	−0015	−0030	−0035	−0020	−1·8	−1·4	−0·7	−0·2

Saint Guénolé looking SE. Since this picture was taken building work has continued

Tidal streams
For streams in the offing see under Penmarc'h (page 49). In the harbour the streams are weak, except in the final approach channel where they can reach 3–4kts.

Depths
2·0m in the approach channel. Depths in the harbour from 2·5m to drying. The deep water is largely taken up with fishing vessels so yachts must be prepared to take the ground.

LIGHTS
1. **Eckmühl** 47°47'·9N 4°22'·4W
   Fl.5s60m23M Horn 60s
   Grey 8-sided tower
2. **Men Hir** 47°47'·8N 4°23'·9W
   Fl(2)WG.6s19m7/4M 135°-G-315°-W-135°
   White tower, black band
3. **Basse Gaouac'h buoy (starboard)**
   47°48'·7N 4°24'·2W Fl(3)G.12s Whis
4. **Passe de Grounilli Ldg Lts 123°**
   Front 47°48'·2N 4°22'·6W F.G.9m9M
   Rear 300m from front F.G.13m9M
   Fluorescent orange-red spheres on white columns with black bands
5. **Scoëdec** 47°48'·5N 4°23'·1W Fl.G.2·5s6m3M
   Green tower
6. **Intermediate Ldg Lts 055°**·
   Front 47°48'·7N 4°22'·7W VQ.5m2M
   Rear 320m from front F.Vi.12m1M
   040°-vis-070°
   Platforms on green and white metal columns
7. **Final Ldg Lts 026·5°** Synchronised
   Front 47°49'·1N 4°22'·6W Q.R.8m4M Red mast
   Rear 51m from front Q.R.12m4M
   Mast, red and white bands

RADIO
VHF Ch 12 day service.

APPROACH AND ENTRANCE
By day
If coming from the south leave Men Hir, white tower with black band, at least 300m to starboard as the reef extends west of it. From a position 300m N of the Basse Gaouac'h whistle buoy bring the leading marks for the Passe de Groumilli into transit, bearing 123°. They are masonry columns with BW horizontal bands, with large fluorescent red spheres as topmarks. They will be seen to the left of Eckmühl lighthouse. The Passe de Groumilli transit leaves the Pellenic rocks, which dry, close to starboard; Scoëdec tower (starboard G) will be seen on the port bow. After ½ mile, before Scoëdec tower

St Guénolé entrance. Intermediate leading marks in transit (arrowed) on 055°

Saint Guénolé harbour

is reached, a port-hand buoy will be left to port and the church of Notre Dame de la Joie, on the coast ½M north of Penmarc'h, will come into transit with Scoëdec tower, bearing 096°.

Passing the buoy, alter to port and steer 055·5° with the two intermediate leading marks (a pair of white columns with green tops) in line. This transit initially passes very close to the reef on which Scoëdec beacon lies so borrow slightly to the left of the transit until Scoëdec bears south. Identify the four entrance-channel buoys (two port and two starboard), followed by the four metal light columns (two port and two starboard) marking the submerged breakwaters, and steer into the harbour.

By night

Only those who are already familiar with the harbour should attempt a night entry.

BERTHS AND ANCHORAGE

Only anchor in an emergency, and do so out of the way of the fishing boats, probably near the lifeboat house. The bottom is rock, covered with muddy sand; it is foul and a tripping line should be used. Normally a yacht should secure alongside temporarily and consult the authorities to be assigned a berth.

FACILITIES

All shops. Shipyard. Several hotels. Buses to Quimper. Museum of prehistoric megalithic culture about 1M distant. Water from the fish market on the quay.

12. Pointe de Penmarc'h

47°48'N 4°22'·5W

Passage notes

GENERAL

The Pointe de Penmarc'h is a low headland, in contrast with the very high octagonal lighthouse (Eckmühl) on it, which is 60m high. There are reefs of rocks extending in all directions from the headland, with numerous towers on them. In bad weather the whole scene is grim, but the point need not be closely approached except when on passage north of the Iles de Glénan. When rounding Pointe de Penmarc'h progress often seems slow, with Eckmühl lighthouse in sight for a long time, as the course follows an arc over 1M offshore.

Charts

BA *2351, 2643, 2646*
Imray *C37*

TIDAL STREAMS

These do not compare in strength with those in the Four channel or the Raz de Sein, as the spring rates are only 1½ to 2kts, except perhaps in the vicinity of the Men Hir tower.

The tidal stream divides at the Pointe de Penmarc'h, the flood setting northerly towards Audierne and easterly towards the Iles de Glénan; the ebb sets in the opposite direction, the streams meeting off the Men Hir tower, where there are overfalls in rough weather.

Pte de Penmarc'h

Steering S to round Pte de Penmarc'h. Men Hir beacon tower left centre, Eckmühl lighthouse with old tower.

N of Penmarc'h the NNW stream begins at about −0540 Brest, the SSE at about +0025 Brest, spring rates 2kts. S of Les Etocs the E and NE stream begins about −0600 Brest, the W and WSW at about HW Brest, spring rates 1½kts. Some 4M S of Penmarc'h the streams are rotary clockwise: N at −0325 Brest, E at −0020 Brest, S at +0240 Brest, WSW at +0600 Brest.

The streams on the coast E of Penmarc'h are much affected by wind.

LIGHTS

1. **Eckmühl** 47°47'·9N 4°22'·4W
   Fl.5s60m24M Horn 60s
   Grey 8-sided tower
2. **Men Hir** 47°47'·8N 4°23'·9W
   Fl(2)WG.6s19m8/5M 135°-G-315°-W-135°
   White tower, black band.
3. **Locarec** 47°47'·3N 4°20'·3W
   Iso.WRG.4s11m9-6M
   063°-G-068°-R-271°-W-285°-R-298°-G-340°-R-063°
   White tank on rock
4. **Lost Moan** 47°47'·1N 4°16'·7W
   Fl(3)WRG.12s8m9-6M
   327°-R-014°-G-065°-R-140°-W-160°-R-268°-W-273°-G-317°-W-327°
   White tower, red top
5. **Cap Caval buoy** (W card) 47°46'·5N 4°22'·6W
   Q(9)15s Whis
6. **Spinec Buoy** (S card) 46°45'·3N 4°18'·8W
   Q(6)+LFl.15s Whis

DIRECTIONS

By day

Give Men Hir a good berth as the reef on which it stands extends over 200m W of it. That apart, there are no hazards outside the lines joining the buoys. However, there is often a heavy swell in the vicinity of Pointe de Penmarc'h and in these circumstances, or in poor visibility, it is safest to stay a good 3M off the land.

By night

There are many lights, in addition to the principal ones listed above on the Pointe, as the approaches and harbours of Ste Guénolé, Kerity and Guilvinec are all lit for the benefit of the many fishing vessels based at them.

13. Le Guilvinec

47°48'N 4°17'W

GENERAL

Situated some 4M east of Penmarc'h, Le Guilvinec (officially Guilvinec, but always called Le Guilvinec) is an important centre for fishing vessels of all kinds, and has processing factories. The town is not a tourist centre and derives its living entirely from the fishing industry. It has the attractions of a busy working town. Provided that care is taken to avoid the outlying rocks, the approach is straightforward and the harbour is sheltered. There is only limited room for yachts, which are tolerated rather than encouraged. There is no local yachting activity. Except in an emergency yachts may not enter or leave between 1600 and 1830 when the fishing fleet is underway.

Charts

BA *3640, 2351*
Imray *C37*

TIDAL DATA

Times and heights

Time differences				Height differences			
HW		LW		MHWS	MHWN	MLWN	MLWS
BREST							
0000 and 1200	0600 and 1800	0000 and 1200	0600 and 1800	6·9	5·4	2·6	1·0
Le Guilvinec							
−0010	−0025	−0025	−0015	−1·8	−1·4	−0·6	−0·1

Tidal streams

Outside, the E stream begins about −0610 Brest, the W at HW Brest, spring rates 1·5kts, but much affected by winds. There is negligible stream in the harbour.

Depths

On the main leading line the least depth is 1·8m, but more water can be found. The harbour is dredged to at least 3m to the inner ends of the fish quays and in the area of the visiting yacht mooring buoys.

LIGHTS

1. **Névez buoy** (starboard) 47°45'·9N 4°20'·0W
   Fl.G.2·5s
2. **Spinec buoy** (S card) 46°45'·3N 4°18'·8W
   Q(6)+LFl.15s Whis
3. **Lost Moan** 47°47'·1N 4°16'·7W
   Fl(3)WRG.12s8m9-6M
   327°-R-014°-G-065°-R-140°-W-160°-R-268°-W-273°-G-317°-W-327°
   White tower, red top
4. **Locarec** 47°47'·3N 4°20'·3W
   Iso.WRG.4s11m9-6M
   063°-G-068°-R-271°-W-285°-R-298°-G-340°-R-063° White tank on rock
5. **Ldg Lts 053°** Synchronised
   Front 47°47'·5N 4°17'·0W Q.7m8M 233°-vis-066° White pylon on starboard mole spur
   Middle 210m from front Q.WG.12m14/11M 006°-W-293°-G-006° Red square on red column
   Rear 1085m from front DirQ.26m8M 051·5°-vis-054·5° Red square on white tower, red stripe
6. **Capelan buoy (starboard)** 47°47'·2N 4°17'·5W
   Fl(2)G.6s
8. **N mole head** Fl(2)R.6s4m5M Red structure
7. **N mole spur** Fl.R.4s11m9M White tower, red top
9. **S mole head** 47°47'·5N 4°17'·1W Fl.G.4s5m7M Round white hut, green top
10. **S mole spu**r Fl(2)G.6s4m5M 078°-vis-258° Green structure

RADIO

VHF Ch 12 intermittent hours.

APPROACH AND ENTRANCE

The landscape E of Penmarc'h is dotted with white houses with grey slate roofs so that Le Guilvinec tends to be inconspicuous among them. The fish

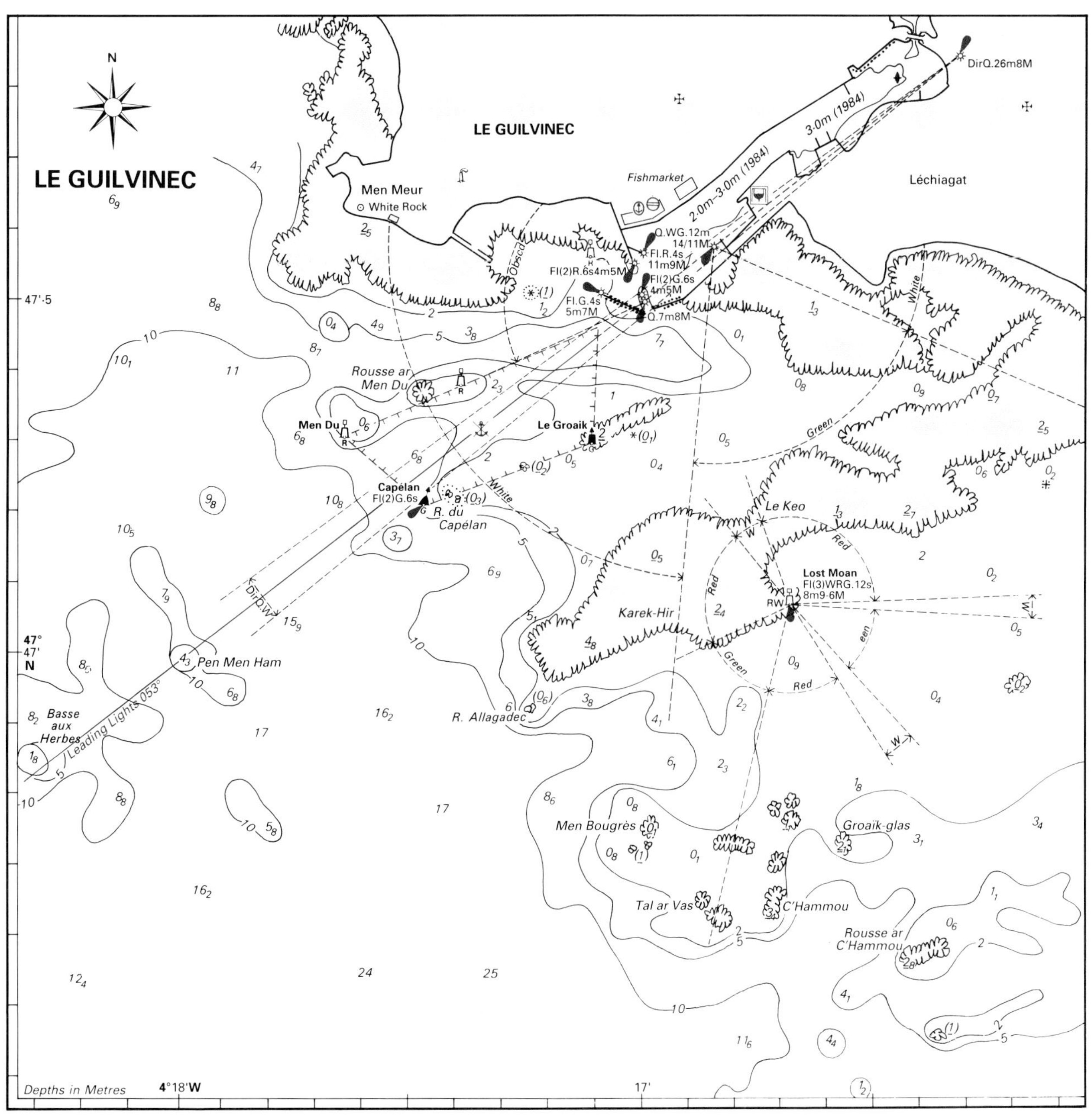

Plan 12

Le Guilvinec

market, which is a long white building is prominent, as are the lighthouse, with a red top on the north mole, a conspicuous large blue travel-lift and the red cylindrical topmarks of the leading beacons.

MAIN CHANNEL

By day

From westward give Les Etocs, a prominent group of above-water and drying rocks, a good berth. Thence make Névez starboard buoy, which lies 900m S of Raguen tower (S cardinal), which is itself on the SE side of Les Etocs. From a position close N of Névez buoy the leading marks are in transit, bearing 053°. They are two large red cylinders on orange-red columns.

The leading line crosses the Basse aux Herbes with a depth of 1·8m. Near low water, especially in rough weather, it may therefore be necessary to borrow 150m to starboard while the Penmarc'h light tower is in line with Locarec tower, bearing 292°. After Basse aux Herbes is passed, return to the leading line, leaving Men Du concrete beacon (port) 200m to port, Capelan conical buoy (starboard) close to starboard, Rousse ar Men Du concrete beacon (port) 140m to port, and Le Groaik tower (starboard) 200m to starboard.

From eastward make for the Basse Spinec whistle buoy (S cardinal), and leave it close to starboard to make for the Névez buoy and enter on the leading line.

Steer to leave the head of the outer S mole (painted white) to starboard and then the N mole head and spur to port. The N mole head has a white rectangle with red border on the end.

By night

Entry by the main channel is straightforward. The synchronised leading lights are easy to identify. If entering at low water when Basse aux Herbes may be a hazard it can be avoided by keeping 150m to starboard of the leading lights when in the red sector of Locarec light[4]. If the unlit beacon towers and Capelan buoy cannot be seen, stay on the leading line until the S mole head light[9] bears 030° distant 200m; it will then be safe to turn to port and head for it.

SOUTHERN CHANNEL

By day

This route should only be used if the marks can be identified with certainty. Make a position 47°45'·5N 4°17'·2W, midway between Ar Guisty S cardinal tower and Spinec S cardinal buoy. Note that Les Fourches rocks 800m NE of this position never cover. Identify the Men Meur white-painted rock, at the W end of the Guilvinec waterfront buildings, and bring it into transit with a slender pyramid with large diamond topmark a mile further inland on a bearing of 352°. Follow this transit for 1¾M to the Capelan buoy (starboard), which is left to starboard to continue as on the main approach.

Le Guilvinec entrance with the western approach leading marks arrowed

Le Guilvinec entrance

BERTHS AND ANCHORAGE
Le Guilvinec is an active fishing port and visitors must not get in the way. Yachts may only secure to a quay or a fishing boat in an emergency. They must proceed to the upper end of the harbour and secure bow and stern to mooring buoys. There are three buoys; by rafting, six visiting yachts may be accommodated. Their stay may not exceed one night and a listening watch on channel 12 is required.

FACILITIES
The main part of town is on N side of harbour. Market day is Tuesday. There are the normal facilities of a moderate-sized town including banks, supermarkets, café-bars and restaurants.

Visitors may find a vacant mooring at the head of the harbour for a single night's stay

14. Lesconil

47°47'N 4°12'W

GENERAL

Lesconil is a small fishing port and yachts are not particularly welcome. It is easy of access except in strong southerly winds. It is less crowded and more attractive than Le Guilvinec 3M to the west. Except in an emergency, yachts must not enter or leave between 1630 and 1830, when the fishing fleet returns.

Charts

BA *3640, 2351, 2352*
Imray *C37*

TIDAL DATA

Times and heights

	Time differences			Height differences			
HW		LW		MHWS	MHWN	MLWN	MLWS
BREST							
0000 and 1200	0600 and 1800	0000 and 1200	0600 and 1800	6·9	5·4	2·6	1·0
Lesconil							
–0008	–0028	–0028	–0018	–1·9	–1·4	-0·6	–0·1

Tidal streams

At the Karek Greis buoy the SW stream starts at about +0100 Brest, the NE stream at about –0500 Brest, spring rates 0·6kt.

Depths

2·6m in the approach, 1·5m in the harbour entrance and 1·5–3m inside.

LIGHTS

1. **Karek-Greis buoy** (E card) 47°46'·1N 4°11'·3W Q(3)10s Whis
2. **Men-ar-Groas** 47°47'·8N 4°12'·6W Fl(3)WRG.12s14m10-7M 268°-G-313°-W-333°-R-050° White tower, green top
3. **E breakwater head** 47°47'·8N 4°12'·6W Q.G.5m5M Green tower
4. **S breakwater head** 47°47'·7N 4°12'·6W Oc.R.4s5m6M Red tripod

RADIO

VHF Ch 12 0800–1200 and1400–1830 LT

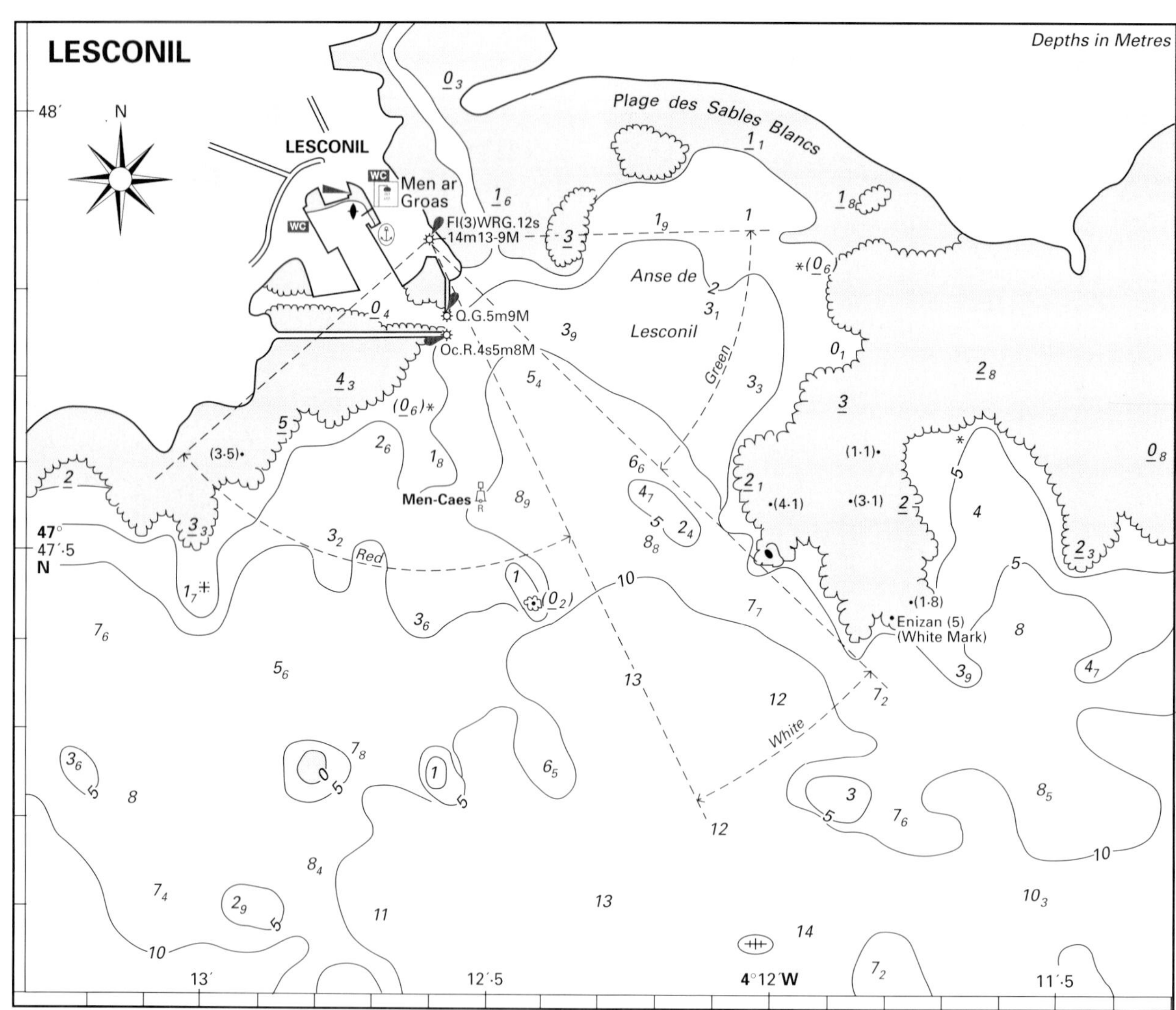

Plan 13

Lesconil harbour is well sheltered, but there is no room for a deep draught yacht except in an emergency when she may be allowed to lie amongst the fishing boats

APPROACH AND ENTRANCE

By day

From a position 600m north of Karek-Greis buoy identify the Men-ar-Groas light. The slender white tower with a green top is situated on the land forming the eastern part of the harbour and is not easy for a stranger to identify. It lies just to the right of a conspicuous white gable end with a large diamond shaped window in it and to the left of a long low grey roof. With the light on a bearing of 325° the belfry of Lesconil church will be just open to the left of it. Proceed on this course, leaving the white mark on Enizan 400m to starboard and Men-Caës red beacon tower 200m to port. Turn to port between the breakwaters and enter the harbour.

Within the harbour red and green unlit buoys mark the deep water towards the fishing vessel berths.

By night

From Karek-Greis buoy steer 325° for Men-ar-Groas[2] remaining in the white sector of the light.

BERTHS AND ANCHORAGE

Except in emergency, yachts are not permitted to lie alongside the quays and if obliged to do so should consult the harbourmaster to be allocated a berth. A yacht which can take the ground may find room to anchor in the western part of the harbour. There is a fair-weather anchorage in 1–3m, sand in Anse de Lesconil immediately to the east of the entrance, but it is open to the south.

Men-ar-Groas light at Lesconil

FACILITIES

Water from the fish market, or standpipes on the quays. Fuel by can. Launderette. Modest shops, café-bars.

15. Loctudy

47°50'N 4°10'W

GENERAL

Geographically Loctudy and Ile Tudy (the peninsula facing Loctudy across the river entrance) lie between Le Guilvinec and Bénodet. Likewise in character they stand midway between the wholly fishing port of Le Guilvinec and the holiday and yachting resort of Bénodet. At Loctudy and Ile Tudy fishing and sailing flourish together. The approach is sheltered from the prevailing westerly winds and the harbour is attractive and secure. The estuary of the Rivière de Pont l'Abbé is now largely full of moorings but the marina at Port Tudy has all facilities. The harbour is very animated when the fishing fleet is in, especially if dinghy racing is taking place as well.

Charts

BA *3641, 2351, 2352*
Imray *C37*

TIDAL DATA

Times and heights

Time differences				Height differences			
HW		LW		MHWS	MHWN	MLWN	MLWS
BREST							
0000 and 1200	0600 and 1800	0000 and 1200	0600 and 1800	6·9	5·4	2·6	1·0
Loctudy							
-0013	-0033	-0035	-0025	-1·9	-1·5	-0·7	-0·2

Tidal streams

In the offing the NE stream begins about −0610 Brest and the SW at HW Brest, spring rates 1·5kts. In the harbour the streams are strong, with spring rates of 3kts on the flood and 3·5kts on the ebb.

Depths

The least water in the approach is 0·9m. Off Loctudy there is 3m. Off Ile Tudy 1·0m or more may be found, and there is a deep pool with 5m on the opposite side of the channel just upstream of Ile Tudy jetty, with depths of 1m or more above and below it. The marina is dredged to 1·5m.

LIGHTS

1. **Pointe de Langoz** 47°49'·9N 4°09'·6W
   Fl(4)WRG.12s12m15-11M
   115°-W-257°-G-284°-W-295°-R-318°-W-328°-R-025°
   White tower, red top
2. **Ile aux Moutons** 47°46'·5N 4°01'·7W
   Oc(2)WRG.6s18m15-11M
   White tower and dwelling
   Auxiliary Light DirOc(2)6s17m24M
   278·5°-intens-283·5°
   Synchronised with main light, same structure
   Lights in Line 000·5°
3. *Front* **Pte de Combrit** 47°51'·9N 4°06'·7W
   Oc(3+1)WR.12s19m12/9M 325°-W-017°-R-325°
   White square tower grey corners
4. *Rear* **Pyramide** 340m from front
   Oc(2+1)12s48m11M White tower, green top
5. **Basse Bilien buoy** (E card) 47°49'·2N 4°08'·0W
   VQ(3)5s Whis
6. **Karek-Saoz** 47°50'·1N 4°09'·3W Q.R.3m2M
   Red truncated tower
7. **Les Perdrix** 47°50'·3N 4°10'·0W
   Fl.WRG.4s15m11-8M
   090°-G-285°-W-295°-R-090°
   Black and white chequered tower
8. **Le Blas** 47°50'·3N 4°10'·1W Fl(3)G.12s5m1M
   Green pylon on pedestal

RADIO

Port VHF Ch 12 Mon–Fri 0630–1200, 1400–1900 and Sat 0800–1200 LT
Marina VHF Ch 9 0730–2100 LT

APPROACH AND ENTRANCE

Note Between 1800 and 1900 when the fishing fleet returns entry is only permitted under power, sailing being prohibited.

By day

From the N and Wt the approach is straightforward using the chart. The reefs to the S of the Penmarc'h peninsula are marked by buoys and beacons. From Menhir beacon, near low water, in heavy weather or poor visibility take the course outside the buoys, Spinec, Karek-Greis, Bas Boulanger and Chenal du Bénodet (E cardinal), the latter marking the Basse du Chenal rocks. Continue N for 500m to clear this

There are many moorings in Loctudy harbour but space can still be found to anchor

Looking west into Loctudy

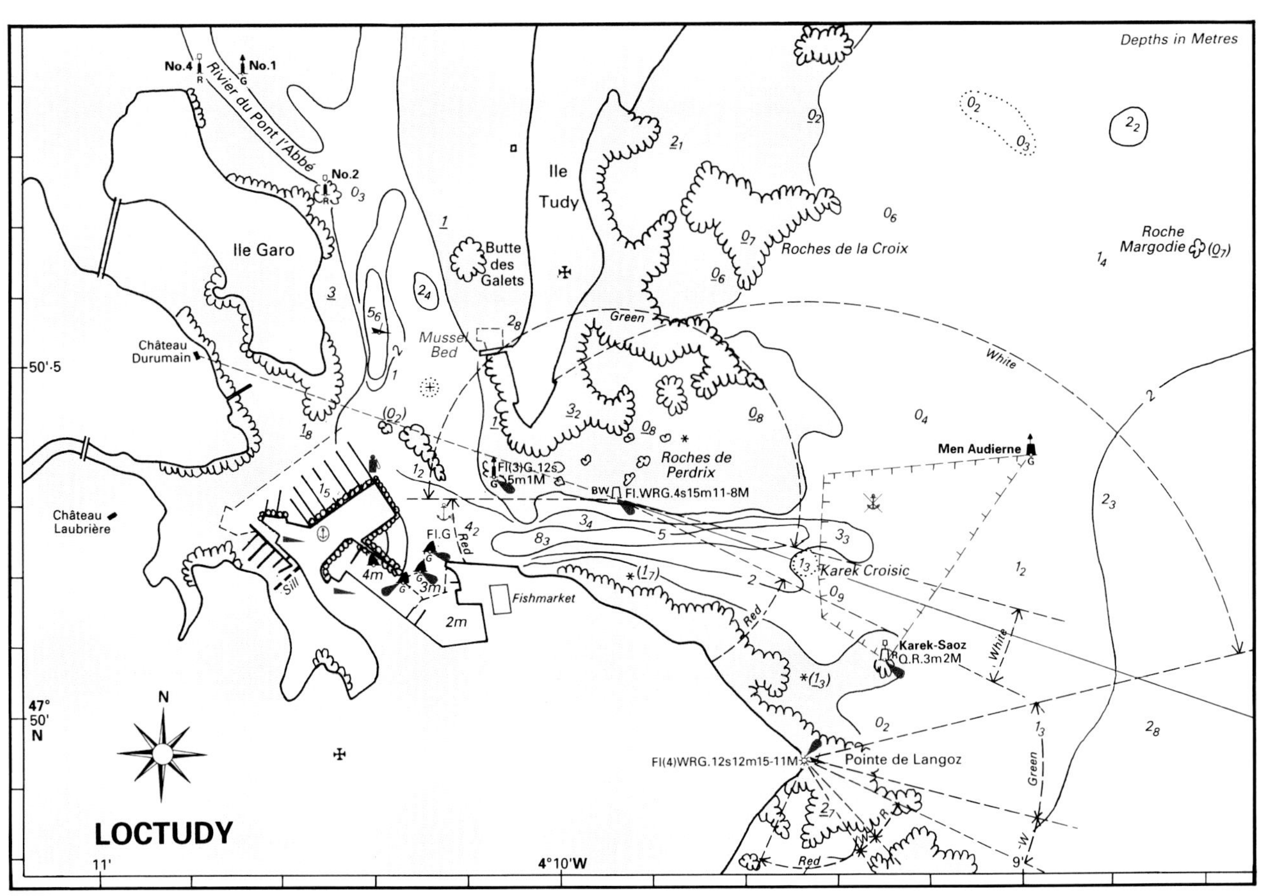

Plan 14

drying reef before turning NW towards Bilien buoy and the harbour entrance.

In good conditions and with sufficient rise of tide passage can be made inside the buoys. Note that the beacons do not all lie on the extreme edges of the reefs they mark and that there are several unmarked drying and shallow patches, in particular the 0·4m Basse Deval in the approaches to Lesconil, Basse St-Oual, also carrying 0·4m, ½M east of Les Bleds beacon and the drying Roche Glinec, 750m S of Men Bret beacon.

From the E and SE leave Ile-Aux-Moutons to port. Thence steer to the NW, leaving both Les Poulains tower (N cardinal) and Men Dehou tower (E cardinal) to port. Half a mile NW of Men Dehou is a rock with 2·1m over it. If necessary, this can be left to the SW by keeping Ile Aux Moutons lighthouse midway between Les Poulains beacon and Men Dehou tower. Thence leave the buoys on Basse Malvic (W cardinal), Basse du Chenal (E cardinal) and Basse Bilien (E cardinal) to port. Note that the that Basse du Chenal rocks lie to the NE of the buoy that marks them.

From the vicinity of the Basse Bilien buoy proceed NW towards Men Audierne green beacon. When Les Perdrix chequered beacon bears 290° steer for it leaving the red beacon on Karek-Saoz 180m to port. 300m from Les Perdrix alter to port and head 270° towards the outer of the three green buoys which mark the entrance to the fishing harbour. When close to this buoy alter to the NW and follow the channel round into the marina.

If proceeding northward to the Ile Tudy anchorage it is best to wait until there is sufficient rise of tide to ignore the rock awash at chart datum lying 180m SW of the end of Ile Tudy jetty. Turn to starboard after passing the Banc Blas beacon (starboard), leaving the middle ground (which dries 1·8m) to port. Steer towards a position some 30m off the end of the jetty at Ile Tudy. 100m N of the jetty head is the Butte des Galets, a shingle patch, on which it is easy to ground when it is covered near high water. It is reported that the drying wreck, shown on the plan and the charts no longer exists, but this cannot be confirmed.

BY NIGHT

From the west

Stay outside the lit buoys marking the hazards S of Pointe de Penmarc'h. Near low water it will not be safe to steer from Basse Boulanger to Bilien as there are shallow patches near the route. In these circumstances a detour to the E must be made. After passing Spinec buoy S cardinal), continue SE until Ile-aux-Moutons light[2] turns from red to white. Keep within this white sector, with the light on a bearing of about 083°, for some 8½M and until the Bénodet lights, Pte de Combrit[3] and Pyramide[4] come into line bearing 000·5°. Turn onto this transit and maintain it until the white sector of Pte de Langoz light[1] is reached. At this point it is safe to turn to the NW, leaving Basse Billien buoy[2] well clear to port.

With sufficient rise of tide it is not necessary to make this lengthy detour towards Ile-aux-Moutons as the lit Karek-Grise, Basse Boulanger and Basse Bilien buoys enable the dangers to be avoided.

Once within the white sector of Les Perdrix[4], head for it until within 400m of the light, leaving Karek-Saoz red light[3] at least 100m to port. There are no navigational lights in the river except for Le Blas[5] and the three lit green buoys which lead into the fishing harbour but there is usually plenty of light from the shore.

From the east

Leave Ile-aux-Moutons[2] light to port and steer northwards to get into the white sector of Pointe de Langoz light[1]. Head for the light staying in the white sector until Basse Bilien buoy[2] is abeam to port. Then alter course to the NE to get into the white sector of Les Perdrix light[4] and proceed as above.

BERTHS AND ANCHORAGE

In the marina yachts berth alongside on both sides of the outer pontoon or on fingers on the next pontoon –pontoon A.

Most of the river N of the marina is now occupied by moorings but one or two spaces remain in which to anchor.

FACILITIES

The marina has all facilities including fuel. Bread is delivered each morning.

In Loctudy there are banks, café-bars, restaurants, shops, a post office, a supermarket just out of town, a launderette and a good vegetable market on Tuesdays. Shipyard, marine engineer and chandler at the fishing port, where there is a top-class fish market at landing each evening.

At Ile Tudy there are also shops and hotels, but it is rather less sophisticated. There is a water tap at the root of the jetty.

Rivière de Pont l'Abbé

As with other rivers, commercial traffic is no longer scouring the channel and it has silted. A visit to the town of Pont l'Abbé is still worth while, but the three-mile journey should perhaps be made in a dinghy with a reliable outboard.

16. Bénodet and Rivière Odet

47°53'N 4°07'W

GENERAL

The port of Bénodet, at the mouth of the river Odet, situated some 16M to the eastward of Penmarc'h, is one of the principal yachting centres in the north of the Bay of Biscay. With marinas and numerous buoys on both sides of the river, it has good moorings and facilities and is a popular port of call for British yachts. The little town itself is a yachting and holiday resort where a yachtsman can get most of the things he needs. The only trouble is that it becomes extremely crowded in summer, so much so that the area below the bridge has lost some of its charm.

The Anse de Bénodet is a wide bay, some five miles across with sandy shores, sheltered from the north and west. The port of Loctudy lies on the west side and to the east lies the Baie de la Forêt, partially sheltered from the west, with marinas at Port de la Forêt and Concarneau. To the south there are the Glénan Islands, only twelve miles away.

The Odet river, which is completely sheltered and very beautiful, is navigable almost as far as the cathedral city of Quimper. There are several peaceful anchorages in the river and its creeks.

Unless the yachtsman is in a hurry to sail south, he has plenty of local sailing to interest him. The whole bay is a centre of intense local sailing activity.

Charts

BA *3641, 2351, 2352*
Imray *C37*

TIDAL DATA

Times and heights

	Time differences		Height differences			
	HW	LW	MHWS	MHWN	MLWN	MLWS
BREST	0000 0600 and and 1200 1800	0000 0600 and and 1200 1800	6·9	5·4	2·6	1·0
Bénodet	0000 –0020	–0023 –0013	–1·7	–1·3	–0·5	–0·1
Corniguel	+0015 +0010	–0015 –0010	–2·0	–1·6	–1·0	–0·7

Tidal streams

In the centre of the bay the streams are rotary clockwise, running N at +0600 Brest, NE at –0330 Brest, SE at +0015 Brest and SW at +0245 Brest, spring rate about 1kt. In the river the flood begins at

Bénodet

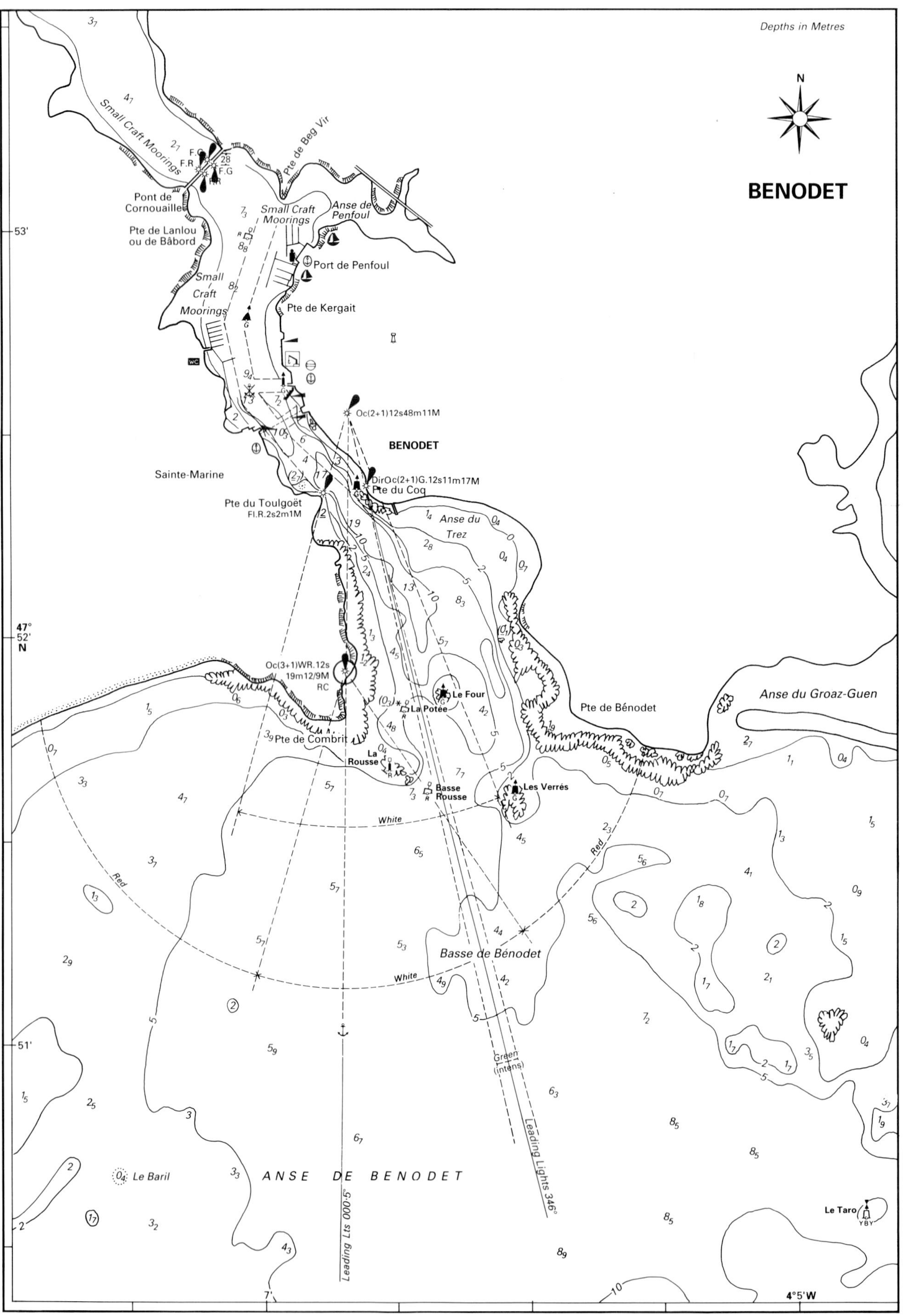
Depths in Metres
N
BENODET
Small Craft Moorings
Pte de Beg Vir
Pont de Cornouaille
F.G
F.R
28
Pte de Lanlou ou de Bâbord
Small Craft Moorings
Anse de Penfoul
Port de Penfoul
Small Craft Moorings
Pte de Kergait
Oc(2+1)12s48m11M
BENODET
Sainte-Marine
DirOc(2+1)G.12s11m17M
Pte du Coq
Pte du Toulgoët
Fl.R.2s2m1M
Anse du Trez
Oc(3+1)WR.12s
19m12/9M
RC
Le Four
La Potée
Pte de Bénodet
Anse du Groaz-Guen
Pte de Combrit
La Rousse
Basse Rousse
Les Verrés
White
Red
Basse de Bénodet
Green (intens)
Le Baril
ANSE DE BENODET
Leading Lts 000·5°
Leading Lights 346°
Le Taro
YBY
53'
47° 52' N
51'
7'
4°5'W

Plan 15

Bénodet is one of the principal, and busiest, yachting centres in Brittany

about −0540 Brest and the ebb at HW Brest, spring rates over 2·5kts.

Depths

The approach and entrance and the river for several miles upstream are deep. Above Lanroz depths in the channel steadily decrease from 3m to less than 0·5m at the bridge below Quimper.

LIGHTS

1. **Pte de Langoz** 47°49'·9N 4°09'·5W
   Fl(4)WRG.12s12m15-11M
   115°-W-257°-G-284°-W-295°-R-318°-W-328°-R-025°
   White tower, red top
2. **Ile aux Moutons** 47°46'·5N 4°01'·7W
   Oc(2)WRG.6s18m15-11M
   White tower and dwelling
   Auxiliary Light DirOc(2)6s17m24M
   278·5°-intens-283·5°
   Synchronised with main light, same structure
3. **Trévignon** 47°47'·6N 3°51'·3W
   Oc(3+1)WRG.12s11m14-11M
   004°-W-051°-G-085°-W-092°-R-127°, 322°-R-351°
   White square tower, green top
   Lights in Line 000·5°
4. *Front* **Pte de Combrit** 47°51'·9N 4°06'·7W
   Oc(3+1)WR.12s19m12/9M 325°-W-017°-R-325°
   White square tower grey corners
5. *Rear* **Pyramide** 340m from front
   Oc(2+1)12s48m11M
   Synchronised with Pte de Combrit light
   White tower, green top
   Ldg Lts 345·5°
6. *Front* **Pte du Coq** 47°52'·4N 4°06'·6W
   DirOc(2+1)G.12s11m17M 345°-intens-347°
   White round tower, vertical green stripe
   Rear **Pyramide** 1180m from front. *See light 5 above*
7. **Pte du Toulgoët** 47°52'·3N 4°06'·8W
   Fl.R.2s2m1M Red mast
   Buoys to SW
8. **Karek Greis** (E card) 47°46'·1N 4°11'·4W
   Q(3)10s Whis
9. **Basse Boulanger** (S card) 47°47'·4N 4°09'·1W
   VQ(6)+LFl.10s
10. **Basse Bilien** (E card) 47°49'·2N 4°08'·0W
    VQ(3)5s Whis
    Buoys to SE
11. **La Voleuse** (S card) 47°48'·8N 4°02'·4W
    Q(6)+LFl.15s Whis
12. **Grands Porceaux** (N card) 47°46'·1N 4°00'·7W
    VQ
13. **Rouge de Glénan** (W card) VQ(9)10s8m8M Whis
    HFPB
14. **Jaune de Glénan** (E card) 47°42'·6N 3°49'·8W
    Q(3)10s Whis

RADIO

Both marinas VHF Ch 9 0800–2000 LT

APPROACH

From the west

By day

Although there are many hazards between Ile aux Moutons and the mainland they are well marked and consequently the approach is not difficult. The usual route, which relies on the buoys, passes between Basse Boulanger (S cardinal) and Helou (W cardinal) and thence between Chenal du

Bénodet (E cardinal) and Bas Malvic (W cardinal) buoys. If the buoys are hard to identify then Pyramide lighthouse at Bénodet (white tower with green top) in line with Pte de Combrit Light (white square tower, grey corners) bearing 000·5° leads safely in from the S leaving Rostolou (E cardinal) buoy and the rocks between it and Helou to port. Once within a mile of Pte de Combrit, alter course to starboard for the entrance.

In good conditions and with sufficient rise of tide several other routes through the shallow patches can be found.

By night

Stay outside the lit buoys marking the hazards S of Pointe de Penmarc'h. After passing Spinec buoy (S cardinal), continue SE until Ile-aux-Moutons light[2] turns from red to white. Keep within this white sector, with the light on a bearing of about 083°, for some 8½M and until the Bénodet lights, Pte de Combrit[4] and come into line bearing 000·5°. Turn onto this transit and maintain it watching the Pointe de Langoz light[1]; it will change colours as one progresses N. When it finally changes from green to white bearing 257°, the way is clear to turn to starboard to bring the Bénodet leading lights[6] in line on 345·5° and enter the river. Many lights other than those described will be seen.

It should be noted that yachts have been wrecked by following the Pyramide/Pte de Combrit transit of 000·5° onto the shore, under the impression that it led into the river.

From the southeast

By day

Pass between Plateau de la Basse Jaune and the mainland. Leave Les Porceaux and Ile Aux Moutons well to port, Les Poulains tower (N cardinal) to port, La Voleuse buoy (S cardinal) to starboard and Men Déhou tower (E cardinal) to port. Once past Men Dehou it is safe to turn towards the harbour entrance leaving Le Taro tower (W cardinal) ½ mile to starboard.

By night

Approach within or just S of the intensified sector of Ile Aux Mouton light[2], leaving Jaune de Glénan buoy[14] to port. Continue in this sector until Pte de Langoz light[1] is identified and Trévignon light[3] has turned from white to green bearing more than 051°.

Alter to starboard to get into the white sector of Pte de Langoz light, bearing about 295° and keep within it until Pointe de Combrit light[4] opens white bearing 325°. Then steer for this light, crossing the green sector of Pte de Langoz light, and bring the Bénodet leading lights[5,6] in transit on 345·5°. Many lights other than those described will be seen.

ENTRANCE

By day

During the season and particularly at weekends the entrance to Bénodet is so busy with pleasure craft of all kinds, including numerous dinghies, as to make entry under sail hazardous. Speed is limited to 3kts above the Pte de Coq beacon, but this rule is widely ignored.

The dangers in the entrance are marked and it is not usually necessary to keep to the transit, nor will it be possible to do so on a busy summer day. The tower of Pyramide light is conspicuous, but the front mark, Le Coq, is less easy to identify. It will be seen some way to the left of the conspicuous letters YCO on the grassy bank in front of the old yacht club building. These two marks in line on a bearing of 345·5° form the transit. In the entrance, two buoys and one beacon (all port-hand) will be left to port and two starboard-hand beacon towers to starboard. When within 400m of Le Coq, alter to port and steer up the middle of the river between Pointe du Toulgoët port-hand beacon and a starboard-hand beacon tower.

By night

Entrance is straightforward, but the river is congested with moorings, and anchoring is prohibited in the channel until well beyond the bridge. The leading lights[5,6] lead clear of all unlit buoys and beacons. When within 400m of Le Coq[6], turn to port to pass halfway between Le Coq and Pte du Toulgoët flashing red light[7]. Fixed red and green lights will be seen on the bridge and the shore lights may give some guidance.

BERTHS AND ANCHORAGE

There is good anchorage during offshore winds in the Anse du Trez on the starboard side of the entrance, especially if arriving in the dark. There is some hazard here from sailboard and Optimist schools, but it becomes peaceful at night. West of the Pointe de Combrit the bay, with a long sandy beach, makes a pleasant lunchtime stop.

There are moorings, some of them for visitors, on both sides of the river up to and well beyond the bridge which has a clearance of 28m. Anchoring is prohibited in this area. There are marinas on the port side above Ste Marine and on the starboard side at the entrance to the Anse de Penfoul. Approach the visitors' berths in both marinas, and the buoys, against the stream and with considerable caution. The currents are strong during both flood and ebb and set across the pontoons; at spring tides it is best to arrive or depart near slack water. The moorings are administered by the marina on the side of the river on which they lie.

It may be possible at tide time to secure to the quay to do any business in the town and then go up the river where there is still room to anchor, but the yacht may be at risk from wash due to the large number of passing craft.

FACILITIES

There are all the facilities of a major yachting and holiday centre with restaurants and hotels on both sides of the river. The food shops are of moderate standard. Facilities are generally more comprehensive on the Bénodet side.

Most repairs can be carried out.

There is a café-bar (which sells some groceries), launderette, and chandlery at the Anse de Penfoul marina.

Fuel is available at the Anse de Penfoul marina, but as the berth lies across the current it should be used with care.

Rivière Odet

The river Odet is a famous beauty spot, with steep, tree-covered banks, and ferries ply regularly from Bénodet to Quimper on the tide. There is 28m clearance under the bridge above Bénodet and there is no difficulty in sailing up the first five miles in depths of 3m or more. The deep water is in the middle and the only obstruction is a rock on the sharp turn to starboard, which is marked by a green beacon.

Above Lanroz the river is shallower, but well marked by beacons as far as the commercial jetties of Corniguel; above that the river nearly dries and the beacons are farther apart. A bridge prevents masted yachts from reaching Quimper, but yachts that can take the ground may anchor or borrow a mooring below the bridge and visit Quimper by dinghy, while motor yachts can carry a depth of drying 1·5m up to the first quays on the port hand in Quimper. The bottom here is hard and uneven for drying out.

There are no facilities on the way up the river, but everything can be got at Quimper, the regional centre and a large and attractive city, famous for its pottery, with an interesting cathedral with nave and chancel out of line.

When looking for a place to anchor in the river it is best to choose a bight out of the worst of the stream where the mud will have settled; in the main channel much of the bottom is rock. Among several suitable places are the Anse de Combrit and the bay opposite Lanroz. There is a beautiful anchorage just below Lanroz in the Anse de Toulven inlet on the eastern side, but care must be taken to avoid a drying rocky plateau on the south side of the narrow entrance where it opens out. Keep close to the north side of the channel. In this pool a large area has 1m depth and 2m can be found in which to swing on short scope. At the end of the first pool there is a rock with 1m or less, on the inside corner of the sharp turn to the north.

The Odet river winds inland through the countryside to Quimper

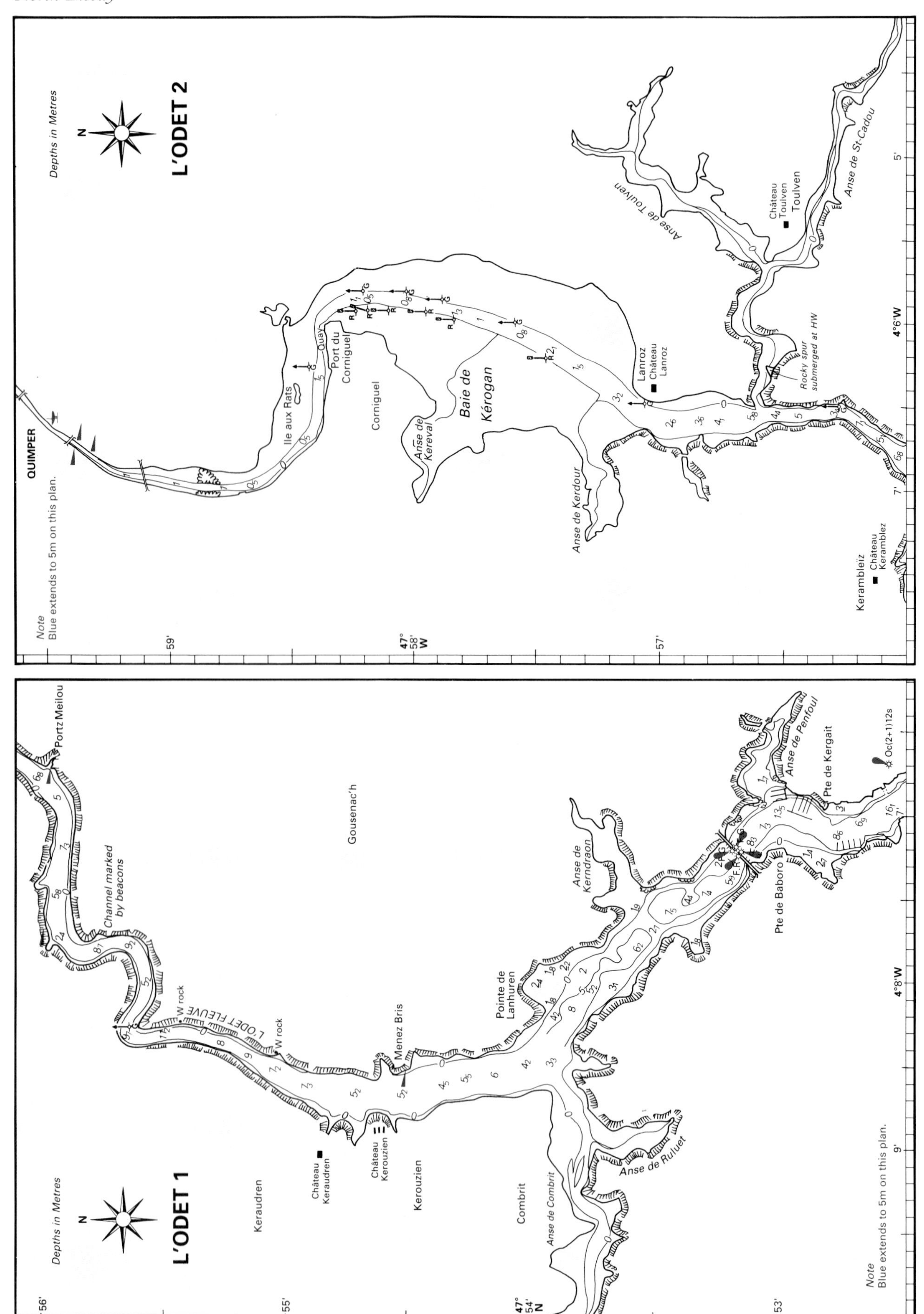
L'ODET 1
Depths in Metres
Note
Blue extends to 5m on this plan.
Portz Meilou
Channel marked by beacons
Gousenac'h
L'ODET FLEUVE
W rock
W rock
Menez Bris
Pointe de Lanhuren
Anse de Kerndraon
Château Keraudren
Château Kerouzien
Keraudren
Kerouzien
Combrit
Anse de Combrit
Anse de Ruluet
Pte de Baboro
Anse de Penfoul
Pte de Kergait
Oc(2+1)12s
F.R
4°8'W
47° 54' N
L'ODET 2
Depths in Metres
Note
Blue extends to 5m on this plan.
QUIMPER
Ile aux Rats
Quay
Port du Corniguel
Corniguel
Anse de Kereval
Baie de Kérogan
Anse de Kerdour
Lanroz
Château Lanroz
Anse de Toulven
Château Toulven
Toulven
Anse de St-Cadou
Rocky spur submerged at HW
Kerambleiz
Château Keramblez
4°6'W
47° 58' W
Plan 16

17. Iles de Glénan

Penfret lighthouse 47°43'N 3°57'W

GENERAL

Situated about 12M south of Bénodet and 10M from Concarneau this beautiful archipelago is an intricate mixture of islands fringed by sandy beaches, rocks and shoals. In character it resembles a miniature Scilly Islands and is the home of the Centre Nautique de Glénans (CNG), the largest sailing school in Europe, which gives young people training at all levels from basic seamanship to cruising and ocean racing. The school's main base is on Ile Cigogne.

The fleets of training boats are in evidence everywhere among the islands. The CNG is very hospitable to visitors, but the latter should be careful not to impose on this hospitality as the *moniteurs* have a full programme.

The islands should be visited only in good weather as all the anchorages are somewhat exposed, at least at high water. They form a fascinating area to explore and practise one's pilotage. It is hoped that the plans in this book will suffice for a quick visit, using the main channels, but for any exploration large-scale charts are essential. The most detailed one is French SHOM *6648* which covers all the islands, despite being called *Iles de Glénan, partie Sud*, but BA *3640* is sufficiently detailed for all but the most intricate parts of the archipelago.

A vessel should be fully provisioned before going to the islands as supplies are very limited.

The islands become very crowded during July and August, particularly during fine-weather weekends.

Charts

BA *3640, 2352*
Imray *C38*

Iles de Glénan from the north

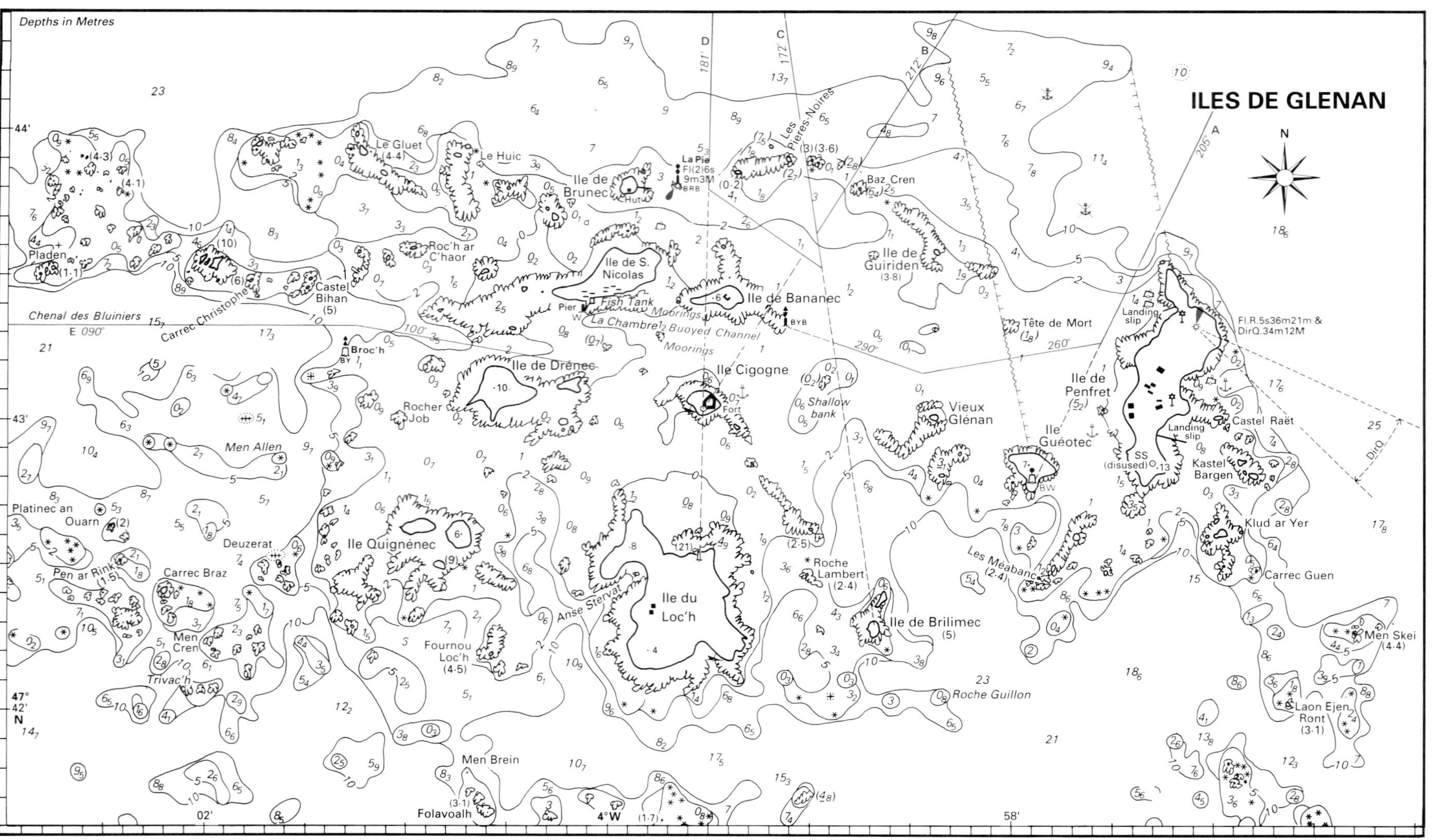
ILES DE GLENAN
Depths in Metres
Ile de Penfret
Ile Guéotec
Vieux Glenan
Ile de Guiriden
Ile de Bananec
Ile Cigogne
Ile de S. Nicolas
Ile de Brunec
Ile de Drénec
Ile du Loc'h
Ile Quignénec
Ile de Brilimec
Les Pieres-Noires
Baz Cren
Le Huic
Le Gluet
Roc'h ar C'haor
Castel Bihan
Broc'h
Rocher Job
Men Allen
Deuzerat
Carrec Braz
Men Cren
Trivac'h
Platinec an Ouarn
Pen ar Rink
Pladen
Chenal des Bluiniers
Carrec Christophe
La Chambre
Buoyed Channel
Moorings
Fish Tank
Pier
Fort
Shallow bank
Tête de Mort
Castel Raët
Kastel Bargen
Klud ar Yer
Carrec Guen
Men Skei
Laon Ejen Ront
Les Méabans
Roche Guillon
Roche Lambert
Fournou Loc'h
Men Brein
Folavoalh
Anse Stervat
La Pie
Fl(2)6s 9m3M
Landing slip
SS (disused)
Fl.R.5s36m21m & DirQ.34m12M
4°W
47° 42' N

Plan 17

Ile St Nicolas from the fort

TIDAL DATA

Times and heights

Time differences				Height differences			
HW		LW		MHWS	MHWN	MLWN	MLWS
BREST							
0000 and 1200	0600 and 1800	0000 and 1200	0600 and 1800	6·9	5·4	2·6	1·0
Ile de Penfret							
–0005	–0030	–0028	–0018	–1·9	–1·5	–0·7	–0·2

Tidal streams

Near the islands the streams are rotary clockwise, less than 1kt at springs. Amongst the islands the streams run in the direction of the channels, the flood setting N and E and the ebb S and W, spring rates up to 2kts.

Depths

There is enough water in the anchorages for most yachts at all tides. Above half tide there is enough water to sail freely in the channels and in the large pool between Penfret and St Nicolas, but near low water the pilotage becomes intricate and a number of the channels cannot be used.

LIGHTS

1. **Ile aux Moutons** 47°46'·5N 4°01'·7W Oc(2)WRG.6s18m15-11M 035°-W-050°-G-063°-W-081°-R-141°-W-292°-R-035° White tower and dwelling
   Auxiliary light DirOc(2)6s17m24M 278·5°-intens-283·5°
   Synchronised with main light
2. **Penfret** 47°43'·3N 3°57'·2W Fl.R.5s36m21M White square tower, red top
   Auxiliary light DirQ.34m12M
   295°-vis-315° Same structure
3. **La Pie** 47°43'·8N 3°59'·8W Fl(2)6s9m3M Isolated danger beacon

APPROACH

The main islands are easily distinguished by the conspicuous lighthouse on Ile de Penfret, the largest and most easterly of the group and by the stone fort on the SE side of Ile Cigogne which has a tall concrete tower, the top of which is painted black. Also conspicuous are a disused factory chimney on Ile du Loc'h, some houses on the SE side of Ile de Drénec and the buildings on Ile de St Nicolas, including the shellfish tank with adjacent house on the south side of the island, which provides a useful mark (but is often hidden behind the yachts in the crowded anchorage). A number of islets stretch out to the west of Ile de St Nicolas and the western edge of the archipelago is marked by Les Bluiniers tower (W cardinal). The southern and southeastern sides are guarded by buoys (see British Admiralty *2352* or Imray *C38*).

ENTRANCE

By day

GPS can be of considerable assistance to a stranger visiting the archipelago provided that the large-scale BA chart (*3640*) is available. If the yacht is positioned on a transit line while still well clear, identification of the particular rocks or islets which comprise the transit will be simplified. GPS may also enable some of the southern entrances to be attempted. When using GPS in these circumstances it is essential to ensure that the datum corrections, noted on the chart, are applied where necessary.

The entrances are described on the basis that one is aiming for La Chambre, the most popular and therefore the most crowded summer anchorage. Once inside the pool between Penfret and Bananec, the various alternative anchorages are easily reached.

Yachts from Bénodet and Concarneau normally use the northern entrances. For a stranger, the easiest entrances are those from the north and

Ile de Penfret lighthouse

La Pie beacon with the Ile du Bananec anchorage beyond

northeast. Once inside, the necessary landmarks can be more easily identified; exit can be made by another channel, which can then be used for a subsequent entry. When manoeuvring in the pool, La Tête de Mort (dries 1·8m) is a well-known hazard to be avoided; another is a shallow patch (drying 0·2m) 700m E of Cigogne.

In the descriptions of the entrances, the paragraph letters refer to the plan.

Northeastern entrance

A. This channel carries a least depth of 1m, but passes close to shoals of 0·7m and should be treated as carrying that depth. Leave the northern end of Le Penfret 300m to port and steer 205° on the stone beacon on Ile de Guéotec. When Ile Cigogne concrete tower bears 260° alter course to make good the bearing, which also holds Penfret lighthouse dead astern. If the E cardinal beacon SE of Bananec can be located, alter course for it when it bears 290° and so avoid the shallow patch to the E of Cigogne. Alternatively alter onto 283°, steering for the wind generator on the W end of St Nicolas. Using either course, leave the E cardinal beacon SE of Bananec to starboard to enter the buoyed channel of La Chambre.

Northern entrances

All three entrances should be regarded as carrying 1m, although with careful pilotage through the pool, using a large-scale chart, more water can be found. In the approach care must be taken to avoid Les Pourceaux rocks, marked on their SE side by Leuriou tower (E cardinal).

The three entrances are taken in order from east to west; the easiest for a stranger is La Pie, the third. The vital clues to the first two entrances are four above-water rocks: Baz Cren (1·5m above MHWS) in the E, then two adjacent rocks of Les Pierres Noires (3·6 and 3m) and finally in the W a single Pierre Noire (2·6m) with others to its SW which seldom cover. All these rocks stand on rocky bases and must be distinguished from Ile de Guiriden to the SE; this has a considerable sandy expanse, which covers near HW, leaving only the rocky head (3·8m).

B. The first entrance leaves Baz Cren 50 to 100m to port steering on Fort Cigogne tower, bearing 212°. Once Baz Cren is fairly passed the vessel can bear to port as convenient. For this entrance the CNG use the chimney on Ile du Loc'h in transit with the E cardinal beacon southeast of Ile de Bananec on 200°. This is a positive transit to pick up but leaves an outlier of Les Pierres Noires, drying 2·8m only 60m to starboard.

C. The second entrance leaves the two adjacent heads of Les Pierres Noires 20 to 60m to port. Steer on Ile de Brilimec, bearing 172°, which leads fairly into the pool. This is a popular entrance for local yachts, but should not be used for a first visit, as Ile de Brilimec and Les Pierres Noires must be positively identified and there is a rocky plateau drying 2·7m, 100m to starboard.

D. For the third entrance, La Pie, bring the chimney on Ile du Loc'h just open to the right-hand side of the Cigogne tower, bearing 181°. Steer so until inside Les Pierres Noires leaving La Pie isolated danger light beacon abeam to starboard. Near low water the chimney dips behind the fort and one must then steer to pass 100m from La Pie beacon. Except near high water there is no problem about knowing when Les Pierres Noires are passed, as a rock 0·2m above MHWS, and thus seldom covered, marks their SW extremity. When La Pie beacon is abaft the beam and in transit with the N side of Ile de Brunec, bearing

The fort on Ile Cigogne

On Ile de Guéotec the wall beacon is a mark for the north-eastern approach

about 280°, steer to port into the pool, unless heading for the anchorage N of Ile de Bananec, in which case steer straight on.

Western entrance

E. The Chenal des Bluiniers carries a least depth of drying 0·5m, but it is safer to regard it as drying 0·8m. If this gives insufficient margin, it is better not to use this entrance, but to skirt the Nedge of the rocks and enter by La Pie. Visibility of three miles is needed for this channel except towards high water.

Make a position 200m S of Les Bluiniers tower (W cardinal); if coming from the NW round this tower at not less than 200m distance. From this point steer E for Le Broc'h tower (N cardinal), keeping at least 100m S of a line joining all the dangers that show to the N and keeping Penfret lighthouse open to the N of Le Broc'h tower, bearing about 090°. Approaching Le Broc'h tower, leave it 100m to starboard and bring the semaphore, near the southern point of Ile de Penfret, open to the left of Fort Cigogne by the width of the fort (not the tower), bearing 100°. Steer so until the eastern part of Ile de Drénec is abeam to starboard; this island is in two clearly defined parts separated by a sandy strip which

Ile de Bananec anchorage in the foreground with La Chambre vedette channel beyond the island. The sandy isthmus is covered at high water

The buoyed approach channel to the Ile de Ste Nicolas landing runs through La Chambre and must be left clear for the vedettes

covers at HW. Thence steer 035° on the summer cottages to the east of the shellfish tank to enter La Chambre. Near HW the detailed directions above can be disregarded; having passed Le Broc'h tower it is only necessary to sail 100m N of Ile de Drénec and then make straight for La Chambre or the pool as required.

For those already familiar with the islands the transits shown on BA chart *3640* may be used, but it is necessary to identify the semaphore mast on Penfret at a distance of 5M as well as the farm buildings on Drénec.

Southeastern entrance

Notes on entry by this route are not included as it should not be attempted until well acquainted with the area.

By night

Night entry is not recommended.

BERTHS AND ANCHORAGE

East of Ile de Penfret

This anchorage is in the sandy bay south of the hill on which the lighthouse stands. Approach with the middle of the bay bearing 270°. This leaves a rock drying 0·5m 200m to starboard and another, awash at the datum, 100m to port. This latter rock lies 150m N of an islet, Castel Raët, which is joined to Penfret by a ridge of rocks. There is a large metal mooring buoy on the N side of the bay, but it is preferable to anchor closer to the beach on sand, taking care to avoid patches of weed. The anchorage is well-protected from the W but should not be used if there is any chance of a *vent solaire* during the night.

S of the islet is another bay with a slip and containing CNG moorings. This bay is unsuitable for anchoring.

Southwest of Ile de Penfret

There is a good anchorage in 2·5m outside the CNG moorings between the island and Ile de Guéotec. The tide runs fairly hard here, but the islands give a good deal of protection from the W and it is well sheltered from the E. This anchorage should normally be approached from the N; from the S the pilotage is intricate and requires the large-scale chart.

East of Ile Cigogne

Anchor in 1 to 1·4m, N of the rocky ledge running SE from Cigogne.

La Chambre

This anchorage S of Ile de St Nicolas is the most popular one for visitors but there are now many moorings. The depths are up to 3m. Do not anchor in the channel used by the *vedettes* and marked by small port and starboard buoys.

Avoid a rocky shoal which extends 350m SE from Ile de Bananec, the end marked by an E cardinal beacon. The bottom is also rocky for about 100m out along the S shores of St Nicolas and Bananec. Between the two islands, however, is sand. At low water they are joined by a sandy ridge, on either side of which bays are formed, drying 1m, which make excellent anchorages for yachts that can take the ground.

Coming from the pool, make for a position 100m S of the E cardinal beacon SE of Ile de Bananec. If La Chambre is full of yachts, follow the marked channel in until a suitable anchorage is found. If the shellfish tank is not obscured, keep it on 285° until Bananec is passed and then bear a little to port if wishing to proceed further into La Chambre. At low water depths of less than 1m may be encountered in La Chambre. The water is clear and it is necessary to look for a sandy patch on which to anchor as there is much weed.

North of Ile de Bananec

There is a popular fair-weather anchorage, with moorings, in the bay NW of Bananec and E of St Nicolas. The depth shoals from 2m; choose a spot according to tide and draught. There is a clean, sandy bottom. The anchorage is exposed to the N and E at high water.

FACILITIES

During the season enterprising vendors tour the anchorages each morning with bread, seafood and, occasionally, fresh vegetables for sale.

There is a famous restaurant and a café-bar on Ile St Nicholas together with a small shop which occasionally stocks very limited provisions.

Fresh water is in short supply and visitors should not expect to obtain any.

18. Port La Forêt

47°54'N 3°58'W

GENERAL

Baie de la Forêt lies just to the NW of Concarneau. It is rectangular in shape, with shoals on each side of the entrance. Anchorage can thus be found in it in most weather, even in SW winds. The shelter is sufficient for many local boats to lie on permanent moorings in the summer off Beg-Meil. The E and NE sides of the bay are foul. The large marina in the estuary at the head of the bay is easy of access and is popular with UK boats. It provides convenient laying-up facilities at a reasonable rate. During the season it is generally less crowded than Bénodet or Concarneau, but is not as attractive as either. The facilities are good and the marina forms part of a planned holiday village complex which is slowly developing.

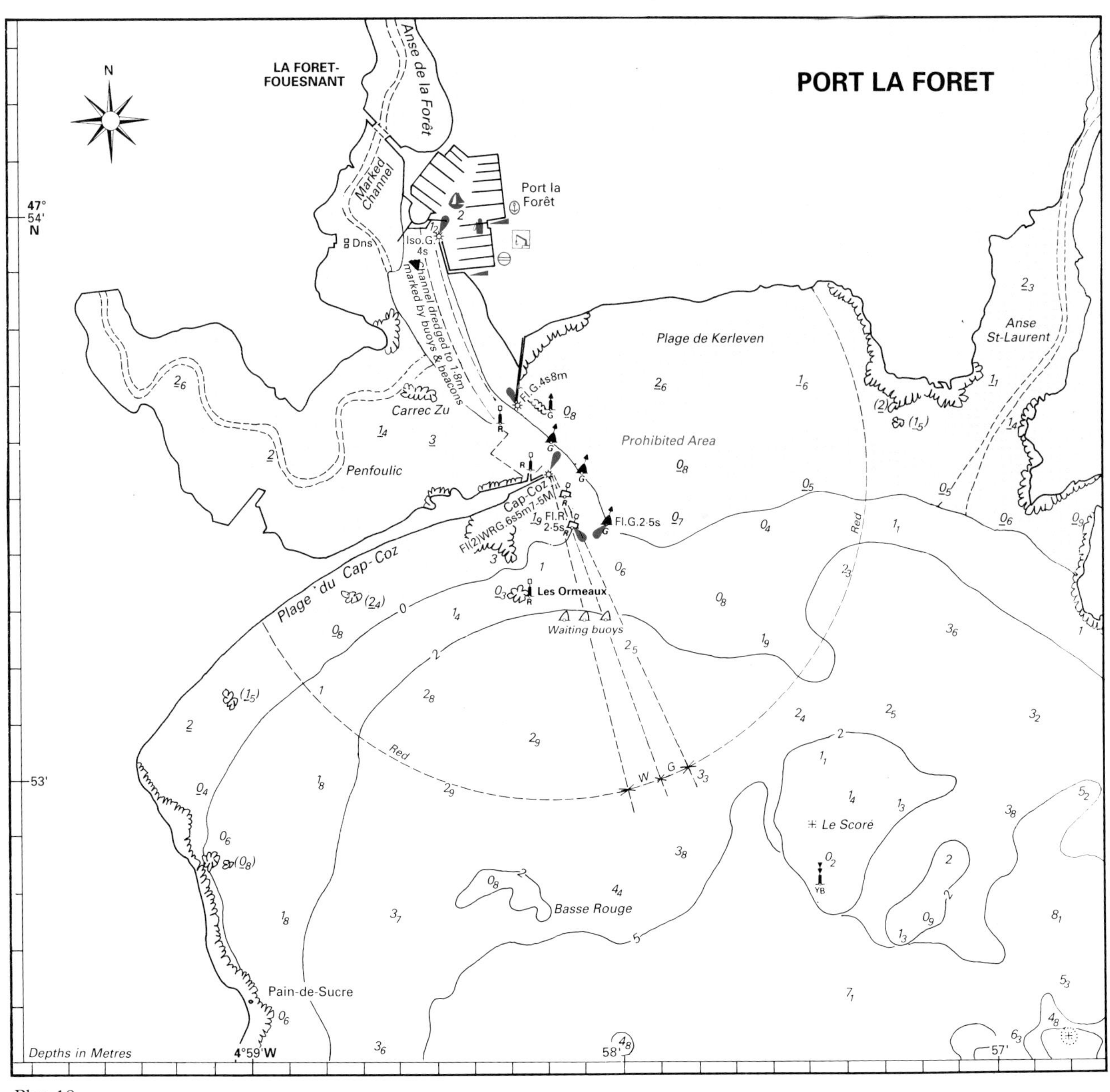

Plan 18

Looking north east into Port La Forêt

Charts

BA *3641*, *2352*
Imray *C38*

TIDAL DATA

Times and heights

Time differences				Height differences			
HW		LW		MHWS	MHWN	MLWN	MLWS
BREST							
0000 and 1200	0600 and 1800	0000 and 1200	0600 and 1800	6·9	5·4	2·6	1·0
Concarneau							
−0010	−0030	−0030	−0020	−1·9	−1·5	−0·7	−0·2

Tidal streams

In the bay the stream is weak. In the entrance, streams are about ½kt.

Depths

The entrance channel was dredged to 1·8m in 1999.

LIGHTS

1. **Cap-Coz (west) mole head** 47°53'·5N 3°58'·1W
   Fl(2)WRG.6s5m7-5M
   shore-R-335°-G-340°-W-346°-R-shore
   Red lantern on grey post, white hut
2. **Kerleven (east) mole head** 47°53'·6N 3°58'·1W
   Fl.G.4s8m Green lantern on grey mast, white hut
3. **Marina mole head** 47°54'·0N 3°58'·2W
   Iso.G.4s5m5M
   Green lantern on grey mast, white hut
4. **Buoys marking entrance of channel**
   SE of Cap Coz mole head starboard – Fl(2)G.2·5s & port Fl.R.2·5s

RADIO

VHF Ch 9 0800–2000 LT

APPROACH AND ENTRANCE

By day

The Baie de La Forêt is entered between the point, Beg-Meil, to the W and the reefs which lie off the entrance to Concarneau to the E. Chausée de Beg-Meil extends 1M SE from the point and is marked by Linuen S cardinal beacon and an E cardinal light buoy. The rocks NNE of the entrance to Concarneau are mainly unmarked, but many of them seldom dry. They can be avoided by keeping the slender Le Score S cardinal beacon open E of the end of Cape Coz breakwater or, more simply, by keeping well off the E side of the bay. The entrance to the estuary lies to the E of the wooded promontory of Cap Coz. Pass between the loose-boulder breakwaters of Cap Coz to port and Kerleven to starboard. The channel is well marked with lateral buoys and beacons. The moorings near the top of the estuary are reserved for fishermen, but there are a number of moorings for yachts the port hand opposite the marina entrance in 2·5m. Turn sharply to starboard to round the marina breakwater head, marked by a named green and white column and pole.

By night

The white sector of Cap Coz[1] light marks the deepest water. The green sector is also safe, except for a patch, Basse Briérou Sud, with only 2·6m over it which may be a hazard near low water. A pair of lit buoys[4] mark the entrance to the channel and a night entry is possible if there is enough light to see any unlit channel buoys and beacons.

BERTHS AND ANCHORAGE

On entering, the visitors pontoon is immediately ahead. Secure here and visit the helpful harbour office to be allocated a berth.

FACILITIES

Fuel, 30-tonne travel-lift, slipway and haul-out area. Engine and yacht repairs undertaken.

Groceries, café-bars, restaurants, launderette and chandlery in the marina. There are pleasant beaches nearby.

One mile upstream of the marina entrance the town of La Forêt-Fouesnant lies on the west side of the estuary and can be reached by dinghy when the tide is up. The lock marked on the charts is now permanently open. There are fairly frequent buses from the port to Quimper and Concarneau.

19. Concarneau

47°52'N 3°55'W

GENERAL

Concarneau is an important fishing port with some commercial traffic and at present the inner harbour is wholly devoted to these activities. The *avant-port*, on the other hand, is wholly devoted to yachting, of which the port is a busy centre. The harbour is easy of access by day or night and the shelter is good

The town is large and contains all resources, making it a good place for victualling. The walled Ville Close is picturesque, but is entirely dedicated to the tourist trade. Though rather off the route to the south, Concarneau is a place of character, well worth a visit. At one time it was the main port in the region for the sailing *thoniers* one whose graveyards is the Blavet river.

Charts

BA *3641, 2352*
Imray *C38*

TIDAL DATA

Times and heights

Time differences				Height differences			
HW		LW		MHWS	MHWN	MLWN	MLWS
BREST							
0000 and 1200	0600 and 1800	0000 and 1200	0600 and 1800	6·9	5·4	2·6	1·0
Concarneau							
–0010	–0030	–0030	–0020	–1·9	–1·5	–0·7	–0·2

Tidal streams

The streams in the narrowest part of the entrance reach up to 2kts at springs.

Depths

The entrance is deep. The marina has 1 to 2·5m, but beware of rocks along the fuel-berth wall, which should only be approached near HW. The Anse de Kersos shoals steadily from 3m.

LIGHTS

1. **Le Cochon** 47°51'·5N 3°55'·5W
   Fl(3)WRG.12s5m9-6M
   048°-G-205°-R-352°-W-048° Green tower
2. **Basse du Chenal buoy** (port) 47°51'·6N 3°55'·6W
   Q.R
3. **Men Fall buoy** (starboard) 47°51'·8N 3°55'·2W
   Fl.G.4s
   Ldg Lts 028·5°
4. *Front* **La Croix** 47°52'·2N 3°55'·1W
   Oc(3)12s14m13M 006·5°-vis-093°
   Red and white tower
5. *Rear* **Beuzec** 47°53'·4N 3°54'·0W 1·34M from front
   DirQ.87m23M 026·5°-intens-030·5°
   Belfry
6. **Lanriec** 47°52'·1N 3°54'·6W Q.G.13m8M
   Green window in white gable
7. **La Médée** 47°52'·1N 3°54'·9W Fl.R.2·5s9m4M
   Red tower
8. **Passage de Lanriec** 47°52'·3N 3°54'·8W
   Oc(2)WR.6s4m9/6M 209°-R-354°-W-007°-R-018°
   Red tower below wall of La Ville Close

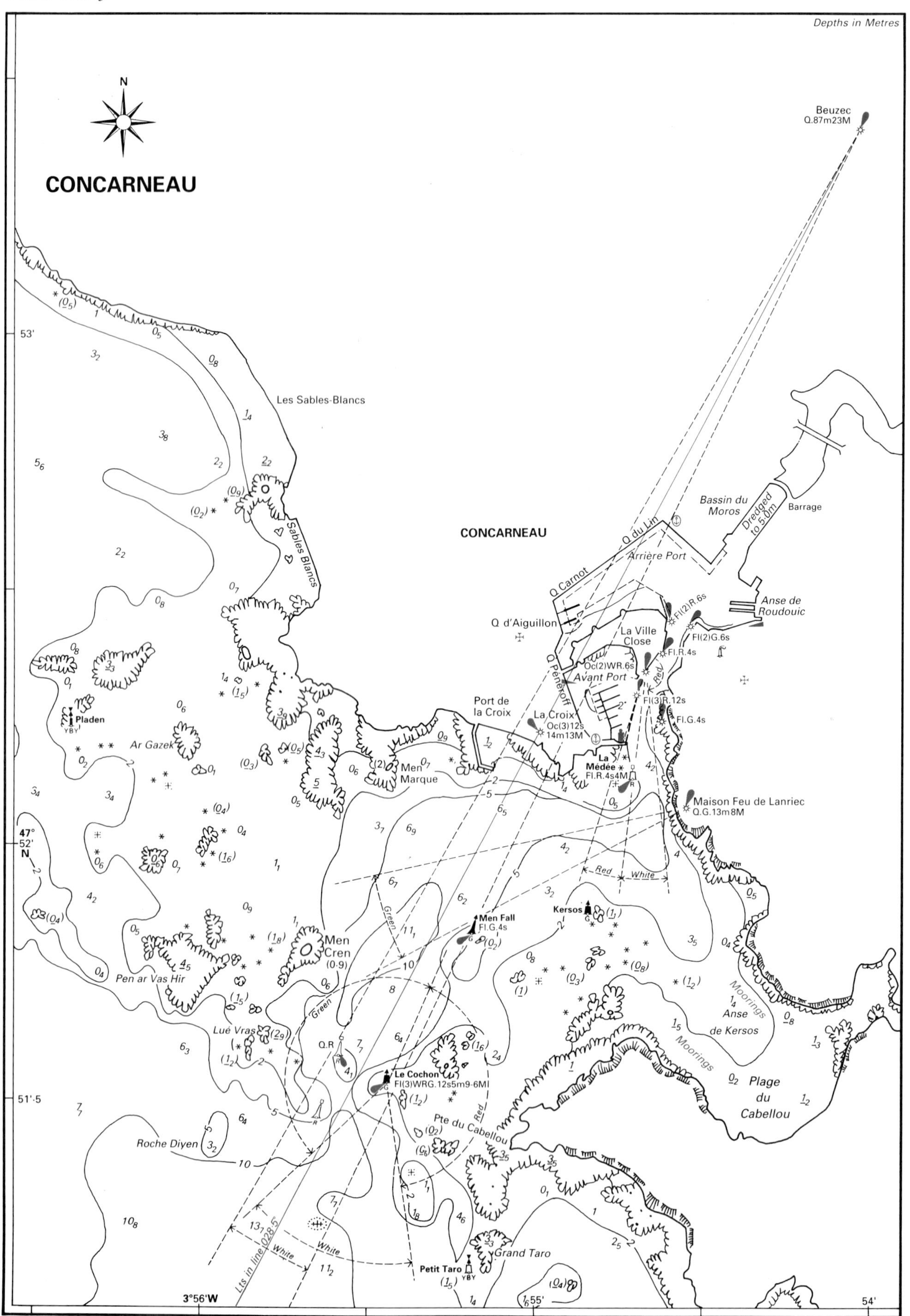
Depths in Metres
CONCARNEAU
Beuzec
Q.87m23M
Les Sables-Blancs
Sables Blancs
CONCARNEAU
Bassin du Moros
Dredged to 5.0m
Barrage
Q du Lin
Arrière Port
Q Carnot
Q d'Aiguillon
La Ville Close
Fl(2)R.6s
Anse de Roudouic
Fl(2)G.6s
Fl.R.4s
Oc(2)WR.6s
Avant Port
Q Pénéroff
Fl(3)R.12s
Fl.G.4s
Port de la Croix
La Croix
Oc(3)12s 14m13M
La Médée
Fl.R.4s4M
Maison Feu de Lanriec
Q.G.13m8M
Pladen
YBY
Ar Gazek
Men Marque
Red
White
Men Fall
Fl.G.4s
Kersos
Men Cren
(0·9)
Pen ar Vas Hir
Green
Moorings
Anse de Kersos
Luë Vras
Q.R
Le Cochon
Fl(3)WRG.12s5m9-6M
Plage du Cabellou
Pte du Cabellou
Roche Diyen
Grand Taro
Petit Taro
YBY
Lts in line 028.5°
White
53'
47° 52' N
51'·5
3°56'W
55'
54'

Plan 19

Concarneau, looking NE with La Ville Close beyond the marina

Men Fall buoy is left to starboard before turning onto 065° for Lanriec light (arrowed)

9. **East side (No. 1) Beacon** 47°52'·2N 3°54'·6W Fl.G.4s4m5M Green round tower
10. **Entrance to Marina** Fl(3)R.12s Red post on N end of wavebreaker

Beyond the marina further red and green lights mark the passage past La Ville Close into the fishing harbour.

RADIO

Commercial Port VHF Ch 12 24hr
Marina VHF Ch 9 0700–2100 LT

APPROACH AND ENTRANCE

By day

Whatever the direction of approach, the buildings on the hill rising up at the back of the town are unmistakable. Steer for a position about half a mile W of the tree-covered promontory, Pointe de Cabellou.

The official leading line is Beuzec belfry, on the ridge a mile inland, in transit with La Croix lighthouse, on the seafront, bearing 028·5°. The belfry is not conspicuous and La Croix is undetectable in front of an apartment block. Le Cochon green beacon tower is more easily identified and it is sufficient to pass midway between it and the two red buoys which mark the dangers to port, on a course of about 030°.

Continue on this course for 600m towards Men Fall starboard-hand buoy. Round the buoy and steer 065° while attempting to identify the next mark, 'Maison Feu de Lanriec'. This is the end gable of a white house, among many white houses, with what appears to be a black window in the upper half. Binoculars may reveal the name in green under the window, and the mark can be identified for future reference on leaving Concarneau.

The channel is wide and, leaving Kersos green beacon tower 200m to starboard, it is sufficient to steer to leave La Médée red beacon tower to port to enter the marina. A floating wavebreaker is connected to the head of the harbour wall, the entrance to the marina is at its northern end. Visitors can secure along the inner side before visiting the harbour office to arrange for a berth.

By night

Approach in the white sector of Le Cochon[1] and bring Beuzec[5] and La Croix lights[4] in transit on 028·5°. Hold this course past Le Cochon and Basse du Chenal buoy[2] towards Men Fall buoy[3]. As Men Fall is passed, Lanriec Q.G light[6] will open. Steer about 070° in the visible sector until the Passage de Lanriec light[8] on the Ville Close opens red. Continue to head for Lanriec until it turns from red to white at which point alter to about 000° to keep in the white sector, leaving La Médée[7] to port and No. 1 beacon[9] to starboard. Round the north end of the floating wavebreaker[10] and secure to the inside or raft to another yacht. The floodlights which illuminate La Ville Close give plenty of background illumination to the marina area. The channel beyond the marina into the inner harbour, past the Ville Close, is marked by further red and green lights.

BERTHS AND ANCHORAGE

Visitors berth either on the inner side of the floating breakwater or on the visitors pontoon which is directly inside the marina entrance. It is claimed that there is less disturbance from the wash of passing vessels at the breakwater berths than there is at the visitors' pontoon. The outside of the wavebreaker is used by ferries; yachts should not use it and those who do risk being damaged.

If moving to a pontoon near the wall beware of the shallow rocky patch by the fuel berth which is a hazard near low water.

Although the authorities do their best to fit everyone in, there may be occasions during the height of the season when there are no places available in this popular harbour. The Anse de Kersos offers shelter from the N through E to SW, but is exposed to the W and NW. To anchor, go in clear of the moorings as far as draught and tide will permit. There are no facilities and it is a long and exposed journey in the dinghy back to Concarneau.

Should the wind be westerly, Beg Meil is not far off and will provide shelter, or a berth can be found at Port La Forêt.

FACILITIES

There are all the facilities of a sizeable town and busy fishing and yachting port. Sailmakers and chandlers near the marina. Fuel berth, slipways. All repairs can be undertaken.

Shops of every kind, banks, hotels and restaurants to suit all tastes. Large supermarket.

There is a delightful beach just over a mile NW of the port. The Musée de Pêche in the Ville Close is interesting. The annual *Fête de Pêche des Filets Bleus* is held on the second-to-last Sunday of August; a cheerful, noisy festival of Breton costume, dancing, music and wrestling, with an illuminated procession of boats.

Bus connection to railway at Quimper and Rosporden.

20. Pointe de Trévignon

47°47'N 3°51'W

Passage notes

GENERAL

There is a 700m-wide passage between Ile Verte and Ile de Raguenès. If using it, care must be taken to avoid the rocks which extend ¼M off each island; those off Ile de Raguenès being marked by a S cardinal beacon. If passing outside Ile Verte Men ar Tréas reef, drying 1·4m is a hazard. It lies 1M SW of Ile Verte and is marked by a S cardinal buoy.

Charts

BA *2352*
Imray *C38*

TIDAL STREAMS

The early part of the flood stream divides at this headland, one branch turning NW towards Concarneau and the Baie de la Forêt, the other turning E, flowing past Ile Verte and along the land. The latter part of the flood flows S and E round the point. This pattern is reversed on the ebb. Between the Pointe de Trévignon and Ile de Groix the stream is weak.

LIGHTS

1. **Chausée Les Soldats – Roche Le Dragon**
   47°47'·9N 3°53'·3W VQ(9)10s6M W card beacon tower
2. **Pte de Trévignon light (Breakwater root)**
   47°47'·6N 3°51'·3W
   Oc(3+1)WRG.12s11m14-11M
   322°-R-351°-obscd-004°-W-051°-G-085°-W-092°-R-127° White square tower, green top

ANCHORAGE

E of La Pointe de Raguenès is a sandy beach off which there are a number of summer yacht moorings. The island gives some protection from westerly winds and a pleasant overnight anchorage can be found in about 4m outside the moorings.

21. Aven and Bélon rivers

47°48'N 3°44'W

GENERAL

These popular and very pretty rivers are both well sheltered. Whilst space to anchor can still be found, they are very crowded with moorings and a visitor should expect to have to use one. There are good restaurants, but not much else in the way of shops except at Port Manec'h and Pont Aven; the Bélon is famous for its oysters. Both rivers have shallow bars, but whereas that of the Bélon is impassable in bad weather, the Aven bar is sheltered and rarely breaks. It is perhaps partly for this reason that the Aven river is the more visited of the two.

In the Bélon, yachts seldom go further upstream than the visitors moorings. The Aven however, can be explored on the tide as far as the town of Pont Aven 2½M above Rosbraz. The channel is adequately marked and a yacht of 2·2m draught can

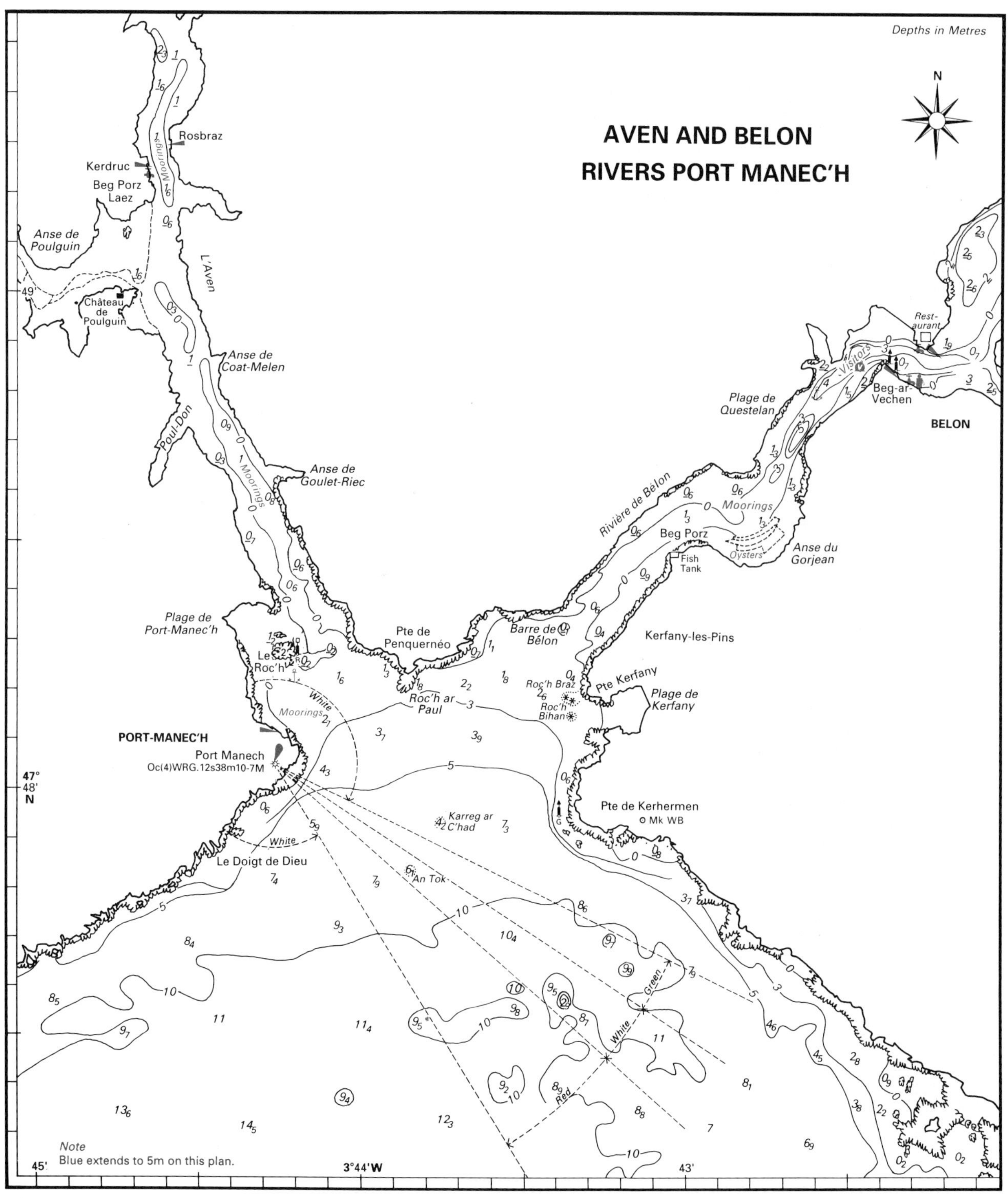

Plan 20

Port-Manec'h and the Aven river

reach the quays just below the town, where it is possible to dry out alongside. Pont Aven is famous as the town where Gauguin lived and painted; it is picturesque and there are many galleries.

Charts

BA *2352*
Imray *C38*
The BA chart is on too small a scale for navigation within the rivers, but the plan on page 77 gives sufficient detail to reach the moorings in the Bélon or Rosbraz in the Aven. For more detailed exploration there is a large-scale plan on SHOM *7138*.

TIDAL DATA

Times and heights

Time differences				Height differences			
HW		LW		MHWS	MHWN	MLWN	MLWS
BREST							
0000 and 1200	0600 and 1800	0000 and 1200	0600 and 1800	6·9	5·4	2·6	1·0
Concarneau							
–0010	–0030	–0030	–0020	–1·9	–1·5	–0·7	–0·2

Tidal streams

The flood runs to the E and the ebb to the W at rates which are uncertain but not very great. The streams in the rivers are stronger and in the narrows at Rosbraz reach over 3kts on the ebb.

Depths

The approach from the SSW and S is deep, but coming from the SE inside Les Verrès there is a shoal with 2·6m over it. The bars into both rivers vary and at times may dry, but the channels over them are usually kept dredged and the rivers are normally accessible above half tide.

Within the rivers depths vary but there are many places where a yacht will remain afloat, even at springs. Above Rosbraz the Aven should be considered as drying 1–1·5m, although to find that depth it is necessary not to stray from the channel. There are occasional deeper pools. In the Bélon there is plenty of water on the visitors buoys.

Boats are moored head and stern on the moorings between Kerdruc and Rosbraz

LIGHTS

1. Port Manec'h (Pointe de Beg-ar-Véchen)
   47°48'·0N 3°44'·4W
   Oc(4)WRG.12s38m10-7M
   050°-W(unintens)-140°-W-296°-G-303°-W-311°-R-328°-W-050°
   Obscd by Pointe de Beg-Moreg when bearing less than 299° White and red tower

APPROACH AND ENTRANCE

By day

The entrance is easy to locate by the lighthouse at Port Manec'h on the west side of the entrance. On the E side there is a large white masonry beacon with a black vertical stripe, on Pointe Kerhermen, with a beacon (starboard) off the tip of the point.

Approach can be made from any direction, having regard to the following dangers. To the W are the unmarked Les Cochons de Rousbicout, drying 0·3m, lying ¼M off a small inlet. To the SE Les Verrès dry 2·6m and are marked by a BRB tower. An outlier, Le Cochon, lies half a mile NW of the tower and dries 0·6m. There is a clear passage between Les Verrès and the land, carrying a depth of 2·6m. Enter as convenient between Port Manec'h and the starboard beacon off Pte de Kerhermen, giving them a berth of 100m.

By night

The white sectors of Port Manec'h light[1] lead in. The red sector covers Les Verrès and the green sector the rocks along the coast to the SE. Having made the entrance, a stranger should anchor or pick up a mooring off Port Manec'h and wait for daylight.

Port Manec'h

On the point below the lighthouse is a white building with a grey roof. The short Port Manec'h breakwater, marked at its head by a red rectangle with a white border, runs upstream from the point. Behind it is a small quay and slipway. E of the breakwater are a number of white visitors' mooring buoys with 2·5m or more for deep-draught vessels. Upstream of them are a number of red mooring buoys. These provide double-ended moorings with heavy chain, but lie in shallower water and are only convenient for boats of less than 10m length. During the season, all of these moorings are likely to be taken by early afternoon. There is room to anchor outside them.

A drying inlet runs W of Le Roc'h, the drying rocks marked by a red beacon at the Aven bar. This inlet shoals towards a sandy bathing beach and provides a convenient anchorage, clear of the bathers, for shallow-draught vessels that can take the ground.

FACILITIES

Land at the quay or on the beach. There is water on the quay and modest shops, restaurants and a hotel. There is a café-bar W of the beach.

Aven river

The river in general is shallow, and the position of the bar, which has been known to dry 1m if it has silted, changes periodically. The channel through the bar is normally kept dredged for the benefit of the many boats which lie on moorings in the river. There are pools up as far as Kerdruc and Rosbras, but these tend to be occupied by moorings for local boats. It is a pleasant river to visit near high water. The river can be explored above Rosbraz on the tide, but if planning to linger, a yacht must be prepared to take the ground.

For a first visit, in case silting has occurred, enter on a rising tide when the rocks marked by the red beacon are covered and one can expect at least 2m over the bar. Leave the beacon comfortably to port and proceed up the centre of the river. Half a mile up there is an inlet called Anse de Goulet-Riec on the eastern side. Here the river deepens for a little and 2m or more may be found.

Farther on the river shoals to dry 0·6m in places and there is a large drying creek branching off to the west with a château at its mouth. Beyond, the river narrows, with the quays and slips of Kerdruc on the W bank and Rosbraz on the E. Between them is a long, deep pool where yachts are rafted on mooring trots on either side in up to 3m. It is possible to dry out alongside the quays on mud at Kerdruc and shingle and mud at Rosbras; alternatively use a mooring. The ebb runs at over 3kts and there is not much room in the river between the moorings. It is difficult for a yacht of over 10m to find space to turn. If mooring, it is essential to secure bow and stern.

On the tide there is plenty of water for a deep keeled yacht to reach Pont Aven

Above the quays the river widens and shoals, but is navigable by yacht (on the tide) or by dinghy and outboard, a further 2½M to Pont Aven. The channel, marked by buoys, is easy to follow and the detailed French chart is not essential. There are quays at the town against which a yacht may berth and dry out, but these tend to be crowded.

FACILITIES

Rosbras can offer a water tap on the upper slip, toilets, and a café-bar a short walk away.

Kerdruc has a bar with food by the quay.

Pont Aven has all the facilities of a market town, including shops, banks, hotels and many restaurants. The picturesque town is a famous haunt of artists and is well worth a visit.

Bélon river

It is best for a stranger to make his first visit to the Bélon river when the tide is well up. Make a position about 100m W of the green beacon off Pte de Kerhermen; that is, about 200m W of the point itself. Thence steer about 005° for the rounded headland on the north side of the entrance. This course leaves a bay with a popular bathing beach,

The Bélon river

the Plage de Kerfany, to starboard and passes close to three small rocks awash at datum off Pte Kerfany, on the east side of the mouth.

With Pte Kerfany abeam to starboard, steer down the middle of the dredged channel on 035°. The small grey hut which used to provide a convenient head mark has now collapsed and the best advice is to keep mid-channel. At Beg Porz, where the river curves to starboard there are the remains of a concrete fish tank, at present (1998) above water at all times, but in a ruinous condition; if it collapses further it will be a hazard. Just past the tank, the channel turns sharply to starboard and the best course is to keep close outside the line of moorings, backed by oyster beds in the large curving bay on the starboard side, leaving to port the inner bar which projects from the NW side of the river.

There are stakes marking oyster beds on this bar, and there are similar stakes planted in the bay and on both sides of the river so that it is not always easy to distinguish the channel. Coming out of the bay the channel leads straight upriver, keeping rather to the E side. Half a mile on, the river turns to starboard, and on the port-hand side of the curve in comparatively still, deep water are three large white metal head and stern mooring buoys for visitors, suitable for rafting.

It is still possible to find a space to anchor below the permanent moorings downstream of the visitors buoys. However, each year the space becomes more limited and it is essential to use two anchors to keep out of the channel.

Further on is a drying slip and a quay. On the starboard bank is a long slip, with the lower end marked by a green beacon and the upper end leading onto the curving quay of Lanroit. Here the river is wide, with many fishing-boat and yacht moorings, but it soon shoals. Above Lanroit, where it dries, there are extensive oyster beds, and yachts should not proceed much beyond the visitors' moorings.

Near high water it is possible to cross the outer bar rather than enter by the channel, but fresh winds from the S or SW quickly bring swell, making the bar impassable and entry by the channel inadvisable.

Facilities

In July and August a shop for campers is open by the Plage de Kerfany.

At Lanroit there is fuel and water on the quay and several café-bars. Near HW fresh seafood can often be bought direct from the fishing boats, but there are no food shops.

On the opposite side of the river is a seafood restaurant of repute.

22. Brigneau and Merrien

47°47'N 3°39'W

GENERAL

These two small harbours lie only ¾M apart about three miles southeast of Port Manec'h.

Brigneau lies in a small inlet and in onshore weather the swell gets right in and it is untenable, but in fine weather it is an interesting and pretty place for a visit. The quay dries out; in very fine weather one can stay afloat at the entrance, anchored or on a buoy. At the beginning of the 20th century Brigneau was a busy sardine port. Now activity is divided between a sailing school and a small fishing fleet.

Merrien is a delightful place to visit, particularly for yachts prepared to take the ground. In calm conditions deep-draught vessels may anchor in 3m or more or secure to a visitors buoy in the bay outside. Inside the entrance is a wide drying pool; above it the river narrows and turns to starboard, leading to the village on the east bank and a trot of visitors' moorings where shallow-draught vessels can expect to lie afloat on most tides in complete shelter. A channel is occasionally dredged from the entrance as far as the quay but is liable to silt and should not be relied on.

Charts

BA *2352*
Imray *C38*

TIDAL DATA

Times and heights

Time differences				Height differences			
HW		LW		MHWS	MHWN	MLWN	MLWS
BREST							
0000 and 1200	0600 and 1800	0000 and 1200	0600 and 1800	6·9	5·4	2·6	1·0
Port Tudy							
0000	–0025	–0025	–0015	–1·8	–1·4	–0·6	–0·1

Tidal streams

Outside the flood sets to the E, the ebb to the W; rates are weak. There is some stream in Merrien creek but little in Brigneau.

Depths

There is 1·7m just outside the entrance to Brigneau and 1m outside the entrance to Merrien. Brigneau dries 1 to 2m, from the quay to the head of the harbour and Merrien dries 0·6m except in the channel, which must be kept clear.

LIGHTS

1. **Brigneau mole head** 47°46'·9N 3°40'·2W Oc(2)WRG.6s7m12-9M 280°-G-329°-W-339°-R-034° White column, red top
2. **Merrien** 47°47'·1N 3°39'·0W Q.R.26m7M 004°-vis-009° White square tower, red top

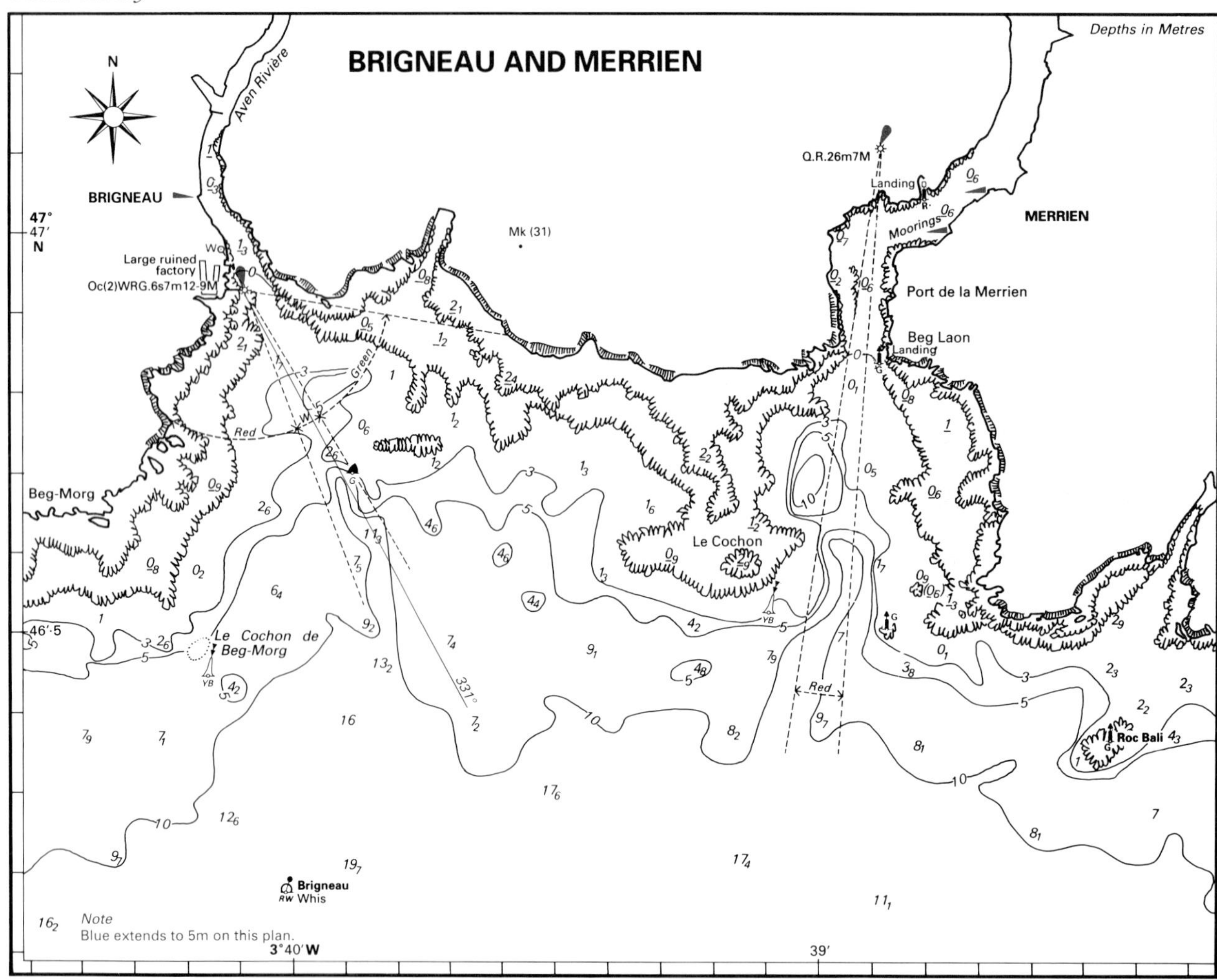

Plan 21

Brigneau

APPROACH AND ENTRANCE

By day

The point to the W of Brigneau falls away to the low rocky spit of Beg Morg, with Le Cochon de Beg Morg, drying 0·3m, 400m off the point. ¾M due S of the entrance is an unlit RW landfall whistle buoy ('Brigneau'). From this point the port can be identified by the large ruined factory building on the west side, with the breakwater below. Steer N for a point E of the breakwater, leaving to port a S cardinal buoy marking Le Cochon de Beg Morg. Leave 200m to starboard a green buoy on a rock awash at LWS and bear to port to enter the harbour, leaving the breakwater head, marked by a red rectangle with a white border, to port.

A leading line is provided on 331° using the Brigneau light structure as front marker and for rear marker a white open tubular frame with a wire mesh rectangle at the top. This is situated just to the right of the lowest house on the west side of the harbour – the only house to the right of the ruined factory.

By night

Entrance can be made without difficulty in calm weather by keeping in the white sector of the mole head light[1] on 335° until close to and then bearing to starboard to take a mooring with the aid of a spotlight. Alternatively anchor outside to starboard of the line, keeping clear of fishing floats.

MOORINGS

There are two trots of moorings on the E side of the harbour, just inside the entrance; the inner (eastern) one is for yachts, whilst the outer one is for fishing boats. The moorings are suitable for lengths of up to about 10m; depths shallow from 2m on the outer pair of buoys to 1·2m on the third pair in. Thereafter they are in increasingly shallow water. There are many moorings which dry further in. Only very small yachts should proceed further up the harbour than the slipway on the port hand as beyond it the harbour is very congested and there is little room to turn.

FACILITIES

There are water taps and electric points along the quay. Small food shop at the top of the square past the crane. Café-bar in the square.

Brigneau

Merrien

APPROACH AND ENTRANCE

The entrance is easy to identify from the W, ¾M E of Brigneau. From the E, the entrance will open after passing a headland topped by some holiday houses, white with grey roofs, 1¾M W of Doëlan.

There are marked dangers on both sides of the entrance. To the W lies a spit of rocks, terminating in the ubiquitous Cochon, guarded by a S cardinal buoy. To the E rocks extend for 100m out along the side of the headland, marked by a green starboard beacon. 500m further E is an isolated rock, Roche Bali, marked by a green beacon.

From a position due S of the entrance to the river the white light tower will be seen at the head of the pool, backed by a large grey-roofed house with a gable on the E end. Keep the light tower on a bearing of 005° to enter the river or to anchor or moor outside.

By night

Entry to the pool is possible, though not advisable, keeping strictly in the narrow red sector of the light[2] on 005°. Should the light disappear it will be hard to make the correct course alteration to bring it back.

MOORINGS AND ANCHORAGE

The three visitors buoys outside are the best place in calm conditions. For a short visit, with enough water, the pool inside the mouth is inviting, with a flat sandy bottom except for a rocky patch (see plan opposite). Keep out of the channel and at least 50m offshore in the outer half as the sides are rocky. There are trots of head and stern moorings for visitors up to about 9m length in depths of about 1m.

After the sharp turn to starboard there is another landing place on the port side, marked by a red beacon; visitors' buoys and Merrien quay and slipways are on the starboard side of the channel. Do not proceed beyond the quay as the river is full of oyster beds.

FACILITIES

For those anchored or on the buoys outside the harbour there are steps on the starboard side of the entrance leading down to a flat stone jetty, submerged at high water and marked by a green beacon. It is a pleasant walk along the headland from them to the port. Water available on the quay. Café-bars and restaurant in the village up the hill, about ½M.

Within Brigneau harbour there is little room and visitors are better off near the entrance

23. Doëlan

47°46'N 3°36'W

GENERAL

The port of Doëlan, though larger than the other small ports on this part of the coast, is still very small. It supports a small but active fishing fleet, and there are a number of yachts which take the ground at the back of the harbour, in shelter provided by a bend in the creek. The outer harbour is exposed to the south and entry should not be attempted except in settled offshore weather. It is a pretty little place and quite a resort for artists.

Charts

BA *2352*
Imray *C38*

Merrien

TIDAL DATA

Times and heights

Time differences				Height differences			
HW		LW		MHWS	MHWN	MLWN	MLWS
BREST							
0000	0600	0000	0600				
and	and	and	and	6·9	5·4	2·6	1·0
1200	1800	1200	1800				
Port Tudy							
0000	–0025	–0025	–0015	–1·8	–1·4	–0·6	–0·1

Tidal streams

Outside the flood sets to the east, the ebb to the west; rates weak. There is little stream in the harbour.

Depths

There is 4m just inside the breakwater and the harbour is dredged to 2m, although it is subject to silting and the depths cannot be relied upon. The inner quays dry 0·7 to 1·5m.

LIGHTS

Ldg Lts 014°

1. *Front* 47°46'·3N 3°36'·5W
   Oc(3)WG.12s20m13/10M
   shore-305°-G-314°-W-shore
   White tower, green band and top
2. *Rear* 47°46'·5N 3°36'·3W 326m from front
   Q.R.27m9M White tower, red band and top

APPROACH AND ENTRANCE

By day

The port is easily recognised by the conspicuous factory buildings with slender chimney on the E side of the entrance and the two lighthouses that provide the leading line. Enter with the lighthouses in line bearing 014°. The transit leaves a red beacon marking Basse La Croix to port and Le Four green beacon to starboard.

By night

Approach and enter with the leading lights[1,2] in line on 014°. Coming from the direction of Lorient, a vessel can avoid the rocks SE of Le Pouldu (Les Grand et Petit Cochons) by keeping out of the green sector of the front light[1], which covers them.

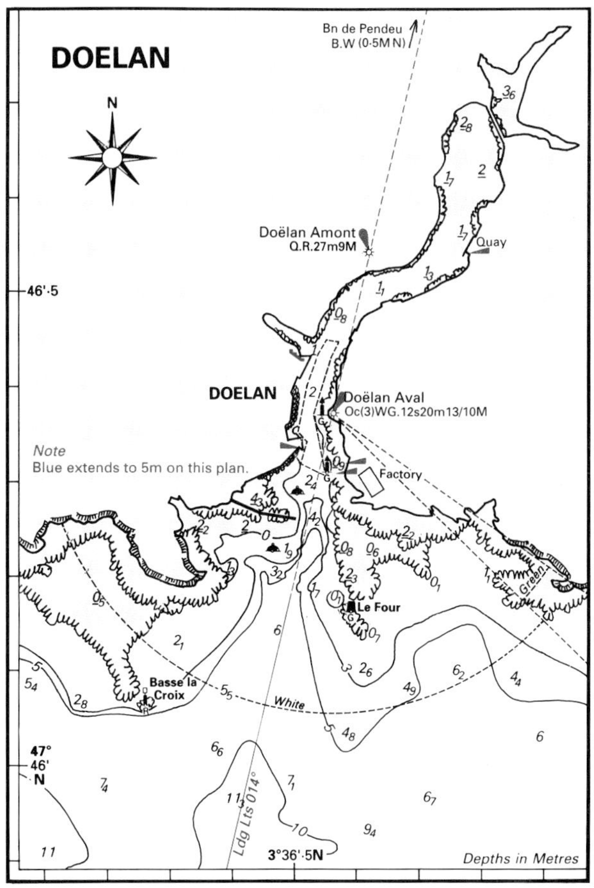

Plan 22

BERTHS AND ANCHORAGE

Visitors may raft with other yachts to a large white metal buoy with a rail round its edge. There is one of these just outside and another inside the breakwater on the W side of the entrance, together with four orange conventional visitors' buoys.

The fishermen are friendly, and it may be possible to borrow one of their moorings; for a yacht that can take the ground, it may be possible to borrow a mooring up-harbour.

The approach to Doëlan with the leading lighthouses almost in transit

Looking NE into Doëlan

Alternatively, one can dry out at one of the quays. Near the entrance to the harbour there is a landing slip and quay on the port side, a pair of slips forming a V on the starboard side. Other quays lie further in. Local advice should be obtained before drying out. The inner quay on the port hand is not suitable as the bottom slopes outwards. The first two quays on the starboard hand should, however, be suitable, the bottom drying about 1·5m.

FACILITIES

Water and electricity are available on the quays and there is a fish market on the outer port-side quay, Quay Neuf. There are bars and restaurants on both sides and provisions may sometimes be obtained and bread ordered from a bar on the W bank (turn right at the top of the square). There is a good chandlery S of the *Hôtel Café du Port*. The nearest shops are at Clohars Carnoet, 3km inland.

24. Le Pouldu

47°46'N 3°32'W

GENERAL

Le Pouldu, at the mouth of La Laïta or Rivière de Quimperlé, has a character quite different from its neighbouring ports. If we can liken the Aven to a miniature Salcombe and Doëlan to a miniature Dartmouth, here we have a miniature Teignmouth. It has a much more open valley, shifting sands and searing tides, and because of these it is much less frequented by cruising yachts.

A visit is only practicable in fine settled weather, as the bar breaks heavily when the wind is onshore and, once inside, a change of wind can make departure impossible for several days. Exploration is an interesting exercise in a bilge-keeler, but is hazardous in a deep-draught vessel, and is best undertaken at mean tides, as there is scarcely enough water at neaps and the tides are uncomfortably strong at springs. At low water the anchorage outside is a deep peaty colour, justifying the name Le Pouldu (The black anchorage).

The marina is small and there appear to be no berths for boats much over 9m, nor much space for visitors.

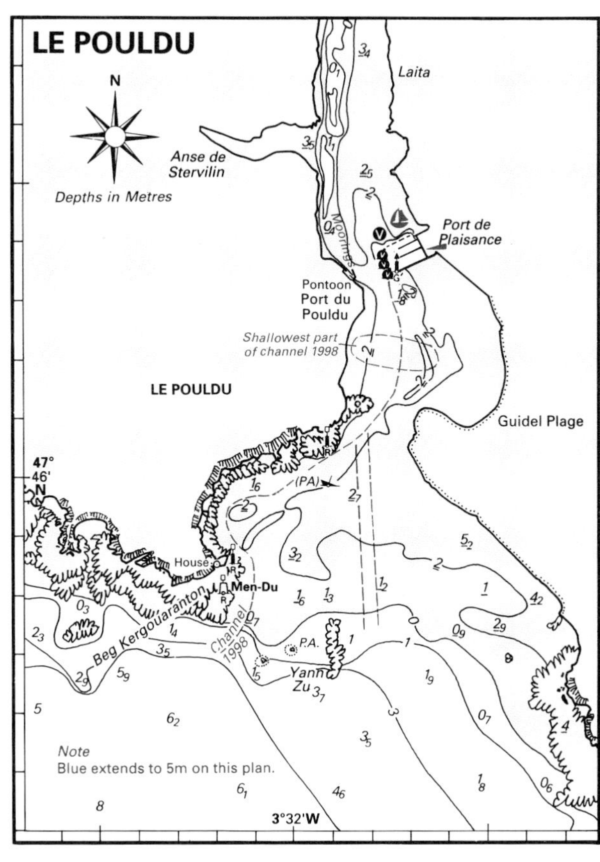

Plan 23

Charts

BA *2352*
Imray *C38*

TIDAL DATA

Times and heights

Time differences				Height differences			
HW		LW		MHWS	MHWN	MLWN	MLWS
BREST							
0000 and 1200	0600 and 1800	0000 and 1200	0600 and 1800	6·9	5·4	2·6	1·0
Port Tudy							
0000	–0025	–0025	–0015	–1·8	–1·4	–0·6	–0·1

Tidal streams

Outside the flood sets to the E, the ebb to the west; the streams are weak. The streams in the river are fierce, up to 6kts springs.

Depths

The bottom is sandy and both the position and the depth of the channel are liable to change. Without prior exploration it should be regarded as drying 2·2m, but it is said that with local knowledge more water can be found. There is a deep pool above Le Pouldu.

APPROACH AND ENTRANCE

Caution The stream runs like a millrace in the river and except near slack water a yacht which grounds will be slewed round uncontrollably and, if small, may be heeled over dangerously.

The entrance to the Quimperlé river is almost completely blocked by sandbars, leaving only a narrow channel on the western side

Men-Du beacon tower and the port-hand beacons beyond it

By day
Approaching from the SE, Le Grand Cochon is marked by a S cardinal buoy. Keep well offshore to avoid the reefs and shallows which lie off Fort Bloque. The harbour entrance can be identified by the former pilot's house, white with a round tower, situated on the headland on the E side. The final approach is made with the headland bearing 010° to avoid rocks drying 0·6m and a shoal drying 1·3m 400m to the SSE.

Without previous reconnaissance near LW or local advice, entry should only be attempted in calm conditions shortly before HW. Under these conditions the flood stream will not dictate the course followed, but there may be no indication of where the channel lies. It can only be misleading to give precise directions, as the channel shifts frequently and unpredictably. In general, a sandy spit runs out from the east side of the entrance, as shown in the plan on page 87.

The main channel follows the W bank and is marked by the red beacon tower at the entrance, followed by a port-hand beacon pole and, after curving to starboard, a second port-hand beacon pole near the end of a small rocky spit. This channel, except for the stream from the river, dries at LW. However, the strong streams sometimes cut through the spit, so that the channel may follow the dotted lines shown on the plan, and a steep-sided sandy island may build up which can on occasion almost block the under-cliff channel. In 1998 this secondary channel was small, only navigable by dinghy, even near HW.

Assuming that the main channel is to be taken, leave the second beacon pole 40m to port and keep this distance off to avoid a rocky shelf. The river opens out, with a wide shallow bay to starboard, and the protecting breakwater of a marina will be seen ahead on the E bank. In 1998 the channel was as shown by the dotted line on the plan and it was necessary to go very well into the bay on the W side. Local reports maintain that this is normally the case, the best water being more likely to be found by following the W shore until the next point is reached, with two hotels and a small jetty.

Thence one can cross to the marina. In 1998 the shallowest area in the entrance channel was as shown on the plan.

The river is navigable by dinghies at HW up to Quimperlé, but a bridge with 10m clearance two miles from the entrance prevents the passage of masted vessels.

By night
There are no lights and a night entry should not be attempted.

BERTHS AND ANCHORAGE
In settled offshore weather anchorage can be found outside the bar. The best spot seems to be with the marina bearing 000° as far in as draught permits, bottom hard sand.

There are red mooring buoys for visitors (reportedly dredged but depth uncertain) off the marina, or one can continue upriver to find deep water (2m or more) for anchoring along the W bank, at the entrance to a shallow creek, above a line of moorings. The holding appears to be good in spite of the stream and some weed. There is a drying sandbank in the middle of the river and there are many small-craft drying moorings on the E side and in the bay downstream.

FACILITIES
The pontoon on the W bank is for fishermen, but dinghy landing is permitted, and there are two hotels close by, with Le Pouldu and its shops a mile down the road. On the E bank by the marina are restaurants catering for a camping site, and a large supermarket is situated a few minutes' walk round the bay towards the entrance.

25. Kerroc'h and Le Pérello

47°42'N 3°27'W

GENERAL

These two small harbours lie on either side of Pte du Talut. Neither of them is particularly attractive, but they provide shelter for a yacht which does not wish to enter Lorient and finds Port Tudy too crowded for comfort. Kerroc'h is well sheltered, although in strong westerly winds some swell may enter near HW. Le Pérello is open to the southeast. There are few facilities

Charts

BA *2352*
Imray *C38*

TIDAL DATA

Times and heights

	Time differences				Height differences			
	HW		LW		MHWS	MHWN	MLWN	MLWS
BREST								
	0000 and 1200	0600 and 1800	0000 and 1200	0600 and 1800	6·9	5·4	2·6	1·0
Port Tudy								
	0000–0025		–0025	–0015	–1·8	–1·4	–0·6	–0·1

Tidal streams

Between Ile De Groix and the mainland the flood stream runs E and the ebb W, spring rates ½kt. In the anchorages the streams are very weak.

Depths

The approach to Kerroch has a 2·8m shoal patch; the approach to Pérello is deep. In Kerroc'h the anchorage is deep. At Pérello depths of 2m or more may be found, shoaling further in.

LIGHTS

1. **Kerroc'h** 47°42'·0N 3°27'·7W
   Oc(2)WRG.6s13m11-8M
   096·5°-R-112·5°-G-132°-R-302°-W-096·5°
   White truncated tower, red top

Kerroc'h

APPROACH AND ENTRANCE

By day

The approach is made between the reef which extends west from the harbour, the outer end of which is marked by a W cardinal beacon, and Les Sœurs, an extensive patch of drying and above-water rocks which lie 500m further west. Approaching

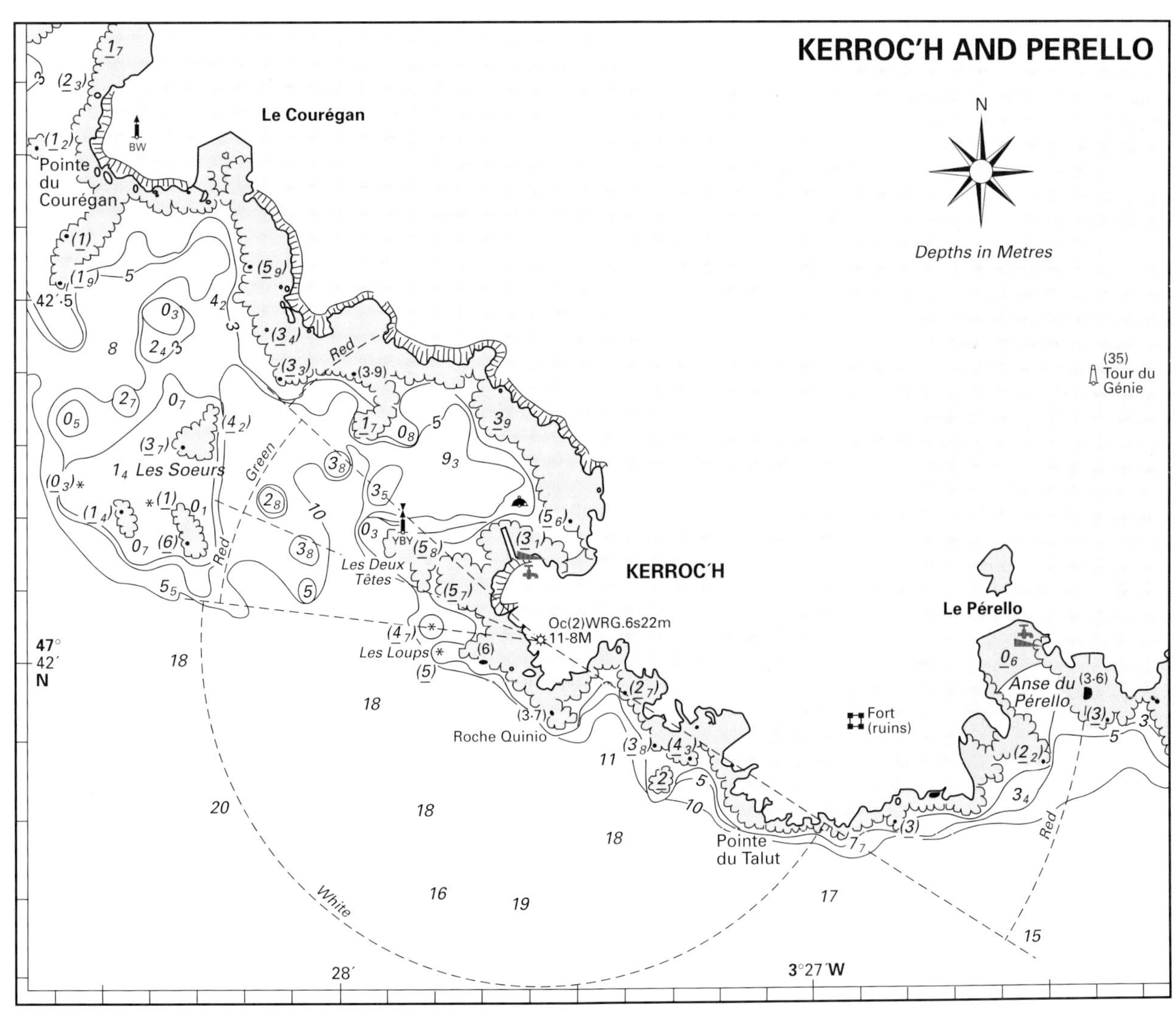

Plan 24

Approaching Kerroch give this west cardinal beacon a fair berth before turning towards the breakwater

Le Pérello. The distinctive grey and white house is the back mark for the transit. The front mark is the elbow on the slipway below. This view is taken from well to starboard of the line.

from the E, give the shore a reasonable berth to avoid Les Loupes, which only cover at HW springs. Once they have been passed, alter northwards to pass 100m from the W cardinal beacon and then turn to the E towards the harbour.

From the W, pass S of Les Sœurs, the S extremity of which is 1m high and steer to pass 50m N of the beacon.

By night

Night entry is not recommended.

BERTHS AND ANCHORAGE

Anchor as far in as draught allows, bottom sand. Do not go too far as the depths shoal quickly once the head of the breakwater has been passed. There are some moorings in the harbour and it might be possible to borrow one.

FACILITIES

There are café-bars and a limited range of shops in the village.

Le Pérello

APPROACH AND ENTRANCE

By day

The approach to this small bay is made from the SSE. The drying rocks on either side of the entrance can be avoided by aligning the elbow of the small slipway on the NE side of the bay with the seaward-facing gable end of the house behind it, on a bearing of 353°. In 1998 the house was distinctive as the left half of the gable and wall are painted grey and the right half painted white (see photograph above). This line takes one into the bay leaving the rocks extending from its SW point 50m to port.

By night

Night entry is not recommended.

ANCHORAGE

There are some moorings in the bay, but there is plenty of room to anchor, bottom sand.

FACILITIES

Café-bar.

26. Lomener

47°42'N 3°26'W

GENERAL

The port of Lomener, with the adjacent Anse de Stole, is a small harbour on the north side of the channel between Ile de Groix and the mainland. Exposed to the south, it would be uncomfortable in fresh southerly winds and dangerous in gales. However, a considerable fleet of fishing vessels and yachts lies on moorings, both in the harbour and in the Anse de Stole, so the shelter must be sufficient for normal summer conditions.

It is sheltered from the north and in fine settled weather, when the *vent solaire* is in evidence, it provides good shelter for a night's stop when on passage; better indeed than Port Tudy opposite, where the excitement in the outer harbour begins in the early hours of the morning when the wind freshens from the northeast.

Lomener has good bathing beaches and the attractions of a small seaside resort.

Charts

BA *2352*
Imray *C38*

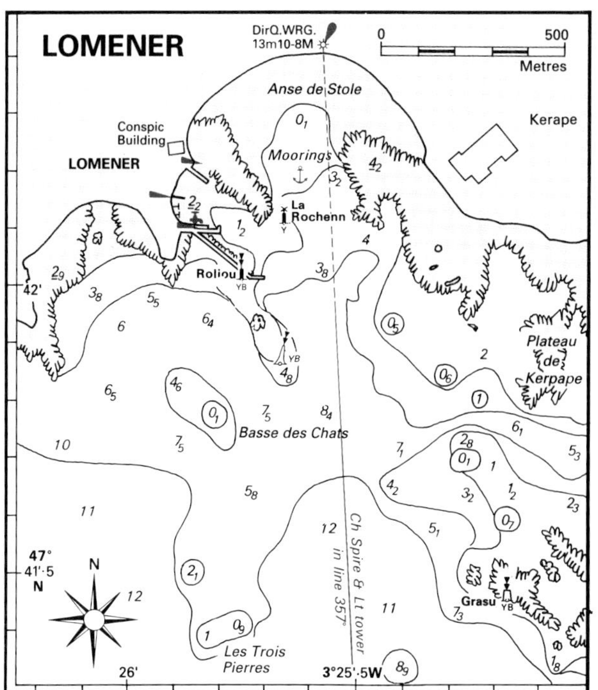

Plan 25

Looking SW over Lomener towards Ile de Groiz, near LW. Anse de Stole lighthouse arrowed

Anse de Stole light tower is sometimes difficult to see amongst the masts of anchored boats

TIDAL DATA

Times and heights

	Time differences				Height differences			
	HW		LW		MHWS	MHWN	MLWN	MLWS
BREST								
	0000 and 1200	0600 and 1800	0000 and 1200	0600 and 1800	6·9	5·4	2·6	1·0
Port Tudy								
	0000	−0025	−0025	−0015	−1·8	−1·4	−0·6	−0·1

Tidal streams

Off the harbour the flood runs to the E and the ebb to the W, spring rates 1kt. There is no stream in the harbour.

Depths

3m abreast the breakwater, shoaling steadily towards the shore.

LIGHTS

1. **Anse de Stole** 47°42'·4N 3°25'·5W
   DirQ.WRG.13m10-8M
   349·2°-G-355·2°-W-359·2°-R-005·2°
   White tower, red top

APPROACH AND ENTRANCE

By day

The harbour is not difficult to identify with a very prominent block of flats behind the breakwater. The approach is between the rocks round the Grasu S cardinal beacon tower and the shoal of Les Trois Pierres (0·9m) if the tide makes the latter relevant. Note that the rocks extend nearly 150m WNW of Grasu tower; this is not clear from the BA chart.

Steer for the white tower with a red top in transit with the Ploemeur church spire (which in 1988 only just showed above the trees) on 357°. A S cardinal buoy marks a rock (drying 0·4m) 200m SSE of the breakwater head and an E cardinal beacon marks Roliou just S of the breakwater.

The plan on page 91 shows the drying, rocky spurs on both sides of the bay and the yellow beacon close to the tip of the western spur.

By night

Enter by keeping in the white sector of Anse de Stole light. Beware of many fishing floats, and further in, moorings.

BERTHS AND ANCHORAGE

Anchor in the Anse de Stole where space and soundings permit, making sure that there is room to swing, or borrow a mooring by arrangement. The beaches behind the breakwater and in the Anse de Stole are excellent for drying out. There is a landing slip on the spur inside the harbour. Avoid the breakwater wall as there are vicious rocks at its foot.

FACILITIES

Water at the root of the quay. All the ordinary shops, café-bars and restaurants of a small seaside resort. Large supermarket close to the quay. Shellfish can often be bought direct from local fishermen.

27. Lorient

with the Blavet river and Locmalo
Harbour entrance 47°42'N 3°22'W

GENERAL

The city of Lorient is a combination of commercial port, fishing harbour and yachting centre. Although laid up warships remain, the naval base in the north of the harbour has now closed, and to the south of the city the massive reinforced concrete submarine pens are a reminder of the Second World War. Bombing devastated the city, but it has been rebuilt and is a thriving place. It is the largest fishing port in Brittany; the fishing vessels, ranging in size up to the largest deep-sea trawlers, have the exclusive use of the Port de Pêche at the south end of the city, to the east of the submarine pens. Further to the north, are the quays used by commercial vessels.

Port Louis, situated near the harbour entrance on the east side, also has a fishing fleet. It is named after Louis XIII, and the fortifications were created by Richelieu.

The principal yachting centres are the marina at Kernével, near the entrance on the west side, Port Louis opposite, the marina at Ste Catherine and the Port de Commerce in the centre of the city. A new marina was under construction in 1998 at Pen-Mané. Most visitors use either the Port du Commerce or Kernével. Although Kernével is conveniently close to the harbour entrance, it is a long way from the city centre and from shops.

In contrast, the Port de Commerce lies in the heart of downtown Lorient. It was the operational base of the French East India Company and it is from this that the city takes its name. There is still very limited commercial activity – the ferries for Port Louis and the Ile de Groix start here – but it is now principally devoted to yachting. At the upper end of the *avant-port* there are pontoons with plenty of space for visitors, and the wet dock has been restored as a yacht harbour for those remaining longer. The area is surrounded with cafés, bars, restaurants and shops of all kinds and is conveniently close to the centre of the city. It attracts many tourists and is full of bustle and vibrant activity.

Lorient is a good place for changing crew, as communications are excellent and there is plenty to explore if one has a day in hand. It hosts an international festival of Celtic music during the second week of August; the centre of the festival is close to the Port de Commerce.

The entrance to Lorient. Kernével marina is on the left

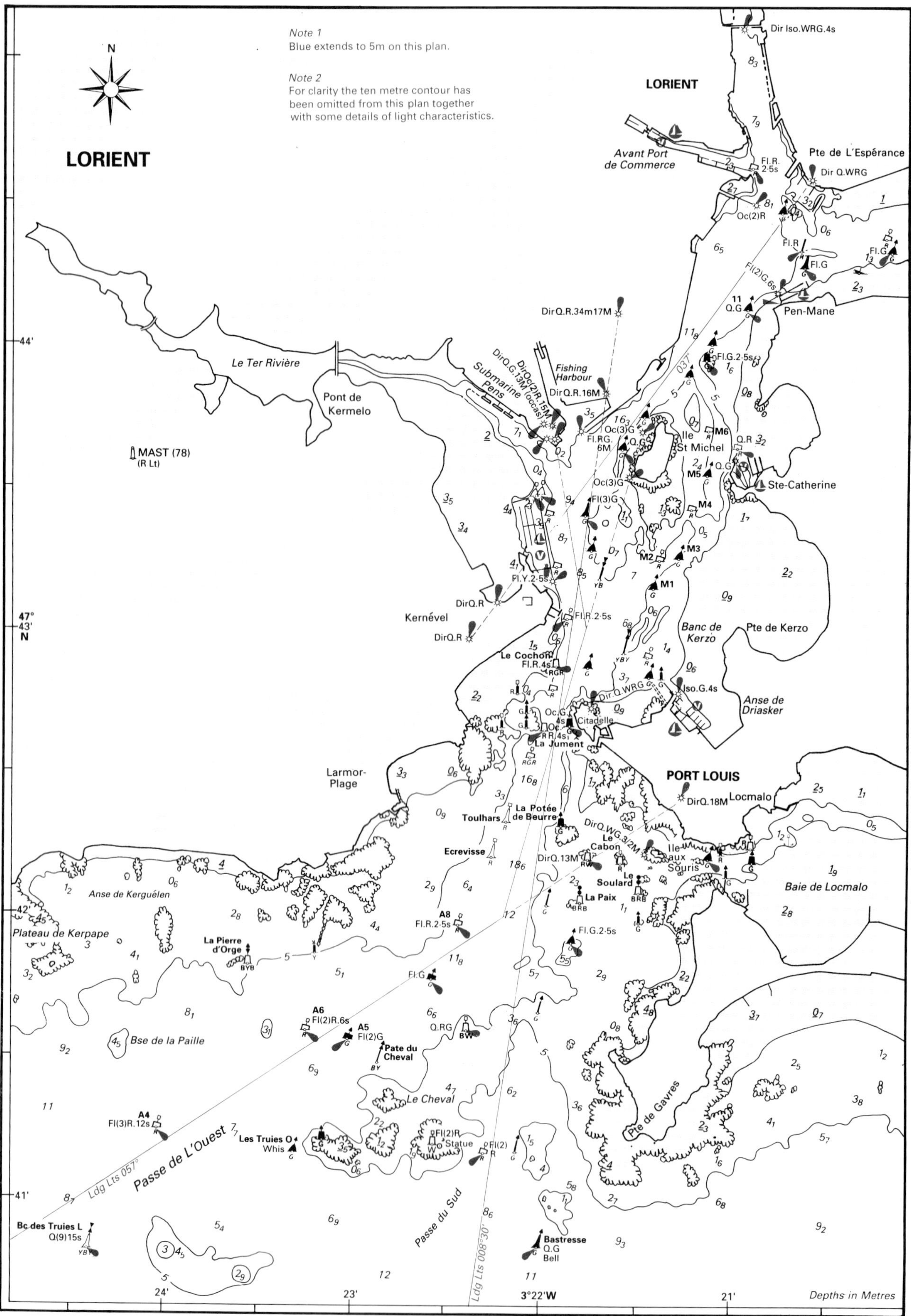
Note 1
Blue extends to 5m on this plan.
Note 2
For clarity the ten metre contour has been omitted from this plan together with some details of light characteristics.
LORIENT
LORIENT
Avant Port de Commerce
Pte de L'Espérance
Dir Iso.WRG.4s
Dir Q.WRG
Pen-Mane
Le Ter Rivière
Pont de Kermelo
Submarine Pens
Fishing Harbour
MAST (78) (R Lt)
Ile St Michel
Ste-Catherine
Kernével
Banc de Kerzo
Pte de Kerzo
Le Cochon
Anse de Driasker
Citadelle
La Jument
Larmor-Plage
PORT LOUIS
Locmalo
Toulhars
La Potée de Beurre
Ecrevisse
Le Cabon
Ile aux Souris
Le Soulard
La Paix
Baie de Locmalo
Anse de Kerguélen
Plateau de Kerpape
La Pierre d'Orge
Bse de la Paille
Pate du Cheval
Le Cheval
Les Truies
Statue
Passe de L'Ouest
Passe du Sud
Pte de Gavres
Bc des Truies L Q(9)15s
Bastresse Q.G Bell
Ldg Lts 057°
Ldg Lts 008°30'
24'
23'
3°22'W
21'
44'
47° 43' N
42'
41'
Depths in Metres

Plan 26

The entrance to Lorient lies between La Jument beacon and the Citadel

The river Blavet sees few visiting yachts. This is a pity as it is attractive and worth exploring. Working the tides, there is plenty of water for a deep draught yacht as far as Hennebont, an interesting walled market town full of character and charm, with a pontoon for visitors. Those with a draught not exceeding 0·8m can enter the Brittany canal system here. After going on up the Blavet to Pontivy one climbs over the hills and down to Redon, whence one can reach St Malo, Nantes or the sea via the Vilaine.

Charts

BA *304, 2352*
Imray *C38*

TIDAL DATA

Times and heights

Time differences				Height differences			
HW		LW		MHWS	MHWN	MLWN	MLWS
BREST							
0000 and 1200	0600 and 1800	0000 and 1200	0600 and 1800	6·9	5·4	2·6	1·0
Port Louis							
+0004	–0021	–0022	–0012	–1·8	–1·4	–0·6	–0·1
Lorient							
+0003	–0022	–0020	–0010	–1·8	–1·4	–0·6	–0·2
Hennebont							
+0015	–0017	+0005	+0003	–1·9	–1·5	–0·8	–0·3

Tidal streams

Outside, between the Ile de Groix and the shore, the flood sets E and SE, the ebb W and NW, spring rates ½kt. The main flood and ebb into and out of the harbour run through the Passe du Sud, spring rate 1½kts. In the Passe de l'Ouest there is a slack for two hours, starting at HW; the spring rates, flood and ebb, are 1kt. The strongest streams occur in the narrows off the citadel of Port Louis, where the spring rate is 3½kts; on extreme tides the ebb may reach 4½kts if the rivers are in flood. The stream in the narrows sets to the W on to La Jument and Le Pot during the last of the flood and the whole of the ebb. Once through the narrows the streams are weaker; spring rates everywhere less than 2kts. Generally the streams flow in the direction of the channels.

Depths

The main channels are deep. Enough water can be found in all the usual marinas and anchorages, except Locmalo, for yachts of normal draught. In the Blavet, which has silted recently, 2·5m or more should still be found at half tide up to Hennebont. The Baie de Locmalo has 3m just inside the entrance, but as little as 0·6m off the pier at Locmalo.

Of the marinas, Kernével has 2–3m, Port Louis 1–1·5m, Ste Catherine 1·5–3m and Pen-Mané 1·5–2m. There is 2·5m at the Port de Commerce pontoons and 2·3m in the wet basin.

LIGHTS

Lights other than those listed are occasionally shown during large-ship movements. There are many lit buoys and non-navigational lights in the harbour, which are not listed here. Lights specific to the marinas are at the end of the list.

Passe de l'Ouest
Ldg Lts 057°

1. *Front* **Les Soeurs** 47°42'·2N 3°21'·7W
   DirQ.11m13M 042·5°-intens-058·5°
   Red tower, white bands
2. *Rear* **Port Louis** 47°42'·4N 3°21'·3W
   740m from front DirQ.22m18M
   White daymark on building, red bands
3. **Les Trois Pierres** 47°41'·5N 3°22'·5W
   Q.RG.11m6M 060°-G-196°-R-002°
   Black tower, white bands

Passe de la Sud
Ldg Lts 008·5°

4. *Front* **Fish Market** DirQ.R.16m17M
   006°-intens-011°
   Red square with green bands on grey metal framework tower
5. *Rear* **Kergroise-La Perrière** 47°44'·1N 3°21'·6W
   515m from front DirQ.R.34m16M
   006°-intens-011° Synchronised with front
   Red square with white stripe on grey metal framework tower

Locmalo

6. **Ile aux Souris** 47°42'·2N 3°21'·4W
   DirQ.WG.6m3/2M 041·5°-W-043·5°-G-041·5°
   Green framework tower

Entrance
Ile Saint-Michel Ldg Lts 016·5°

7. *Front* 47°43'·5N 3°21'·6W DirOc(3)G.12s8m16M
   014·5°-intens-017·5° White tower, green top

8. *Rear* 47°43'·7N 3°21'·5W 306m from front DirOc(3)G.12s14m16M 014·5°-intens-017·5° Synchronised with front White tower, green top
9. **La Citadelle** 47°42'·6N 3°21'·9W Oc.G.4s6m6M 009°-vis-193° Green concrete tower
10. **La Jument** 47°42'·6N 3°21'·9W Oc.R.4s5m6M 182°-vis-024° Red concrete tower
11. **Le Cochon** 47°42'·8N 3°22'·0W Fl.R.4s5m5M Red tower, green band

Harbour

Kéroman Submarine Base Ldg Lts 350°

12. *Front* 47°43'·7N 3°21'·9W DirOc(2)R.6s25m15M Red house, white bands
13. *Rear* 95m from front DirOc(2)R.6s31m15M 349°-intens-351° Synchronised with front red and white topmark on grey pylon, red top

Kernével Ldg Lts 217°

14. *Front* 47°43'·1N 3°22'·3W DirQ.R.10m15M 215°-intens-219° Red truncated cone on red and white metal framework tower
15. *Rear* 47°42'·9N 3°22'·4W DirQ.R.18m15M 215°-intens-219° White square tower, red top
16. **Pte de L'Espérance** 47°44'·6N 3°20'·6W DirQ.WRG.8m10-8M 034°-G-036·7°-W-037·2°-R-047° (White sector covers Kernével Ldg Lts 14, 15) White tower, green top
17. **Fishing harbour entrance, E side** 47°43'·7N 3°21'·8W Fl.RG.4s7m6M 000°-G-235°-R-000° White truncated tower, green top
18. **Pengarne** 47°43'·9N 3°21'·1W Fl.G.2·5s3m3M Green tower
19. **Ro Ro terminal jetty head** 47°44'·5N 3°20'·9W Oc(2)R.6s7m6M Red structure
20. **Gueydon bridge** 47°45'·1N 3°21'·0W DirIso.WRG.4s6m11-9M 350°-G-351·5°-W-352·5°-R-355·5° White square hut

Marinas

Kernével

21. **South basin, E Breakwater head** 47°43'·2N 3°21'·9W Fl.Y.2·5s4m2M
22. **North basin entrance E side (buoy)** 47°43'·5N 3°22'·0W Fl.Y.2·5s Conical yellow buoy, can topmark
23. **North basin entrance W side (buoy)** 47°43'·5N 3°22'·0W Fl(4)Y.15s Conical yellow buoy, triangle topmark

Port Louis (Porte de la Pointe)

24. **Jetty Head** 47°42'·8N 3°21'·3W Iso.G.4s7m6M 043°-vis-301° White tower, green top.

Locmiquélic (Ste Catherine)

25. **Breakwater head (S side of entrance)** 47°43'·6N 3°21'·0W Q.G.5m2M Green post
26. **N side (buoy)** 60m N of 24 Q.R Red can buoy, can topmark

Pen-Mané

27. **Breakwater elbow** 47°44'·2N 3°20'·8W Fl(2)G.6s4M

Port de Commerce

28. **Entrance, S side (No. 8 buoy)** 47°44'·6N 3°20'·9W Fl.R.2·5s Red can buoy, can topmark

RADIO

Commercial Port c/s *Vigie Port Louis* VHF Ch 16, 12 24hr
Lorient marina (Port de Commerce) VHF Ch 9 0800–1230 and 1330–2000 LT
Kernével marina VHF Ch 9, 0800–2000 LT
Locmiquélic (Ste Catherine) marina VHF Ch 9 0800–1200 and 1500–2000 LT
Port Louis Marina VHF Ch 9 0730–1200 and 1500–2030 LT

APPROACH AND ENTRANCE

The approaches to Lorient are partly sheltered by the Ile de Groix, some four miles to the SW. They are well marked and the huge white grain silo in the commercial port is conspicuous. There are two approach channels, the Passe du Sud and the Passe de l'Ouest. At a first visit, not all the leading marks are easy to identify, but it is seldom necessary for yachts to use the transits as the numerous buoys and beacons make navigation by day easy. On a clear dark night, the plethora of lights can confuse and it may be difficult to locate the buoys against the background lights of the city.

The whole of the harbour is deemed to be a narrow channel for the purposes of the Collision Regulations. Yachts should navigate out of, or on the edges of, the channels wherever possible and should keep out of the way of all large vessels, which have very little room to manoeuvre. In particular yachts should keep well to the appropriate side of the entrance at the Citadelle and not on the Ile Saint-Michel transit, whether or not a large ship is present.

Traffic signals on the simplified system are made, for large ships only, from the signal station on the citadel of Port Louis. Yachts may not enter the narrows when one of these signals is shown. Appropriate announcements are also made on VHF and yachts are required to maintain watch on Ch 16 when underway in the harbour.

Passe de l'Ouest

By day

This channel, well buoyed, starts ¾M S of the conspicuous Grasu tower (S cardinal). The outer leading mark is the red and white tower on Les Soeurs rocks. The rear marker, seen to the right of the conspicuous spire of St Pierre church, is the red and white banded daymark above the walls of the citadel. These are in transit on a bearing of 057°.

When Les Trois Pierres beacon tower (BW horizontal bands) is abaft the beam to starboard, the narrows will open, and when the two white towers with green tops on the W side of Ile Saint-Michel come into line bearing 016°, either turn towards this transit to pass through the narrows, or enter the Chenal Secondaire, described below, on the W side of the narrows.

By night

The intensified sector of the leading lights[1,2] on 057°

covers the channel and all the lateral buoys are lit. While in the outer part of the channel identify other relevant lights, particularly Les Trois Pierres[3], as the turn to port is made when it is abaft the beam. Look for La Citadelle[9] and La Jument[10], marking the narrows. Ignore the green lights[7,8] of the Ile Saint-Michel transit and when the red leading lights[4,5] over the fish market come into line on 008·5°, turn towards them and pass through the entrance.

Passe du Sud

By day

The approach to this channel lies NE of the E end of Ile de Groix and ½M W of Pointe de Gâvres on the mainland. From an initial position of about 47°40'N 3°22'·5W, steer for the citadel on 010° until the leading marks are made out, or the yacht's position is confirmed by the channel buoys. The first buoy is Les Bastresses Sud. To port will be seen Les Errants beacon tower, white with black square topmark, and further up channel is the conspicuous Les Trois Pierres black and white beacon tower. This is also left to port, after passing between Les Bastresses Nord (starboard buoy) and Les Errants (port buoy). The main channel, the Passe de l'Ouest, is then joined and is well marked to the citadel.

The day leading marks bearing 008·5° are on and behind the Fish Market Hall at the S end of Lorient; the front mark is a red square with green bands and the rear one red square with a white stripe. These lead up the channel and through the narrows.

By night

The Q.R leading lights[4,5] on 008·5° have an intensified sector extending out beyond both sides of the channel. Do not assume that if you are in the intensified sector you are in the channel, as some of the buoys are unlit. The transit passes through the narrows, where La Citadelle[9] and La Jument[10] mark the port and starboard sides.

Chenal Secondaire

By day

This channel passes over Le Cochon (dries 1m) but is convenient, given sufficient water, when making for Kernével marina or when the narrows are congested. Illuminated depth indicator panels have been situated on shore at each end of the channel as an experiment. These give the height of the tide above the datum and so 1m must be subtracted from the reading to allow for Le Cochon.

A RGR spar buoy, 180m S of La Jument marks the entrance to the channel. Leaving this buoy to starboard, the channel is seen to be marked by red and green beacons up to Le Cochon beacon tower (RGR), to be left to starboard, after which the main channel is re-entered.

By night

The Chenal Secondaire is unlit and should not be used at night.

PROCEEDING UP THE HARBOUR

Once through the narrows, the harbour opens out ahead. Navigation is straightforward within the harbour, the dangers are marked, and the chart is the best guide.

By day

If bound for the Port de Commerce or the Blavet river, either the channel to the E or to the W of Ile Saint-Michel may be used. Note that there is an unmarked shallow patch, with 0·5m over it, on the edge of the E channel.

By night

Although there is often enough background light for the unlit buoys in the eastern channel to be seen, the usual route up harbour is to the W of Ile Saint-Michel. The shallow area SSW of this island (Banc du Turc) will be a hazard below half tide, so until the Fl(3)G.12s buoy marking its western extremity has been definitely identified, keep near to line of the 350° leading lights[12,13]. The white sector of Pte de L'Espérence light[16] then leads all the way up the harbour, but once the Ro Ro terminal light[18] has been identified course can be altered towards it and thence to No. 8 buoy[29] and the entrance to the Port de Commerce.

The entrance to the Blavet channel is marked by lit port and starboard lateral buoys and the starboard-hand buoys in the lower reaches of the river are also lit. Using these a yacht can enter the river and find a temporary anchorage out of the channel.

Kernével marina, on the west side of the harbour is a long way from the city centre

ANCHORAGE
Yachts seldom anchor in the harbour, though it is possible to do so on the bank SE of Pen-Mané or in the shallow water E of Ile Saint-Michel. Neither place is particularly convenient and both are subject to the wash of passing traffic, and in places the bottom is foul. It is possible to find fair-weather anchorage off the beaches to the south and east of Larmor-Plage, but to do so the large-scale chart is essential as there are many rocks.

Port de Plaisance Kernével

Entrance
A line of floating wavebreakers secured to piles protects the marina. The southern entrance leads only to the fuel pontoon; the northern entrance is used when looking for a berth.

Facilities
Fuel berth, slipway for hauling out. Scrubbing berths.

There are no shops or restaurants within walking distance in Kernével but bicycles are available from the helpful marina staff in the *capitainerie*, which is a large, late 19th-century mansion. Two large supermarkets are situated about a mile NW round the bay and there is a frequent bus service to Lorient, where chandlers, workshops and engineers can be found.

The construction of a new *capitainerie* building, which will include shops, chandlers, café-bars and restaurants, is planned and should be completed during the lifetime of this edition.

Port de Commerce

The wet dock is a fully pontooned yacht harbour in pleasant surroundings, as the roads are set well back. At busy times yachts arriving will be met by marina staff in a launch and directed to a pontoon; otherwise tie up where convenient and arrange a berth with the helpful staff in the *capitainerie*. Only those planning a stay of more than a few days usually berth in the wet basin. Entry to it past the bridge and sill is only possible for one hour either side of HW springs and less at neaps.

The pontoons between the entrance to the *avant-port* and the Ile de Groix ferry terminal are reserved for local boats.

Facilities
Except for a fuel berth, everything is at hand for the wet dock and the outer pontoons. Fuel is obtainable at Kernével.

Shops, banks, main post office, chandlery; shipyards and sailmakers, slipway and crane or travel-lift in the *avant-port*. The rail and bus services for Lorient are good and there are flights to Paris from Quimper.

Port Louis

There are many moorings in the shoaling bay to the E of the citadel; some of these are available to visitors on application to the yacht club.

To enter Port Louis marina leave the green can buoy which marks a ruined wharf to starboard. Just beyond it a green beacon marks the starboard side of the channel leading into the Anse Driasker and the marina where there are usually visitors berths available. Keep in the channel close to the pier as there are obstructions in the bay.

Port Louis itself is a very interesting 18th-century walled town, with an excellent museum in the citadel, all ordinary facilities and a recommended Hôtel du Commerce.

Locmiquélic (Ste Catherine)

This marina has all the normal facilities and space for visitors can usually be found. It is entered from the channel E of Ile Saint-Michel. There is a wreck with only 0·4m over it, marked by M5 green conical buoy, just S of the marina entrance and a yacht should pass to the W of this buoy when the tide is low.

The old commercial docks of the French East India company have been converted into a yacht harbour

Port Louis, just within the entrance is attractive, has a small marina and some pontoons for visitors, seen here

Locmiquélic (Ste Catherine) marina lies on the east side of the harbour

The first bridge across the Blavet river

The railway viaduct just below the town has a clearance of 22m

Enter the marina between the floating breakwater to the S and the red buoy to the N and secure temporarily before being allocated a berth. Access is possible at night as both the breakwater and red buoy have lights[26,27] but as the channel is unlit it is easiest for the stranger to approach from N of Ile Saint-Michel.

There are shops and the usual facilities of a small township 500m from the marina.

Pen-Mané Marina

This marina was under construction in 1998. There appeared to be no berths allocated to visitors and, at that time, no facilities ashore whatsoever. It is understood that a *capitainerie* will be built and this may contain some shops. At present it is a long walk even to buy bread.

Blavet river and Hennebont

The upper reaches of this little-visited river are most attractive and interesting, with an abundance of bird-life. At half tide it is possible to find plenty of water all the way to Hennebont. The two shallowest patches lie just after the first and second road bridges where only 1·5m could be found at LW neaps.

Three bridges cross the river between the entrance and Hennebont. The first two have 22m clearance and the last – railway bridge – 21m. Power cables also cross the river above the second road bridge. Their height is unknown but they appear to be higher than the bridges.

The channel is buoyed or beaconed up to the first road bridge two and a half miles from Pen-Mané with extensive mudbanks on the S side. Above the bridge the river narrows and winds a further four miles to Hennebont.

A concrete obstruction which dries is reported to lie under the second road bridge, approximately one third of the way out from the left supporting column (heading upriver). When passing under the bridge keep to the centre, or to starboard if proceeding upriver.

There are many possible anchorages on the way up to Hennebont, where there is a short-stay pontoon. This is reputed to have 2m but in 1998 there was less depth, but as the bottom is very soft mud an overnight stay is possible. There are head and stern visitors' moorings suitable for yachts less than 10m.

Facilities

Hennebont is a very pleasant walled market town (market in the square on Thursday mornings) with all shops (including a large supermarket), banks and restaurants. Fuel can be obtained from a garage close to the bridge on the port bank and there is a water tap in the toilets close to the pontoon. Good rail connections.

Locmalo (plan page 94)

A pleasant anchorage in the bay S of Port Louis. For the stranger, entry is only possible by day using the large-scale chart, BA *304*, and with sufficient rise of

Locmalo. Looking SW over the Baie de Locmalo towards Ile de Groix. Locmalo entrance centre, the citadel and Rade de Port de Louis far right

Locmalo is a pleasant anchorage just outside the entrance to Lorient

tide. It is essential to grasp the scale – within 500m of Le Cabon reef there are seven beacons. Either of two approaches may be used.

The first, easier, route is to pass N of La Potée de Buerre with the N side of Ile aux Souris in transit with the end of the ferry slip on the S side of the entrance to the Baie de Locmalo, bearing 112°. This transit leads in between the rocks. On approaching Ile aux Souris, with a green light tripod on its western side, alter course to leave the islet to starboard and steer on the N side of the channel, leaving a green buoy to starboard, to pass between the red and green beacon towers. The channel then curves NE towards the jetty at Locmalo.

For the second approach, from the S, start at the green conical buoy and head for Ile aux Souris, on a heading of about 045°. It is important to realise that once Le Soulard BRB beacon is abeam a definite alteration of course to port is needed to pass between Le Cabon reef and Ile aux Souris. Neither the beacon on Le Cabon, nor the light beacon on Ile aux Souris mark the extremities of the dangers. Le Pesquerez green pole beacon astern should be kept open W of Le Soulard isolated danger mark. After Ile Aux Souris has been passed the channel described above is joined.

Anchorage

There are many moorings off Pen-er-Run and it might be possible to borrow one. The pool due E of the Grand and Petit Belorc'h beacons is clear of moorings and offers good anchorage in depths of up to 4m. There are also moorings off Ban-Grâves and it is possible to take the ground at Ban-Grâves jetty.

Facilities

There are all shops, banks and restaurants at Port Louis. The easiest dinghy landing is at Locmalo jetty.

28. Ile de Groix

Port Tudy 47°38'N 3°28'W

GENERAL

The Ile de Groix was formerly a centre for tunny-fishing as Port Tudy was easy to make and leave under sail. Today, only some inshore fishing activity remains and now the island is chiefly concerned with tourism. It offers a busy yachting harbour, pleasant walks in peaceful countryside and a small town with adequate shops but there are few sophisticated facilities.

The island is fairly high, edged for the most part by cliffs, but falling away to the low Pointe des Chats in the southeast. Although the coast is rocky, the western part of the island is reasonably free from dangers. On the other hand, the eastern end is foul. East of Port Tudy rocks extend 600m offshore, off Pointe de la Croix the sandy shoals extend 300m seaward and there are several dangerous wrecks further out; south of Pointe des Chats the rocks extend one mile.

The main harbour, and the only completely secure one, is Port Tudy, halfway along the north shore, a very popular staging point for English and French yachts on passage.

Half a mile west of it is Port Lay, a small drying harbour protected by a breakwater. As it is wide open to the north it is suitable for a day visit only. Port Lay is in a prohibited anchorage zone, but there are a number of moorings, laid by the sailing school, which might be used for a short time by arrangement.

At Pte de La Croix and down the east side of the island are sandy beaches. In settled weather day anchorage can be found here.

On the south side of the island is the pretty little harbour of Loc Maria, which is well worth a visit under the right conditions, but is dangerous if the wind comes in from the south. Further west, Port St Nicholas is nothing more than a cleft in the cliffs, wide open to the southwest, but in settled weather it is a peaceful, isolated anchorage with only the seabirds for company.

Charts

BA *2352*
Imray *C38*

TIDAL DATA

Times and heights

Time differences				Height differences			
HW		LW		MHWS	MHWN	MLWN	MLWS
BREST							
0000 and 1200	0600 and 1800	0000 and 1200	0600 and 1800	6·9	5·4	2·6	1·0
Port Tudy							
0000	–0025	–0025	–0015	–1·8	–1·4	–0·6	–0·1

Tidal streams

Between the Ile de Groix and the mainland the flood runs to the E, the ebb to the W; spring rates ½kt. Off Pointe de la Croix, at the eastern end of the island, the flood runs to the S, the ebb to the N; spring rates ½kt. To the SE of Les Chats, the southernmost point, the streams are rotary clockwise, the greatest rates being ESE ½kt at –0130 Brest and SW 0·6kt at +0230 Brest.

Depths

At Port Tudy 2m on the moorings. The inner harbour 1–2·5m and 2–3m in the wet basin. At Loc Maria 3–0·5m in the anchorage; the jetty dries. At Port St Nicholas 2m or more in the anchorage

LIGHTS

1. **Pen Men** 47°38'·9N 3°30'·5W Fl(4)25s59m29M 309°-vis-275° White square tower, black top
2. **Pointe des Chats** 47°37'·3N 3°25'·3W Fl.R.5s16m19M White square tower and dwelling
3. **Les Chats buoy (S card)** 47°35'·7N 3°23'·6W Q(6)+LFl.15s Whis
4. **Pointe de la Croix** 47°38'·1N 3°25'·0W Oc.WR.4s16m12/9M 169°-W-336°-R-345°-W-353° White pedestal, red lantern

Port Tudy

5. **East mole head** 47°38'·7N 3°26'·8W Fl(2)R.6s11m6M 112°-vis-226° White round tower, red top
6. **North mole head** 47°38'·7N 3°26'·7W Iso.G.4s12m6M White tower, green top

RADIO

Port Tudy VHF Ch 9 0630–2100 LT

Port Tudy

This is the only completely protected harbour in Ile de Groix. It is a good one except in easterly and especially northeasterly winds, when the swell penetrates the outer basin between the pierheads. If the *vent solaire* is in evidence this happens in the early hours of the morning and as yachts lie rafted on the moorings in the outer harbour a disturbed night is had by all. The harbour is very crowded, often uncomfortably so, during the season, particularly at weekends. The high-speed, noisy ferries run from early morning to late evening embarking and disembarking crowds of day trippers. All in all, although it is an attractive place, Port Tudy cannot be described as peaceful.

APPROACH AND ENTRANCE

By day

The harbour is easily identified and the approach from the W and N is straightforward; there are some mooring buoys and a fish farm off Port Lay, but no other dangers. From the E and SE care must be taken to avoid the dangers off the coast, which extend in places outside the line of buoys and beacons. A safe course is with the harbour lighthouses in transit bearing 217°. This passes close to an E cardinal buoy ½M off the entrance; the buoy marks a wreck with more than 9m over it. The transit then leaves a rock, with 0·6m over it, 200m to port, with other dangers marked by a red beacon closer inshore.

Port Tudy, Ile de Groix

Approach to Port Tudy

When close to the entrance bear to port and enter midway between the breakwater heads, steering in parallel to the N breakwater; there are rocks at the base of the head of the E breakwater. If the ferry to the mainland is manoeuvring to enter or leave, stand off, as it needs all the room there is.

By night

The buoys in the approaches are unlit. The E breakwater light[5] is obscured over the dangers to the E of the harbour, so it is safe to steer in with this light showing and just open to the left of the N breakwater light[6]; if they are in transit, the rear light is obscured.

ANCHORAGE AND MOORING

In settled weather it is possible to anchor outside the harbour but it is essential not to obstruct the frequent ferries. Their wash makes the anchorage uncomfortable.

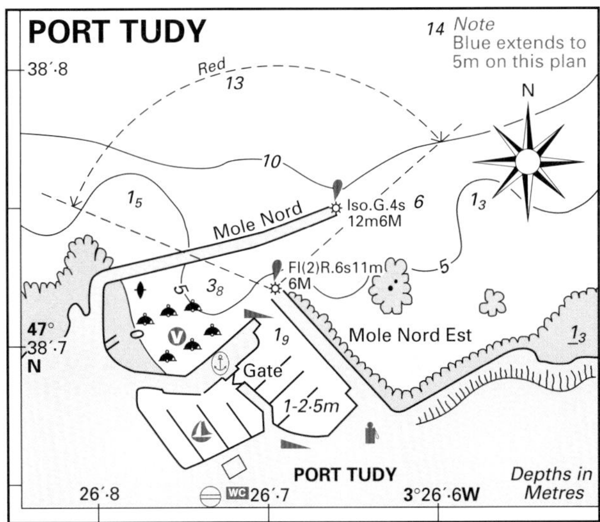

Plan 27

There are pontoon berths on the south-eastern side of the harbour in the basin in front of the gate to the inner basin

In the season yachts entering may be met by a high-speed harbour launch and directed to a berth. In the outer harbour yachts moor between the large white mooring buoys, ensuring that there is room for the ferry to manoeuvre. Long warps are necessary and springs to neighbouring yachts advisable to ensure that spreaders will not foul when the swell gets up. The landing slip is reserved for ferries. There is no room to anchor in the harbour and the bottom is foul.

The inner harbour shoals inwards, but there is plenty of water for most yachts. There are pontoon berths and yachts lie rafted together.

A wet dock has been formed from half of the inner harbour by installing a retaining wall and gates with a swing footbridge. Entry is possible during the day some two hours either side of HW. While waiting for the gates to open it is best to tie up temporarily on a pontoon as the inner landing slip has a stone shelf protruding below the top end of the slip near the gates.

Visitors will be directed to a berth in from 2m to 3m. The wet basin is even more crowded than the rest of the harbour; yachts are rafted on the pontoons. Unless planning a long stay there seems little point in using it.

FACILITIES

Fuel is available from the depot at the SE corner of the inner harbour. It will have to be carried. Marine engineer with hauling-out slip. Some chandlery. Launderette on quay. There are café-bars around the harbour and bread may be obtained nearby. Up the hill in the town are all other shops, a supermarket and hotel.

Bicycles may be hired to explore this picturesque island. Frequent ferries run to Lorient.

Pte de la Croix

There are several pleasant small beaches south of Pte de la Croix together with a larger one extending westwards from the point itself. Anchorage may be found off any of them in settled weather and they offer good bathing. The usual approach is from the N or E, but except at very low water a yacht may approach from the S, passing inside the W cardinal beacon off the Pointe des Chats. Anchor as close in as depth allows, but keep outside any lines of yellow buoys which mark the areas reserved for swimmers. The water is crystal clear and a good lookout needs to be kept for snorkellers and divers who frequent the area.

Loc Maria

This charming unspoilt little harbour is situated on the S of Ile de Groix, ¾M west of Pointe des Chats. The approach is open to the Atlantic, but the harbour itself is well sheltered from the W through N to E. The harbour within the jetties dries but outside there is space to anchor in depths of 1m or more; most yachts will be able to lie afloat except perhaps at springs.

APPROACH AND ENTRANCE

The distant approach must be made from the chart. If coming from the east or southeast it will be necessary to make a detour round Les Chats.

From an initial position of about 47°36'N 3°25'W the bay will be open. On the eastern side the harbour and village will be seen, together with a green beacon tower offshore and a white masonry beacon on the land. On the western side is another smaller village. Between the two villages is a small group of houses on the NW side of the bay, with a small white masonry beacon in front of them.

Approach with the green beacon tower bearing 005° until the houses and beacon to the NW of the harbour have been identified. The lead for the entrance is the masonry beacon in transit with the centre window of a white cottage bearing about 350°. There are several cottages in the area but this is the lowest one, the right-hand one of a group of

Loc Maria. The entrance transit is arrowed

three, (the left-hand one of which is end on) which appear joined. It has blue shutters and has the left-hand cottage of a group of four above it (see photos below and opposite).

Follow this transit, passing between a port and a starboard beacon, until the vessel is about halfway between the two cardinal beacons to starboard, marking the middle ground; near low water, deeper water may be found by borrowing to the W when the outer port-hand beacon comes abeam. Then bear to starboard for the pierhead, keeping rather closer to the inner port-hand beacon. There is a shallow channel for local boats to the east of the middle ground, marked by a port and a starboard beacon, but it should not be used.

There are no lights and a night entry should not be attempted.

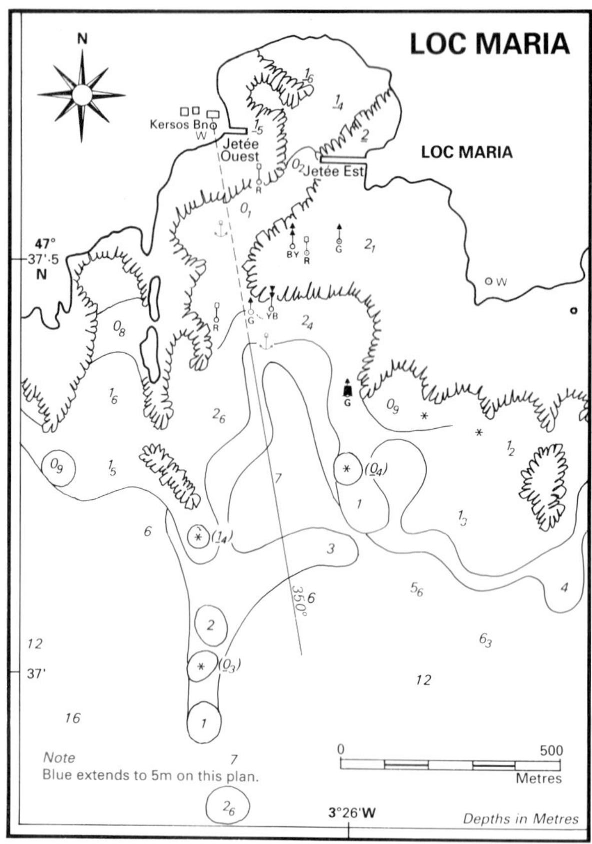

Plan 28

The transit in close up. The white masonry beacon is in line with the right hand of this group of three cottages

ANCHORAGE

The harbour is choked with small-boat moorings and there is no room to anchor and remain afloat. Vessels that can take the ground may anchor with a kedge astern after inspecting the bottom for rocky patches. At neaps, others may anchor outside the harbour with good holding just W of the leading line, with the outer middle-ground beacon (S cardinal) in transit with the green beacon tower, and the head of the jetty bearing about 060°. Alternatively there is a good anchorage just outside the reef, S of the S cardinal beacon, in about 2m. Lying alongside the jetty is impossible owing to the lines on small-boat moorings, but it may be used for landing.

FACILITIES

Shops, a bar and a *crêperie* in the village. A pleasant mile and a half walk to Port Tudy. Good bathing beaches.

Port Saint Nicholas

This cleft in the cliffs lies on the south coast of Ile de Groix, 1½M E of Pen Men. It can be identified by the black and white daymark 900m to the west of the cove. The anchorage is wide open to the SW but is sheltered from the *vent solaire*.

Approaching from the E, give Pte St-Nicholas a berth of at least 400m to clear the rocks which lie off it. From the W, maintain a minimum of 200m from the shore. To enter, keep the left-hand edge of a conspicuous anvil-shaped rock in the centre of the bay on a bearing of 070°. This takes one into the centre of the bay. If proceeding well in, keep S of the centreline after passing the entrance in order to avoid a group of rocks extending across the northern half of the cove. There is little room to swing and two anchors are recommended. After exploration at low water a route into the northern arm of the inlet can be found.

This is a delightful spot in settled conditions and is a haven of peace in an otherwise crowded area.

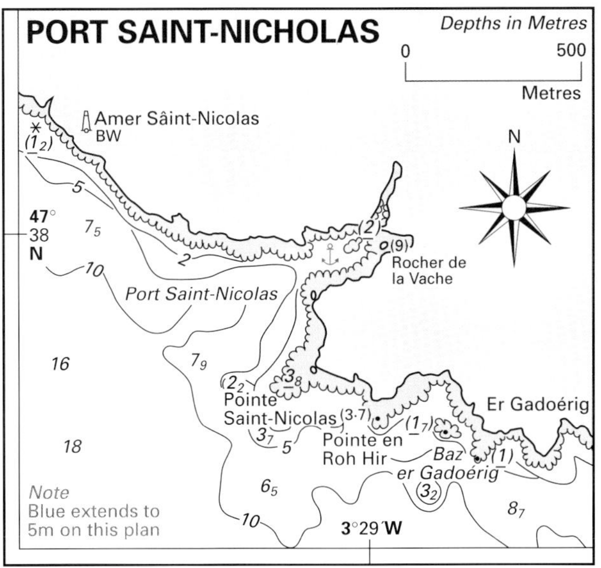

Plan 29

29. Etel

47°39'N 3°13'W

GENERAL

The Etel river is a delightful place, with its clean blue water and extensive sands. In settled weather it is easy of entrance, but should not be approached by night, in bad visibility, or on the ebb. First visits are not recommended in strong onshore winds. Otherwise, Etel is fun.

The miniature inland sea, La Mer d'Etel lies upstream. This large sheltered expanse of water with many islands cannot be reached in a masted yacht, but is interesting to explore by dinghy. The large amount of water moving up and down the river to and from La Mer gives rise to very strong streams. There is a shallow sandy bar across the mouth of the river and entry should normally be made on the last of the flood.

Charts

BA *2352*
Imray *C38*

TIDAL DATA

Times and heights

	Time differences				Height differences			
	HW		LW		MHWS	MHWN	MLWN	MLWS
BREST								
	0000 and 1200	0600 and 1800	0000 and 1200	0600 and 1800	6·9	5·4	2·6	1·0
Port d'Etel								
	+0020	−0010	+0030	+0010	−2·0	−1·3	−0·4	+0·5

Tidal streams

The tidal streams offshore do not exceed 1kt and are much affected by wind. Streams in the river attain 6kts at springs, but are somewhat weaker for 1½ hours after high water and low water. The streams continue to run the same way for about one hour after high water and low water. That is to say, a vessel arriving on the bar at high water will find that the tide is still flowing strongly into the river. On spring tides there is hardly any slack.

Depths

The bar varies greatly; it usually has about 0·5m, but has been known to dry 4·5m. Once over the bar the channel is deep but narrow for a short section 400m inside the entrance (see plan page 106). Above the marina 8m can be expected in the channel as far as the bridge.

LIGHTS

1. **Plateau des Brivideaux** 47°29'·2N 3°17'·4W
   Fl(2)6s24m10M Black tower, red bands
2. **West side of entrance** 47°38'·7N 3°12'·8W
   Oc(2)WRG.6s13m9-6M
   022°-W-064°-R-123°-W-330°-G-022°
   Red metal framework tower
3. **Epic de Plouhinec head** 47°38'·6N 3°12'·8W
   Fl.R.2·5s7m2M Red structure
4. **Roche Saint-Germain** 47°39'·0N 3°12'·5W
   Fl(2)G.6s6m1M Green pylon

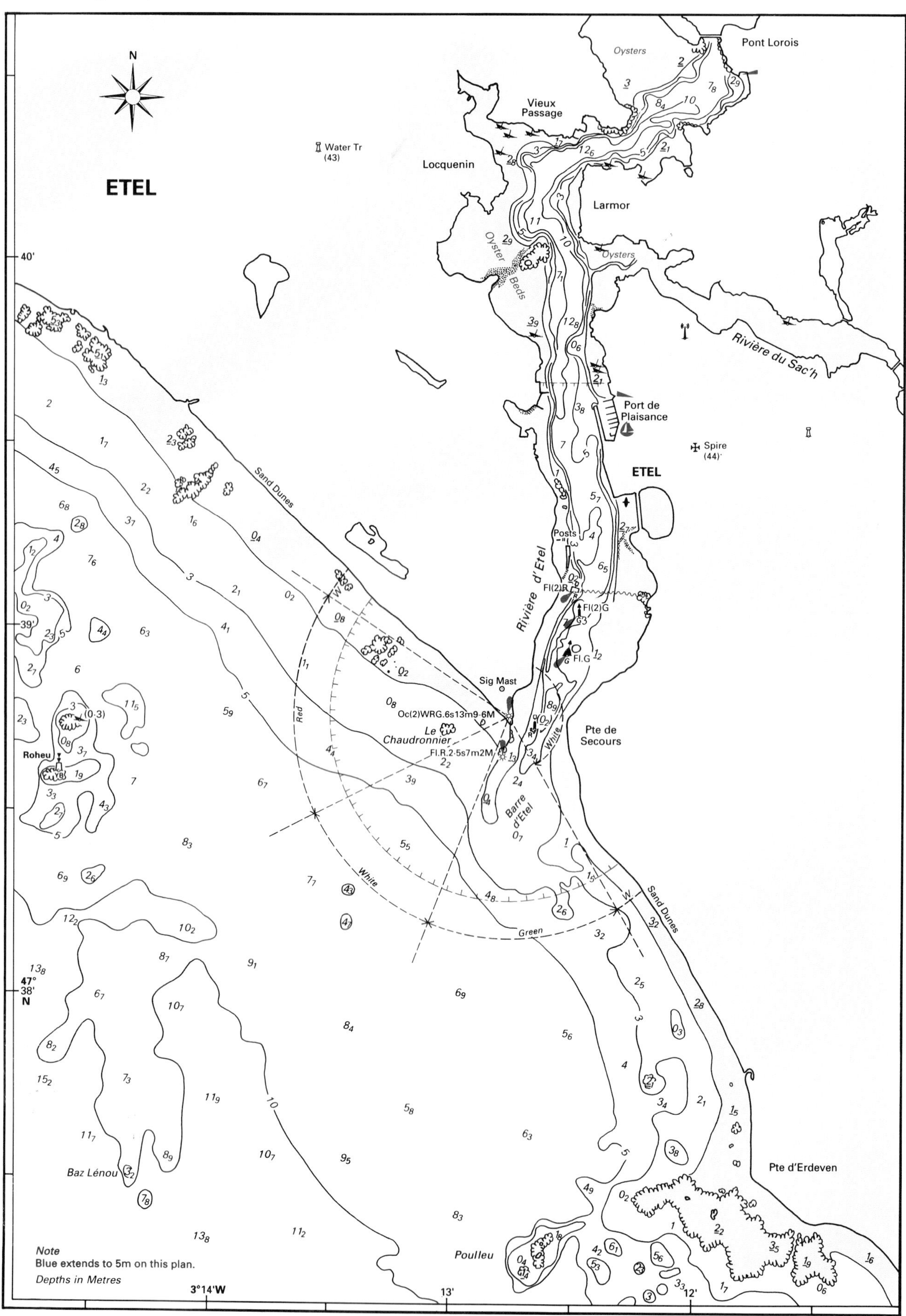
N
ETEL
Water Tr (43)
Locquenin
Vieux Passage
Pont Lorois
Oysters
Larmor
Oyster Beds
Oysters
Rivière du Sac'h
Port de Plaisance
Spire (44)
ETEL
Posts
Rivière d'Etel
Fl(2)R
Fl(2)G
Fl.G
Sig Mast
Oc(2)WRG.6s13m9·6M
Le Chaudronnier
Fl.R.2·5s7m2M
Pte de Secours
Barre d'Etel
Sand Dunes
Red
White
Green
Roheu
Baz Lénou
Poulleu
Pte d'Erdeven
40'
39'
47° 38' N
3°14'W
13'
12'
Note
Blue extends to 5m on this plan.
Depths in Metres
Plan 30

The Etel river

The entrance to the river

RADIO

Semaphore d'Etel VHF Ch 16, 13 3hrs before to 2hrs after HW

Marina VHF Ch 13, Mon–Sat 0800–1200, 1400–1800 LT, Sun 1000–1200 LT

APPROACH AND ENTRANCE

By day

During the approach it is essential to make contact with the semaphore station and until then to keep at least ½M off as the bar lies further out than one might imagine. The visual signals displayed are as follows:

- Arrow horizontal: sea too rough, no entry for any vessels.
- Black ball: no entry for undecked vessels under 8m length.
- Red flag: Not enough water or pilot not on duty.

The pilot, Madame Josiane Pene, is famous in France as the only woman pilot. Once VHF contact has been established, she will give instructions in clear, simple French. It is as well to have a felicitous phrase ready for when she signs off as one enters the river proper.

Etel marina. Boats over about 11m long should berth on the ends of the pontoons

The semaphore is now hardly ever used for entry although it might be possible to arrange it for some special reason by telephoning 02 97 55 35 59 in advance and giving an ETA. The following signals would be used:

- Arrow vertical: continue on course.
- Arrow inclined left: steer to port.
- Arrow inclined right: steer to starboard.

The position of the deepest water across the bar varies considerably. In 1998 there was no particular deep channel and entry was made in the centre of the river mouth, with the shallowest depth being 0·5m at the datum. The outer face of the bar was like a cliff, the sounding going instantly from over 10m to 5m. Strong winds or a gale may change the situation, literally, overnight so one cannot rely on previous experience to find the channel.

The stream is weak outside the bar, but may reach six knots as the port-hand beacon is passed. Shortly after entering the river continue up along the W side, where the best water is likely to be found, leaving an unlit red beacon to port, a green buoy and beacon to starboard and a final red buoy to port. From there, keep centre channel where the water is deep.

By night

A stranger should not attempt to enter at night

BERTHS AND ANCHORAGE

There is a marina behind the fishing jetty with places for visitors of less than 15m overall in a least depth of 2·5m. Do not secure to the main jetty, which is reserved for the fishing fleet, and keep clear of the ferry berth on the innermost pontoon.

It is now hard to find an anchorage in the river that is not full of moorings, and when anchoring it is necessary to get far enough in (by sounding) to be out of the main stream, especially at springs. A kedge is essential to stop swinging into the shallows. Keep clear of oyster beds and look out for mooring buoys, which can run under in the current and only show at slack water.

Just above Etel the holding is good on both sides of the river, but springs run at 6kts and there are oyster beds in the shallows. There is a good anchorage just above Vieux Passage, but do not go far into the bay as the bottom is foul. Finally, an anchorage recommended by some is just into the northern side of the bay on the E bank below Pont Lorois. The southern part of this bay is foul.

FACILITIES

The small town has shops, bars and good restaurants and an excellent supermarket with fresh oysters and fish for sale in front of it. The town caters well for holidaymakers; market day Tuesday. The marina staff are helpful. It is worth visiting the *capitainerie* to see the awesome aerial photograph of the bar during a southerly gale and a spring ebb.

There is a memorable and highly recommended tuna festival on the second Sunday in August when the town gives itself over to fun and feasting.

La Mer d'Etel

The description below has been retained in the present edition even though a visit involves passing under the bridge at the entrance to La Mer d'Etel, which should only be attempted after first consulting the harbourmaster, and then only with a robust dinghy, fitted with a powerful motor.

Above the bridge, Pont Lorois, said to have a clearance in the region of 9m, there is a wide expanse of water, the arms of which extend 5M inland. No official charts are available for the Mer d'Etel, which, except for the currents (up to 10kts under the bridge) and a larger tidal range, might be compared with Poole Harbour. There is 2m in the main channel for the three miles up to La Pointe du Verdon. While this is no place for a seagoing yacht, it is an interesting place to explore in a dinghy with sufficient power to cope with the currents. There is an ancient oratory at St Cado, which is a good place for a picnic, as are the many islands in this inland sea.

After passing under the bridge keep to port to round a green beacon. Then cross over to leave the red beacon to port. The river up to this point is strewn with islets and submerged rocks over which strong eddies swirl. From there on up the stream should be weaker.

30. Presqu'île de Quiberon

47°30'N 3°08'W

Charts

BA *2357, 2353*
Imray *C38, C39*

GENERAL

The name of Quiberon is familiar because it was the scene of the great sea-battle in 1759, when, in a November gale and gathering darkness, Hawke led his fleet into the bay and to victory among the rocks, shoals and strong tides which will be described.

The peninsula itself is about 5M long and is joined to the mainland by a sandy neck which is little over 100m wide. North of this a narrow arm of sand dunes continues for some three miles before widening to merge with the broader mainland. The total length of the projection seawards is about 8M. The geological formation continues for nearly 15M to the SE, in the shape of an archipelago of rocks, islets and shoals, between which are navigable passages, described in Chapter 34. Houat and Hoëdic are the only inhabited islands in this archipelago.

Presqu'île de Quiberon itself looks somewhat sinister from seaward; it is sandy in the north but rocky towards the south, and was formerly strongly fortified. Ashore, however, the whole peninsula is dotted with seaside resorts, for it has a long coastline and the sandy beaches are ideal for bathing. The town of Quiberon is the capital and there are two harbours a little over half a mile apart, Port Maria on the SW side and Port Haliguen on the NE. Quiberon has a population of about 4,000, a railway station, an airport and many shops, for it serves the whole district. Accommodation varies from the luxury hotel to the camping site.

Port Maria is closed to yachts except in an emergency. The harbour is very crowded with fishing boats and the ferries to Belle Ile. Port Haliguen, the yacht harbour for Quiberon, has all the facilities of a marina. The NE side of the peninsula is sheltered from the prevailing winds and there are several anchorages available in winds from NW to S. At Port d'Orange, 2½M farther north, there is merely a jetty and a somewhat indifferent anchorage. There are oyster beds in parts of the NW corner of the Baie de Quiberon, marked by orange buoys.

Yet further north on the NE side of Quiberon peninsula is an almost landlocked bay, but it is very shallow in both the bay and the approaches, except for a winding unmarked channel. Here is the Anse du Po, which is only one mile from Carnac, where the alignments of standing stones form one of the greatest sites of the megalithic culture.

The only other harbour on the Quiberon peninsula is Portivi, on the west side. This is exposed to the west, and when there is a heavy swell the sea is said to break nearly one mile to seaward. The anchorage is, however, a pleasant one in fine weather.

31. Port Maria

47°28'N 3°07'W

GENERAL

This is an artificial harbour, sheltered from all winds, situated just E of Beg el Lan on the SW extremity of the Quiberon peninsula. There is a conspicuous château with towers on this point. The harbour is used by many fishing vessels and is the terminal for the frequent, large, high-speed ferries to Belle Ile. Yachts are tolerated in an emergency rather than welcomed and a notice on the port-hand wall in the entrance, stating that any stay is limited to 72 hours, gives the restrictions. Except in an emergency, use the marina at Port Haliguen.

Charts

BA *2353, 2357*
Imray *C38*

TIDAL DATA

Times and heights

	Time differences				Height differences			
	HW		LW		MHWS	MHWN	MLWN	MLWS
BREST	0000 and 1200	0600 and 1800	0000 and 1200	0600 and 1800	6·9	5·4	2·6	1·0
Port Maria	+0010	−0025	−0025	−0015	−1·6	−1·3	−0·5	−0·1

Tidal streams

Some 3M SW of Port Maria the streams are rotary clockwise, the main strength being SE (1½kts at −0300 Brest) and NW (1½kts at +0400 Brest). There is no stream in the harbour.

Depths

Maximum 2·3m; much of the harbour dries.

LIGHTS

1. **Main light** 47°28'·8N 3°07'·5W
   Q.WRG.28m14-10M 246°-W-252°, 291°-W-297°-G-340°-W-017°-R-051°-W-081°-G-098°-W-143°
   White tower, green lantern

Ldg Lts 006·5°

2. *Front* 47°28'·7N 3°07'·2W DirQ.G.5m13M
3. *Rear* 230m from front DirQ.G.13m13M
   005°-intens-008°
   White truncated tower, black band and top
4. **Les Deux Frères** 47°28'·4N 3°07'·2W
   Fl.R.2·5s6m2M 175°-vis-047° Red beacon
5. **East mole head** 47°28'·6N 3°07'·4W
   Iso.G.4s9m7M White tower, green lantern
6. **S breakwater head** 47°28'·5N 3°07'·3W
   Oc(2)R.6s9m7M White tower, red lantern

APPROACH AND ENTRANCE

By day

The approach is well marked. Coming from the W or NW leave Le Pouilloux S cardinal whistle buoy to port. Then steer 070° until the leading marks, two white masonry beacons with black bands and black tops, E of the breakwater, come into line, bearing 006°. Follow the transit, leaving Les Deux Frères red beacon about 70m to port and Fregate unlit

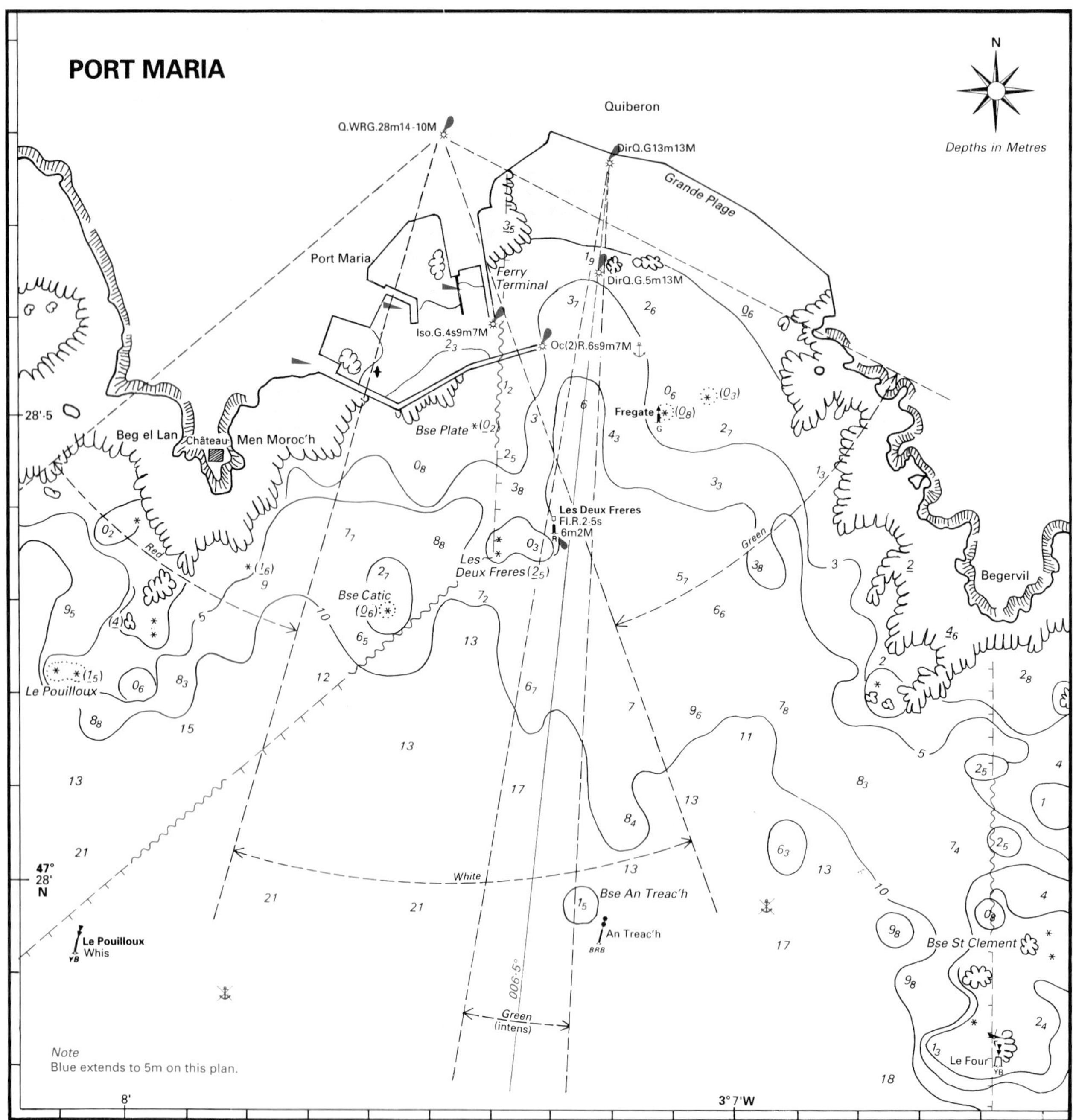

Plan 31

green beacon 150m to starboard, until the harbour entrance opens up behind the breakwater and it is safe to steer in.

By night

The main light[1] has 5 white sectors. Approach in the white sector where the light bears N or between 340° and 017° (an arc of 37°). In good time bring the leading lights[2,3] into line and steer on the transit, leaving Les Deux Frères[4] to port, until the entrance between the S breakwater head[6] and E mole head[5] opens up.

BERTHS AND ANCHORAGE

In settled weather from the north it is possible to anchor clear of the fairway and E of the seaward leading light. Do not anchor inside the yellow buoys which define the swimming and pedal-boat area. Subject to fishing-boat and ferry wash. Should it be necessary to find a berth in the harbour, apply to the harbour authorities.

The deep water (1·4 to 2·2m) lies on the SE side of the harbour parallel with the southern mole, and rocks and rocky bottom lie on the landward side. There are rocks at the base of the mole, which should not be approached too closely. The berth at the E mole is used by the ferries to Belle Ile and anchoring in the harbour is not permitted. Much of that which remains is taken up by fishing-boat moorings.

The rock formations of the peninsula of Presqu'île de Quiberon continue beyond the point forming the reefs, shoals and islets between the mainland and Houat and Hoëdic

The leading lights

The approach to Port Maria

FACILITIES

Water tap at ferry terminal. Several hotels, restaurants and shops of all kinds. Ferries to Belle Ile and Houat. Bus service to Carnac and Auray. Railway (seasonal) and airfield at Quiberon (1km). Good chandlery.

The harbour has a blind entrance. Beware of the high speed Belle Ile ferry which may leave unexpectedly

32. Belle Ile

Le Palais 47°21'N 3°09'W

GENERAL

Belle Ile is the largest island off the Brittany coast, being about 10M long and up to 5M wide. The NE coast is fairly free of outlying dangers except at its ends, off Pointe des Poulains and Pointe de Kerdonis. This side of the island is sheltered from the prevailing winds and has two harbours. Le Palais, when not overcrowded, is one of the best in Brittany, and Sauzon has an excellent drying inner harbour for vessels that can take the ground. Sauzon also has an outer harbour with moorings and visitors moorings outside, both comfortable except during the *vent solaire*.

The Atlantic side of the island is rugged and deeply indented, and has a profusion of rocks. It is picturesque and the island attracts many tourists. The only inlet on this side that provides any kind of harbour is the Port du Vieux Château (Ster Wenn), 1M south of Pointe des Poulains. This has no quay, roads or facilities, but has become a popular objective for yachts since attention was drawn to it in the first edition of this book. The danger is that the Atlantic swell can rise and bar the entrance.

Belle Ile has a long and interesting history. It was captured in 1761 by the British under Admiral Keppel; for their heroic storming of the apparently impregnable citadel the Royal Marines were awarded the laurels which surround their cap badge to this day. Two years later the island was restored to France in exchange for Nova Scotia. A number of Nova Scotian families returning to Europe settled in the island and introduced the potato some years before the vegetable became popular on the mainland.

During the Second World War a contingent of German soldiers occupied the barracks in the citadel at Le Palais. The prison there, which only closed in 1961, has had some notable inmates including, briefly, Karl Marx.

Charts

BA *2353*
Imray *C39*

TIDAL DATA

Times and heights

	Time differences				Height differences			
	HW		LW		MHWS	MHWN	MLWN	MLWS
BREST	0000 and 1200	0600 and 1800	0000 and 1200	0600 and 1800	6·9	5·4	2·6	1·0
Le Palais	+0007	−0028	−0025	−0020	−1·8	−1·4	−0·7	−0·3

Tidal streams

In the channel to the NE of Belle Ile the streams set NW at low water, SE at high water; spring rates up to 1½kts at the north end and in the middle and about 1kt at the south end. The streams probably run harder close to the north and south points of the island. The streams in the harbours are weak.

Depths

The approaches to the harbours are deep. Le Palais has 3m on the visitors moorings and 2–2·5m in the wet basin; the inner harbour dries. Sauzon inner harbour dries; 1m or more should be found in the outer harbour and 2·5m or more on the visitors moorings. Port du Vieux Château (Ster Wenn) has about 1·5m.

LIGHTS

1. **Goulphar** 47°18'·7N 3°13'·6W Fl(2)10s87m26M
   Grey tower, red lamp
2. **Pointe des Poulains** 47°23'·3N 3°15'·1W Fl.5s34m23M
   White square tower and dwelling, red lamp
3. **Pointe de Kerdonis** 47°18'·6N 3°03'·6W Fl(3)R.15s35m15M
   White square tower, red top and white dwelling

Le Palais

4. **South jetty head** 47°20'·8N 3°09'·1W Oc(2)R.6s11m11M White round tower, red lantern
5. **North jetty head** 47°20'·9N 3°09'·1W Fl(2+1)G.12s11m7M White tower, green top

Sauzon

6. **West jetty** 47°22'·4N 3°13'·1W Q.G.9m5M
7. **NW jetty head** 47°22'·5N 3°13'·0W Fl.G.4s8m8M
   White tower, green top
8. **SE jetty head** 47°22'·5N 3°13'·0W Fl.R.4s8m8M
   White truncated tower, red top

RADIO

Le Palais VHF Ch 9 0800–1200 and 1400–2000 LT
Sauzon VHF Ch 9 0700–2100 LT

Le Palais

Once a principal sardine-fishing port, Le Palais is now mainly a holiday resort, though some fishing continues. It is very popular, not only with yachts on passage, but also with the large fleet from the Baie de Quiberon, so that in the afternoon the harbour fills rapidly, especially at weekends. The town is the capital of Belle Isle with shops of all kinds. In the season it is very crowded with day tourists.

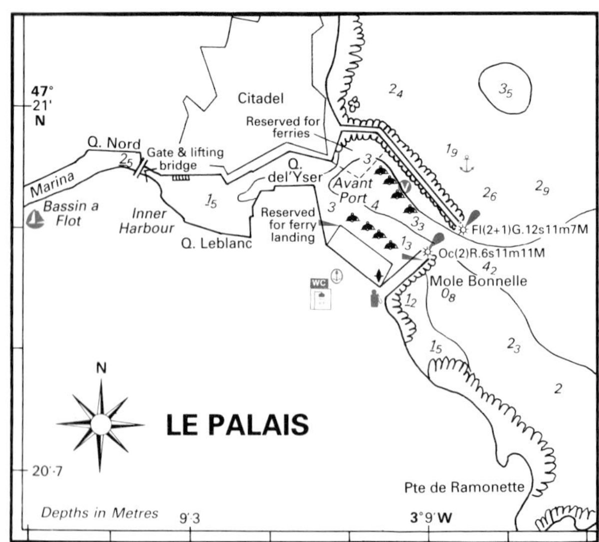

Plan 32

Le Palais provides good shelter, and there is an adequate anchorage outside in offshore winds. The harbour can, however, become uncomfortably overcrowded in July and August. It has a narrow entrance facing SE, but some swell can enter. Very strong NE winds cause seas to break over the breakwater. Even strong NW winds can cause some swell in the harbour, but it is well sheltered from the S and W.

In the approach and within the harbour, the ferries must operate at considerable speed (so as to maintain steerage way). There is little room for them to manoeuvre and it is *vital* for other craft to keep out of their way.

If the outer harbour becomes too uncomfortable it is possible to dry out in the inner harbour or go into the wet dock, which has a marina.

APPROACH AND ENTRANCE

By day

The citadel makes identification easy and there are no dangers in the approach. Steer for the lighthouse on the end of the northern jetty. Keep a sharp lookout for the frequent ferries from Quiberon, which enter and leave at speed, taking up most of the channel. If the way is clear, enter giving a wide berth to the southern pierhead, which has a rock at its base, and to the northern one, where the bottom is foul for some distance in along the wall.

By night

As by day, keeping a sharp lookout for the unlit buoys which are sometimes moored near the entrance.

ANCHORAGE AND MOORING

Outside the harbour, anchor to the east of the N jetty in 3m, keeping well clear of the fairway. This is a safe anchorage, with good holding ground, in offshore winds. Anchoring is prohibited between the citadel at Le Palais and the approaches to Sauzon, because of cables, but the anchorage noted above is just clear of the prohibited area, and two large mooring buoys have been placed here for visitors' use.

Inside the harbour, yachts raft fore and aft between three rows of mooring buoys or between the inncr row of buoys and chains suspended from the breakwater wall. The dinghy will be needed to get ashore. Check that your neighbour's spreaders will not foul, as yachts are subject to movement from wash and to any incoming swell. Yachts also secure between rows of buoys to port inside the entrance.

Le Palais, Belle Ile

The entrance to the inner harbour and basin lies between the citadel and the ferry berth

In the inner harbour it is possible to dry out bow to the N wall on either side of the grid, with a stern mooring if one is available or, if a space can be found, alongside. Consult the harbourmaster as in places the bottom is foul. White stripes on the walls reserve spaces for fishing boats, and anchoring is forbidden in the harbour.

Because the outer harbour is now often so crowded, more yachts enter the wet-dock than previously. The gates are opened from 1½ hours before to 1 hour after high water between 0600 and 2200 LT. Beyond the wet dock and a lifting bridge opening daily at 0700 lies La Saline marina, completely secure, with water and electricity on the pontoons.

FACILITIES

Water, showers and toilets by the *capitainerie*. Fuel by long hose from the root of the S breakwater. Haul-out facilities, marine and electrical engineers, chandlery. Banks, hotel, restaurants, café/bars and a good selection of shops. Frequent ferry service to Quiberon. It is possible to hire bicycles and cars to explore the island.

Sauzon

Situated less than two miles SE of Pointe des Poulains, this once peaceful little harbour is now full of yachts in season, but is still a very pleasant place to visit, and is a secure haven for vessels which can take the ground. The moorings in the outer harbour and outside are sheltered from the S and W but offer no comfort when the *vent solaire* blows. There is some local fishing and active sailing.

APPROACH AND ENTRANCE

By day

The harbour is easy to identify. The Gareau beacon tower (starboard) off the Pointe du Cardinal north of the entrance will be seen if approaching along the coast in either direction. The ends of the two outer breakwaters are marked by low white lighthouses with red and green tops, while behind them can be seen the old taller lighthouse, also white with a green top.

By night

The main light[6] and the two jetty head lights[7,8] are obscured by the Pointe du Cardinal when approaching from the NW. Pick up a buoy on the W side of the entrance, or enter using a good spotlight, as the harbour is very crowded and there is little background light from the shore.

ANCHORAGE AND MOORING

There are visitors' moorings outside the outer north mole, with room to anchor outside them clear of the fairway, although the harbourmaster discourages anchoring.

Between the outer and inner moles on the E side there are some mooring buoys for single mooring with better shelter; the old port tower still stands there and the bottom round it is foul. Between the moles on the W side there are two rows of mooring buoys. Yachts moor bow and stern and when the

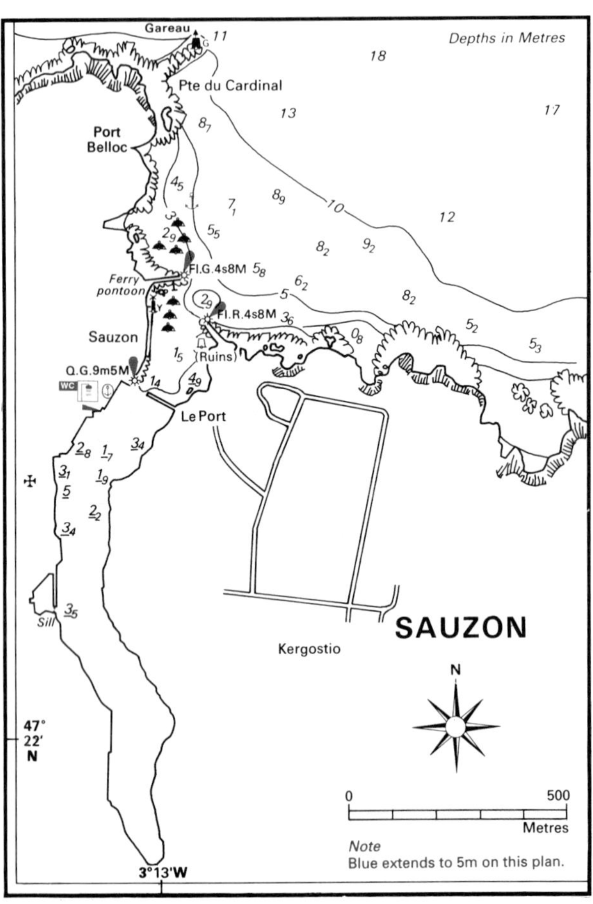

Plan 33

Looking into Sauzon

Inside Sauzon harbour visitors can lie afloat between head and stern buoys

harbour is crowded during the summer up to eight yachts may be rafted between two buoys.

The inner harbour dries to a firm sandy bottom. Yachts able to take the ground may moor among the local boats, secured bow and stern in the lines of buoys inside the entrance, or further up the harbour on their own anchors. It may also be necessary to dig the anchor in as the bottom is hard sand and shingle. Single-keel yachts may find a space to lie against a wall after consulting the harbourmaster.

The creek is over 500m long and if there is a crowd near the entrance there is plenty of room higher up for those prepared to dry out for longer each tide.

FACILITIES

Water tap at the root of the inner W jetty. Showers and toilets on the west wall of the inner harbour at the harbourmaster's office. Hotels, restaurants and café-bars. There are some food shops, but many have been converted to cater for tourists. Bicycles may be hired.

Port du Vieux Château (Ster Wenn)

This anchorage is in a fjord on the west coast of Belle Ile, a little over a mile S of Pointe des Poulains. It was described in the first edition of this work as one of the most beautiful in France; in consequence it has become also one of the most overcrowded by day visitors. It has also been likened to a lobster pot: easy to get into and hard to get out of. The onset of bad weather, or heavy swell, which can be caused by bad weather elsewhere, would make the entrance a deathtrap and yachts should be prepared to clear out at short notice.

The directions and plan should be used with caution, as the largest-scale chart published is on too small a scale to show much detail. The names Pointe Dangereuse and Pointe Verticale are fictitious, though appropriate; the name Pointe du Vieux Château (Beg en Nuet) on the plan is attached to what is believed to be the correct point – official charts differ.

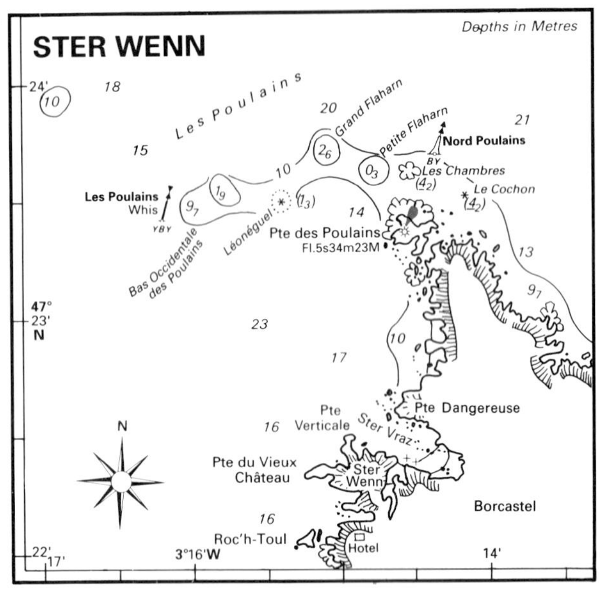

Plan 34

Looking into a very uncrowded Ster Wenn

APPROACH AND ENTRANCE

In the approach from northward the dangers off the Pointe des Poulains must be avoided. A detour may be made round Basse Occidentale des Poulains buoy or, if the rocks of Les Chambres and Le Cochon are showing (as they generally will be), the Pointe des Poulains may safely be rounded close inside them.

The Port du Vieux Château is divided into two parts: the main inlet, called Ster Vraz, which is seen from seaward, and a smaller inlet called Ster Wenn, which opens out on the south side of Ster Vraz. Ster Vraz is 400m wide and 900m long. Ster Wenn is only 50m wide and 500m long.

The entrance to Ster Vraz is harder to locate than it appears on the chart, as there are several inlets

The entrance to Ster Wenn is a blind corner and the first indication of the anchorage is likely to be the masts of other yachts within

looking similar from seaward, but on nearer approach it is easy to identify. The N side of Ster Vraz is encumbered with rocks as much as 300m off Pointe Dangereuse, but the southern side is steep-to, there being 15m almost alongside. Pointe Verticale forms a cliff on the south side of the entrance and it is this cliff which makes identification easy.

Some ¾M S of Pointe Verticale the Hôtel de l'Apothicairerie is conspicuous on the skyline.

Pointe Verticale, then, lies one mile SE from the Basse Occidentale des Poulains buoy, but it is better not to approach the last half mile on the direct line as an approach from a more westerly direction gives a good berth to the sunken rocks off Pointe Dangereuse and the northern arm of Ster Vraz. The stream weakens as Ster Vraz is entered, and so does the swell, especially in southerly winds.

The cliffs along the southern shore of Ster Vraz may be skirted in safety. Unless a yacht is entering or leaving, no sign of the existence of Ster Wenn will be seen until, quite dramatically, the entrance opens up to starboard. Open Ster Wenn fully, when course may be altered sharply to starboard to enter.

If Ster Wenn is overcrowded, there is a possible day anchorage further up Ster Vraz; use it only in calm weather. Keep to starboard and look out for many rocks as the beach is approached. Most of the rocks occupy the northern half of the inlet; they provide some shelter for local fishing boats.

ANCHORAGE

Ster Wenn is deep near the entrance and shoals gradually up to a sandy beach after a small fork. A cable is slung across the inlet at the fork to provide moorings for small fishing boats. On both sides iron rings are set into the rock above the high-water line. Drop anchor in the middle of the inlet (1·5m or more) and take a stern line ashore to one of the rings. The holding is good, but make sure that the anchor is well dug in before going ashore. Do not allow other yachts to raft to you with slack cables and shore lines if you are to survive a *vent solaire* during the night.

The water is smooth in all winds except NW. It seems inconceivable that any sea can make the double turn to enter this snug retreat, even in a severe gale. It is stated, however, that surge enters when there is a heavy onshore wind, and that the anchorage is then dangerous. Accordingly, the anchorage must be regarded only as a fair-weather one.

FACILITIES

There is a dinghy landing on the beach and a path leading up the valley to the road. Turn left and Sauzon can be reached after a walk of some 3M. Turn right and visit the Grotte de l'Apothicairerie (¾ mile), a cave that is worth seeing, so named after the rows of cormorants that sometimes line the ledges, looking like the jars of coloured liquid in an old chemist's shop. There is a tourist shop and café above the cave.

33. Houat and Hoëdic

Positions: Houat 47°2'N 2°58'W
Hoëdic 47°2'N 2°52'W

GENERAL

These two low islands are the only inhabited elements of the chain of rocks and islets which forms the southeasterly extension of the Quiberon peninsula and provides shelter to Quiberon Bay. Both are small – although only 2M long Houat is nearly twice the size of Hoëdic – and they support slender permanent populations of farmers and fishermen. In the summer they are busy with tourists who visit to enjoy the peace, the outstanding beaches and the profusion of wild flowers.

Houat and Hoëdic offer the same attractions to the yachtsman. Each island has a small harbour, but neither Port Saint Gildas on Houat or Port de l'Argol on Hoëdic has much room for visitors. But both islands have several anchorages and one sheltered from the prevailing weather can usually be found.

Houat is pronounced 'What', rhyming with 'that'

Charts

BA *2357, 2353*
Imray *C39*

TIDAL DATA

Times and heights

	Time differences				Height differences			
	HW		LW		MHWS	MHWN	MLWN	MLWS
BREST								
	0000 and 1200	0600 and 1800	0000 and 1200	0600 and 1800	6·9	5·4	2·6	1·0
Ile de Houat								
	+0010	–0025	–0020	–0015	–1·7	–1·3	–0·6	–0·2
Ile de Hoëdic								
	+0010	–0035	–0027	–0022	–1·8	–1·4	–0·7	–0·3

Tidal streams

In the Passage du Beniguet the NE stream begins at −0540 Brest and the SW at +0040 Brest, spring rates 2kts. In the Passage des Sœurs the NNE flow begins +0540 Brest and the SW at −0030 Brest, spring rates 2kts. North of Hoëdic the NE stream begins at −0600 Brest, the SW stream at HW Brest; spring rates 1½kts. Half a mile E of Les Grands Cardinaux the flood runs NNE, the ebb SW; spring rates 1½kts.

Depths

In Port St Gildas harbour at Houat there is 2 to 2·5m near the breakwater; the S side of the harbour dries. Half Argol harbour on Hoëdic dries but there is 2m in the entrance. In the anchorages there is normally plenty of water, but at Port de La Croix on Hoëdic the harbour dries 2·8m; however in the pool most yachts will be able to remain afloat, except perhaps at LW springs.

LIGHTS

1. **Houat, Port St Gildas N mole** 47°23'·5N 2°57'·4W Fl(2)WG.6s8m9/6M 168°-W-198°-G-210°-W-240°-G-168° White tower, green top
2. **Hoëdic, Port de l'Argol breakwater head** 47°20'·7N 2°52'·5W Fl.WG.4s10m9/6M 143°-W-163°-G-183°-W-203°-G-143° White tower, green top
3. **Grouguéguez (Les Grands Cardinaux)** 47°19'·3N 2°50'·1W Fl(4)15s28m13M Red tower, white band

Houat

Houat is a strangely shaped island about 2M long, lying 7M east of Le Palais and 10M south of La Trinité. At its eastern end there are long promontories. En Tal, on the NE, is low; the southern one is higher, with off-lying rocks. Between these headlands lie the remarkable sands of Tréac'h-er-Goured, and the old port Er Beg, destroyed by a violent tempest in 1951. The new harbour, Port St Gildas, lies to the west of En Tal. This harbour is very snug and well protected from the swell, but it is small and the local fishing boats nearly fill it.

Port St Gildas is named after St Gildas de Rhuys, a 6th-century British missionary who established a monastery near the entrance to the Morbihan. St Gildas died in 570 when visiting Houat, and in accordance with his wishes his body was placed in a boat and pushed out to sea. Two months later, on 11 March, the boat was washed ashore at what is now the entrance to Crouesty Marina. A chapel was built at the spot, and according to Baring-Gould, writing in 1920, a procession leaves St Gildas annually to visit the site. The chapel can be seen on the south side of the marina entrance. It has been rebuilt several times, having suffered damage in storms. Its history is recorded on a plaque by the porch.

APPROACH

By day

The easiest approach is from the N and E. From the N one will try to come down with the ebb stream, but if planning to enter the harbour it is better to avoid arriving near low water, so as to have room to manoeuvre inside.

From the N steer towards the E end of the island. Nearly one mile N of it is the conspicuous rock La Vieille (14m high) and NNE of it a mussel bed marked by a N cardinal and an E cardinal buoy to

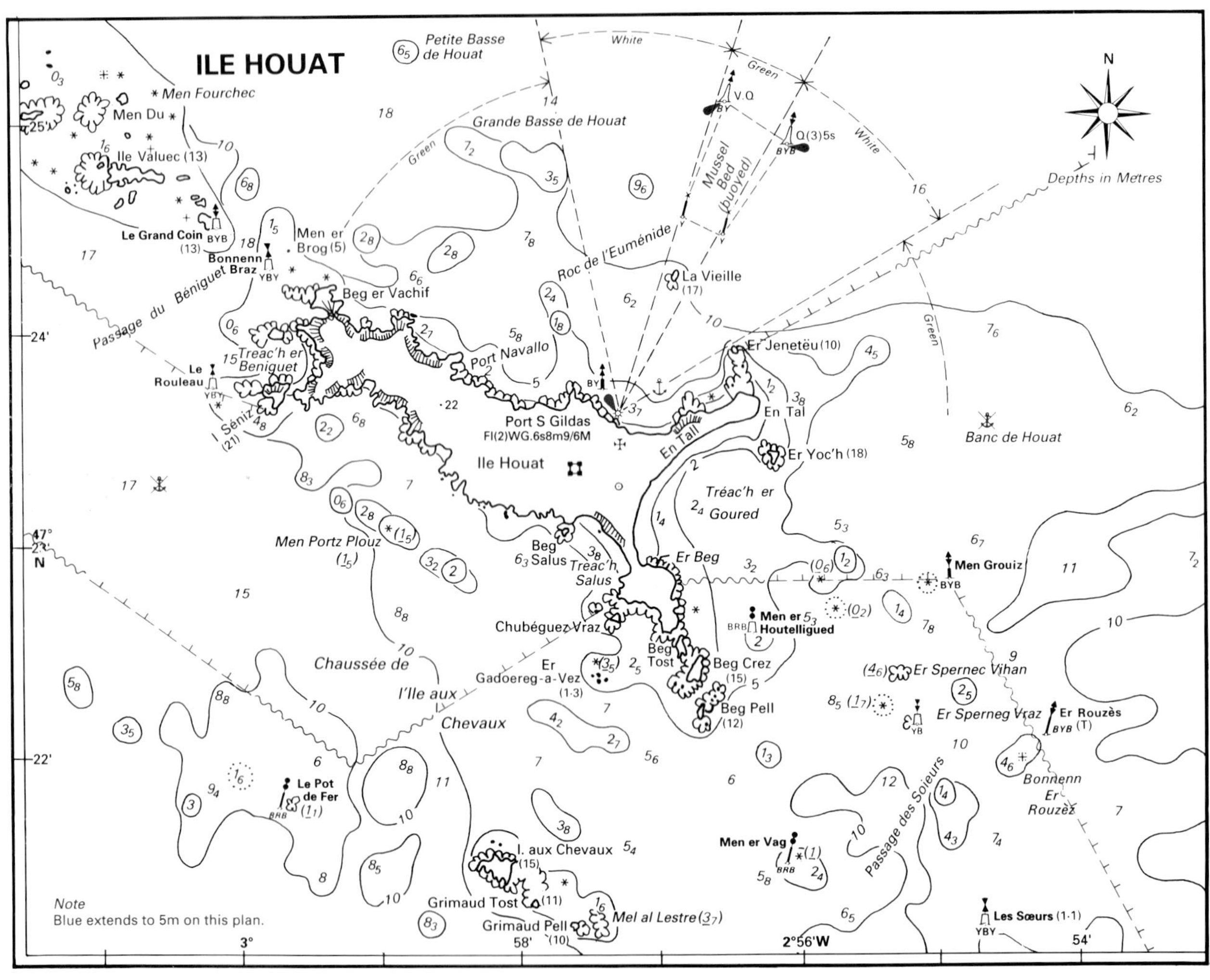

Plan 35

Port St Gildas on Houat

The approach to the harbour

the N and two yellow buoys to the S. Once La Vieille is identified it is easy to locate the harbour, which bears 200°, ¾M from it. Pass either side of the shellfish zone and La Vieille, which is clean to the N and E but less so to the SW; shoals extend about 200m to the S.

From the E the outer NE rock, Er Jenetëu (16m high), can be passed at a distance of 100m. There are rocks near the direct line from it to the harbour, and a yacht should stand well out into the bay before shaping up for the harbour.

By night

Green sectors of the breakwater light[1] cover La Vieille and also the dangers to the E and W of the harbour. Approach in either white sector and anchor off the harbour, or enter if there is enough light to berth. The shellfish zone lies in the green sector of the breakwater light, and the N cardinal buoy marking the N corner and the E cardinal buoy marking the NE corner are both lit.

BERTHS AND ANCHORAGE

Port St Gildas is small and a yacht much over 10m is unlikely to find a berth. There is a row of head and stern moorings for yachts running parallel to the breakwater, which is reserved for fishing boats. Enter between the breakwater and the first row of moorings if there is room to pick one up or raft to another yacht. Do not obstruct the access for the ferry. If the harbour is full, as is likely during the season, anchor in the bay to the east in 2m. The holding here is not good and in fine weather it is exposed to the *vent solaire*. Port Navallo, a small bay one mile to the W, offers better holding, as does the next bay W, which has a sandy beach.

Many yachts anchor off Tréac'h-er-Goured and Tréac'h-Salus, despite the fact that these are shown on charts as prohibited because of underwater high-tension cables. Treac'h-Salus offers good protection from the *vent solaire* in fine weather. The anchorage in Tréac'h-er-Beniguet is also attractive, sheltered

Treac'h-er-Goured, a bay whose sandy beach rivals the Caribbean. Despite being, in theory, a prohibited anchorage it is usually more crowded than this during the season

from N through E to S. If approaching it from the north do not head into the bay too soon, but rather come in on an easterly heading from a point close N of Le Rouleau W cardinal beacon.

FACILITIES
Water from the public tap in the centre of the pretty village or at the toilets on the pier. The shops can supply simple needs, but they are limited. Small hotels, café-bars. Medical centre, post office. Good shrimping and cockling off Tréac'h-er-Goured. The island is noted for its succession of wild flowers: roses in May, carnations in June, yellow immortelles in July and sand lilies in August. There are wonderful beaches on the north side of En Tal, at Tréac'h-er-Goured in the east, Tréac'h-Salus in the SE and Tréac'h-er-Beniguet in the west.

Hoëdic

This island, rather over 1M long and ½M wide, lies about 4M SE of Houat. There are many detached rocks off its W, S and E coasts. There are two harbours. Argol harbour, on the N side, is very small; most yachts will prefer to lie outside. Port de la Croix, the southern, drying, harbour, and its approaches are dangerous in winds from the S and E, but in settled fine weather offer the best and most attractive anchorage.

APPROACH
By day
From the N make for the centre of the island, taking care to avoid La Chèvre marked by an isolated danger beacon, in the close approach. From Houat, leave Men Groise E cardinal beacon and Er Rouzèz E cardinal buoy to starboard. Thence steer for the north side of the island, passing SW of La Chèvre. From the E, making for the N side of the island, leave Beg Legad, the NE point of the island, about 400m to port to clear a drying rock (marked by a N cardinal beacon) NW of the point and continue into the bay.

The approach from the S and W will be made through either the Passage des Soeurs or Passage de l'Ile aux Chevaux which are described in Chapter 34.

By night
Approach in one of the white sectors of the harbour light[4]. Green sectors cover La Chèvre and dangers to the east and west of the approach.

ANCHORAGES
L'Argol harbour has room for 20 to 30 visiting yachts in settled weather. To avoid sunken rocks in the approach and outside anchorage, do not bring the head of the eastern jetty to bear more than 180°. The bottom shoals steadily; anchor in 2m, 60m from the beach, just inside the entrance to port or raft in less water with other yachts, using one of the moorings. A road leads to the village.

The southern harbour, Port de la Croix, is best visited using BA chart *2353*. The harbour itself dries 2·8m and is often crowded; most yachts will prefer to anchor outside, where there is good shelter from the *vent solaire* in fine weather.

The simplest approach from the north is to pass outside Les Grands Cardinaux and the associated rocks and then steer SW until the S cardinal tower Madavoar comes into line with the right-hand edge of the fort, bearing 320°. Maintain this transit and

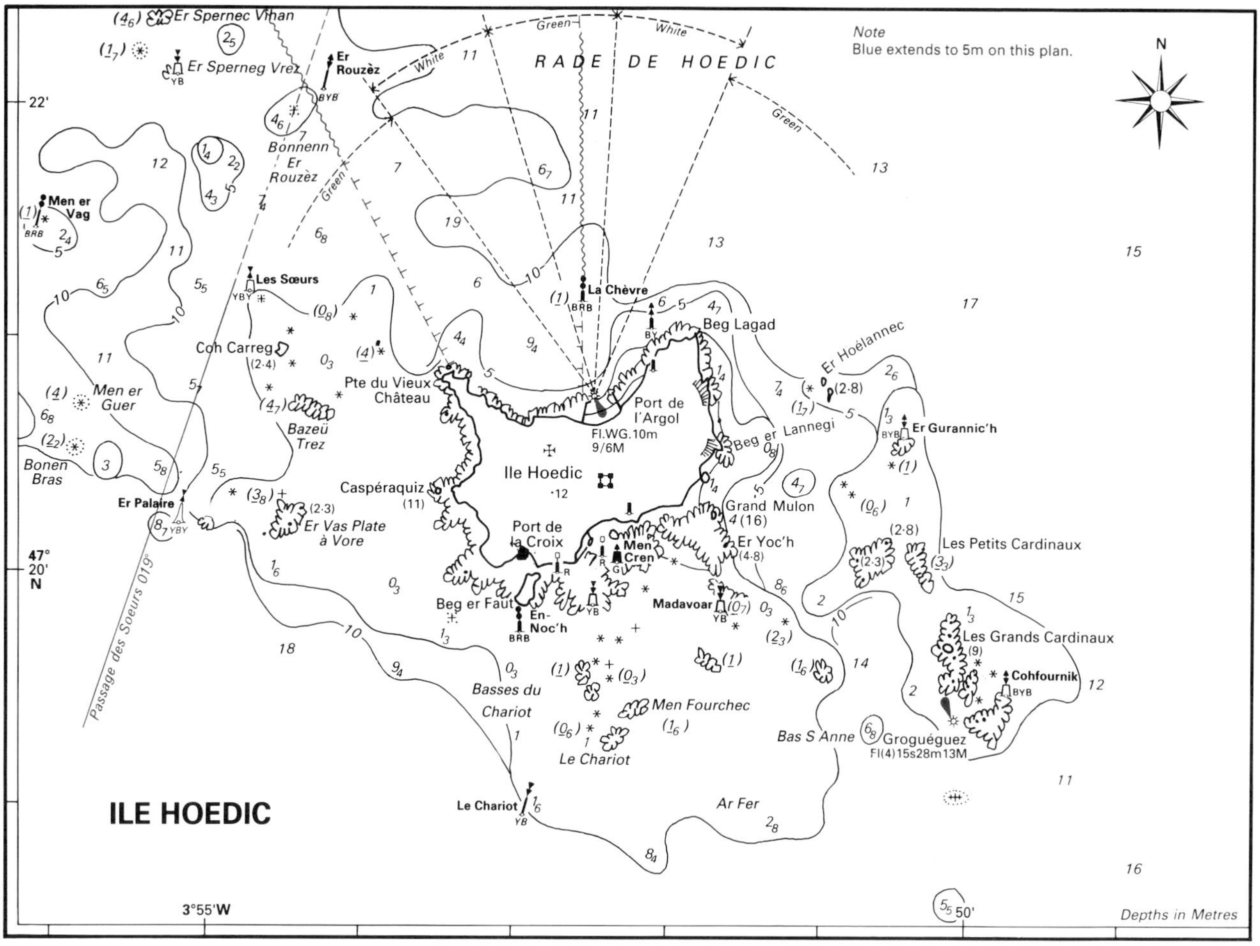

ILE HOEDIC

Note
Blue extends to 5m on this plan.

RADE DE HOEDIC

Er Spernec Vihan
Er Sperneg Vrez
Er Rouzèz
Bonnenn Er Rouzèz
Men er Vag
Les Sœurs
Coh Carreg
Men er Guer
Bonen Bras
Er Palaire
Bazeü Trez
Pte du Vieux Château
Caspéraquiz
Er Vas Plate à Vore
La Chèvre
Beg Lagad
Port de l'Argol
Fl.WG.10m 9/6M
Ile Hoedic
Port de la Croix
Beg er Faut
En-Noc'h
Men Cren
Madavoar
Beg er Lannegi
Grand Mulon
Er Yoc'h
Er Hoélannec
Er Gurannic'h
Les Petits Cardinaux
Les Grands Cardinaux
Cohfournik
Groguéguez
Fl(4)15s28m13M
Bas S Anne
Basses du Chariot
Men Fourchec
Le Chariot
Ar Fer
Passage des Soeurs 019°

22'
47° 20' N
3°55'W
50'

Depths in Metres

Plan 36

Port de l'Argol, Hoëdic

Port de La Croix on the south side of Hoëdic dries, but there is a pleasant anchorage off it in northerly weather

on close approach, leave Madavoar to starboard and make for a point to the S of Men Cren starboard beacon tower, fetching a slight curve northwards to avoid rocks which must be left to port SE of Men Cren.

Alternatively, with sufficient rise of tide, the route from the north inside the reefs can be taken. The only hazards which cannot be avoided easily by reference to the chart or plan are the patch which dries 2·3m, 500m east of Madavoar beacon, and an isolated pinnacle, drying 0·7m, 170m SE of Madavoar. This rock is cleared by making the passage with sufficient rise of tide to float over it and the one further out avoided by staying within 400m of the beacon, or by keeping Er Gurannic'h E cardinal beacon bearing not less than 035° astern. Once past Madavoar, join the route described above.

Anchor S of Men Cren tower. Yachts which can take the ground, and others at neaps, can pass between Men Cren tower and the port-hand beacon and anchor in the pool if room can be found amongst the permanent moorings. Thence the way to the harbour is open.

There is an anchorage suitable for a visit by day off a sandy beach north of Grand Mulon, a rock 14m high rising out of rocky flats which cover (see plan on page 121). This is approached from Beg Lagad, the NE point of the island, keeping 300m offshore and avoiding a rocky spur extending SE from Beg-er-Lannegi, the northern headland of the bay. Anchor with soundings on sand, avoiding any patches of weed. Other anchorages around the island can be found – the water is so clear that in calm weather and at slow speed, many of the submerged hazards can be seen and avoided.

The best anchorage is to the south of Men Cren beacon. The pool inside it dries

FACILITIES

Yachts should be adequately provisioned and watered before visiting Hoëdic. The island boasts a small hotel, a food shop and baker, together with café-bars and *crêperies*, There is a shower and toilet block with fresh-water tap on the right on the way up from the harbour.

34. La Teignouse, Le Beniguet, Ile aux Chevaux, Les Soeurs

Passage notes

GENERAL

For a distance of some 15M southeast of Quiberon there are islets, reefs and shoals together with the two inhabited islands of Houat and Hoëdic. Between the reefs and rocks there are several navigable passages, but only the main four will be described. The Passage de la Teignouse is the big-ship route and the only one that is lit; it is about 3M from Quiberon. The Passage du Beniguet, which lies close NW of Houat, is narrow but quite straightforward. The Passage des Soeurs lies between Houat and Hoëdic; it is wider than Le Beniguet. The Passage de l'Ile aux Chevaux is the short route between Le Palais and Hoëdic.

With the aid of the large-scale chart other routes into Quiberon Bay can be found, particularly towards high water. Even if the tides are only neaps, at HW many of the dangers will have more than 2m of water over them and most of those that remain a

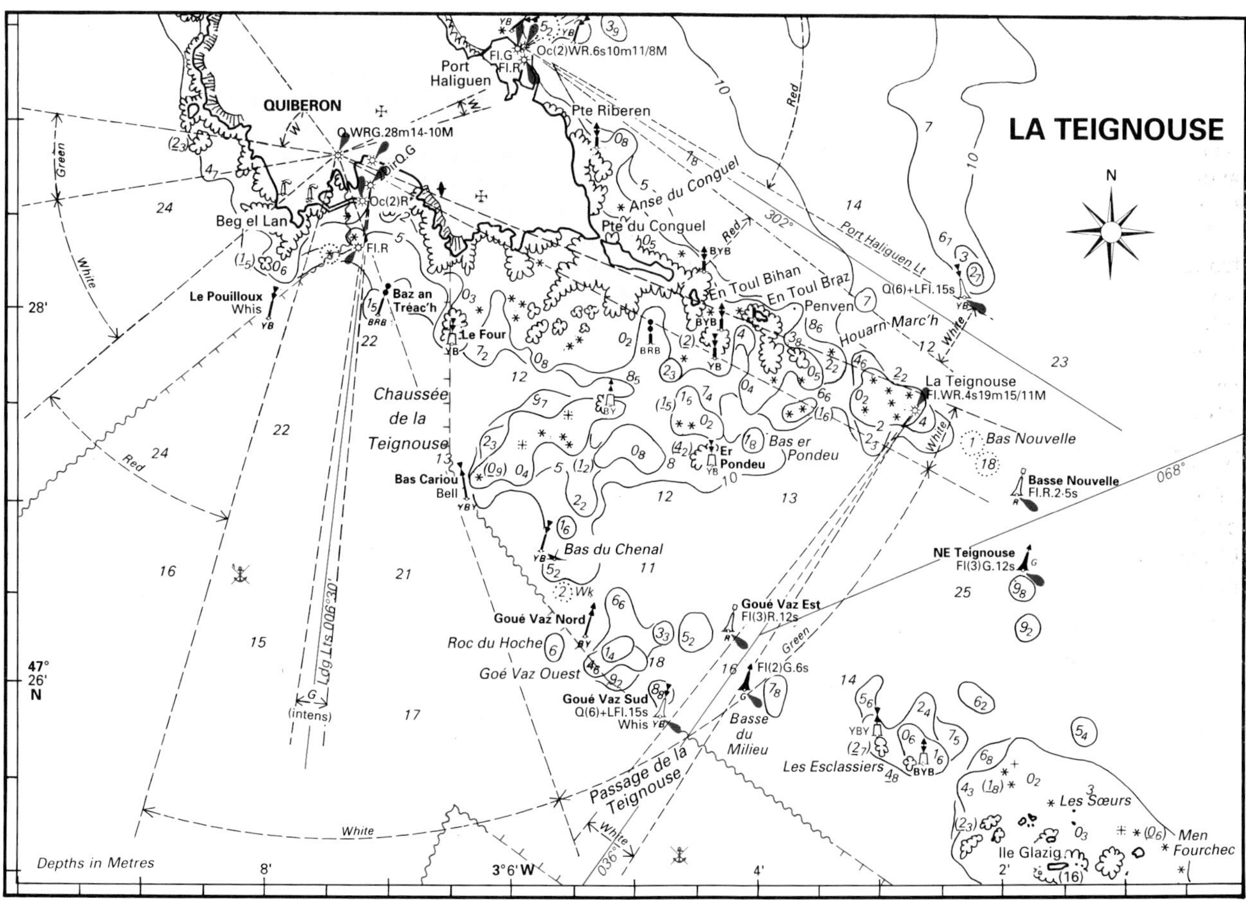

Plan 37

La Teignouse light from the NW

hazard are marked or permanently above water. Allowance must be made, however, for any swell which may be running.

Charts
BA *2357, 2353*
Imray *C39*

TIDAL DATA

Times and heights

Time differences				Height differences			
HW		LW		MHWS	MHWN	MLWN	MLWS
BREST							
0000 and 1200	0600 and 1800	0000 and 1200	0600 and 1800	6·9	5·4	2·6	1·0
Port Maria							
+0010	–0025	–0025	–0015	–1·6	–1·3	–0·5	–0·1

Tidal streams

La Teignouse NE stream begins –0600 Brest, SW stream begins HW Brest, spring rates 2·5kts.

Le Béniguet NE stream begins –0540 Brest, SW stream begins +0040 Brest, spring rates 2kts.

Ile aux Chevaux (rounding the SE point of Houat) and **Les Soeurs** NNE stream begins +0540 Brest, SSW stream begins –0030 Brest, spring rates 2kts.

Depths
All four channels are deep.

Passage de la Teignouse

LIGHTS

1. **Port Maria main light** 47°28'·8N 3°07'·5W Q.WRG.28m14-10M 246°-W-252°, 291°-W-297°-G-340°-W-017°-R-051°-W-081°-G-098°-W-143° White tower, green lantern
2. **La Teignouse** 47°27'·5N 3°02'·8W Fl.WR.4s19m15/11M 033°-W-039°-R-033° White round tower, red top
3. **Goué Vaz Sud buoy (S card)** 47°25'·8N 3°04'·8W Q(6)+LFl.15s Whis
4. **Basse du Milieu buoy (starboard)** 47°26'·0N 3°04'·0W Fl(2)G.6s9m2M Green triangle on green HFPB
5. **Goué Vaz E buoy (port)** 47°26'·3N 3°04'·2W Fl(3)R.12s
6. **NE Teignouse buoy (starboard)** 47°26'·6N 3°01'·8W Fl(3)G.12s
7. **Basse Nouvelle buoy (port)** 47°27'·0N 3°01'·9W Fl.R.2·5s
8. **Port Haliguen, New breakwater head** 47°29'·4N 3°06'·0W Oc(2)WR.6s10m11/8M 233°-W-240·5°-R-299°-W-306°-R-233° White tower, red top
9. **Sud Banc de Quiberon buoy (S card)** 47°28'·1N 3°02'·3W Q(6)+LFl.15s

GENERAL

This is a well-marked channel, ¼M wide, and small vessels have plenty of margin, as there is deep water on either side of the marked channel. There are no difficulties other than those caused by bad visibility or bad weather. The strong tides cause a steep sea when wind and tide are opposed, so that with a contrary wind the passage should be taken as near slack water as possible.

Even on a flat calm day there are overfalls in the Passage du Beniguét. When there is a fresh wind against the stream it is rough

From the southwest

By day

Bring the white lighthouse on La Teignouse to bear 036°. This line leads S of Goué Vaz Sud buoy (S cardinal), which must not be confused with Goué Vaz Nord buoy (N cardinal), situated ½M to the NW of it. Steer on this course, 036°, leaving Goué Vaz Sud S cardinal buoy to port, Basse du Milieu green buoy to starboard and Goué Vas Est red buoy to port.

When this last buoy is abeam alter course to 068°. The official lead for this is the church at St Gildas, 10M away, bearing 068°, but it is only necessary to steer out between Basse Nouvelle buoy to port and La Teignouse NE buoy to starboard.

From the east

Reverse the above courses.

From the southwest

By night

Enter the white sector (033°–039°) of La Teignouse light[2] before Port Maria main light[1] turns from white to green. Steer in this sector between the buoys. When the vessel is approximately between Basse du Milieu[4] and Goué Vaz Est buoys[5] alter course to 068° to pass between the Basse Nouvelle[7] and NE Teignouse[6] buoys.

From the east or north

Avoid the dangers off La Teignouse by keeping in the white sector of Port Haliguen light[8] 299°–306°. Enter between the Basse Nouvelle[7] and NE Teignouse[6] buoys and steer 248° to pass between Basse du Milieu and Goué Vaz buoys[4,5]. Steer out 216° between the buoys in the white sector of La Teignouse light[2]. When Port Maria main light[1] turns from green to white all dangers are passed.

Passage de Béniguet

For the plan of this passage see under Houat in the previous chapter, page 118.

This is an easy daylight passage, lying immediately to the NW of the island of Houat, and is often used by yachts going between Belle Ile and Houat.

Coming from the SW, leave Le Rouleau tower (W cardinal) about 600m to starboard and steer about 030° to pass between Le Grand Coin tower (E cardinal) and Bonnenn Braz tower (W cardinal). Keep closer to Le Grand Coin tower and well clear of Bonnenn Braz and the shoals with a least depth of 1·5m which extend 600m to the NNE of it. Le Grand Coin tower bearing 240° (and in transit with Le Palais citadel, if the visibility is good) clears these shoals.

Use this transit when leaving Baie de Quiberon and alter to 210° when Le Grand Coin is 400m distant.

Passage de l'Ile aux Chevaux

For this passage see plan on page 118. This is the direct fine-weather route from Le Palais to Hoëdic, and is an attractive alternative to Le Beniguet for reaching Houat.

Steer E from Le Palais for the Ile aux Chevaux. The Pot de Fer, 1M NNW of Ile aux Chevaux dries 1·1m and may be passed on either side. Keep 400m N of the rocks, 0·7m high, N of Ile aux Chevaux.

Bound for Houat, steer to leave Beg Pell (12m high) 200m to port; there is a rock with 1·3m over it about ½M to the SE. Beg Pell and the rocks N of it are steep-to. Thence, leave the Men er Houtelligued BRB tower 100m to starboard. To port will be seen the dramatic sweep of Tréac'h-er-Goured, one of the sights of Brittany.

It is a magnificent beach for bathing. British Admiralty chart *2353*, and the French charts, mark it as being within a prohibited anchorage area and, officially, yachts found to be at anchor are liable to prosecution. This rule seems to be honoured more in the breach than the observance, as both bays are crowded with yachts at anchor on most days throughout the summer.

Cross the bay if proceeding to Port St Gildas, leave the rock Er Yoc'h (18m high) 100m to port and the beach on the point En Tal well to port, and round Er Jenetëu (10m high), leaving it 100m to port, to enter Port de St Gildas.

Bound for Hoëdic, leave Men er Vag shoal, drying 1m, marked by a BRB spar buoy, to starboard. Thence, leave Les Soeurs tower (W cardinal) to starboard and follow the directions for the Passage des Soeurs given below.

Passage des Soeurs

For this passage see plan page 121.

Make a point 400m W of Er Palaire W cardinal buoy (which replaced the destroyed beacon tower in 1998). Steer 019° to leave Les Sœurs tower (W cardinal) 100m to starboard. The official alignment is Er Rouzèz W cardinal buoy (or the beacon tower if it has been replaced) in line with S Gildas-de-Rhuys church, but the latter is 10M to the N and is not likely to be seen. The channel is quite wide and it is not necessary to follow the transit closely, but if beating Men er Guer and Bonen Bras shoals, which dry 4m and 2·2m respectively, are a hazard. They can be avoided by keeping Er Spernec Vraz S beacon tower open to the left of Men Grouiz N beacon tower. Having passed Les Soeurs tower, steer out as requisite.

Bound for Hoëdic, do not let Les Soeurs tower bear more than 255° until the W side of Hoëdic is shut in behind the Pointe du Vieux Château, bearing 175°. This point is the NW headland of Hoëdic, and shoals extend northwards of a line between the point and Les Soeurs.

Bound north, leave Er Rouzèz E cardinal buoy at least 200m to port.

35. Port Haliguen

47°29'N 3°06'W

GENERAL

Port Haliguen is the yachting harbour for Quiberon. A simple village encircles the old drying harbour. Every yachting facility is provided by the marina, there are excellent beaches handy and the resources of Quiberon are only a mile away. This is a pleasant harbour, but the facilities are some distance from the visitors' pontoon.

Charts

BA *2357, 2353*
Imray *C39*

TIDAL DATA

Times and heights

	Time differences				Height differences			
	HW		LW		MHWS	MHWN	MLWN	MLWS
BREST								
	0000 and 1200	0600 and 1800	0000 and 1200	0600 and 1800	6·9	5·4	2·6	1·0
Port Haliguen								
	+0015	−0020	−0015	−0010	−1·7	−1·3	−0·6	−0·3

Tidal streams

Off the harbour the N stream begins at −0600 Brest and the S stream at +0100 Brest; spring rates 1kt.

Depths

The approach is deep. In the harbour there is up to 3m.

LIGHTS

1. **Port Maria main light** 47°28'·8N 3°07'·5W Q.WRG.28m14-10M 246°-W-252°, 291°-W-297°-G-340°-W-017°-R-051°-W-081°-G-098°-W-143° White tower, green lantern
2. **Marina, new breakwater head** 47°29'·4N 3°06'·0W Oc(2)WR.6s10m11/8M 233°-W-240·5°-R-299°-W-306°-R-233° White tower, red top
3. **Old breakwater head** 47°29'·3N 3°06'·0W Fl.R.4s10m5M 322°-vis-206° White tower, red top
4. **NW mole head** 47°29'·4N 3°06'·1W Fl.G.2·5s9m6M White column, green top
5. **Pier head** 49°29'·3N 3°06'·0W Fl.Vi.2·5s5m Purple column

RADIO

VHF Ch 9 0800–1230 and 1400–2000 LT

APPROACH AND ENTRANCE

By day

The approach to the Baie de Quiberon through the Teignouse is described in the previous chapter. Port Haliguen is situated less than 2M NW of the SE extremity of the Quiberon peninsula. The immediate approach is easy, passing midway between La Teignouse lighthouse and the S cardinal buoy Sud Banc de Quiberon on a course of 305°, leaving to starboard the S cardinal buoy Port Haliguen.

Enter between the breakwaters and turn to starboard for the visitors' pontoon, which runs along the inside of the breakwater. Report to the harbour office, which will allocate a permanent berth if the authorities wish you to move.

By night

Approach in the white 246°–252° sector of Port Maria light[1], or in one of the white sectors of Port Haliguen Marina light[2]. Keep a lookout for unlit buoys and avoid the protective spur off the E breakwater head on entering.

MOORING

Anchoring is not permitted in the harbour. Visitors secure to the pontoon along the wall of the northwestern basin. Mooring buoys for very large yachts may be available in the northwestern basin. Should the visitors' berths be full, the reception pontoon is beside the fuel pontoon in the southeastern basin.

FACILITIES

All the facilities of a major marina. Fuel pontoon, slip, crane, travel-lift, engineers, club. Bread available at café at the port. A 15-minute walk on the road towards Quiberon is a large supermarket with fish and oysters on sale outside. Hotels, restaurants, banks and all shops in Quiberon, 1M away, where there are connections by bus, train and plane to all parts.

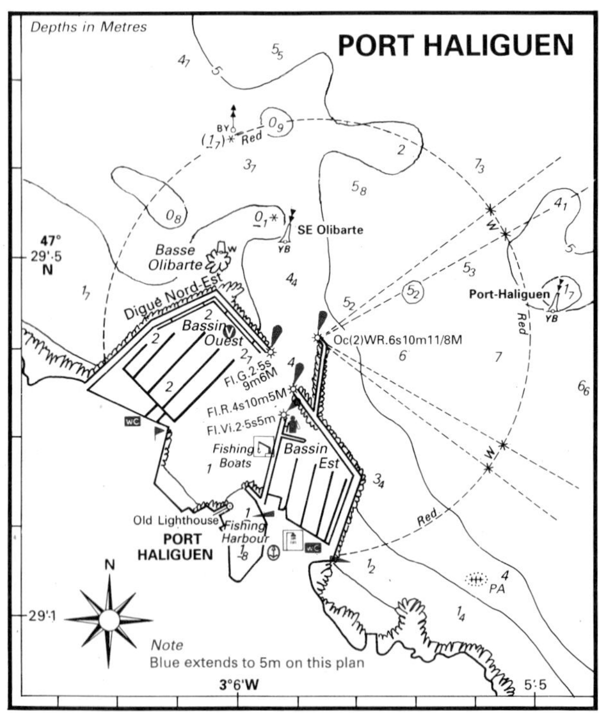

Plan 38

Port Haliguen

The entrance to Port Haliguen is not immediately obvious as the breakwaters appear to merge

Once the entrance to Haliguen has been opened the way in is clear

The old lighthouse and the inner harbour, which dries

36. La Trinité

47°35'N 3°01'W

GENERAL

La Trinité, situated 1½M up the river Crac'h on the west side, is one of the most popular yachting centres in the Bay of Biscay. It is not in itself exceptionally pretty, but it is the centre for a remarkably interesting cruising area which also affords good courses for racing. It is, in consequence, more of a place to yacht from than to visit, though visitors are made welcome and all reasonable needs can be met.

In the marina the shelter is excellent from all except strong S and SE winds, which send in a sea near high water when La Vaneresse, the sandbank protecting the harbour, is covered. In addition to its yachting activity, La Trinité is a great centre for oyster culture.

The town has good facilities for the visitor, including many restaurants, and La Trinité is an excellent place to visit, and in which to shop, if it is planned to spend time in the more remote parts of the Morbihan.

The Carnac Alignments

The Quiberon district is famous for the large number of megaliths, stone circles, tombs and stone rows in the area. A visit to the Carnac Alignments is highly recommended and La Trinité is an ideal base from which to start. There is a bus service to Carnac, from which the Alignments can be reached on foot; the ancient tomb, built in a huge artificial mound now surmounted by a Chapel of St Michael, can be visited en route. An alternative is to hire a bicycle for the visit.

There has been much debate as to the purpose of the Alignments and the surrounding megaliths. One theory is that the area was a vast astronomical observatory for predicting solar and lunar events.

Charts

BA *2357, 2358, 2353*
Imray *C39*

The west side of the Crac'h river is buoyed. Do not stray outside the channel as there are shellfish beds

La Trinité, looking north, with homecoming yachts funnelling into the channel

TIDAL DATA

Times and heights

Time differences				Height differences			
HW		LW		MHWS	MHWN	MLWN	MLWS
BREST							
0000 and 1200	0600 and 1800	0000 and 1200	0600 and 1800	6·9	5·4	2·6	1·0
La Trinité							
+0020	–0020	–0015	–0005	–1·5	–1·1	–0·5	–0·2

Tidal streams

The currents outside vary from point to point. 4M S of La Trinité the flood sets NNE, the ebb SW; spring rates 2kts. In the river, the stream reaches 3kts on the ebb at springs.

La Trinité marina, looking south

Depths

The river is deep in the channel until the last reach, approaching the marina, where there are patches with only 1·8m. Within the marina, depths are up to 4m.

LIGHTS

La Trinité Ldg Lts 347°

1. *Front* 47°34'·1N 3°00'·4W Q.WRG.11m10-7M 321°-G-345°-W-013·5°-R-080° White tower, green top
2. *Rear* 560m from front DirQ.21m15M 337°-intens-357° Synchronised with front White round tower, green top
3. **La Trinité-sur-mer Dir Lt 347°** 47°35'·0N 3°01'·0W DirOc.WRG.4s9m13-11M 345°-G-346°-W-348°-R-349° White tower
4. **Le Petit Trého buoy (port)** 47°33'·5N 3°00'·7W Fl(4)R.15s
5. **S pier head** 47°35'·1N 3°01'·5W Oc(2)WR.6s6m10/7M 090°-R-293·5°-W-300·5°-R-329° White tower, red top
6. **Marina pierhead** 47°35'·3N 3°01'·5W Iso.R.4s8m5M White framework tower, red top

RADIO

VHF Ch 9 0800–1300 and 1400–2000 LT

APPROACH AND ENTRANCE

The river becomes almost impossibly crowded during summer weekends and entry is best made under power. There is a speed limit of 5kts but it is widely ignored. Power vessels over 20m overall, barges and oyster-culture vessels under tow have priority over all other vessels.

By day

Approaching from La Teignouse, a wooded hill about 30m high will be seen to the W of the

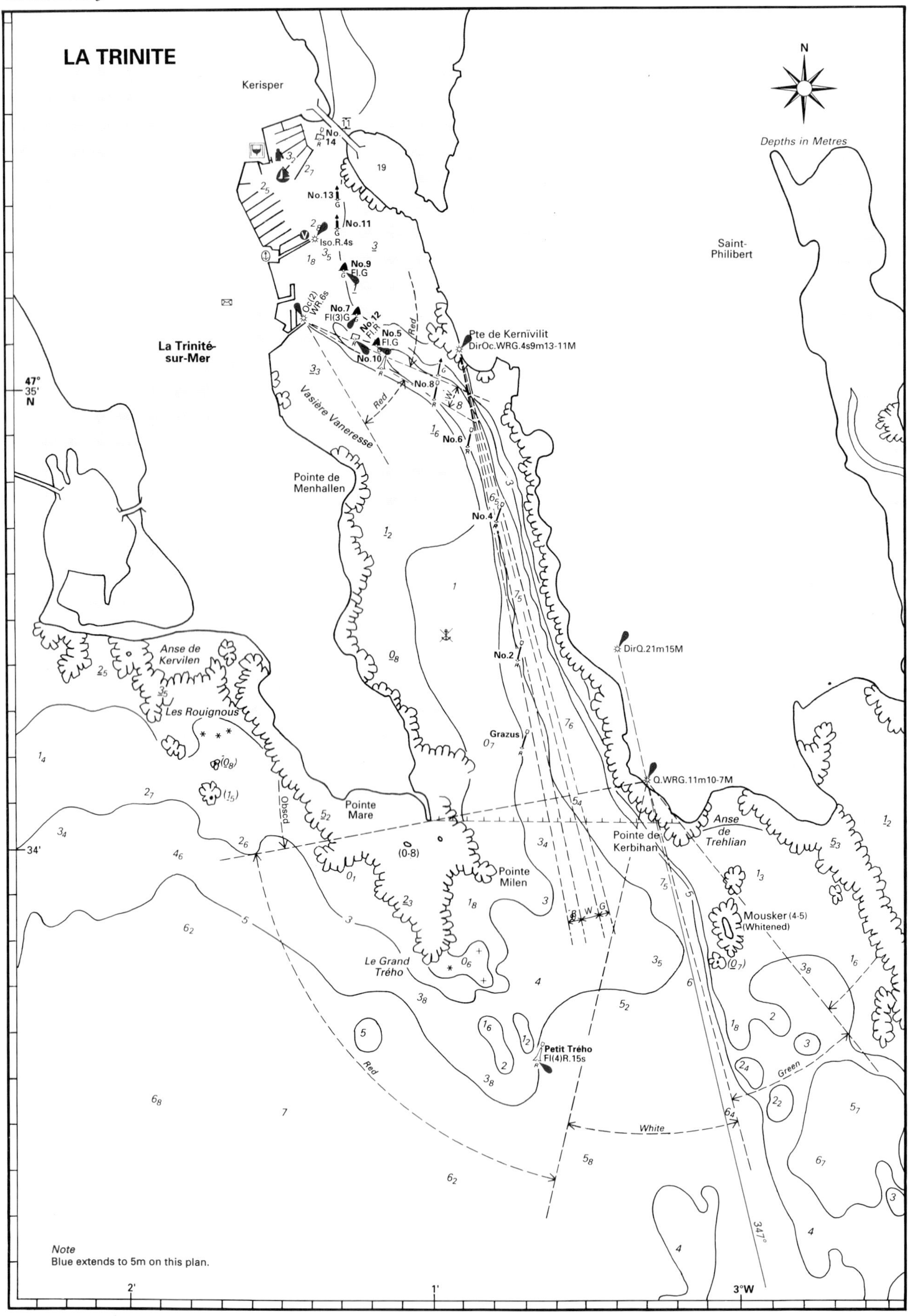
LA TRINITE
Kerisper
Depths in Metres
No.14
No.13
No.11
Iso.R.4s
No.9
Fl.G
Oc(2)WR.6s
No.7
Fl(3)G
No.12
Fl.R
No.5
Fl.G
No.10
No.8
No.6
No.4
No.2
Grazus
Pte de Kernïvilit
DirOc.WRG.4s9m13-11M
DirQ.21m15M
Q.WRG.11m10-7M
Saint-Philibert
La Trinité-sur-Mer
Vasière Vaneresse
Pointe de Menhallen
Anse de Kervilen
Les Rouignous
Pointe Mare
Pointe Milen
Pointe de Kerbihan
Anse de Trehlian
Mousker (4·5) (Whitened)
Le Grand Trého
Petit Trého
Fl(4)R.15s
Red
Obscd
White
Green
347°
47° 35' N
34'
2'
1'
3°W
Note
Blue extends to 5m on this plan.

Plan 39

entrance. La Trinité nestles behind it, but there are some villas on it. To the E the lighthouse will be seen. Some two miles S by W of the entrance lies Le Souris BRB spar buoy. From a position 500m E of Le Souris buoy, Le Petit Trého buoy (port), 1½M due N will be easy to find; this buoy marks the outer dangers on the W side of the entrance to the river.

From the S or SE leave the conspicuous island of Méaban and the Buissons de Méaban buoy (S cardinal) to starboard and make for the leading line, the two lighthouses in transit bearing 347°. Many of the dangers on the E side of the leading line are marked by beacons, but Roche Révision, with 0·2m over it, is unmarked.

The river is entered between Mousker rock (4·5m high), painted white on top, to starboard and Le Petit Trého buoy to port. Follow up the channel, which is well marked by buoys, as shown on the plan.

By night

It is not necessary for a yacht to approach with the leading lights[1,2] in transit but she should stay in the white sector of the front light. Get into the white sector of the directional light[3] by the time Petit Trého buoy comes abeam and steer up the river in this sector, which becomes very narrow. When the S pier head light[4] turns from red to white alter to port and stay in the white sector for about 500m, when the channel, marked at this stage by lit (and unlit) red and green buoys turns to starboard towards the marina head light[5].

There are unlit navigation and mooring buoys throughout the channel, as well as fishing floats.

BERTHS AND ANCHORAGE

Anchoring is prohibited between the entrance to the river and the bridge (clearance 11m). Visitors' berths at the marina are on the first or second pontoon above the breakwater. A marina launch will normally meet a visiting yacht and direct her to a berth.

FACILITIES

All the facilities of a major yachting centre and small town, including launderette, ice, fuel, crane, 25-tonne travel-lift, chandlers, shipyard, repairs of all kinds, agents for many marine equipment suppliers. Scrubbing berth, with a level concrete bottom, by the yacht club.

In the town there are banks, hotels, restaurants and all shops. Good fish market at the head of the marina. Bus to Auray and other localities.

37. Morbihan

Entrance 47°33'N 2°55'W

GENERAL

This inland sea, which receives the waters of three rivers, though it is fed mostly by the tide, has an area of about 50 square miles. Since the megalithic era the land has sunk, or the sea level has risen, by some 10m, and a partly submerged stone circle can be seen on the islet Erlannig to the south of Gavrinis island. The islands of the Morbihan are said to be equal in number to the days of the year, but in fact there are no more than 60 and this figure includes the isolated rocks. Many are wooded and all, with the exception of Ile aux Moines and Ile d'Arz, are privately owned. Most are uninhabited, and in these cases landing is not objected to. Ile Berder is a convalescent home, and it is usual for visitors wishing to penetrate inland to ask permission. Ile aux Moines, with its pine woods, restaurants, good shops and beach, is the island most visited.

Ile d'Arz has picturesque walled farms, such as Ker Noel. The Séné peninsula (known as L'Angle and lying east of Boëdig) was the home of the Sinagots, a separate community of fishermen. On Gavrinis, a guide will conduct visitors coming by launch from Larmor Baden round the celebrated carved tumulus. Sadly, landing from yachts is no longer permitted.

Vannes, 10M from the entrance has a perfectly sheltered marina, accessible on the tide, near the city centre and is an interesting town to visit. It has excellent communications, and is a good place to change crew or to leave a yacht

As a cruising ground the Morbihan is exceptionally interesting, a beautiful expanse of sheltered water, with a profusion of bird life in the less crowded parts in the east. Only near the narrow entrance off Port Navalo is it open to the sea. Navigation is not difficult as the islands are easy to identify. There is deep water in the main channels and the dangers are marked by beacons and buoys.

The tidal streams are a major factor for yachts cruising the Morbihan. Often they are fast enough for their direction to be seen from their surface appearance. Except in the vicinity of Le Grand Mouton, the streams tend to follow the directions of the channels. Sometimes they run on one side of the channel and there is a slack or reverse eddy on the other, with a clear dividing line between them. Using the eddies, those with local knowledge can make surprising progress against a foul tide. When leaving the main channel, begin to turn in good time, to avoid being swept past your destination. The best time for cruising is at neaps but even then the speed across the ground with a fair stream will be considerable.

The Morbihan becomes very crowded during the season and moorings now fill most of the traditional anchorages. Some of them still have places where a yacht can lie on her own ground tackle, but they are becoming harder to find and are likely to be in the

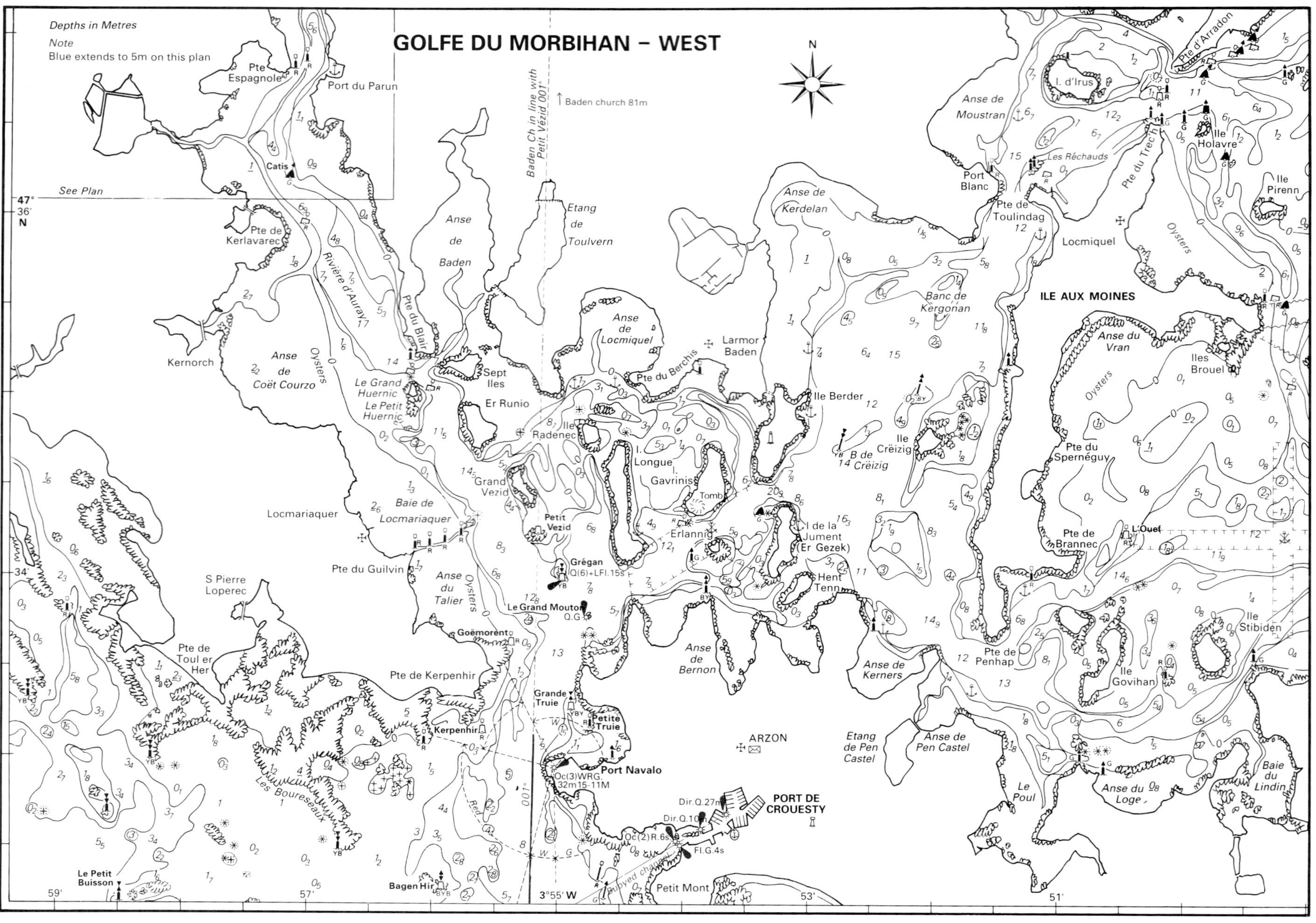
GOLFE DU MORBIHAN – WEST
Depths in Metres
Note
Blue extends to 5m on this plan
See Plan
Baden church 81m
Baden Ch in line with Petit Vézid 001°
ILE AUX MOINES
Locmiquel
Port Blanc
Pte de Toulindag
Anse de Moustran
Les Réchauds
I. d'Irus
Pte du Trec'h
Pte d'Arradon
Ile Holavre
Ile Pirenn
Oysters
Iles Brouel
Anse du Vran
Pte du Sperneguy
Pte de Brannec
L'Ouef
Ile Stibiden
Ile Govihan
Baie du Lindin
Anse du Loge
Le Poul
Pte de Penhap
Anse de Pen Castel
Etang de Pen Castel
Anse de Kerners
Ile Creizig
B de Creizig
Banc de Kergonan
Anse de Kerdelan
Ile Berder
Larmor Baden
Pte du Berchis
I de la Jument (Er Gezek)
Hent Tenn
Erlannig
I. Gavrinis
I. Longue
Tomb
ARZON
PORT DE CROUESTY
Anse de Bernon
Petit Mont
Port Navalo
Petite Truie
Grande Truie
Grégan
Le Grand Mouton
Petit Vezid
Ile Radenec
Anse de Locmiquel
Etang de Toulvern
Anse de Baden
Sept Iles
Er Runio
Grand Vezid
Pte du Blair
Le Grand Huernic
Le Petit Huernic
Baie de Locmariaquer
Anse du Talier
Goëmorent
Kerpenhir
Pte de Kerpenhir
Pte du Guilvin
Locmariaquer
Bagen Hir
Les Boureseaux
Rivière d'Auray
Port du Parun
Pte Espagnole
Catis
Pte de Kerlavarec
Anse de Coët Courzo
Kernorch
S Pierre Loperec
Pte de Toul er Her
Le Petit Buisson
Red
Buoyed channel
Dir.Q.27m
Dir.Q.10m
Fl.G.4s
Oc(2)R.6s
Oc(3)WRG 32m15-11M
Q(6)+LFl.15s
Q.G
3°55'W
47° 36' N
34'
59'
57'
53'
51'

Plan 40

The Morbihan is a miniature inland sea with a myriad islets

stream. Many *vedettes* ply their trade in summer and some of them are large, so when anchoring it is important not to obstruct the channels.

In general, only the popular places have been described here, but with the aid of the chart many other anchorages can be found.

Charts
BA *2358* (which is recommended if it is intended to explore)
Imray *C39*

TIDAL DATA
Note Tidal information for the interior of the Morbihan is given under the headings *Auray river, Vannes channel* and *Southern and eastern Morbihan.*

Times and heights

Time differences				Height differences			
HW		LW		MHWS	MHWN	MLWN	MLWS
BREST							
0000 and 1200	0600 and 1800	0000 and 1200	0600 and 1800	6·9	5·4	2·6	1·0
Port du Crouesty							
+0013	–0022	–0017	–0012	–1·6	–1·2	–0·6	–0·3
Port Navalo							
+0030	–0005	–0010	–0005	–2·0	–1·5	–0·8	–0·3

Tidal streams
Off Port Navalo the flood begins −0400 Brest, the ebb at +0100 Brest, spring rates 5kts or more. Within the entrance, off Grand Mouton rock and south of Ile Longue, Gavrinis and Ile Berder, the streams attain over 9kts at springs tides. They are also fierce in the narrows between the islands, but farther from the entrance they moderate and in the upper reaches are not strong.

Depths
The approach and entrance are deep.

LIGHTS
1. **Port Navalo** 47°32'·9N 2°55'·1W Oc(3)WRG.12s32m15-11M 155°-W-220°, 317°-G-359°-W-015°-R-105° White tower and dwelling

Port de Crouesty Ldg Lts 058°

2. *Front* 47°32'·6N 2°53'·8W DirQ.10m19M 056·5°-intens-059·5° Red panel with vert white stripe on white metal framework tower
3. *Rear* 315m from front DirQ.27m19M 056·5°-intens-059·5° White tower
4. **Crouesty N jetty head** 47°32'·5N 2°54'·2W Oc(2)R.6s9m7M White square tower, red top

Grégan and Petit Vézid beacons in the Morbihan entrance

5. **Crouesty S jetty head** 47°32'·5N 2°54'·2W Fl.G.4s9m7M Green and white square tower
6. **Le Grand Mouton beacon (starboard)** 47°33'·8N 2°54'·8W Q.G.4m3M Green tripod
7. **Grégan** 47°33'·9N 2°55'·1W Q(6)+LFl.15s3m3M Black beacon, yellow top

RADIO

Crouesty Marina VHF Ch 9 0830–2000 LT

APPROACH AND ENTRANCE

By day

The outer approach to the Morbihan presents no difficulty. Peering above the trees is Port Navalo lighthouse, on the east side of the entrance, with a second tower like a lighthouse close to it; more conspicuous from the southwest are the Petit Mont, a hill 42m high, on the peninsula 1M to the SE of it, and the white lighthouse within Crouesty marina.

Make Basses de Méaban S cardinal buoy and, leaving it to port, approach the entrance and identify the leading marks. These are the white pyramid on Petit Vézid in transit with Baden church spire 3M behind it, bearing 001°. Follow this transit through the narrows, leaving Petit Mont ¾M to starboard, Bagen Hir E cardinal tower ½M to port and Port Navalo lighthouse 200m to starboard. This transit leads close to the Pointe de Port Navalo. On the ebb there can be a strong eddy, running along the shore from the entrance towards Crouesty marina and round the point.

The flood sweeps past the Pointe de Port Navalo and swings across towards the Pointe de Kerpenhir, then back towards Grégan tower. The approach is rough on the ebb if there is an onshore wind. The entrance channel is marked on its W side by two red towers, Kerpenhir and Goëmorent, and on its E side by the Grande Truie tower (W cardinal), on the N side of Port Navalo bay.

For further directions for the Auray river see page 135, and for the Vannes channel page 139.

By night

There are no lights or lit buoys in the Morbihan with the single exception of Roguédas beacon in the Vannes Channel. If it is not quite dark it is possible to use the Port Navalo lighthouse to get into Port Navalo and wait for daylight, but it is easier to enter Crouesty marina, which has leading lights.

For Port Navalo, enter the white sector of Port Navalo light[1] on about 010° and keep on the west side of the sector. Petit Mont (42m) will be left to starboard; when the Crouesty leading lights are in transit, bear a little to port, just into the red sector. Round the lighthouse at a distance of 150m and, passing into the white sector of the light, pick up a vacant mooring clear of the pier in 1m or less. The bay is full of moorings and it is not advisable to anchor in the dark.

For Le Crouesty approach in the white sector of Port Navalo light[1]. When the Crouesty leading lights[2,3] come into transit on 058°, turn to starboard onto this transit and steer into the marina, passing between the pier head lights[4,5].

BERTHS AND ANCHORAGE

Le Crouesty

This marina is in the bay S of Port Navalo and is useful if arriving at the entrance to the Morbihan at the wrong tide. It has a large supermarket, at the head of the north basin, with a fish market outside. This is excellent for storing ship before entering to explore the Morbihan.

The entrance opens on passing Petit Mont, and it is only necessary to follow the buoyed channel, carrying 1·8m, to pass between the outer piers. Leading marks are the lighthouse and a red panel with a vertical white stripe. The marina is dredged to 2m. Visitors less than 14m long can go in beyond the travel-lift area and berth below the marina office if there is room; or they may secure with the larger visitors to the pontoons on the right-hand side 200m inside the breakwater, where yachts can expect to be rafted during the season.

FACILITIES

Fuel, launderette. Café-bars and food shops round the marina, excellent supermarket. Chandlers, engineers, crane, scrubbing berth, 45-tonne travel-lift. All repairs. Other shops, bank and PO at Arzon (½M).

Port Navalo

There is a tolerable anchorage in depths of 1·5m off the end of the pier, if space can be found among the moorings, but it is exposed to the S and W and disturbed by the wash from ferries. The shoaling bay

Le Crouesty marina

is full of moorings and it may be possible to arrange to borrow one.

FACILITIES
Land at the outer jetty, but dinghies must not be left blocking the way for passengers on the ferries. Alternatively, at tide time, land at the eastern jetty by the village. Simple shops, café-bars and restaurants. Ferries to Auray and Vannes.

The entrance to Le Crouesty

Auray River

GENERAL
This fine river on the west side of the Morbihan provides eight miles of varying scenery. The town of Auray, at the head of the navigable river, stands on a steep hill on the west side, with the old port of St Goustan on the east side. Auray is quite a large town; much of it is fifteenth century, with the steeples of the church and chapel standing on the hill. ¼M below the town a bridge, with 14m clearance, crosses the river.

The old port of St Goustan is now small, but at one time had a substantial trade. Benjamin Franklin landed here from America to negotiate a treaty with France during the War of Independence. The river runs between wooded shores, through a narrow cleft at Le Rocher, then gradually widens out between mud banks and oyster beds until near the entrance it merges into the Morbihan scene of islands and fast tidal streams.

The river is often visited by English yachts, but is relatively less popular with the local people, so that one can easily find quiet spots away from the crowds. Auray has good communications, making it a suitable place for changing crew.

Port Navalo bay is crowded with moorings

TIDAL DATA

Times and heights

	Time differences				Height differences			
	HW		LW		MHWS	MHWN	MLWN	MLWS
BREST								
	0000 and 1200	0600 and 1800	0000 and 1200	0600 and 1800	6·9	5·4	2·6	1·0
Auray								
	+0055	+0000	+0020	+0005	-2·0	-1·4	-0·8	-0·2

Tidal streams

The flood begins −0455 Brest, ebb begins +0020 Brest, spring rates 3 to 3½kts.

Depths

The river is deep as far as Le Rocher, though the last mile of the deep channel is narrow, so that it may be better to regard it as carrying 1m. Above Le Rocher it shoals rapidly and the bottom is only just below datum. The mooring areas at Auray in midstream have been dredged to 1·5–2·4m, but most of the quays dry, bottom mud.

The moorings at Le Bono are deep.

THE RIVER

In passing the Morbihan entrance (see page 134), keep nothing E of the 001° transit of Le Petit Vézid pyramid and Baden church. When the tide is up a bit one can pass fairly close to Goëmorent tower (port), but there is only 0·9m some 200m E of it and near LW the leading line must be held.

The tidal set over Le Grand Mouton at the entrance to the Vannes channel presents a real hazard at this point, whether a vessel intends to proceed up to Auray or to Vannes.

If bound for Auray, when Goëmorent is on the port quarter leave the leading line, alter to port and steer 345° for the centre of Er Runio (Ile Renaud). When Petit Vézid beacon is abeam, steer towards E Harnic (port) buoy to the right of Le Grand Huernic islet. Leave the buoy close to port and pass between N Harnic buoy (port) and a green beacon off Pte du Blair.

N of this the channel is wide, though there is a big shallow bay, the Anse de Coët-Courzo, to port. A course of 325° will take the yacht to the port-hand buoy off the Pointe de Kerlavarec and on to the Catis buoy (starboard). Here the channel is narrower and there are extensive mud flats on either hand. The yacht should be steered in a gradual

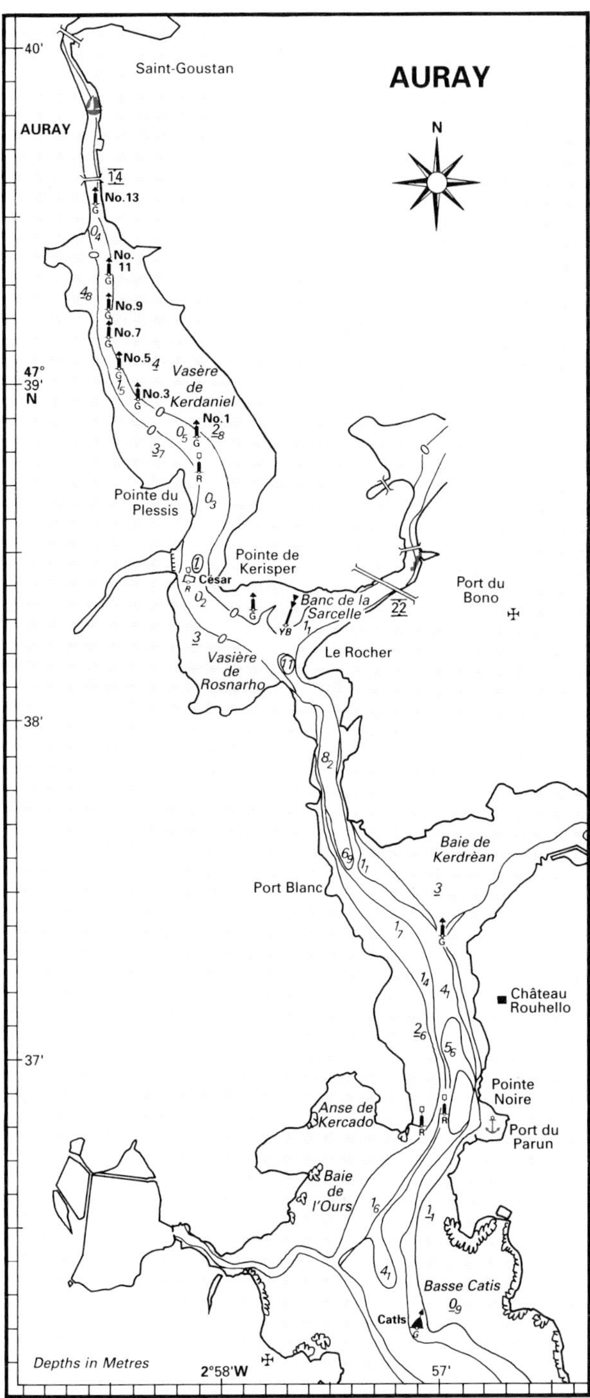

Plan 41

sweep round the mud on the starboard hand until she heads for the middle of the narrows off Pointe Espagnole. The withies on the oyster beds help to identify the channel.

Above Pointe Espagnole the deep water lies initially on the east side. Then, as the Baie de Kerdréan opens, the channel bears to port towards the narrows seen ahead. The shallow bay is left to starboard, together with the green beacon marking the edge of the mud and the channel now crosses to the other side. This is the narrowest part of the river, which becomes much prettier, passing between steep, rocky shores and thick woods to Le Rocher.

Since the river's deep part ends above Le Rocher, it can only be navigated up to Auray with sufficient rise of tide. The channel almost dries, but there is plenty of water in the pool at Auray. The channel is clearly marked, the trickiest part being where it crosses the remains of a Roman bridge ½M above Le Rocher. There is a drying shoal in midstream marked by César, a red buoy, which should be left to port. The only visible remnant of the bridge is a flat square of turf over stones on the bank to port.

ANCHORAGES

Locmariaker This village is on the west side of the river near the entrance, opposite the Vézid islands. There is a channel to it, with about 1m, marked by port-hand beacons, but it is narrow and used by the ferries. The quay dries 1·5m. Yachts can take the ground between the village quay and the *vedette* jetty or deep-keeled yachts might dry out against the outer side of the jetty. It is possible to anchor off the entrance and go in by dinghy, but this is rather exposed and subject to strong tides.

Larmor Baden This village lies 1M to the east of the Auray river, between it and the Vannes channel. It can be approached from the Auray river by passing between Grand Vézid and Er Runio (Ile Renaud), leaving Ile Radenec to starboard and keeping in the northern half of the channel to avoid a rock 200m N and a drying patch 200m NE, of Radenec. It can also be approached from the Vannes channel by passing close east of Ile Longue, or more simply between Gavrinis and Ile Berder. It is possible to anchor near Pointe de Berchis. Closer to the pier there are many moorings and anchoring appears to be forbidden. The tides run hard through the channel (flood E, ebb W), and it is best to work into one of the bays as far as draught and depths allow.

Le Rocher Once an excellent and popular anchorage, but now full of permanent moorings. If one is available, land at the small inlet downstream on the east side.

Port du Bono An inlet to starboard just north of Le Rocher. There is over 1m as far as the jetty. The basin and quays dry. There is now no room to anchor, but there are visitors' head and stern moorings, in deep water, just beyond the new bridge (clearance 22m); when arriving or departing be aware that the tide runs very hard through them. A dinghy excursion can be made to the hamlet and chapel of St Avoye; land on the port side ½M above the old bridge at Le Bono.

St Goustan The clearance of the road bridge just below the port is 14m, but the river occasionally rises above MHWS after heavy rain.

There are moorings in the middle of the river opposite the quays and for high-masted yachts there are also visitors' fore and aft moorings below the bridge. There is enough water at most tides over a considerable length. The water shoals rapidly on the

Evening in the Auray river

The basin at Le Bono dries, but there are visitors' head and stern moorings between these quays and the high road bridge where a deep draught yacht can remain float

Yachts with tall masts (over 14m) can use the visitors' buoys below the bridge at Auray

Above Le Rocher the river is shallow but Auray can be reached on the tide

turn to the old, low bridge in the town; at springs, the ebb pours violently through this bridge and eddies make the upper end of the mid-stream moorings an uneasy berth. The quay should be used only as a temporary berth at high water, and the large floating restaurant-cum-sightseeing vessel must be given plenty of room to manoeuvre and berth. There is a dinghy pontoon near the old bridge which is useful at low water to avoid the mud.

FACILITIES

Shops café-bars and restaurants at Locmariaker, Larmor Baden and Le Bono, but nothing at Le Rocher. At St Goustan, a harbour office and showers; there are simple shops and restaurants on the quay, a good fish market in the square, and all the facilities of a substantial town at Auray, including a marine engineer. Market day Monday. Good train service, though the station is some way from the town and further from St Goustan. Buses to all parts, including La Baule for the airport and Carnac for the megaliths.

Vannes channel

TIDAL DATA

Times and heights

Time differences				Height differences			
HW		LW		MHWS	MHWN	MLWN	MLWS
BREST							
0000 and 1200	0600 and 1800	0000 and 1200	0600 and 1800	6·9	5·4	2·6	1·0
Arradon (47°37'N 2°50'W)							
+0155	+0145	+0145	+0130	–3·7	–2·7	–1·6	–0·5
Vannes							
+0220	+0200	+0200	+0125	–3·6	–2·7	–1·6	–0·5

Tidal streams

Inside the Morbihan entrance the stream divides, a weaker portion running up the Auray river. Part of this sweeps back past Larmor Baden and rejoins the main Vannes channel at the south end of Ile Berder, where it causes turbulence and a back eddy close to the shore. The main torrent follows the main channel; the spring rate is about 8kts. The irregularities of the channel produce whirlpools. The way the water climbs up the Grand Mouton is remarkable.

Once through the narrows S of Ile Berder the rate decreases a little, but the stream continues in a narrow jet towards Ile Crëizig, and thence passes near the Ile aux Moines to the narrows NW of that island. Here the stream is fierce, sweeping across from the Pointe de Toulindag in a wide curve along the mainland side and south of Ile d'Irus. This sets

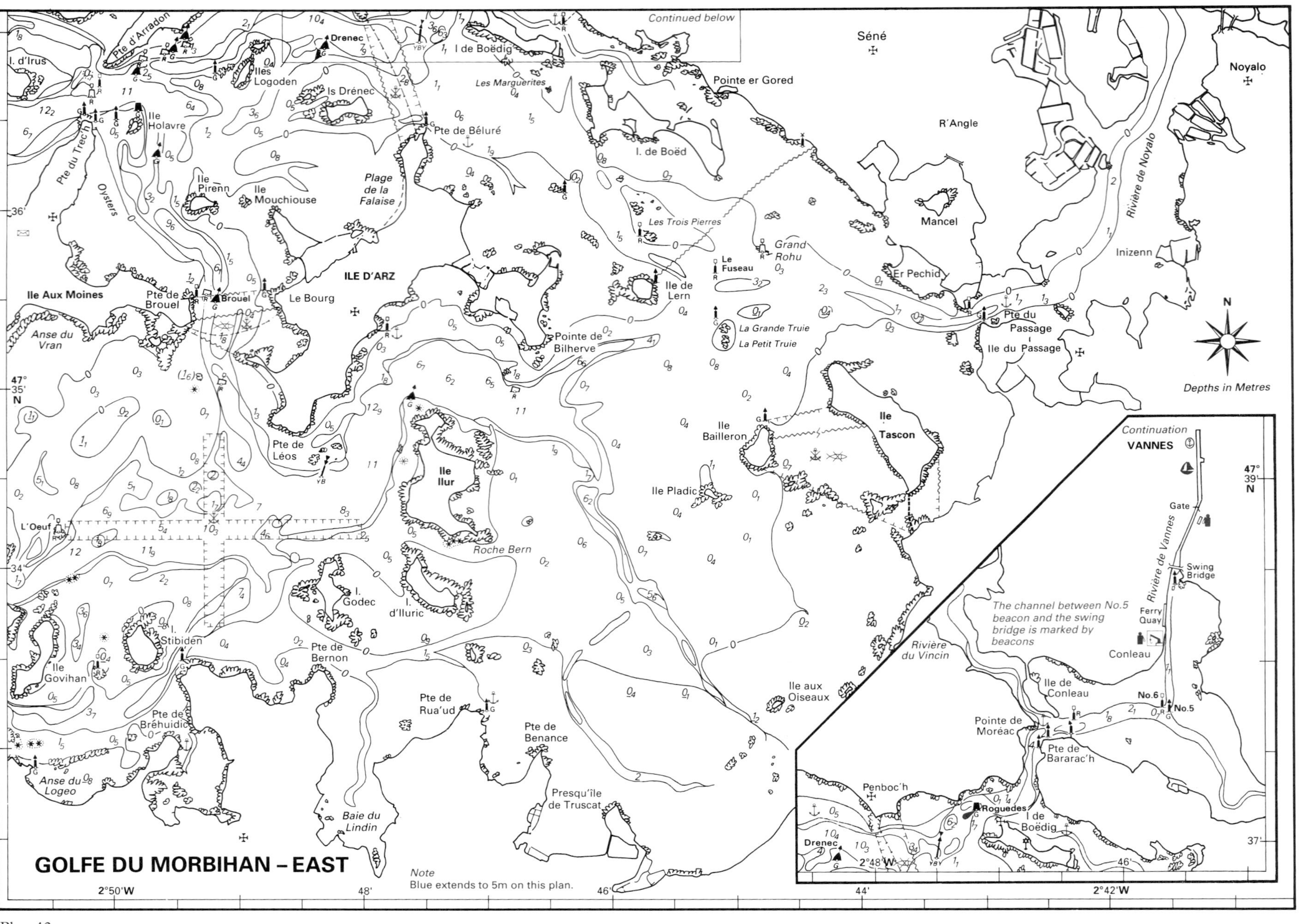

GOLFE DU MORBIHAN – EAST
Note
Blue extends to 5m on this plan.
Depths in Metres
Continued below
Continuation
VANNES
Rivière de Vannes
Gate
Swing Bridge
Ferry Quay
The channel between No.5 beacon and the swing bridge is marked by beacons
Conleau
Ile de Conleau
No.6
No.5
Pointe de Moréac
Pte de Bararac'h
Rivière du Vincin
Penboc'h
Roguedes
I de Boëdig
Drenec
Noyalo
Rivière de Noyalo
Inizenn
Séné
Pointe er Gored
R'Angle
Mancel
Er Pechid
Pte du Passage
Ile du Passage
Grand Rohu
Le Fuseau
Ile de Lern
La Grande Truie
La Petit Truie
Ile Tascon
Ile Bailleron
Ile Pladic
Ile aux Oiseaux
Les Trois Pierres
I. de Boëd
I de Boëdig
Les Marguerites
Pte de Béluré
Drenec
Is Drénec
Iles Logoden
Pte d'Arradon
I. d'Irus
Ile Holavre
Pte du Trec'h
Oysters
Ile Pirenn
Ile Mouchiouse
Plage de la Falaise
ILE D'ARZ
Le Bourg
Pointe de Bilherve
Ile Aux Moines
Pte de Brouel
Brouel
Anse du Vran
Pte de Léos
Ile Ilur
Roche Bern
I. Godec
I. d'Iluric
L'Oeuf
I. Stibiden
Pte de Bernon
Ile Govihan
Pte de Bréhuidic
Anse du Logeo
Pte de Rua'ud
Pte de Benance
Presqu'ile de Truscat
Baie du Lindin

Plan 42

up an eddy, so that NW of Ile aux Moines the current runs SW almost continuously.

After passing the narrows north of Ile aux Moines the stream fans out and becomes weaker, nowhere exceeding 4kts. The ebb stream roughly reverses the flood, but one must keep towards the S side of the narrows between Ile Berder and Ile de la Jument to avoid being swept up the channel W of Ile Berder to Larmor Baden. It is important to realise not only that high water is progressively later as one goes up the channel (1½ to 2hrs between Port Navalo and Vannes), but also that the streams do not turn until about 1½hrs after local high water or low water.

Depths

The channel is deep to Ile aux Moines; thence deep water can be carried to Ile de Boëdig, but the deep channel is very narrow in places and it is easier to regard it as carrying 2m. Thence to just downstream of Conleau it carries 3·2m, after which it shoals progressively with a shallowest depth before the bridge of 0·7m. There is thus adequate depth for vessels approaching or leaving Vannes near high water. The marina is maintained at 2·4m.

MARINA ACCESS

The lock is open by day (during the season 0800–2200 LT) from 2½hrs before to 2½hrs after local HW.

The swing bridge, 1000m to seaward of the lock, opens as follows:

- For the first and last half-hour that the lock is open – on demand
- On the even hour whilst the lock is open
- In addition, from 15 June–15 September, and at weekends – every even half-hour whilst the lock is open

There are waiting pontoons, which reportedly have 2·5m, below the bridge. During busy periods the bridge may open at other times so yachts should be prepared to move at once.

The traffic signals are as follows:

- 2 red lights – no passage
- 2 flashing red lights – prepare to move
- 2 green lights – passage permitted
- 2 green flashing lights – proceed only if already underway and passage is clear

LIGHTS

1. **Roguédas** 47°37'·2N 2°47'·2W Fl.G.2·5s4m4M Green tower

RADIO

Marina VHF Ch 9 Mon–Sat 0800–2000 LT. Sun 0800–1900 LT

Swing bridge VHF Ch 9 HW±2½

THE CHANNEL

Before entering the Morbihan for the first time it is advisable to plot the succession of compass courses up to Vannes on the chart. This will make it easier to identify the islands and the relevant gaps between them as the yacht speeds up the channel. Tick the islands off on the chart as they flash past.

After passing the entrance (see page 134), immediate steps must be taken to avoid being swept

The upper reaches of the Vannes channel, looking north. Ile de Boëdig is in the foreground

The swing bridge at Vannes

Vannes marina

by the tide onto the Grand Mouton rock, which lies to starboard and is marked by a green beacon with a green triangular topmark. Hold the Baden/Petit Vézid transit and turn sharply to starboard only when the Grand Mouton is safely abaft the beam. The channel is now clear before you. Leave Ile Longue to port, a green beacon and the islet of Erlannig to starboard, Gavrinis to port (there is a landing place here, marked by beacons), a green buoy and Ile de la Jument to starboard, and Ile Berder to port.

A wide expanse of water, some of it shallow, now opens, but it is best to keep in the jet of the tide setting towards the small Ile Creïzig. Leave the two cardinal buoys marking middle grounds to port, steering midway between the second and the N end of Ile Creïzig. After passing this, turn towards the N, keeping fairly close to (but not less than 200m off) the Ile aux Moines shore. This avoids the Kergonan shoal, which dries in places.

The stream sets strongly through the narrows between Ile aux Moines and the mainland, and Les Réchauds rocks, marked by two green beacons, are left to starboard. Thence the channel is straightforward, the critical points being well marked.

Leave Ile d'Irus to port, two green beacons on Pointe du Trec'h to starboard, a red tower and a red beacon on the rocks S of Pointe d'Arradon to port and a green buoy E of the Pointe d'Arradon to starboard. The yachting centre of Arradon, and the five buoys off it, three red and two confusingly green, are all left to port. Steer to leave the green beacon W of Iles Logoden 100m to starboard and round Le Petit Logoden, leaving it 100m to starboard and Drenec green buoy to starboard.

The channel continues in a curve to the NE, leaving Boëdig W cardinal buoy and Roguedas tower to starboard. North of Ile de Boëdig the continuation of the channel is not obvious from a distance. As one passes N of Boëdig the narrow gap opens up dramatically. When it is fully open turn sharply to port and steer through it. Coming out of this narrow passage, the yachting centre of Conleau is to port and a wide expanse of shallow water lies ahead. The channel through this is marked by beacons; at the far end it takes a very sharp turn to port. Thence the channel is very narrow, though well marked by beacons, and there is only just room to pass oncoming traffic.

A short distance past the *vedette* quay is the swing bridge. This is operated from the *capitainerie* at the Vannes wet basin. Closed-circuit television cameras show the situation on the road and in the channel. If the bridge is not open, secure to the waiting pontoon on the starboard side.

In the season, a launch is likely to meet visiting yachts and direct them to a berth, but in the absence of this, secure to the visitors' pontoons which are on either side of the marina, just before the *passerelle* bridge.

ANCHORAGES

Ile Longue There is a NE-facing bay on the SE end of this island where the water is slack when the tide is running hard in the channel. The bottom shelves rapidly, but there is room to anchor outside the moorings on soundings. There is a slipway, the end of which is marked by a white post with a red top. The island is private and landing is not allowed.

Larmor Baden see page 137.

Ile de la Jument On the east of the island between the two most easterly points, out of the tide. Go in as far as depth allows. There are no moorings here. Access from the south of Ile de la Jument is possible with the large-scale chart, passing either east or west of Hent Tenn. A good place to wait for a fair tide.

Ile Berder To the E of the island, NW of the S cardinal buoy, or farther N in the Mouillage de Kerdelan. A good anchorage with little stream, but moorings occupy the best areas.

Ile aux Moines There is a small marina on the NW corner at Locmiquel with a few pontoon berths for visitors and some visitors' moorings. It might be possible to find an anchorage here but one is likely to be in the stream as the bottom shelves gradually. There is a fine-weather anchorage exposed to the W and SW south of Pte de Toulindag but it is uncomfortable as there is a back eddy and boats lie at all angles in the stream.

Anse de Moustran This is the bay just N of Port Blanc on the opposite side of the narrows to Ile aux Moines. The best spots are occupied by moorings, so that one is pushed out into deeper water where the tide is strong. If the wind comes up against the tide the yacht sheers about.

Pen er Men N of Ile d'Irus there is room to anchor off the north shore, clear of the moorings.

Arradon A popular yachting centre. Moorings for visitors but now little room to anchor. Rather exposed in southerly weather near high water.

Ile de Boëdig There is a pleasant, secluded, sheltered anchorage off the bight at the NE end of the island. The island is private and there is no landing.

Pointe de Beluré Anchor E of the green beacon which marks the end of the ferry slip.

Conleau The inlet to the SW of the peninsula is full of moorings. The best anchorage is in the bight on the port side just before the far end of the narrows. There are usually some fishing boats here.

FACILITIES

There are no facilities at all at Iles de la Jument, Berder and Boëdic. Facilities are limited at Arradon. At Port Blanc (Anse de Moustran) fuel and water are available, with a *capitainerie* and tourist bureau. At Pen er Men there is a café-bar. On Ile de Conleau there is a good restaurant. At Ile aux Moines there are all the usual village shops and hotels and restaurants near the quay.

Vannes is an attractive cathedral city of historic interest with banks, hotels, restaurants and all the facilities of a large town. Market day is Tuesday. Yacht yard with fuel berth outside the gates and chandlers in the town. Vannes is a main rail centre and communications by rail and bus (including a direct bus to Roscoff) are good, making it a suitable place for a change of crew. Buses from Conleau and Vannes marina pass the railway station. There is an airfield north of the city and a regular ferry service from below the swing bridge to Conleau, Ile aux Moines, Port Navalo, Auray and other points in the Morbihan.

There are plans to excavate a new, large marina below the swing bridge and this work may be undertaken during the lifetime of this edition. Whilst this will be convenient for local boats, it will be a long way from the centre of Vannes and it is to be hoped that visitors will still be able to use the existing marina.

Southern and eastern Morbihan

GENERAL

An interesting alternative after passing between Iles Berder and Ile de la Jument is to proceed south of Ile aux Moines. Beyond the narrows the channels, though well marked, wind between mud flats and are probably best taken by a stranger on a rising tide. The tidal streams are not so fierce as in other parts of the Morbihan. Between Ile aux Moines and Ile d'Arz the flood runs to the S. If bound for Le Passage it is also possible, on a rising tide, to take the passage SW of Ile de Boëdig and Ile de Boëd.

Although still crowded, the south shore of the Morbihan is less visited by yachts and is more peaceful. A yacht is more likely to find space to anchor here than en route to Vannes or Auray.

TIDAL DATA

Times and heights

	Time differences			Height differences			
	HW		LW	MHWS	MHWN	MLWN	MLWS
BREST							
	0000 0600 and and 1200 1800		0000 0600 and and 1200 1800	6·9	5·4	2·6	1·0
Le Logeo (47°33'N 2°51'W)							
	+0155 +0140		+0145 +0125	–3·7	–2·7	–1·6	–0·5

ANCHORAGES

Anse de Kerners Anchor outside the local boats. Water, showers and provisions in season from the campsite.

Anse de Pen Castel Anchor outside the moorings. No facilities.

Anse de Penhap This is a peaceful spot in the S of the Ile aux Moines, much the nicest place in the area. There is plenty of space to anchor. Get in as far as draught and soundings will allow to be out of the stream.

Between Ile aux Moines and Ile d'Arz Those requiring solitude may find it SW of Ile Pirenn. Shallow-draught vessels must keep clear of the oyster beds. Land at the Pointe de Brouel. All shops on Ile aux Moines in Locmiquel, 1M walk.

Ile d'Arz There is an anchorage in the bay on the east side. Beware of going too far in as the depths shoal quickly – there is room to anchor outside the moorings. Land at the jetty/slipway, marked by a red beacon. It is five minutes walk to the pretty village of Le Bourg where there are modest shops, café-bars, post office.

Ile du Passage This is the most easterly anchorage where one can lie afloat. However, the depths in the channel appear to alter from year to year, and a vessel drawing 2m should proceed with caution.

Whether approaching from the W, S of Pointe de Bilhervé, or from the NW, N of Ile de Lern it is easy to lose one's bearings in the large expanse of water and islets E of Le Passage. Grand Rohu red beacon tower (47°35'·8N 2°44'·8W) is conspicuous in the area and once this has been located all becomes clear.

Approaching Le Passage anchorage do not pass too close to the red beacon on the northern shore. This lies beyond the point and marks the end of a slipway and not the southern extremity of the point.

Anchor midstream in the narrows to the N of the island if space can be found among the moorings. Alternatively, in settled weather anchor E of the narrows; the tide is strong. Quiet and rural, Le Passage has no supplies.

38. Pénerf

47°30'N 2°39'W

GENERAL

This quiet and unspoilt river, 6M west of the entrance to La Vilaine, is sheltered from the Atlantic swell by groups of rocks and the peninsula on which Pénerf is situated. The village is small, combining oyster culture with being a minor holiday centre. A good number of yachts and fishing boats are moored off the village of Pénerf, with others off Cadenic, on the other side of the river ½M further up. There are many rocky ledges near the entrance. They are well marked with beacons, but the channels are very

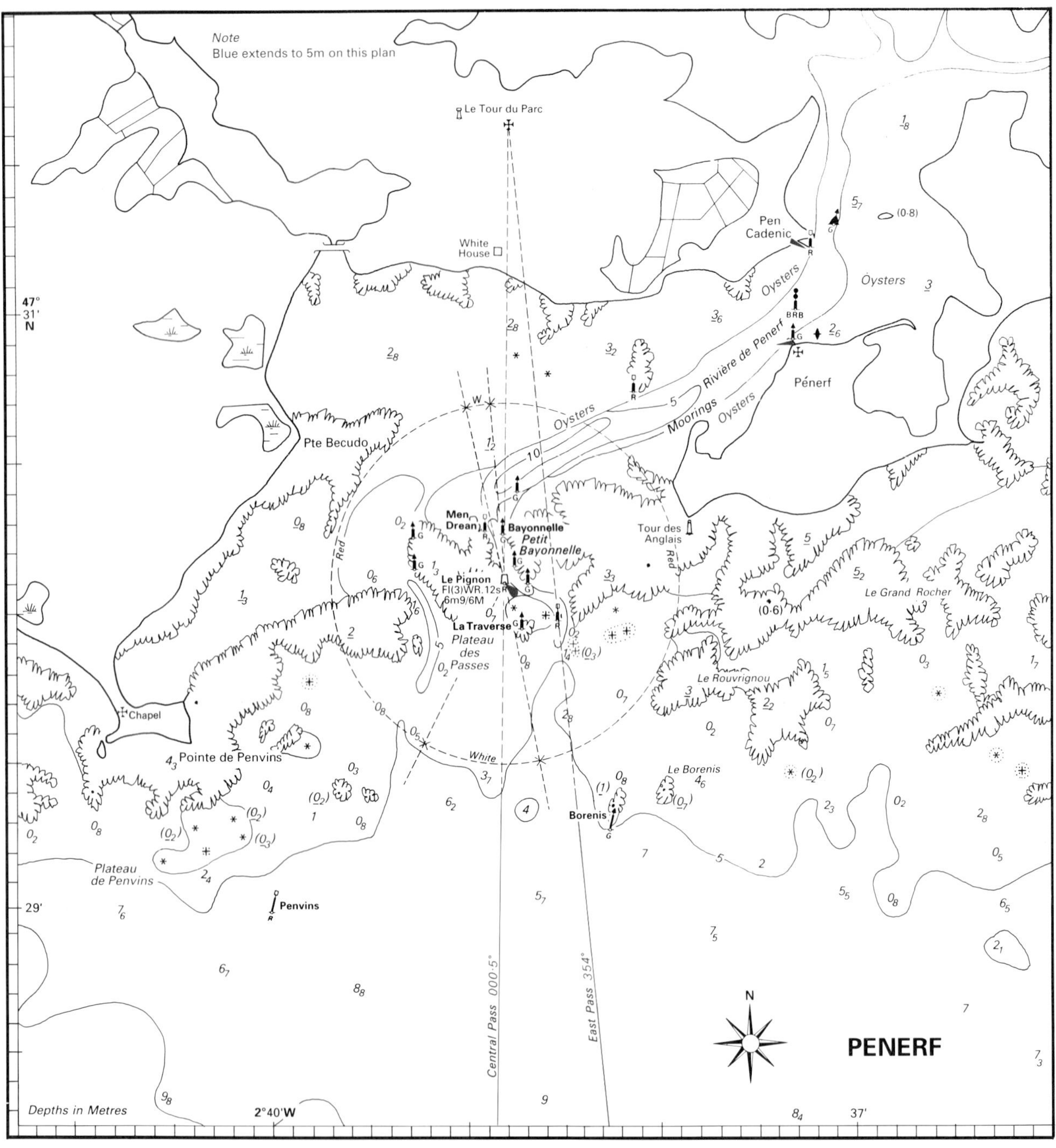

Plan 43

narrow; it is not safe for the stranger in bad weather or poor visibility.

Loss of trees during the storm of October 1987 made the main leading mark, the spire of Le Tour du Parc, visible once more. It was for some years obscured from view. In 1998 the top of the spire was visible, but the trees were growing again and it is likely to become obscured soon.

A first visit should be made in settled weather and above half tide.

Charts

BA *2353*
Imray *C39*

TIDAL DATA

Times and heights

Time differences				Height differences			
HW		LW		MHWS	MHWN	MLWN	MLWS
BREST							
0000 and 1200	0600 and 1800	0000 and 1200	0600 and 1800	6·9	5·4	2·6	1·0
Pénerf							
+0020	–0025	–0015	–0015	–1·5	–1·1	–0·6	–0·3

Tidal streams

Along the coast to the west of the river mouth the flood has a spring rate of 1kt, the ebb 1½kts. In the passes the streams run 3kts springs when the rocks are uncovered, but only 2kts when the rocks are covered.

Depths

In the central pass 0·5m, in the east pass 4·5m. Inside, the river is deep as far as Cadenic.

LIGHTS

1. **Le Pignon** 47°30'·1N 2°38'·9W
   Fl(3)WR.12s6m9/6M
   028·5°-R-167°-W-175°-R-349·5°-W-028·5°
   Red square on tower

APPROACH AND ENTRANCE

By day

The chart shows the off-lying dangers which are buoyed and thus easily avoided. Beware of heavy fishing netting in the approach.

Make an initial position of about 47°29'N 2°39'W where the Tour des Anglais, which resembles a white chess castle is roughly in transit with Pénerf church bell-tower, bearing about 030°. Before entering, identify:

1. Le Pignon red beacon tower
2. a conspicuous water tower to the north and thus a prominent white house with a single gable, on the shore to the right of the water tower,
3. the steeple of Le Tour du Parc church, if it is visible above the trees, to the right of the white house.

There are three passes into Pénerf. Although the W pass is preferred by the local fishermen in strong westerly winds, it is not well enough marked for strangers. The central pass is the easiest, but is not deep enough to be used at low water. The E pass is less easy to follow but is deep.

Pénerf, looking east over Le Pignon red beacon tower (foreground)

Le Pignon beacon at the entrance to Pénerf

It must be appreciated that although the plan shows a profusion of rocks and reefs, above half tide all that will be seen between Pointe Penvins and Tour des Anglais will be an expanse of water with the conspicuous red tower of Le Pignon near the centre. The remaining beacons are thin and inconspicuous from a distance.

Central pass

If the steeple is visible, bring it in line with Le Pignon tower bearing 000°. Should the spire become obscured, Le Pignon in transit with the white house bearing 359° will serve.

These transits will leave Borenis spar buoy 800m to starboard and La Traverse beacon 150m to starboard, with a port-hand beacon for the east pass beyond it.

On close approach to Le Pignon tower, bear to starboard and leave the tower 40m to port. Thence steer to leave the Bayonelle beacon, replacing the Grand Bayonelle tower (destroyed), 20m to starboard; this course leaves two beacons on the S end of Le Petit Bayonelle rocks to starboard, and Men Drean beacon to port.

After passing between the Bayonelle beacon and Men Drean beacon, hold the same course for nearly 200m, until another starboard-hand beacon has come into transit with Pénerf village. Then alter course to steer ENE for the boats on moorings off the village over one mile away. Leave the beacon 100m to starboard, and a red beacon halfway to the village about 200m to port, as it is well up on the mud.

East pass

This pass is narrow and there are rocky shoals close E of it which must be avoided. Before finally committing the yacht to the pass, the following marks should be positively identified:

1. The port-hand beacon lying to the E of La Traverse.
2. The Men Drean beacon (port) beyond Le Pignon tower.
3. The starboard beacon, Bayonelle, E of Men Drean.
4. The two starboard beacons E of Le Pignon.

Approach on 030° with Pénerf church tower just open to the left of the Tour des Anglais. When the Tour du Parc steeple and the port-hand beacon marking La Traverse come into line bearing 354°, turn onto this transit to enter the pass. If La Traverse port-hand beacon has not been identified by the time Borenis spar buoy (starboard) is abeam, about 600m distant, do not attempt the pass.

The transit leaves a rock with 1·4m over it very close to starboard. When within 100m of La Traverse port-hand beacon, alter course to leave it 20m to port. After passing it, continue to steer about 355° for another 100m until a course of 300° will lead between Le Pignon tower and the southernmost of the two green beacons on Le Petit Bayonelle, to the E of Le Pignon. Steer this course and alter as necessary to leave the two green beacons 30m to starboard and Le Pignon to port. Thence, passing between Bayonelle beacon and Men Drean beacon, follow the directions given above for the central pass.

When leaving by the E pass, it is important to bring La Traverse beacon (port) in transit with Le Tour du Parc steeple quickly in order to avoid the eastern rocks.

By night

Although Le Pignon[1] is lit, strangers should not attempt a night entry.

ANCHORAGE

The most convenient anchorage is off Pénerf slip, the end of which is marked by a green beacon (starboard), but moorings now extend downriver for several hundred metres below the slip as well as above it. Two of these moorings, just to the S of the lifeboat, are marked *'visiteurs'* but in 1998 were occupied by local boats. About 200m upstream is an isolated danger beacon, which should be left to port. N of this the channel tends to the W bank, where there is a slip, the end marked by a red beacon, with moorings in 3·5m, mostly occupied by the fishing boats of Cadenic. A green buoy on the other side of the channel marks the edge of the extensive mud flats and oyster beds on the east side of the river. A quiet overnight anchorage may be found upstream of the Cadenic moorings, but there is not much room and the holding has been reported as poor.

FACILITIES

Shops, café and restaurant at Pénerf. Gas. Café but no shops at Cadenic, but a travelling shop calls daily in the summer; orders for it could, no doubt, be left at the café. Excellent oysters and other seafood can be bought from the fishermen on the quays.

There is a very beautiful little chapel at Pénerf, with two traditional hanging Breton model boats.

39. La Vilaine

47°30'N 2°31'W

GENERAL

On a summer's day few places are prettier than La Vilaine, meandering through meadows where cows graze, or between rush-covered banks or rocky cliffs.

There is a dam at Arzal, with a large lock. This is not a tidal power scheme like that on the Rance in north Brittany, with its rapid changes of level. The intention rather has been to improve the river for drainage and navigation. Little commercial traffic uses La Vilaine at present, which is now principally a yachting centre and holiday area. There are marinas at Arzal and the town of La Roche Bernard, which is as far inland as most yachts venture, has extensive pontoons for visitors as well as moorings in the stream.

The river is navigable by seagoing yachts for 48km inland, as far as the town of Redon. The journey passes through beautiful and peaceful countryside. There are several possible stops and a yacht could be left in safety either at Le Foleaux, or in Redon itself. There, the river connects with the Breton canal system by which shallow-draught vessels can travel between the Bay of Biscay and St Malo.

Charts

BA *2353*
Imray *C39*
There is no chart cover above the Arzal dam, but navigation presents no difficulties as far as Redon.

TIDAL DATA

Times and heights

Time differences				Height differences			
HW		LW		MHWS	MHWN	MLWN	MLWS
BREST							
0000 and 1200	0600 and 1800	0000 and 1200	0600 and 1800	6·9	5·4	2·6	1·0
Tréhiguier							
+0035	–0020	–0005	–0010	–1·4	–1·0	–0·5	–0·3

Tidal streams

In the approach the streams are weak. In the river, below the dam the flood runs at up to 2kts and the ebb to 3kts or more depending on the amount of rain. Above the dam the stream is almost invariably to seaward, the rate varying with the amount of recent inland rain – it is not normally strong.

Depths

The construction of the Arzal Dam has caused silting in the estuary and the line of the buoyed channel is subject to alteration. There is at least 0·8m on the bar and 1m in the channel to Arzal. Above the dam a figure of 1·3m is quoted, but the datum to which this is referenced is not known. There is certainly much more water than this and the channel is definitely well over 3m to La Roche Bernard. From there to Redon it is reported to have 3·5m – this is not confirmed, but certainly deep draught yachts and occasional coasters make the passage.

LIGHTS

1. **Basse de Kervoyal** 47°30'·4N 2°32'·6W DirQ.WR.8/5M 269°-W-271°-R-269° S card beacon tower
2. **Basse Bertrand** 47°31'·1N 2°30'·7W Iso.WG.4s6m9/6M 040°-W-054°-G-227°-W-234°-G-040° Green tower
3. **Penlan** 47°31'·0N 2°30'·2W Oc(2)WRG.6s26m15-11M 292·5°-R-025°-G-052°-W-060°-R-138°-G-180° White tower, red bands
4. **Pointe du Scal** 47°29'·7N 2°26'·8W Q.G.8m4M White square tower, green top

RADIO

Arzal lock VHF Ch 18 (irregular hours)

Arzal-Camoël marina VHF Ch 9 0830–1230 and 1400–2000 LT

Note: To obtain the lock opening times small craft should call the marina not the lock.

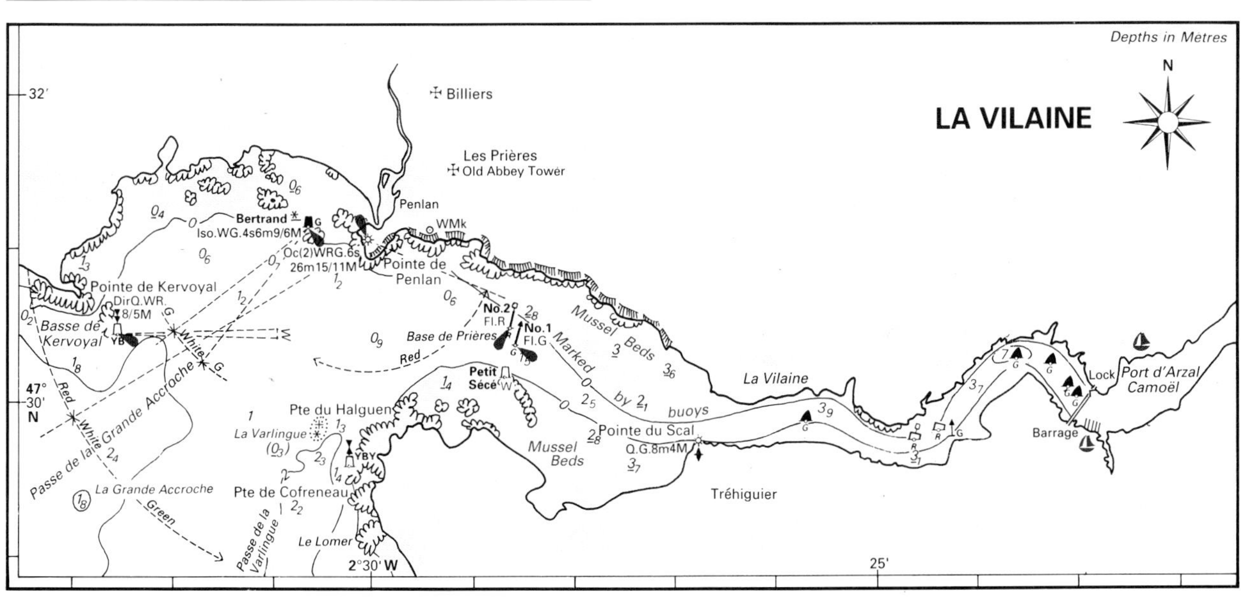

Plan 44

The landing pontoon and moorings at Tréhiguier near the entrance to La Vilaine

APPROACH

In the approach to La Vilaine the depths on the outer bar are not less than 0·8m, except for La Varlingue, a rock drying 0·3m, situated only ½M off Pointe du Halguen, which marks the SE side of the entrance. In good weather, with a sufficient rise of tide, it is only necessary to steer a midchannel course. When there is much sea or swell, conditions are rough on the bar, especially on the ebb, and at these times it is better to enter or leave on the flood.

Directions for the recommended passes across the bar are given below, for use when the conditions call for them. The landmarks shown on the charts and described in earlier editions of the pilot are virtually impossible to see from a yacht due to the growth of trees. For the Passe de la Grande Accroche and for the SW approach one must employ the Pointe de Penlan lighthouse. The Passe de la Varlingue should only be attempted if the tide is sufficiently high to enable La Varlingue to be ignored, or if the leading marks can be positively identified.

The western pass, Passe de la Grande Accroche, carries 1·2m least water to the bar and is lit, but the sea breaks heavily in it in strong onshore winds. Passe de la Varlingue, the E one, carries 1·3m and is not lit, but is preferable in heavy W or SW weather, as the shallow part is inshore and gets some protection from the Grande Accroche bank to seaward.

By day

Passe de la Grande Accroche

Make Les Mâts S cardinal buoy and, leaving it 300m to port, steer on 058° for Pointe de Penlan lighthouse. Leave Basse de Kervoyal tower about 600m to port and La Grande Accroche shoal about 300m to starboard. When the Pte de Kervoyal tower bears 270° alter to 090° into the estuary to pick up the port and starboard buoys that mark the channel.

The SW approach

Pass Ile Dumet on either hand and steer for Pointe de Penlan lighthouse, keeping it on a bearing of between 025° and 040°. Billiers church tower will be open to the left of the lighthouse. This will leave La Varlingue to starboard and La Grande Accroche shoal to port. When Pointe de Kervoyal tower bears 270° alter to 090° into the estuary to pick up the port and starboard buoys that mark the channel.

Passe de la Varlingue

This pass carries 1·3m to the bar and leads through a narrow channel between a W cardinal tower off Pointe de Cofrenau and La Varlingue, which is unmarked; unless the tide is well up the transit must be closely held. The leading marks are the tower of the old abbey at Les Prières in transit with a white wall beacon (in front) and Avalec Mill (1½M behind), bearing 023°; the wall beacon is not easy to locate. Follow this transit until the white Petit Sécé tower bears 105°, then steer to make good 090° into the estuary to pick up the port and starboard buoys that mark the channel.

ENTRANCE

When steering 090° for the outer pair of port and starboard channel buoys N of the white Petit Sécé tower, there may be as little as 0·8m of water. Follow the narrow channel defined by port and starboard buoys, but beware that silting has occurred and the mud has built out between the buoys in places. Take the curves wide. In particular, in 1998 it was necessary to give No. 6 buoy a wide berth and not to go directly from it to No. 8. Mussel beds occupy the mud flats on either side of the channel.

After Tréhiguier there are fewer marks, but the channel is still easy to follow with red and green buoys and the occasional beacon. The approach to the lock is marked with starboard-hand buoys.

The Arzal dam from seaward

The lock gets crowded and plenty of fenders are needed

By night

A night entry should only be attempted by a stranger when weather and tide conditions are very favourable. Approach in the white sector of Penlan light[3], bearing between 052° and 060°. The sectors of Basse Bertrand light[2] can be disregarded. When Basse de Kervoyal light[1] turns from red to white, steer 090° in the narrow white sector to pass between the first pair of red/green channel buoys and follow the channel buoys to Tréhiguier, beyond which the channel is not lit.

THE LOCK

The lock is on the N side of the river, adjacent to the conspicuous control tower. The lower gates are normally left open so that yachts arriving from sea can enter to await locking. If they are not, there are some mooring buoys below the dam and there is room to anchor. The danger area above the dam spillway is marked off by yellow buoys.

The lock is worked in daylight hours between 0700 and 2200, during the season. The lockings are on the hour, but not every hour. In the morning there is almost invariably one at 0800, and usually others at 0900 and 1000. In the afternoon and

La Roche Bernard

The marina is peaceful and well sheltered

evening there are usually lockings at 1500, 1700, 1800, 2000 and 2100. A forecast of times is available at most of the marinas between Port Haliguen and Pornic, or can be obtained by telephone (☎ 02 97 45 01 15).

The sill level is 2m below datum, but there is only 1m just outside, preventing use close to LW; the level above the lock is maintained at 4·5m above datum (3·5m during floods). At HWS there may therefore be a small drop on passing through the lock into the river. The road bridge above the lock is raised as necessary to allow masted vessels to pass.

Securing in the lock can be awkward as there is sometimes substantial turbulence. If alongside the wall, rather than rafted to a boat, pass bow and stern warps round the chains hanging down the walls and tend them and your fenders as the level rises or falls. Do not be in a hurry to unmoor as there will be further turbulence when the gates open and salt and fresh water mix. The lock becomes very crowded in the summer and plenty of fenders are needed on both sides.

THE RIVER

Above the dam a midchannel course should be followed. Be careful not to cut corners; rather tend to keep to the outside. A few special dangers are marked on the lateral system.

The river, which has great charm, runs through hills for some distance above La Roche Bernard; further up, the hills give way to meadows and woods. Masted vessels can go all the way up to Redon, which is a town of some character. There is a swing bridge at Cran, 30km above the dam, which operates from 0630–1200 and from 1300–1930. Sound three blasts on your horn on approach or telephone in advance (☎ 99 90 21 93). A power cable with 23m headroom crosses the river downstream of the Cran bridge, halfway between the bridge and Foleux.

ANCHORAGE AND MOORING

There are many places in the river where anchoring is possible. Below the dam find a spot on the edge of the channel and sound the area carefully before anchoring, as in places the depths shoal rapidly when the channel is left. Two anchors may be necessary.

Above the dam one can anchor almost anywhere, but be alert for signs marking where underwater cables cross the river, and take care to leave the fairway clear.

Tréhiguier A convenient anchorage near the entrance; it is exposed to W and NW winds. Anchor outside the moorings in soft mud. Land at the slip; restaurant.

Arzal There is a large marina (Arzal) on the north bank above the dam and a smaller and quieter one (Camoël) on the south side.

La Roche Bernard is 7km above the dam. There are many moorings in the river; space can be found to anchor. Port du Rhodoir marina is in the Vieux Port, the small inlet below the town, but it is mainly used by local boats. There is a larger marina, Port Neuf in the river below the bridge, with a visitors' pontoon running along the bank downstream of the finger pontoons.

Foleux lies some 7km above Roche Bernard, in peaceful surroundings by the old ferry slips, there are moorings and pontoons on both sides of the river.

Redon is 42 km above the dam. A marina has been built in the old dock, surrounded by picturesque warehouses.

FACILITIES

Tréhiguier has very limited shops and a restaurant.

Arzal-Camoël All the facilities of a major marina complex. The south side is very much more peaceful than the north, but has no facilities other than showers and toilets. Fuel, all repairs, 15-tonne crane, masting, haul out, laying up outside or under cover. There are café-bars and restaurants, but no shops closer than 2M. The dam has a fish pass which is worth seeing.

La Roche Bernard is a sizeable town with facilities to match. All shops, banks and post office. There is a boatyard and repairs can be carried out. 8-tonne crane, masting. Port Neuf is administered from the camp site office. Bread can be delivered to yachts each morning. There are excellent restaurants in the town and an interesting museum.

Foleux has very limited facilities with toilets and showers. A small crane for masting and a café-bar.

Redon is a regional centre and there are the resources of a city. Fuel, crane for masting, chandlery. Major rail centre with good communications.

The basin at Redon where the Breton canals join La Vilaine

40. The Breton canals

GENERAL

The canals offer a convenient route for shallow-draught yachts which do not relish the long haul round the western end of France, where the seas can be rough. Any yacht which can safely reach the Channel Islands can get from there to St Malo and thence have a most pleasant rural passage to the interesting and relatively sheltered waters of the Baie de Quiberon.

The passage is especially attractive to motor yachts, but there are cranes at each end which the crew can use to lay the mast of a sailing yacht on deck; they should be sufficiently experienced to do this without calling on outside help.

The normal, and quickest, route is from St Malo to Rennes by the Canal d'Ile et Rance, from Rennes to Redon by La Vilaine Canalisé and thence to the sea via the lower reaches of the Vilaine, about 130M with 62 locks. The locks are worked from 0800 to 1930, with a short lunch break. There are speed limits of 6km/h (3·2kts) in the canal north of Rennes, and 10km/h (5·4kts) in the river between Rennes and Redon. By keeping going reasonably hard the passage can be made in five days. It is also possible to turn aside at Redon and go up to Josselin, carrying on from there over the hill to Lorient. For Nantes, leave the Vilaine at Bellions lock, below Redon; the canal direct from Redon is now closed.

PRACTICAL INFORMATION

Dimensions

Limits on size dictate that beam must not exceed 4·5m and headroom above the waterline 2·5m. Permissible draught varies, but will never be more than 1·2m, and 1·1m is the more usual official limit. If rainfall has been low, 0·9m draught may be the maximum. The draught limit between Redon and both Lorient and Nantes is 0·8m.

Charges

At present no permit is required, nor is any charge made for a single return journey.

Closures (chomages)

The French Government Tourist Office (FGTO), 178 Piccadilly, London, W1V 0AL ☎ 0906 824 4123, should be applied to for a list of dates on when sections of the canals are closed for maintenance.

Guides

The Cruising Association publish an excellent introduction to the French Inland waterways which is worth consulting when planning the passage. It is desirable before setting out to obtain an up-to-date copy of the *Carte Guide: Navigation Fluviale de Voies Navigables de Bretagne*, produced by Grafocarte. This has strip maps of the canals with directions in French, English and German and, if not available locally, can be obtained from Imray, Laurie, Norie & Wilson Ltd.

Locks
The lock-keepers are careful when letting in the water, and with ordinary care no damage is to be expected. A plank slung across fenders, with an apron to protect the ship's side, should suffice during the passage. Motor tyres are no longer allowed in French canals, as they have a tendency to break off, sink and jam the lock gates.

There are strong currents as a lock fills, and the yacht must be securely moored and the lines tended as the water rises; moor near the lower gates if possible.

It may help to fit blocks at bow and stern so that the mooring lines can be led to the cockpit and tended by one person, who could use the sheet winches in a sailing yacht. Officially the lock-keepers are not required to help with mooring lines and a crew member should be put ashore before entering the lock to handle the lines; help with the gates is appreciated and will speed the passage. S of Rennes the locks are larger and it is less easy to get ashore; here the lock-keepers will usually help willingly with the shore lines.

Masting
There are cranes for masting at Dinan and Redon, the limits which can be reached by masted vessels; there are cranes at St Malo, La Roche Bernard and Arzal-Camoël but these deprive one of some pleasant sailing. There are also cranes at Nantes and Lorient for those using these variants.

THE ROUTE

St Malo–Dinan Accessible to masted vessels. The lock at Le Chatelier is only available for about 4 hours during the high water period in the Rance. Information on the times of operation of the Barrage and Le Chatelier locks may be obtained in St Malo. The upper reaches are shallow out of the channel, but this is clearly marked.

Dinan–Rennes Ile et Rance canal. A straightforward canal section, with 47 locks, of which 11 in quick succession (L'Escalier) climb to the top. Yachts of draught near the maximum will have trouble with soft mud in places. This mud is carried in by watercourses joining the canal. If you begin to drag, try to see which side the flow has come in; the best water will be near the opposite bank. Having found it, open up the engine and force a way through; the bad patches are not very long. The engine water-cooling intake should be inspected regularly, as it may become blocked with weed or grass cuttings from the towpath.

Rennes–Redon Canalised portion of the river Vilaine. There are 12 locks. The river is wider here; the best water is usually about one third of the way from the towpath bank (left bank to Pont Réan, right bank thereafter). There is a channel of the requisite depth all the way, but it is easy to get out of it and go aground. In some places the distance of the channel from the bank is indicated by notices on the towpath, with an arrowhead and a figure indicating the distance in metres.

However, there are other shallows, and the echo sounder should be used between Boel and Malon. Do not trust the advice of fishermen; they have seen shallow-draught vessels travelling in parts of the river outside the proper channel and imagine that all boats can take the same course. Beware of the fisherman, who can sometimes leave four rods and lines poking out through the reeds while he lunches elsewhere, expecting yachtsmen to avoid them. It is a courtesy to slow down when passing fishermen. The river is closed to navigation in times of flood.

Entering Redon, you will come to a stop-gate for flood control. Check the signs to see that it is open before passing through. The locks on either side directly below the stop-gate are no longer in use. After passing the stop-gate, turn sharp right at the junction if you want to enter the dock, or go straight on and turn left for the sea.

FACILITIES

Nearly all the villages on the route have a café-restaurant which can supply a very adequate meal at a reasonable price; one is off the tourist route and does not have to pay tourist prices. They also have food shops. Beware, however, as some shops will close for a month in the summer and a whole village has been known to be closed for August. A number of the lock-keepers sell farm and garden produce. Water can be had at many places along the route.

The main road runs alongside the canal in Rennes and there is traffic noise all night, but it is well worth making a stop for supplies and fuel by day. Excellent hypermarket and banks in a shopping precinct on the right bank close to the yacht berths, and a garage from which fuel may be obtained on the left bank after passing through the lock into the Vilaine.

41. Piriac-sur-Mer

47°23'N 2°33'W

GENERAL

Piriac is a fishing and holiday village on the west side of Quiberon bay. The drying harbour is used by local fishing boats which lie on head and stern buoys – a yacht which can take the ground may find space here and the bottom is flat.

A new wet basin for yachts, maximum length 12m, has been constructed, accessible over a sill which has a lifting gate which is raised to maintain the water depth in the marina as the tide ebbs.

The village is attractive, with narrow streets and fishermen's cottages, many now converted to holiday homes. There are adequate facilities, but Piriac becomes crowded with holidaymakers in summer.

Charts

BA *2353*
Imray *C39*

TIDAL DATA

Times and heights

	Time differences				Height differences			
	HW		LW		MHWS	MHWN	MLWN	MLWS
BREST	0000 and 1200	0600 and 1800	0000 and 1200	0600 and 1800	6·9	5·4	2·6	1·0
Piriac	+0017	–0032	–0017	–0015	–1·5	–1·1	–0·6	–0·3

Tidal streams

In the offing the ebb runs SW and the flood NE, spring rates 0·7kt.

Depths

In the approach there is an unmarked 0·3m patch 500m NW of the Grand Norven beacon and another reef, also unmarked, with 0·6m over it, 600m W of Le Rhotrès beacon tower. The channel to the harbour shoals from 2·6m NE of Grand Norven to dries 0·7m, directly in front of the wet basin sill. The inner harbour dries from 1 to 1·5m.

The lifting gate to the wet basin operates automatically, controlled by the water level. When it is in the shut (raised) position there is no access. It opens (lowers) to sill level when there is 1·4m of water over the sill, which dries about 1·0m; that is the gate opens when there is about 2·4m of tide. It remains open until the same level is reached with the tide falling. The depth inside the wet basin is 2·4m.

LIGHTS

1. **Inner Mole Head** 47°23'·0N 2°32'·6W
   Oc(2)WRG.6s8m10-7M
   066°-R-148°-G-194°-W-201°-R-221°
   White column
2. **East Breakwater head** 47°23'·0N 2°32'·7W
   Fl.R.4s4m4M White structure, red top
3. **West breakwater head** 47°23'·0N 2°32'·7W
   Fl.G.4s5m5M White structure, green top

RADIO

VHF Ch 9 (hours unknown)

APPROACH

By day

The belfry in the town of Piriac-sur Mer is conspicuous. The harbour cannot be entered until the tide is well up. If approaching from the W near low water the hazards W of Les Rhotrès (N cardinal tower) and north of Grand Norven must be avoided. This is best done by keeping at least 1¼M off the land until the belfry is in transit with Grand Norven N cardinal beacon, bearing 178°.

Leave Grand Norven beacon 100m to port and turn onto a heading of about 155°, which will put slender red and green beacons onto the starboard bow. Continue on this course until the red beacon

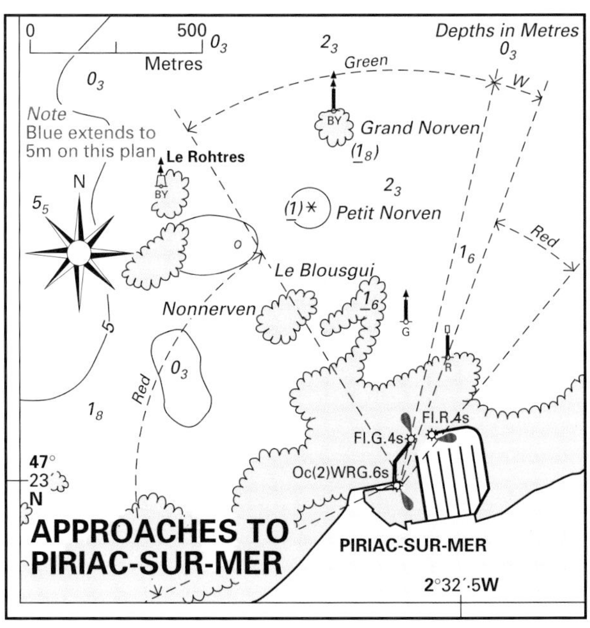

Plan 45

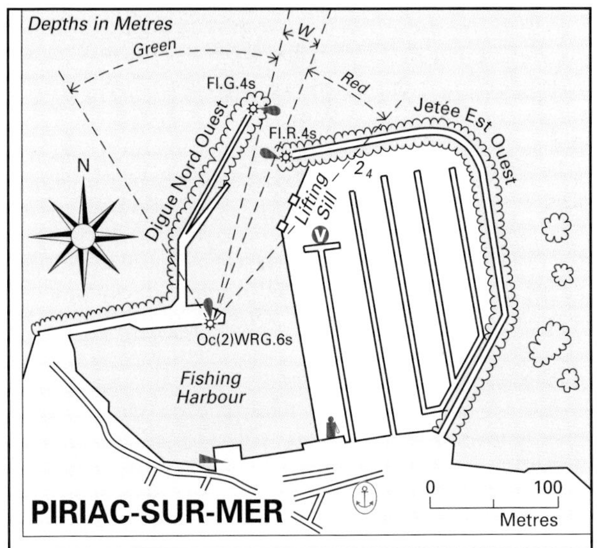

Plan 46

Piriac-sur-Mer. The line of the sill, retaining water in the wet basin, can be seen

comes into line with the E breakwater head, on which there is a white tower with a red top. Then turn towards the harbour entrance leaving the green beacon 100m to starboard and the red beacon close to port.

The entrance to the wet basin is to port, immediately inside the breakwaters. It is only about 50 feet wide and is marked by 2 red and 2 green beacons. Red flashing lights indicate that the gate is closed – even though it may not be visible, whilst green flashing lights indicate that it is lowered. The yellow beacons, between the green beacons and the shore, mark the inner wall of the wet basin.

By night

Approach in the white sector of the Inner Mole light[1] and remain in this sector to the breakwaters[2,3].

BERTHS AND ANCHORAGE

In settled weather temporary anchorage, to wait for the tide, can be found east of the Grand Norven beacon in about 2·5m.

In the marina, the visitors pontoon is immediately ahead on entering and yachts should secure there and report to the harbour office to be allocated a berth.

FACILITIES

Piriac has modest shops and the facilities of a holiday village with many café-bars and restaurants. Fuel is available in the wet basin.

42. La Turballe

47°21'N 2°31'W

GENERAL

La Turballe is a busy fishing port two miles north of Le Croisic, with a fleet of some 60 trawlers based in the Basin de Garlahy. The inner harbour has been dredged and developed with half of it for smaller fishing-boats and the other half a modern marina, with berths for some 280 yachts. 20 pontoon berths are available to visitors, but there are few for boats of over 11m.

Entry is possible in onshore winds of force 5 or 6 and the land provides good shelter from stronger winds from the east.

La Turballe is a holiday resort with quite a large summer population and provides all facilities. There are good sandy beaches to the southeast of the harbour. Although it is crowded in summer, access to the marina in La Turballe is easier than entry to Le Croisic, making it a useful stopping place on this part of the coast.

Charts

BA *2353*
Imray *C39*

TIDAL DATA

Times and heights

	Time differences				Height differences			
	HW		LW		MHWS	MHWN	MLWN	MLWS
BREST								
	0000 and 1200	0600 and 1800	0000 and 1200	0600 and 1800	6·9	5·4	2·6	1·0
Le Croisic								
	+0015	–0040	–0020	–0015	–1·5	–1·1	–0·6	–0·3

Tidal streams

In the middle of the Rade du Croisic the streams are weak. At HW Brest the direction is southerly and at LW Brest it turns northerly, spring rates ½kt. Between the Pointe du Croisic and the Plateau du Four the pattern is similar, but the rates may be greater.

Depths

2·2m in the approach. The marina is dredged to 2m.

LIGHTS

1. **Jetée de Garlahy (W breakwater head)** 47°20'·7N 2°31'·0W Fl(4)WR.12s13m10/7M 060°-R-315°-W-060° White pylon, red top

Ldg Lts 006·5°

2. *Front* 47°20'·8N 2°30'·8W DirF.Vi.11m3M 004°-intens-009° Metal mast, orange top
3. *Rear* 110m from front DirF.Vi.19m3M 004°-intens-009° Metal mast, orange top
4. **Digue Tourlandroux (N end)** 47°20'·8N 2°30'·8W Fl.G.4s4m2M Siren 1 long every 10 minutes White pedestal, green top

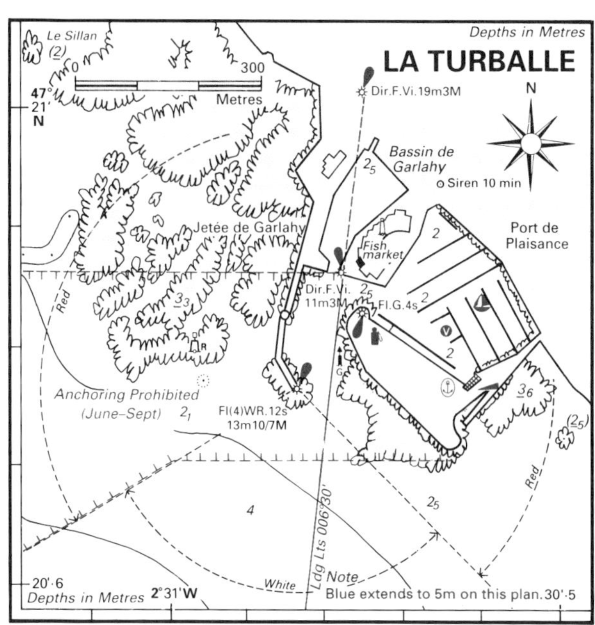

Plan 47

RADIO

VHF Ch 9 0700–1100 and 1500–2100 LT

La Turballe

APPROACH AND ENTRANCE

By day

Rocky shoals extend offshore to the N of the harbour, which should be approached from the SW. Seen from the W, the long white-walled fish market, with a water tower some distance behind, makes a good landmark, and a red beacon tower is situated just W of the entrance. S of the entrance there is 2m to within 300m of the long sandy beach.

Entry is made on a course of about 005° (the leading lights being on 006·5°), as the deep water is nearer the west breakwater. Once past the inner breakwater head, turn sharply to starboard to enter the yacht harbour.

By night

Approach in the white sector of the W jetty head light[1]. Enter with the leading lights[2,3] in line. After passing the W breakwater head, make a sharp turn to starboard round the green light[4], marking the starboard side of the entrance to the yacht harbour.

BERTHS AND ANCHORAGE

In offshore winds there is pleasant anchorage off the long sandy beach to the S of the harbour. In the marina the visitors pontoon is signed. It is often crowded and yachts must expect to be rafted.

FACILITIES

Fuel berth, 16-tonne crane, 140-tonne travel-lift and slipway. Boatyard can take yachts of up to 16m; all repairs undertaken. Chandlers, banks, shops, restaurants and bars close to the marina in the town.

43. Le Croisic

47°18'N 2°31'W

GENERAL

The pretty and interesting harbour of Le Croisic is situated in the SE corner of the Rade du Croisic. The town is a popular holiday resort with a busy fishing fleet, and is associated with Batz and La Baule to the eastward to form a district noted for its bathing sands and holiday amenities. There is a large yard for building trawlers and a substantial new fish market. There is a yacht builder, and much yachting activity takes place.

The entrance channel is shallow and in fresh onshore winds it is rough, owing to the irregular bottom. Otherwise, if approached on the flood and with sufficient rise of tide, it presents no difficulty.

Yachts that can take the ground may use the basin of the Port de Plaisance and there is a good sheltered anchorage in the pool, though it is crowded with permanent moorings.

Charts

BA *2353, 2986*
Imray *C39, C40*

TIDAL DATA

Times and heights

Time differences				Height differences			
HW		LW		MHWS	MHWN	MLWN	MLWS
BREST							
0000 and 1200	0600 and 1800	0000 and 1200	0600 and 1800	6·9	5·4	2·6	1·0
Le Croisic							
+0015	–0040	–0020	–0015	–1·5	–1·1	–0·6	–0·3

The marina at La Turballe is well sheltered with good facilities

Tidal streams

In the middle of the Rade du Croisic the streams are weak. At HW Brest the direction turns S and at LW Brest it turns N, spring rates ½kt. Between the Pointe du Croisic and the Plateau du Four the pattern is similar, but the rates may be greater.

The streams in the entrance to the harbour are very strong; W of the Mabon rocks they exceed 4kts at springs 3 hours before and 2½ hours after HW Brest.

Depths

On the leading line the depths shoal to 0·7m just outside the breakwater head. From there, the channel is dredged to 2·3m to the Fish Quay. A narrow channel, with about 0·5m then runs some 30m out from the wall to the Port de Plaisance, which dries 1·7m. In the pool, up to 2m can be found.

LIGHTS

1. **Jetée du Tréhic head** 47°18'·5N 2°31'·4W
   Iso.WG.4s12m14/11M
   042°-G-093°-W-137°-G-345° Grey tower, green top
2. **Basse Hergo tower** 47°18'·7N 2°31'·6W
   Fl.G.2·5s5m3M Green beacon tower

First Ldg Lts 156°

3. *Front* 47°18'·0N 2°31'·0W DirOc(2+1)12s10m19M
   154°-intens-158°
   Orange topmark on white metal framework tower
4. *Rear* 116m from front DirOc(2+1)12s14m19M
   154°-intens-158° Synchronised with front
   Orange topmark on white metal framework tower

Second Ldg Lts 174°

5. *Front* 47°18'·0N 2°31'·2W
   Q.G.5m11M 170·5°-vis-177·5°
   Yellow can topmark, green stripe on green and white pylon
6. *Rear* 48m from front Q.G.8m11M 170·5°-vis-177·5° Yellow can topmark, green stripe on green and white pylon
7. **Le Grand Mabon** 47°18'·1N 2°31'·0W
   Fl.R.2·5s6m2M
   Red framework structure and pedestal

Final Ldg lights 134·5°

8. *Front* 47°17'·9N 2°30'·8W DirQ.R.6m8M
   125·5°-intens-143·5°
   Red and white chequered rectangle on white pylon, red top
9. *Rear* 52m from front DirQ.R.10m8M
   125·5°-intens-143·5° Synchronised with front
   Red and white chequered rectangle on pylon, on fish market roof

RADIO

VHF Ch 9 0800–2000 LT

APPROACH AND ENTRANCE

The streams are strong and for this reason, at springs, the best time for entry is within the last hour of the flood, when the current is weakening. It is difficult to enter against a spring ebb. At neaps there is more latitude and by following all the transits a yacht can use the channel at any state of tide. On the

Le Croisic

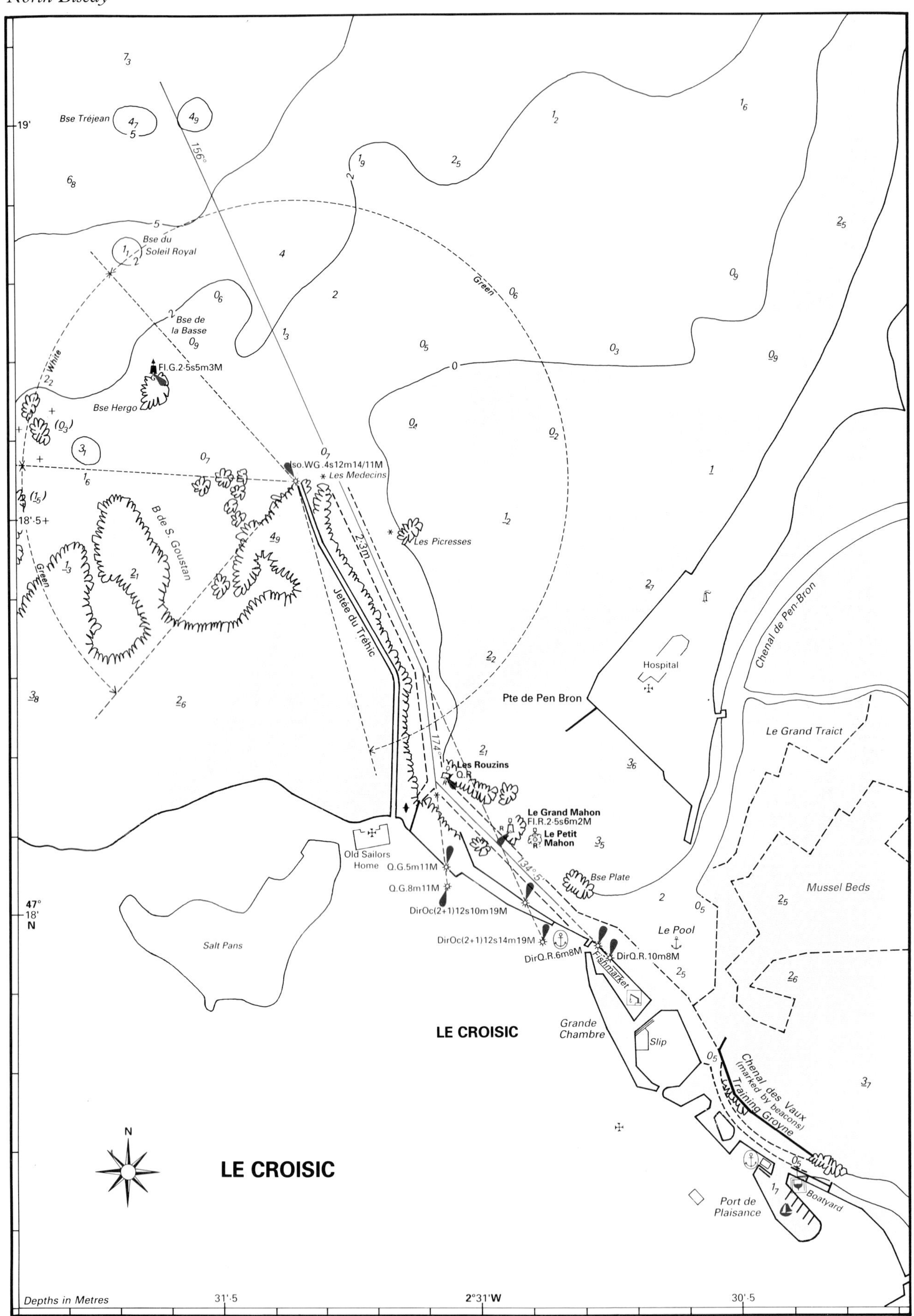

Bse Tréjean
Bse du Soleil Royal
Bse de la Basse
Fl.G.2·5s5m3M
Bse Hergo
Green
White
Iso.WG.4s12m14/11M
Les Medecins
B de S. Goustan
Jetée du Tréhic
Les Picresses
Hospital
Pte de Pen Bron
Chenal de Pen-Bron
Le Grand Traict
Les Rouzins
Q.R
Le Grand Mahon
Fl.R.2·5s6m2M
Le Petit Mahon
Bse Plate
Mussel Beds
Old Sailors Home
Q.G.5m11M
Q.G.8m11M
DirOc(2+1)12s10m19M
DirOc(2+1)12s14m19M
DirQ.R.6m8M
DirQ.R.10m8M
Le Pool
Fishmarket
Salt Pans
LE CROISIC
Grande Chambre
Slip
Chenal des Vaux (marked by beacons)
Training Groyne
Port de Plaisance
Boatyard
LE CROISIC
N
Depths in Metres
31'·5
2°31'W
30'·5
19'
18'·5
47° 18' N
156°
174°
134°·5

Plan 48

The first, red, set of leading marks for Le Croisic are just to the left of the belfry

The second, green, leads are difficult to see. Here they are well open as the turn to the next heading is made

ebb, with strong winds from between WSW and N the entrance is dangerously rough and should not be attempted until the tide has turned and is well up.

If entering on the flood and heading for the yacht basin, take particular care not to be swept onto the submerged training wall in the approach to it.

By day

Approaching from the W or NW, steer into the bay until the leading marks are identified. The church tower, with an unusual near-Byzantine belfry, is conspicuous as is the isolation hospital on the Pen Bron peninsula, to the E of the entrance.

Approaching from the S, the extensive Plateau du Four with its conspicuous lighthouse lies on the W side and the Pointe du Croisic with its off-lying rocks to the E. Near the eastern side of this passage is the Basse Castouillet, with a least depth of 0·6m, marked by a W cardinal buoy.

Steer in with the church belfry bearing 157° until the orange leading marks have been identified – this is not easy as they are in gaps in the trees. Bring them into line bearing 156°; the Basse Hergo green tower will be left 300m, and the end of Jetée du Tréhic 100m, to starboard. Maintain the transit until the bend in the breakwater, then steer 174° on the line of the second leading marks, a pair of yellow

The final transit is at the fishmarket

The channel up to the yacht basin at half tide. The training wall is covered at high water

rectangles with a green vertical stripe situated in a little bay at the root of the breakwater.

Approaching the lifeboat slip the final leading marks, a pair of red and white chequered rectangles, will be seen beyond Le Grand Mabon tower. The rear mark is on the fish market roof, with the front mark on the quay. The turn onto this transit of 134° is marked by red and green buoys which are moved as necessary to mark the channel.

Hold the transit until close to the fishing quay to avoid Basse Plate, drying 2·5m; then, if bound for the yacht basin, steer to leave the quays about 50m to starboard. A training wall of stakes on the port side of the narrow channel is marked by red beacon poles. If looking for an anchorage or mooring, turn to port when the fish market is abeam to starboard and search 'Le Pool'.

By night

In the approach, note that the white sector of Jetée du Tréhic light[1], which leads clear of the distant dangers, such as Le Four and Ile Dumet, leads onto the rocks nearer to the harbour entrance; the close approach must be made in the green sector. The three transits are easier to identify by night than by day and it is only necessary to keep on them. The street lighting on the quays is good and there is no difficulty once they are reached.

BERTHS AND ANCHORAGE

Le Pool is a fair size, and provides good anchorage, though much of it is occupied by moorings. Mussel beds cover the drying banks of Le Grand Traict, but the narrow and steep-sided Chenal de Pen Bron runs up the E side of the peninsula, containing more moorings and a possible anchorage at neaps. There are no visitors' buoys, but it might be possible to borrow a mooring in Le Pool or Chenal de Pen Bron. If anchoring, use a trip-line, as the bottom is foul with old chain. The ebb runs very hard in the Chenal and even in Le Pool the streams are strong.

The harbour has a curious pattern of islands called *jonchères*, with drying basins (*chambres*) behind them in which vessels lie. The original character has been changed by the building of bridges to the islands so that only one remains in its original isolated state.

Yachts should make for the Port de Plaisance in the Chambre des Vases. Deep-keel yachts can dry out against the wall outside on a hard, level bottom and those that can take the ground can enter and secure bow-to a pontoon with a stern mooring.

FACILITIES

The facilities are those of a holiday resort and a fishing and yachting port. Banks, hotels, restaurants and all shops. At present there is no fuel berth for yachts, but fuel may be obtained from a garage in the town. Travel-lift and yacht yard with haul-out facilities, marine engineer and good chandlery.

44. La Baule – Le Pouliguen & Pornichet

Le Pouliguen 47°16'N 2°25'W
Pornichet 47°16'N 2°21'W

GENERAL

La Baule is a sophisticated international beach resort with a casino and innumerable hotels and restaurants of all grades. It may be reached by train or by air to St Nazaire, or its own smaller airport. The bay is sheltered from northerly and westerly winds and is often smooth in summer. There are two harbours, Le Pouliguen and Pornichet.

The approach to Le Pouliguen dries and it is essential for strangers to enter around high water. Yachts berth on pontoons in the river close to the centre of the town which, whilst busy during the season, is moderately attractive. In contrast, Pornichet is a modern, purpose-built and quite characterless marina connected to the shore by a road-bridge. It provides 1,150 berths for yachts of all sizes. It is available at all states of the tide and has good yachting facilities, but otherwise has few attractions for most cruising yachtsmen.

Both harbours are very crowded in high season and yachts of over 10m are often turned away from Le Pouliguen.

Charts

BA *2989, 2986, 2353*
Imray *C39, C40*

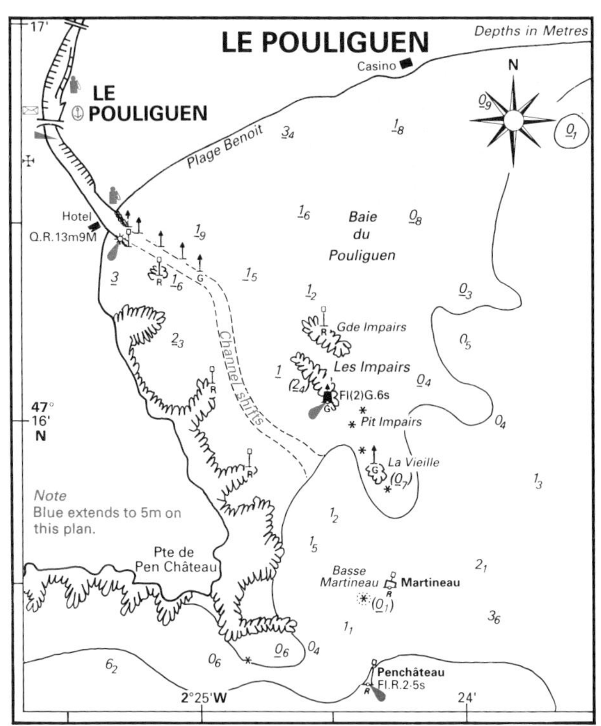

Plan 49

Le Pouliguen

The approach to Le Pouliguen at half tide. The light tower on the west pier head is arrowed

TIDAL DATA

Times and heights

Time differences				Height differences			
HW		LW		MHWS	MHWN	MLWN	MLWS
BREST							
0000 and 1200	0600 and 1800	0000 and 1200	0600 and 1800	6·9	5·4	2·6	1·0
Le Pouliguen							
+0020	−0025	−0020	−0025	−1·5	−1·1	−0·6	−0·3
Pornichet							
+0020	−0045	−0022	−0022	−1·4	−1·0	−0·5	−0·2

Tidal streams

Approaching the Baie du Pouliguen from the W, the stream 1M S of the Pointe de Penchâteau runs E from −0530 Brest, maximum rate 1kt, turning westerly at +0030 Brest.

The tidal streams in the Baie du Pouliguen are irregular in direction, the flood running generally N round the Pointe de Penchâteau and NE towards Pornichet, while the ebb runs S or SW, rates up to about 1kt. In the N of the bay itself the tide tends to run always W. In the Pouliguen river the tidal streams can attain 4kts at springs and care must be taken when approaching or leaving a pontoon.

Depths

The Le Pouliguen channel dries and the rocky sill should be assumed to dry 1·2m. In the pool there is water to float vessels drawing up to 2m. The marina at Pornichet has up to 2·5m in the main berths.

LIGHTS

1. **Les Guérandaises buoy** 47°15'·1N 2°24'·2W Fl.G.2·5s Starboard-hand pillar buoy
2. **Penchâteau buoy** 47°15'·3N 2°24'·3W Fl.R.2·5s Port-hand pillar buoy
3. **Petits Impairs** 47°16'·0N 2°24'·6W Fl(2)G.6s6m2M Green triangle on tower
4. **Le Pouliguen, S jetty** 47°16'·4N 2°25'·4W Q.R.13m9M 171°-vis-081° White column, red lantern
5. **Pornichet, W breakwater head** 47°15'·5N 2°21'·1W Iso.WG.4s11m10/7M 084°-G-081°-W-084° White tower
6. **Pornichet entrance west** 47°15'·5N 2°21'·1W Q.G.3m1M
7. **Pornichet entrance east** 47°15'·5N 2°21'·1W Q.R.3m2M

RADIO

Le Pouliguen VHF Ch 9 0800–2000 LT
Pornichet VHF Ch 9 0800–2100 LT

Le Pouliguen

APPROACH AND ENTRANCE

The best approach from any direction is the western passage between the Pointe de Penchâteau and Les Guérandaises buoy which marks the end of the ledges and rocks extending to the SE as far as the Grand Charpentier lighthouse. From the E approach can most easily be made along the Chenal du Nord which runs outside Le Grand Charpentier and these reefs and then through the western passage. Alternatively there is an inshore passage which can be followed using BA chart *2986*; this channel joins the western passage south of La Vieille beacon.

The harbour entrance is sheltered from the N through W to SW, but southerly swell breaks in the shallow water, and it is fully exposed to the SE. As the sands shift, entrance should only be made around high water.

By day

Leave the Pen Château red pillar buoy 100m to port. Thence steer 020° to leave the Basse Martineau red buoy to port. Leave La Vieille beacon and Les Petits Impairs tower well to starboard, and two red beacons 150m to port. Close to the harbour entrance are five green starboard beacons, the third and fourth a triangular arrangement of three parallel poles. The fifth, a slender wooden pole, marks the tip of a spur of the training wall, covered at HW. To port there are two red beacons, the inner one

Pornichet marina

marking the edge of the entrance channel. The channel usually lies closer to the red beacons than to the starboard ones.

Enter with the church spire open between the pier heads. The lighthouse on the W pier head is a very slender white structure with a red top. This is left to port and the vessel then proceeds between stone embankments. Special care must be taken on near approach to the entrance as the channel is narrow, between high sands on either side. The slender wooden beacon on the starboard side lies well inside the line of rather thicker iron beacons marking the approach and must not be overlooked.

By night

A stranger should not attempt the entry by night as there are few lights. The passage past Pointe de Pen Chateau can be made however as it lies in the white sector of Pornichet light[5], and is marked by lit port and starboard buoys[1,2].

BERTHS AND ANCHORAGE

If waiting for the tide temporary anchorage can be found in about 1m some 400m N of Martineau buoy.

Inside the harbour, the W side of the river is mainly reserved for fishing boats. There are yacht pontoons along the E bank all the way up to the road bridge, with visitors' berths near the entrance.

FACILITIES

All the facilities of a sophisticated yachting centre. The yacht club, with showers and toilets, is a large and clearly labelled building on the La Baule side above the first road bridge. It is hospitable to visitors. There are all shops handy in Le Pouliguen, and yacht yards, chandlers and marine engineers are all close at hand. There are many hotels and restaurants in this holiday town.

Pornichet

APPROACH AND ENTRANCE

By day

From the W, pass between the Penchâteau and Guérandaises light buoys. The forest of yacht masts, together with the white lighthouse at the end of Pornichet outer mole can be made out amongst the buildings at the eastern end of La Baule, bearing 083°, and course should be altered towards them. An unlit green conical buoy marking the northermost extremity of the Guérandaises shoal is left to starboard.

From the S and E, either make the outside passage northwest to the Pointe de Penchâteau and approach as above, or take the passage between the Grand and Petit Charpentier and approach the marina from the SE. One of the detailed charts, BA *2986* or *2989*, are needed for this latter passage as there are unmarked rocks to be avoided.

The entrance to the marina faces N, and it is not until close approach that the red and green beacons marking the underwater projections from the pierheads become clear; course must be altered to pass between them.

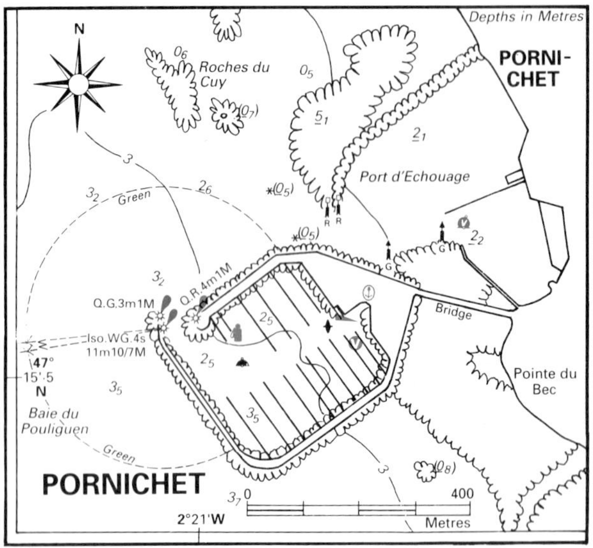

Plan 50

By night

The approach is covered by the white sector of Pornichet pierhead light[5]. This sector just excludes the Penchâteau and Guérandaises light buoys[1,2]. The beacons in the marina entrance show Q red and green lights[6,7].

BERTHS AND ANCHORAGE

There are 10 pontoons (A-J) on the southern side of the harbour and 4 (K-N) on the northern. The heads of all these are allocated to visitors, together with the whole of pontoon J and the outer side of pontoon I, although these two pontoons are only suitable for boats of under 10m length. All the main berths carry a depth of 2·8m. As the bottom is soft mud, vessels of deeper draught will sink their keels into it and remain upright.

If there are no berths available yachts may secure to the large mooring buoy inside the harbour entrance, rafted to other visitors.

FACILITIES

A fully equipped marina. Fuel pontoon immediately to port on entry, chandlery, restaurants, café-bars and a wine merchant in the marina, but no food shops or bakery. Yacht yard with travel-lift; large slipway and grid.

Across the causeway to the mainland there are many shops, hotels and restaurants.

45. The Loire with St-Nazaire and Nantes

GENERAL

The Loire is France's longest river and its ports account for a third of her maritime trade. It is navigable by ocean-going ships as far as Nantes, one of the largest cities in the country, which lies 36M from the river mouth. The marinas of Pornichet and Pornic lie on either side of the entrance, but in the river there are facilities for yachts only at St-Nazaire and Nantes where the Breton canal system joins the Loire. From there shallow draft yachts can reach the English Channel at St Malo (see Chapter 40).

The river is wide and deep and, until Paimbœuf is reached, a significant sea can build up. Further upstream there can still be a considerable chop in strong winds. The channel is so well marked with buoys and beacons that, at a pinch, the passage to Nantes could be made without the detailed chart. It is well lit, but a night passage is not recommended. Just above St-Nazaire a spectacular road bridge arches across the river.

The major port and city of St-Nazaire suffered extensively from bombing during the Second World War, but has been rebuilt. A section of one of the commercial basins has been reserved for yachts with space ashore for laying up, but it is in the heart of the docks, a long way from the centre of town. Few yachts visit.

The passage to Nantes is seldom made by yachts and cannot be described as particularly attractive, although it is interesting. Nantes itself is a historic city. The small marina at Trentemoult is set in a quiet, leafy suburb.

Charts

BA *2646, 2986, 2989, 2985*
Imray *C40*

TIDAL DATA

Times and heights

Time differences				Height differences			
HW		LW		MHWS	MHWN	MLWN	MLWS
BREST							
0000 and 1200	0600 and 1800	0000 and 1200	0600 and 1800	6·9	5·4	2·6	1·0
St-Nazaire							
+0030	–0040	–0010	–0010	–1·1	–0·8	–0·4	–0·2
Cordemais							
+0055	–0005	+0105	+0030	–0·7	–0·5	–0·7	–0·4
Nantes							
+0135	+0055	+0215	+0125	–0·6	–0·3	–0·8	–0·1

Tidal streams

The streams follow the direction of the channel. In the approach, off the Grand Charpentier, the flood reaches 1·4kts and the ebb 1·7kts, off St-Nazaire, flood and ebb, 4kts and off Paimbœuf, flood and ebb 2·5kts, all spring rates.

Above St-Nazaire the current is very much influenced by the fresh water flow in the river and when it is in spate the strength of the flood is much reduced and the ebb much increased.

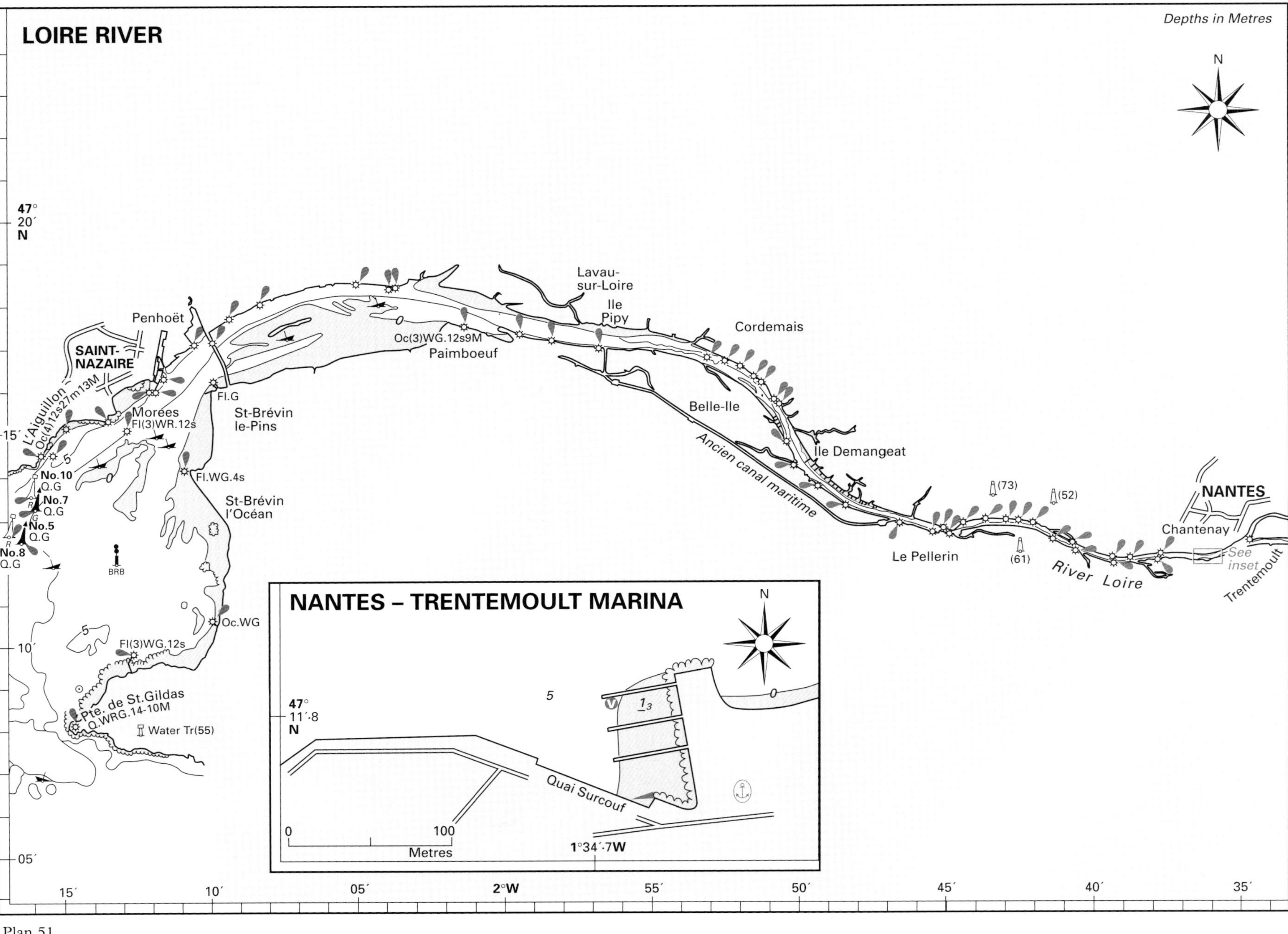
LOIRE RIVER
Depths in Metres
N
47° 20´ N
Penhoët
SAINT-NAZAIRE
L'Aiguillon
Oc(4)12s27m13M
Morées
Fl(3)WR.12s
No.10
Q.G
No.7
Q.G
No.5
Q.G
No.8
Q.G
BRB
Fl.G
St-Brévin le-Pins
Fl.WG.4s
St-Brévin l'Océan
Oc.WG
Fl(3)WG.12s
Pte. de St.Gildas
Q.WRG.14-10M
Water Tr(55)
Oc(3)WG.12s9M
Paimboeuf
Lavau-sur-Loire
Ile Pipy
Cordemais
Belle-Ile
Ancien canal maritime
Ile Demangeat
(73)
(52)
(61)
Le Pellerin
River Loire
NANTES
Chantenay
See inset
Trentemoult
NANTES – TRENTEMOULT MARINA
47° 11´·8 N
Quai Surcouf
0
100
Metres
1°34´·7W
15´
10´
05´
2°W
55´
50´
45´
40´
35´

Plan 51

Depths

The channel is deep. In St Nazaire, the approach to the E lock and the basins are deep. Trentemoult marina largely dries, very soft mud, but there is about 0·5m on the end of the outer pontoon.

LIGHTS

Only the principal lights necessary to reach St Nazaire are given. There are numerous other lights in the approaches.

1. **La Blanche** 47°10'·6N 2°28'·1W Fl(2+1)WR.15s22m15/11M 266°-R-280°-W-266° Black tower, white bands
2. **Ile du Pilier** 47°02'·6N 2°21'·6W Fl(3)20s33m29M Grey pyramidal tower
   Auxiliary light Q.R.10m11M 321°-vis-034° same structure
3. **Le Grand Charpentier** 47°12'·8N 2°19'·1W Q.WRG.22m14-10M 020°-G-049°-W-111°-R-310°-W-020° Grey tower, green lantern
4. **Pointe de St-Gildas** 47°02'·6N 2°14'·8W Q.WRG.20m14-10M 264°-R-308°-G-078°-W-088°-R-174°-W-180°-G-264° Metal framework tower on white house
5. **Pointe d'Aiguillon** 47°14'·6N 2°15'·8W Oc(4)WR.12s27m13/10M 207°-W(unintens)-233°-W-293°, 297°-W-300°-R-327°-W-023°, 027°-W-089°

Ldg lights 025·5°

6. *Front* 47°14'·6N 2°15'·4W DirQ.6m22M 024·7°-intens-026·5° White column on dolphin
7. *Rear* 47°15'·3N 2°14'·9W DirQ.36m24M 024°-intens-027° Synchronised with front, shown throughout 24 hours
   Black square, white stripe on metal tower
8. **Villè-es-Martin, jetty head** 47°15'·3N 2°13'·7W Fl(2)6s10m10M White tower, red top
9. **Morées** 47°15'·1N 2°12'·9W Fl(3)WR.12s11m6/4M 058°-W-224°, 300°-R-058° Green truncated tower
10. **St-Nazaire, Jetée Ouest head** 47°16'·0N 2°12'·2W Oc(4)R.12s11m8M White tower, red top
11. **St-Nazaire Jetée Est head** 47°16'·0N 2°12'·1W Oc(4)G.12s11m11M White tower, green top
12. **SE Vieux mole buoy** 47°16'·3N 2°11'·6W Fl.R.2·5s Red can buoy
13. **Basse Nazaire Sud buoy** 47°16'·3N 2°11'·5W Q(6)+LFl.15s S card pillar buoy
14. **Old mole head** 47°16'·3N 2°11'·8W Oc(2+1)12s18m11M White tower, red top
15. **Beacon** 47°16'·4N 2°11'·7W Q.Y.5m1M Yellow pile
16. **Entrée Est, S side** 47°16'·5N 2°11'·8W Fl(2)R.6s9m9M Red framework tower
   Fixed red leading lights, shown when necessary, lead through the lock

RADIO

To be aware of large ship movements yachts should, if possible, monitor VHF Ch 19 and 12 when in the Loire channels.

St-Nazaire Port VHF Ch 16, 06, 12 (preferred), 14, 67, 69 24hr

Donges Port VHF Ch 16, 12, 69 24hr

Nantes Port VHF Ch 16, 06, 12 (preferred), 14, 67, 69 24hr

APPROACH

By day

The approach is straightforward. The big ship channel is well marked by buoys, but it is not necessary to adhere to it until past Pte d'Aiguillon as there is plenty of water for a yacht on either side. There are some isolated dangers in this shallower water, however, and buoys and beacons mark these. The chart is the best guide. After Pte d'Aiguillon a yacht will need to keep closer to the main channel, but there is generally space for her to pass outside the buoys and she should do so if necessary to avoid commercial traffic.

By night

Because of the dangers outside the channel, the majority of which are not lit, it is best to keep close to, or within, the buoys. The Passe des Carpenters leading lights[6,7] are very conspicuous. At Pointe

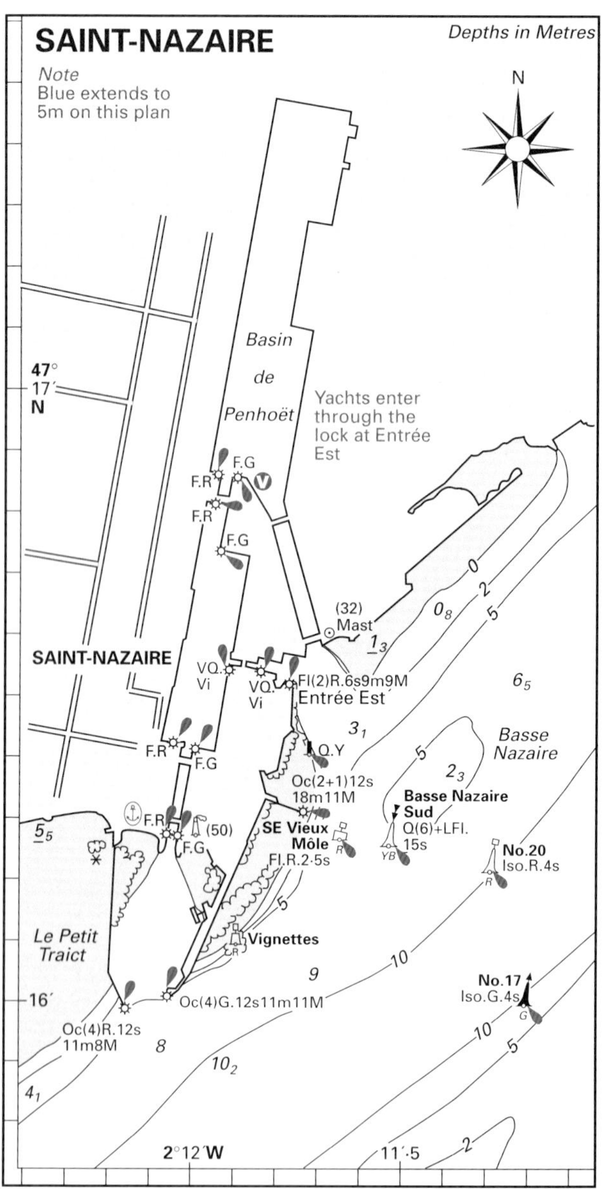

Plan 52

d'Aiguillon the channel turns to starboard, becoming Chenal de Bonne-Anse, and runs between lit buoys

Saint-Nazaire

ENTRANCE

Yachts and fishing boats use the E lock. Exit takes place on the even hours and entry 10 minutes later.

By day

Approach along Chenal de Bonne-Anse leaving the two long breakwaters, which mark the big-ship entrance to the docks, to port. Leave the main channel at this point and head about 030° to pass between the red SE Vieux Môle buoy and the Basse de St Nazaire S cardinal buoy. Continue to turn to port onto about 340°, leaving Vieux Môle jetty and a yellow beacon to port. The entrance to the lock, which lies E/W, will open up to port.

By night

Follow the lit channel until the St Nazaire jetty lights[10,11] are abeam to port. Head 045° for the Basse Nazaire Sud buoy[13]. Leaving it to starboard, alter to about 340° leaving to port the SE Vieux Môle buoy[12], the Vieux Môle[14], an isolated beacon[15] and the lock entrance light[16]. The lock will then open on the port hand. There is a great deal of background light.

FACILITIES

Once locked through, a yacht must turn to starboard and pass through the gate and swing bridge into the Basin de Penhoët, where yachts berth at the S end. There are few facilities but in a port of this size any repairs could probably be arranged. Yachts can be lifted out and stored ashore in a locked compound.

St-Nazaire has all the facilities of a major town, but it is a long walk into the centre. The massive submarine pens, built by the Germans, dominate the docks. Adjacent to the E lock is the French Navy submarine museum, where the *Espardon* can be visited berthed in a reinforced concrete covered lock, a relic of the war. There is a café-bar on the roof of the blockhouse.

THE RIVER

There are no difficulties in navigating from St-Nazaire to Nantes. The channel is well marked by buoys and beacons, most of them lit. In general the deep water lies on the outside of the curves.

It is thirty miles from St-Nazaire to Nantes and HW Nantes occurs between 7 and 7¾hrs after LW at St-Nazaire. It is thus possible for a yacht that can maintain a reasonable speed to enjoy a favourable stream for the entire up-river passage. It is best to leave St-Nazaire about an hour before low water. Heading downriver however, LW St Nazaire is only between 4½ and 5 hours after HW Nantes and so it is likely that some foul tide must be endured, unless the river is running fast. It is best to leave Nantes well before local HW.

The few yachts that visit St Nazaire must berth in the commercial basins which are not particularly attractive

Trentemoult marina at Nantes

Below Ile Demangeat it is possible to find room to anchor and wait for the tide clear of the channel, but it is unlikely to be either comfortable or attractive. Further upstream there are few suitable places. Trentemoult marina lies on the S bank, 1·4M above the only bridge to cross the river after St-Nazaire.

FACILITIES

Trentemoult marina has no facilities other than water and electricity, showers and toilets. It is possible to arrange for a mobile crane for masting. Nearby, there are local café-bars, restaurants and a bakery and it is a 10-minute walk to a shopping centre with a large supermarket. Buses run into Nantes where there is every facility and much to interest the visitor.

46. Saint-Gildas

47°08'N 2°15'W

GENERAL

This small harbour, also known as Anse du Boucau, lies directly to the north of Pointe de Saint-Gildas. It is well sheltered from the south and, at neaps, from the west but it is open to the north. The inner part of the harbour dries, but further out there is room to anchor and there are many yachts on moorings.

There are few facilities but in settled conditions the harbour offers an alternative to Pornic for those who prefer to anchor or to lie on a mooring.

Charts

BA *2986*
Imray *C40*

TIDAL DATA

Times and heights

Time differences				Height differences			
HW		LW		MHWS	MHWN	MLWN	MLWS
BREST							
0500 and 1700	1100 and 2300	0500 and 1700	1100 and 2300	6·9	5·4	2·6	1·0
Pointe de Saint-Gildas							
–0045	+0025	–0020	–0020	–1·3	–1·0	–0·5	–0·2

Tidal streams

Off the harbour the flood runs north-east and the ebb south-west, spring rates about 1kt.

Depths

There is a 1·5m shoal 750m N of the breakwater head. Much of the harbour dries, but on the moorings there is 1·5m.

LIGHTS

1. **Pointe de St-Gildas** 47°02'·6N 2°14'·8W
   Q.WRG.20m14-10M
   264°-R-308°-G-078°-W-088°-R-174°-W-180°-G-264°
   Metal framework tower on white house
2. **Breakwater head** 47°08'·5N 2°14'·7W
   Fl(2)G.6s3M Metal post

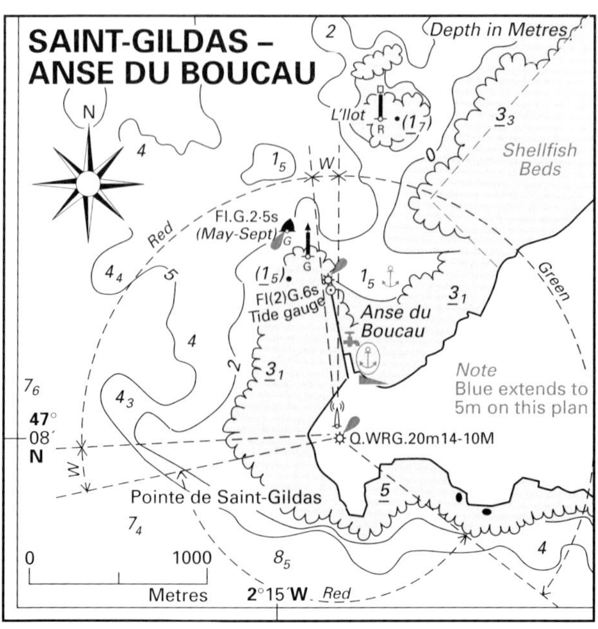

Plan 53

APPROACH AND ENTRANCE

By day

From the S, the extensive shallow Banc de Kerouars, lying 1¾M S of Pointe de St-Gildas, is a hazard. At its W end is La Couronnée, a rocky patch, part of which dries, marked by La Couronnée starboard-hand light buoy. This buoy is one of the big-ship channel marks and can be left up to ¾M to port. From the vicinity of the buoy a course of about 065° leads toward the harbour.

If coming from Pornic, Banc de Kerouars can be left to port as the channel between it and the shore is over a mile wide. A N cardinal buoy, Nord Couronnée, marks the drying rock. Give Pointe de St-Gildas a berth of at least 500m as the rocks extend a long way from the shore. There is also a 1·5m shoal patch ½M W of the lighthouse which may be a hazard near low water.

The harbour lies to the E of a long breakwater. A starboard-hand beacon off the breakwater head marks the end of the rocks and in summer a green light buoy is laid as well. To the N lies the extensive drying reef L'Ilot on which is an unlit port-hand

The approach to Saint-Gildas harbour. The green buoy is only laid during the summer

Saint-Gildas harbour is pleasant and offers an alternative to Pornic for those who prefer to be at anchor or on a mooring

beacon. If coming from the N, give this beacon a good berth as it is in the centre of the patch.

By night

The white sector of Pointe de St-Gildas light[1] (174°-180°) leads into the harbour. There is a light[2] on the end of the breakwater.

ANCHORAGE AND MOORINGS

Yachts which can take the ground may do so on the sandy beach at the head of the harbour. Alternatively anchor as close in as depth allows, clear of the moorings, or it may be possible to borrow one.

FACILITIES

There is a tap at the dinghy pontoon in the inner corner of the harbour. Café-bars, restaurant, hotel. Modest shops at Préfailles, 1·5km.

47. Pornic

47°06'N 2°07'W

GENERAL

Pornic is the best harbour for the visiting yachtsman on this stretch of the coast. It is situated halfway along the northern shore of the Baie de Bourgneuf and is easy of access in reasonable weather. The old harbour in the town is mostly used by fishing boats and dries, but the yacht marina has plenty of water and supports considerable local yachting activity. Visitors are made most welcome, there are good facilities on site and it is only a short, pleasant walk along the river bank to the town. Pornic itself is a pretty place which is well worth a visit. Bluebeard's castle overlooks the harbour just seaward of the quays. There are good beaches to the west of the marina.

Charts

BA *2986, 2981*
Imray *C40*

TIDAL DATA

Times and heights

Time differences				Height differences			
HW		LW		MHWS	MHWN	MLWN	MLWS
BREST							
0500 and 1700	1100 and 2300	0500 and 1100	1100 and 2300	6·9	5·4	2·6	1·0
Pornic							
–0050	+0030	–0010	–0010	–1·1	–0·8	–0·4	–0·2

Tidal streams

Outside the flood runs E and the ebb W, 2kts springs. The streams in the harbour are weak.

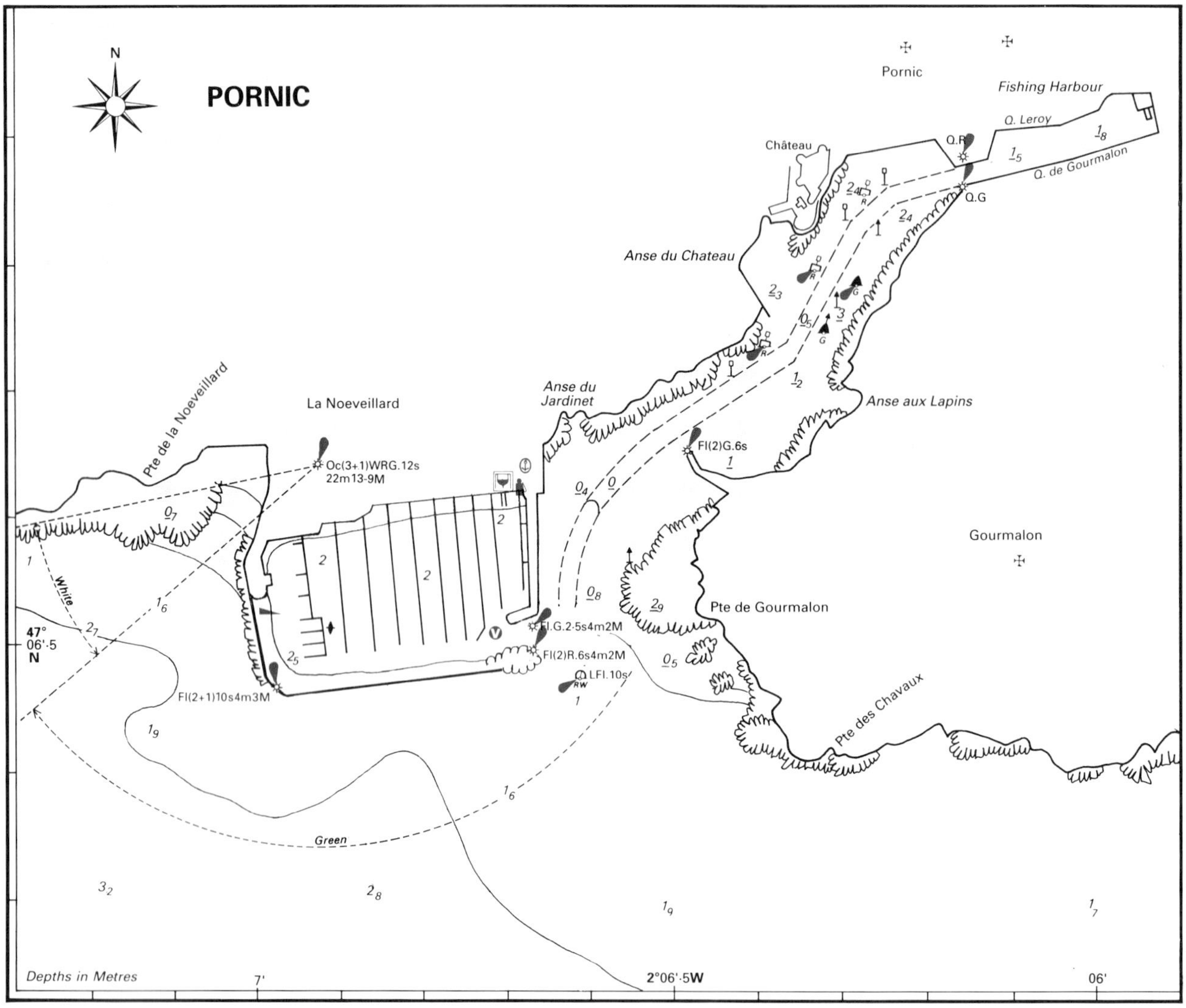

PORNIC

N

Pornic

Fishing Harbour

Q. Leroy

Château

Q.R

Q. de Gourmalon

Q.G

Anse du Chateau

Anse du Jardinet

Anse aux Lapins

La Noeveillard

Pte de la Noeveillard

Fl(2)G.6s

Oc(3+1)WRG.12s 22m13-9M

White

Gourmalon

Pte de Gourmalon

47° 06'·5 N

Fl.G.2·5s4m2M

Fl(2)R.6s4m2M

LFl.10s

Fl(2+1)10s4m3M

Pte des Chavaux

Green

Depths in Metres

7'

2°06'·5W

06'

Plan 54

Pornic, looking north-east

The fairway buoy and entrance to Pornic marina

Depths
There is 1·0m to the fairway buoy. The marina and entrance is dredged to 2m but can silt between dredgings and in 1998 there was about 1·3m in the entrance and 1·5m or more on the visitors pontoon. The old harbour and the channel to it dries.

LIGHTS

1. **Pointe de St-Gildas** 47°02'·6N 2°14'·8W
   Q.WRG.20m14-10M
   264°-R-308°-G-078°-W-088°-R-174°-W-180°-G-264°
   Metal framework tower on white house
2. **Pointe de Noëveillard** 47°06'·6N 2°06'·9W
   Oc(3+1)WRG.12s22m13-9M
   shore-G-051°-W-079°-R-shore
   White square tower, green top, white dwelling
3. **Marina elbow** 47°06'·5N 2°07'·0W
   Fl(2+1)10s4m3M Grey structure
4. **Marina entrance, S side** Fl(2)R.6s4m2M
   Black column, red top
5. **Marina entrance, N side** Fl.G.2·5s4m2M
   Black column, green top
6. **Fairway buoy** 47°06'·5N 2°06'·6W LFl.10s
   Red and white buoy

RADIO
VHF Ch 9 24hr

APPROACH AND ENTRANCE
By day

In the outer approach from the SW the outlying dangers to the N of Ile de Noirmoutier are well marked by a series of buoys and towers. From the NW care must be taken to avoid the Banc de Kerouars, which is unmarked except for a buoy, La Couronnée, one of the channel buoys for the Loire entrance, one mile off its W end and the N cardinal Nord Couronnée buoy, marking a rock which dries 2·2m. The least depth on the bank near the eastern end is 0·7m and is unmarked. To the N of the bank there is a passage over ½M wide and ½M off the land, or entry can be made S of the bank if it is not safely covered.

Leave the BRB tower of Notre Dame (topmark two spheres) about ½M to starboard and steer for the RW fairway buoy at the entrance to Pornic, leaving it to starboard on arrival.

Enter only with sufficient rise of tide – because of the possibility of silting it is best to consider the entrance as having about 1m. Pass between the two red and the green columns, which are placed in the entrance and not on the breakwater heads. Once inside keep clear of the S wall, which is lined with submerged rocks. The E breakwater head is also foul, with a partly submerged knuckle extending diagonally into the marina.

By night

The white sector of the main light[2] clears the Banc de Kerouars and Notre Dame rock. Approach in this sector and leave the fairway buoy[6] to starboard and enter the marina between the entrance lights[4,5].

BERTHS AND ANCHORAGE
The reception berth in the marina is directly ahead on entering and is clearly marked. Secure there and visit the marina office who may ask you to move to a vacant space. There is plenty of room for visitors.

Although yachts are encouraged to use the marina, those that can take the ground may find room to do so in the old harbour. The channel, which should be considered as drying 1·8m, is marked by buoys and beacons and although some of these are lit a stranger should not attempt it by night unless a prior reconnaissance has been made by day.

FACILITIES
There are the facilities of a major marina including fuel, 30-tonne travel-lift, storage ashore. Repairs can be undertaken and there are engineers and sailmakers. The marina staff are particularly helpful.

On the north side of the marina are café-bars, restaurants and chandlers. There are no food shops but some of the bars supply bread and croissants in the early morning. It is a ten-minute walk along the river bank to the town, where there are all shops, banks, hotels and restaurants.

48. Ile de Noirmoutier

L'Herbaudière 47°02'N 2°18'W

GENERAL

The Ile de Noirmoutier is a flat sandy island measuring about 9M from northwest to southeast. It is separated from the mainland by the narrow Goulet de Fromentine. North of the Fromentine bridge is a causeway carrying the old road from the mainland to the island. It is so high that although it covers at high water it is not safe for a deep-keel boat to attempt to cross over.

This is an interesting island to explore by bicycle – it is flat – and bicycles can be hired. The causeway to the mainland is unusual; at a weekend low water it is busy with visitors gathering shellfish. The island is covered in salt pans, many of which are still in use. It has a profusion of sandy beaches.

Noirmoutier has a strategic position guarding the Loire river and was invaded by the English in 1388, by the Spanish in 1524 and by the Dutch in 1674, but is now invaded only by crowds of summer holidaymakers. Port de Morin on the west side is a

The salt pans on Noirmoutier are still in use

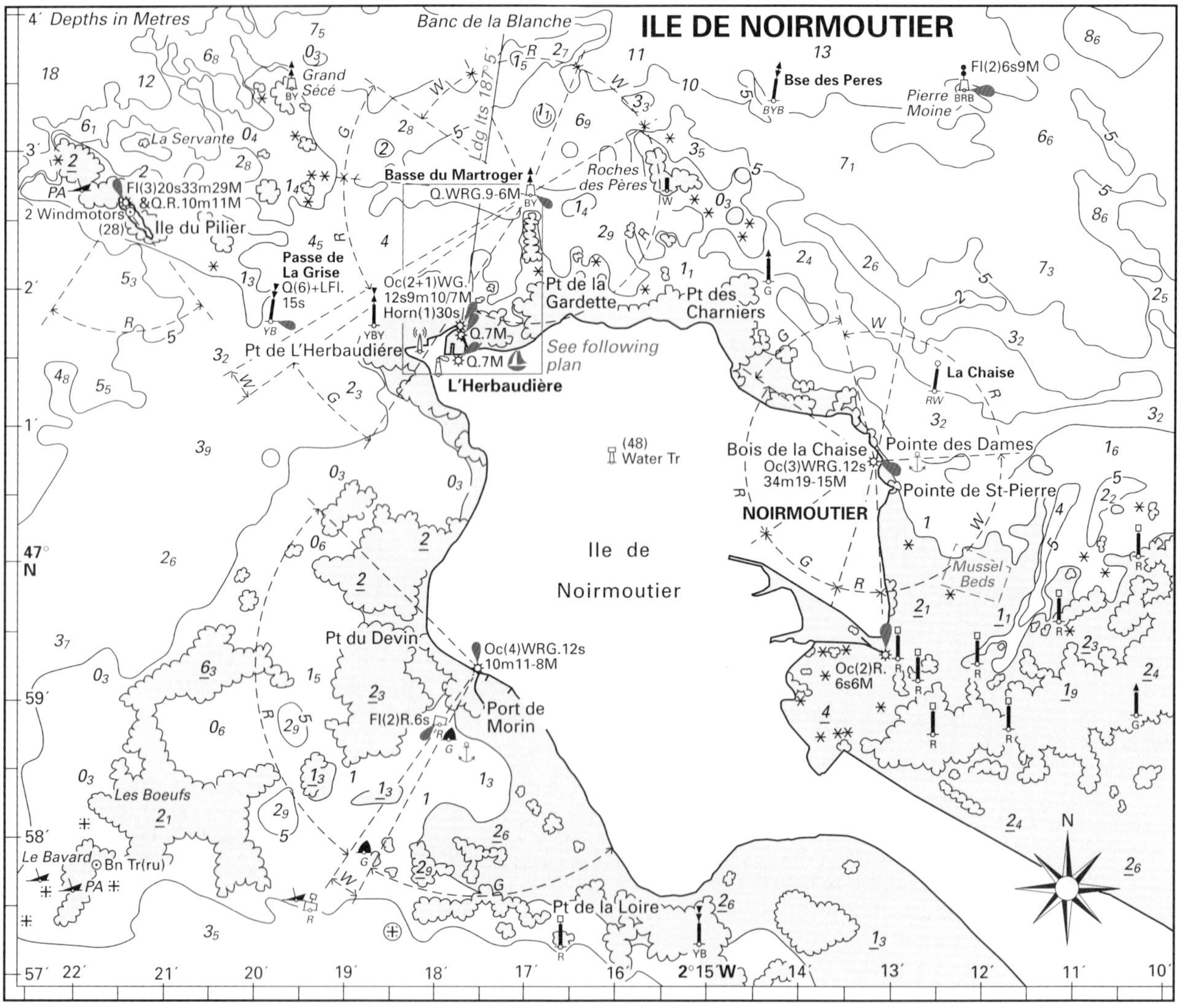

Plan 55

fair-weather anchorage and drying harbour. L'Herbaudière, in the north, has a small marina and is a convenient passage stop. In the east, Bois de la Chaise is an open anchorage, though with enough shelter to be the summer base for yachts. Noirmoutier town dries and can only be reached near high water and Fromentine, on the mainland by the bridge, is approached over a shallow bar exposed to westerly winds and swell, though it is easily accessible at high water in offshore weather. There are shoals and rocks extending a long way off the island but they are adequately marked.

South of the Loire, one must keep a lookout for the *nombreux orins de casiers*. Further to the north, a line of lobster pots is usually marked only by a dan buoy at each end. From Noirmoutier south, the practice is for a line of very small floats to connect the two dan buoys and one should avoid crossing the line.

Charts

BA *2981*
Imray *C40*

TIDAL DATA

Times and heights

	Time differences				Height differences			
	HW		LW		MHWS	MHWN	MLWN	MLWS
BREST								
	0500 and 1700	1100 and 2300	0500 and 1700	1100 and 2300	6·9	5·4	2·6	1·0
L'Herbaudière								
	–0047	+0023	–0020	–0020	–1·4	–1·0	–0·5	–0·2

Tidal streams

In the middle of the entrance to the Baie de Bourgneuf the tide is rotary clockwise: at +0425 Brest, NW 1·5kts springs; at –0325 Brest, 1·7kts SE; at –0025 Brest, turning to SW; at +0225 Brest, NW 1·0kt springs.

In Chenal de la Grise, at the NW end of the island, NE stream begins at –0625 Brest, 1·5kts springs; SW begins –0100 Brest, 2kts springs.

Off Bois de la Chaise SE stream begins –0600 Brest, NW begins –0040 Brest, spring rates 1·5kts.

Depths

L'Herbaudière has 1·5 to 2·2m at the pontoons; the entrance channel is dredged to 1·5m. Bois de la Chaise has about 1m. Noirmoutier dries about 2·5m. Port de Morin has about 1m in the pool, but the harbour dries.

LIGHTS

1. **Ile du Pilier** 47°02'·6N 2°21'·6W Fl(3)20s33m29M
   Grey pyramidal tower
   Auxiliary light Q.R.10m11M 321°-vis-034°
   Same structure
2. **Pointe de St-Gildas** 47°02'·6N 2°14'·8W
   Q.WRG.20m14-10M
   264°-R-308°-G-078°-W-088°-R-174°-W-180°-G-264° Metal framework tower on white house
3. **Pointe du Devin** 46°59'·1N 2°17'·6W
   Oc(4)WRG.12s10m11-8M
   314°-G-028°-W-035°-R-134°
   White column and hut, green top
4. **Basse du Martroger** 47°02'·6N 2°17'·1W
   Q.WRG.11m9-6M
   033°-G-055°-W-060°-R-095°-G-124°-W-153°-R-201°-W-240°-R-033°
   N card beacon tower
5. **Passe de la Grise S card buoy** 47°01'·7N 2°19'·9W Q(6)+LFl.15s
6. **La Pierre Moine** 47°03'·4N 2°12'·4W
   Fl(2)6s14m7M Isolated danger tower
7. **Pointe des Dames** 47°00'·7N 2°13'·3W
   Oc(3)WRG.12s34m19-15M
   016·5°-G-057°-R-124°-G-165°-W-191°-R-267°-W-357°-R-016·5° White square tower
8. **Port de Noirmoutier jetty head** 46°59'·3N 2°13'·1W Oc(2)R.6s6m6M White column, red top

L'Herbaudière

9. **West jetty head** 47°01'·6N 2°17'·9W
   Oc(2+1)WG.12s9m10/7M Horn 30s
   187·5°-W-190°-G-187·5°
   White column and hut, green top

Ldg Lts 188°

10. *Front* 47°01'·6N 2°17'·8W Q.5m7M 098°-vis-278°
    Grey mast
11. *Rear* 47°01'·4N 2°17'·9W Q.21m7M 098°-vis-278°
    Grey mast
12. **East jetty head** 47°01'·6N 2°17'·9W
    Fl(2)R.6s8m4M Red tripod
13. **Lifeboat slip** Fl.R.2·5s Red box

RADIO

L'Herbaudière VHF Ch 9 0800–1200 and 1530–2000 LT (July and August 0730–2230 LT)

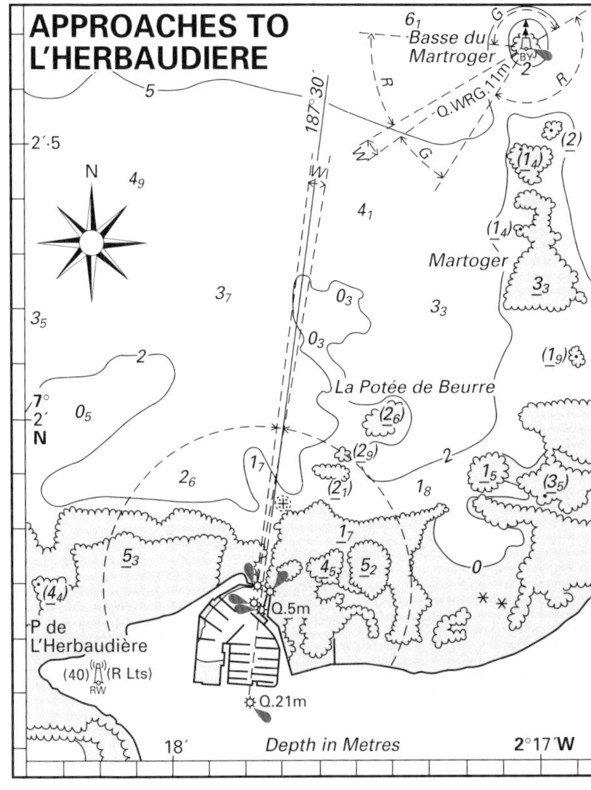

Plan 56

L'Herbaudière

APPROACH AND ENTRANCE

By day

If making for L'Herbaudière, the entrance lies 500m E of a tall red and white radio mast. The large blue 140-tonne travel-lift is also conspicuous.

Make a position 600m W of Basse du Martroger tower. There are shallow patches of 1·1m and 1·5m north of the tower so, from the N near low water the approach to it should be made with it on a bearing of between 125° and 155° or between 200° and 240°. If coming from the SW, through Passe de la Grise, leave the S cardinal buoy to port and the W cardinal beacon off Pte de l'Herbaudière well to starboard as rocks extend N of it.

From this position, W of Basse du Martroger, the harbour entrance will be seen bearing 190°. It is marked by one port and two starboard buoys and by two port-hand beacons.

In conditions of poor visibility it is not easy to identify the marks and in 1993 the leading lights[7] were established. These are automatically switched on in daylight if visibility is reduced. The channel is no wider than the entrance, so do not stray. Alter to starboard on passing the W breakwater and then round the slipway and lifeboat station to port.

By night

From N, approach in either of the two northerly white sectors of Basse du Martroger light[4] and then in the white sector of L'Herbaudière breakwater head light[9] bearing 187·5° to 190°. Identify the

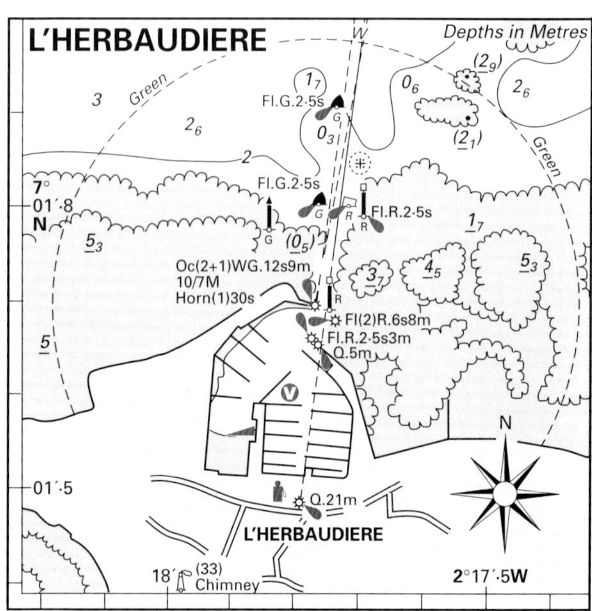

Plan 57

leading lights[10,11] on 188° and follow this transit into the harbour, leaving the red and green lit buoys to port and starboard.

From the south, approach through the Chenal de la Grise in the white sector of Basse du Martroger light[4], bearing between 055° and 060°. When the breakwater head light[9] turns white, steer in this sector on 187·5° to 190° and pick up the transit of the leading lights[10,11] on 188° leading into the harbour.

L'Herbaudière

When a northerly wind blows straight in through the harbour entrance the visitors' pontoons, seen here, can become uncomfortable

BERTHS
Visitors berth on the pontoon directly ahead on entering and must expect to be rafted during the season. This berth is exposed to the harbour entrance and may be uncomfortable if the wind is from the N.

FACILITIES
Fuel berth, 30-tonne crane, slipway and grid. Café-bars, supermarket close to the marina. Sailmaker, engineers and chandlers. In the small town there are the usual shops, bank, hotels and restaurants.

Bois de la Chaise
This open anchorage is sheltered from the W and S. It is exposed to the N and E, but the fetch is not more than 5M and, in summer, yachts lie on moorings here. It is an attractive situation, though the facilities are limited. There are some moorings for visitors and space to anchor.

APPROACH
By day
Bound for Bois de la Chaise, it is best to pass at least 1½M N of Martroger tower to avoid the Banc de la Blanche, with a least depth of 1·5m. Passing close to the S of Banc de la Blanche N cardinal buoy, steer for Pierre Moine BRB tower and alter to leave Basse des Pères E cardinal buoy close to starboard, with Pierre Moine tower 1·3M to port. From this point a course of 153° should lead to the small RW buoy marking the Bois de la Chaise anchorage NW of the Pointe des Dames. A wooden pier projects from this headland, which is steep and tree-covered, with only the top of the lighthouse showing above the trees.

By night
Approach in the northerly white sector of Pointe de Dames light[7].

ANCHORAGE
There are a few moorings for visitors inshore of the RW buoy and there is plenty of room to anchor in from 1·5 to 3m NE or SE of the pier. Land at the steps halfway along the pier; the end must be kept clear for the ferries.

FACILITIES
Two restaurants, a paper shop and a small food shop. Good shops in Noirmoutier, 1½M walk. There is a big camp site behind the beach to the south. In the summer a general shop opens to serve the camp, with a butcher in July and August. To reach them, it is easier to land on the beach to the south of the anchorage than to walk round from the pier.

Noirmoutier
This port is reached by a long, straight, narrow channel. It should be regarded as drying 2·5m and is therefore not accessible to deep-draught yachts at neaps. Should a visit by sea be intended it is strongly recommended that an inspection at low water be made beforehand. Bicycles can be hired at L'Herbaudière and the ride is pleasant over this flat island.

Noirmoutier is a busy port and the quays are occupied by fishing boats and the flat barges used for oyster culture. The bottom is hard rock with a mud overlay and on occasion the channel is scoured by opening the sluices to the inland water. This takes away a foot or so of mud and leaves the sloping mud banks along the quays in an unstable condition.

Enter with the tide; not all the outside berths will have mud, and it is best to pick a berth using a sounding pole to test for mud, and then to tend warps until safely grounded. It will probably be necessary to raft to another yacht, and on occasion rafted boats may tip and cross masts, or even fall outwards into the scoured channel.

APPROACH AND ENTRANCE
S of the channel training wall a rocky shelf, covered with oyster beds, stretches out some four miles to the ENE, with several passages marked by beacons. The old approach runs N of a curving line of 5 red (port) beacons on the northern edge of the shelf. This approach does not dry as far in as Atelier, the second beacon out from the training wall, but since there is a drying 2·5m patch at the entrance it is more convenient to wait until there is sufficient water in the channel and use the line of green beacons to approach along the shore.

Coming S from the Bois de la Chaise anchorage, when there is considered to be enough water, keep about 400m offshore, passing over a sandy bottom (drying 1·6m) inshore of a mussel bed. A line of green (starboard) beacons marking the ends of stone groynes will be seen along the shore, curving to starboard into the entrance of the channel. Follow the line of beacons round to the entrance and continue up the marked channel to the town. The best water at the entrance is on the S side near the training wall. Night entry is not recommended.

BERTHS
Moor to the first quay on the starboard hand, just before the crane is reached. Farther up the quays are shallower. The mud is very soft, so the keel will probably sink in, with any luck leaving the yacht upright.

FACILITIES
All shops; restaurants and hotels. Shipyard, chandlers and marine engineer. A pleasant town.

Port de Morin
This recently built drying harbour is on the west side of the island at the north end of a spectacular sandy beach. It is a pleasant place with a smooth sandy bottom for small yachts which can take the ground. There is a pool with about 1m in which, at neaps those with deeper draught can find a pleasant fair-weather anchorage. In 1998 work was continuing in the approaches and more channel markers may be laid, or dredging carried out.

APPROACH
From an initial position of about 46°56'·5N 2°20'W identify the harbour breakwater and the masts of the yachts within. Head towards it on a course of about 033° leaving the small red buoy marking a drying wreck to port and a green buoy, ½M further on, to starboard. The approach then passes over a bank which dries 1·3m. Deeper water lies to starboard. It is possible that this part of the channel will be buoyed in the future.

Continue toward the breakwater and, if planning to enter the harbour pass between the red and green buoys before rounding the breakwater head close to port. For the pool, sound in on a NE heading to find the deepest water.

Fromentine
46°54'N 2°10'W

GENERAL
The Goulet de Fromentine, between the south of Ile de Noirmoutier and the mainland, is very seldom visited by yachtsmen, as the entrance is on a lee shore if the wind is in any westerly direction; in addition the bar of sand dries and shifts in position. The streams are very strong in the narrows and run seaward for 8½ hours, from about 1½hrs before high water to 1½hrs after low water. The channel is, however, well buoyed, and as it is used all the year round by the Ile d'Yeu ferry it may be regarded as fit for navigation in reasonable weather conditions. The anchorage is uncomfortable.

The directions for crossing the causeway between Noirmoutier and the mainland are based on a survey made by a yachtsman in 1987. The editor could find no-one on the coast who has made the passage in a yacht since then and in 1998, when researching for this edition in *Margaret Wroughton* with 2m draught, tides did not make enough for it to be possible. In view of the age of the last visit the directions given here should be treated with *considerable caution.* The passage should only be attempted using BA chart *2981* (or a large-scale French chart) after prior reconnaissance at LW. The editor would welcome any information gained. A visit to the causeway by land is interesting.

TIDAL DATA
Times and heights

	Time differences				Height differences			
	HW		LW		MHWS	MHWN	MLWN	MLWS
BREST	0500 and 1700	1100 and 2300	0500 and 1700	1100 and 2300	6·9	5·4	2·6	1·0
Fromentine	−0045	+0020	−0015	+0005	−1·7	−1·3	−0·8	−0·1

Tidal streams
Ingoing stream begins −0530 Brest, 5kts springs; outgoing begins −0130 Brest, 8kts springs.

Depths
The bar varies in position and depth; it dries about 1·5m.

The approach to Fromentine

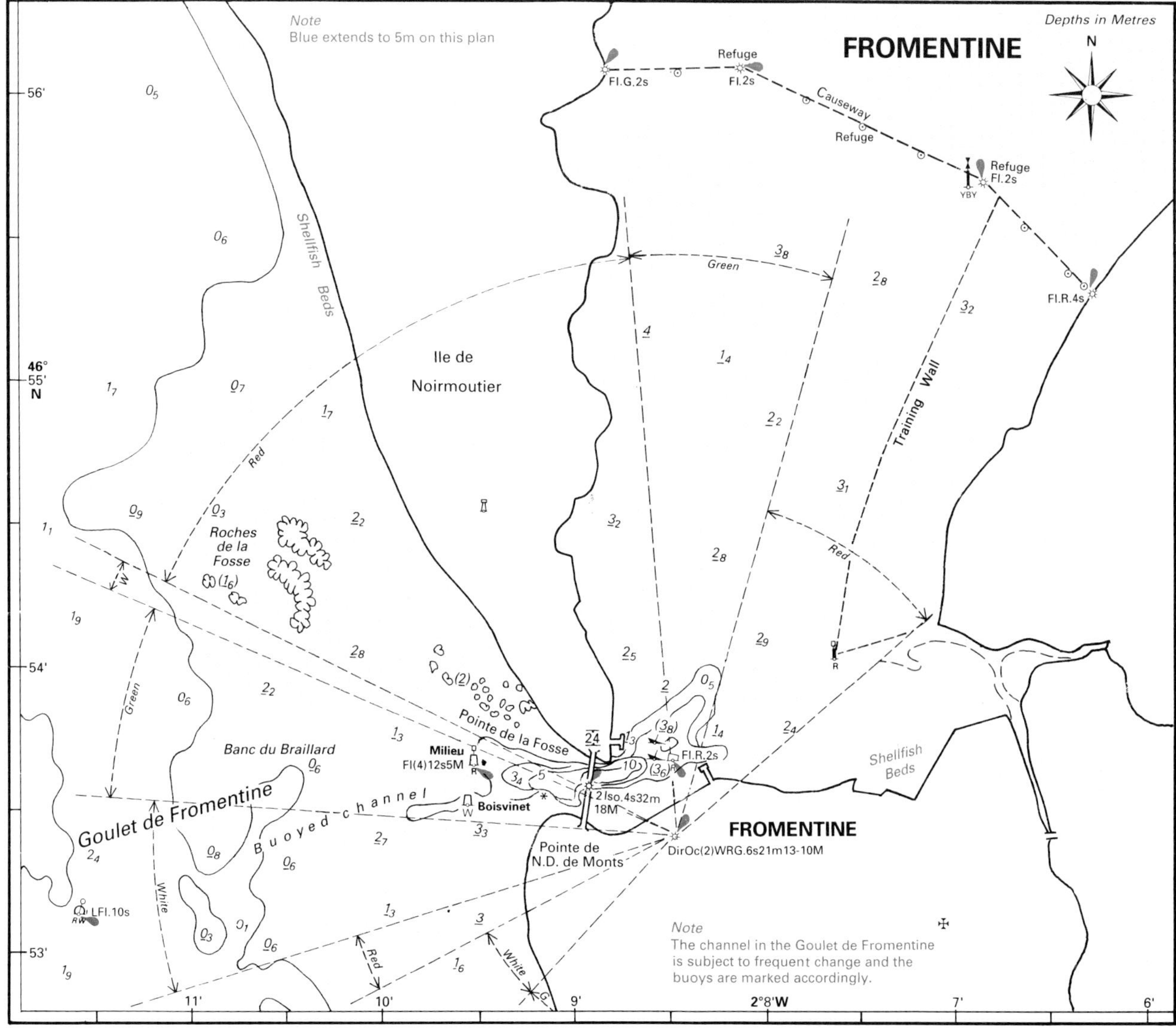

Plan 58

LIGHTS

No lights are included here as it is not advisable to attempt entry at night.

APPROACH AND ENTRANCE

The coast of Noirmoutier and the mainland S of it merge together into a line of sand dunes when viewed from seaward. There are several windmills painted white with black tops on the Noirmoutier side, and a very conspicuous water tower. Notre Dame des Monts lighthouse, with a water tower in the background, is at Fromentine. Half a mile seaward of the bridge are two beacon towers, the northern one red and the southern one white.

Although the Ile d'Yeu ferry uses the port near HW, strangers would be unwise to attempt it in a strong onshore wind, or if there is a swell high enough to break on the shoals. If it is not rough and the approach is made during the last two hours of the flood, there will be plenty of water over the outer shoals, the shallowest being Basse de l'Aigle, with 2·9m over it.

The approach starts at the Basse de l'Aigle buoy, from which course is set for the landfall buoy, situated 1·95M at 264° from Fromentine lighthouse. On the flood tide there is a set to the S. Before reaching the landfall buoy a large water tower on the S end of Noirmoutier and the very large bridge joining the mainland and the island will be seen. From the landfall buoy, pairs of red and green buoys mark the channel across the bar to the beacon towers, one red and one white. The buoys are moved when necessary by the ferry operators. Passing between the beacons the channel deepens and a starboard-hand buoy indicates the way to the main navigation arch of the bridge, clearance 27m, which is clearly marked. A red buoy (port) marks the lead of the channel to the Fromentine pier. To the N of this buoy are two wrecks, exposed at LW.

ANCHORAGE

Depending on draught, either off the jetty on the E side of Pte de la Fosse (Noirmoutier), with less tidal stream, or off the shore just W of the ferry jetty off

Fromentine and just E of the cable area. The streams in the fairway are very strong, about 5kts, but they moderate towards the shore. Anchor as far in as draught and tide will allow.

Owing to the strength of the tide it is said to be unwise to leave a yacht unattended while at anchor, and this would certainly be true at the top of springs. If going in to the Pte de la Fosse side, beware of the wrecks just N of the channel; they lie between the first and second red buoys after you pass under the bridge, so turn in either before the first red buoy or after the second. It is not practical to row across the stream to Fromentine in the dinghy and the bridge is a long way round.

FACILITIES

Water at the ferry jetties; ask the ferry operators. Fromentine is a small holiday resort with hotels, restaurants and shops. Ferry to Ile d'Yeu. At Pte de la Fosse, on Noirmoutier, there is a small hotel, which combines a café-bar, tobacconist and small shop for bread, about 3 minutes' walk from the ferry office. Alternatively, take a walk or taxi over the bridge to Fromentine.

Passage north from Fromentine over causeway

French directions state that there should be more than 1·5m over the causeway 2hrs before HWS but not more than 1m at HWN.

The directions below are compiled from Mr Paul Dane's survey in *Pampa Mia*, a bilge-keel ketch drawing 1·1m, in July 1987. The chart used was French, SHOM *5039P*, but BA *2981* now shows the area in great detail.

The causeway is about 2M long and 30m wide, constructed of stones and small rocks. The roadway is about 10m wide. It is the highest object in the immediate area, and calculations put the height as being 2·64m above the datum. (Note: BA *2981* shows sand drying over 3m directly north and south of the easterly refuge.)

There are three refuges or *bals à hune* on the causeway. On either side of the eastern refuge are beacons to indicate the best place to cross. The refuge is a wooden structure mounted on a stone and concrete plinth, the top of which is 2·1m above the level of the causeway. From this it follows that when the plinth is just covered the causeway may be crossed between the refuge and the port-hand beacon with a minimum depth of 2·1m.

The tide makes from the south, comes in quickly and runs over the causeway across the sands to meet the tide rising on the north side. From a position 100m off the end of the Fromentine ferry jetty, make good a course of 030° up the channel to pass 15m to the east of a spar which is located approximately 400m from the eastern *bal à hune* on a bearing of 199°. Do not borrow east, as there is a training wall further E, covered at HW. After passing the *bal à hune*, set course to make good 355° to clear the oyster beds.

Fine on the port bow you will see a prominent water tower bearing 351° from the *bal à hune*, and on the starboard bow, north of Pornic, another water tower with a RW radio mast close west bearing 002° from the *bals à hune*. This course crosses La Préoire rocky plateau, drying 2·9m. To avoid it, turn onto 040° 2½M from the *bals à hune*, when the water tower on the southern end of Noirmoutier bears 205°. This course will lead to Le Fain channel, where there is sufficient water to leave Goeland lateral starboard buoy to starboard (although it is a starboard-hand channel buoy when going south) and a green (starboard) beacon to port.

The way is then clear to Pornic. As an alternative, those equipped with a detailed chart can find their way across the extensive rocky shelf S of the port of Noirmoutier to an anchorage off Bois de la Chaise.

49. Ile d'Yeu

Port Joinville 46°44'N 2°21'W

GENERAL

The Ile d'Yeu, situated about halfway between Belle Ile and La Rochelle, is the furthest offshore of the islands in the Bay of Biscay. It measures about 5M long and 2M across. The only deep harbour, Port Joinville, is an important fishing port, especially for tunny. The marina has been extended and now has adequate room for visitors and there is an anchorage outside sheltered from the prevailing winds. The town is a pleasant one, with excellent facilities, as the island is popular with visitors.

The south coast is very rocky and deeply indented by the action of the Atlantic seas. There are two bays that can be used as temporary anchorages in offshore winds. In one of these is the narrow winding inlet which forms Port de la Meule which, although Lilliputian, is the only harbour apart from Port Joinville in the island. The other is Anse des Vieilles, near the southeast corner of the island.

Despite its lack of good harbours Ile d'Yeu appears very prosperous, perhaps because the fishing and tourist industries are so active. The houses are whitewashed, with brightly painted doors and shutters. The whole island seems trim and well cared for and is pleasant for walking or cycling.

The coastline is magnificent, especially on the south side, where, overlooking a rock-studded bay, there are the ruins of an 11th-century castle, much damaged by the English, complete with dungeons and moats. In recent history Marshal Pétain was imprisoned near Port Joinville and his simple tomb can be seen in the cemetery there. The island is well worth a visit and it provides a convenient port of call when bound to or from La Rochelle.

Charts

BA *3640, 2663*
Imray *C40*

TIDAL DATA

Times and heights

Time differences				Height differences			
HW		LW		MHWS	MHWN	MLWN	MLWS
BREST							
0500 and 1700	1100 and 2300	0500 and 1700	1100 and 2300	6·9	5·4	2·6	1·0
Port Joinville							
−0025	+0010	−0030	−0030	−1·7	−1·3	−0·6	−0·2

Tidal streams

There is considerable variation in the directions and rates of the streams round the island and a tidal stream atlas and charts should be consulted. Generally the streams are weak, but there are local variations close inshore and there can be 2kts at springs off the NW tip of the island, running NE at −0400 Brest and SW at +0200 Brest.

Depths

The entrance to Port Joinville has 1·2m and the marina is dredged to 1·5 to 2·5m. Port de la Meule dries, but there is an anchorage outside that can be used in offshore winds, as can that further east in Anse de Vieilles.

LIGHTS

1. **Petite Foule** 46°43'·1N 2°22'·9W Fl.5s56m24M
   Square white tower green lantern
2. **Les Chiens Perrins** 46°43'·6N 2°24'·6W
   Q(9)WG.15s16m8/5M
   330°-G-350°-W-200° W card beacon tower
3. **Pointe des Corbeaux** 46°41'·4N 2°17'·1W
   Fl(2+1)R.15s25m20M
   White square tower, red top
4. **La Sablaire buoy** (S card) 46°43'·7N 2°19'·4W
   Q(6)+LFl.15s
5. **Port Joinville NW jetty head** 46°43'·8N 2°20'·7W
   Oc(3)WG.12s9m11/8M Horn(3)30s
   150°-W-232°-G-279°-W-285°-G-shore
   White metal tower, green top

Quai du Canada Ldg Lts 219°

6. *Front* 46°43'·8N 2°20'·9W Q.R.11m5M
   169°-vis-269° Pylon
7. *Rear* 85m from front Q.R.16m5M 169°-vis-269°
   Pylon
8. **Galiotte breakwater, inner end**
   46°43'·7N 2°20'·8W Fl(2)R.2·5s1M
9. **Quai du Canada pier head** 46°43'·8N 2°20'·8W
   Iso.G.4s7m6M White truncated tower, green top
10. **Port de la Meule** 46°41'·7N 2°20'·6W
    Oc.WRG.4s9m9-6M
    007·5°-G-018°-W-027·5°-R-041·5°
    Grey square tower, red top

RADIO

Port Joinville marina VHF Ch 9 0800–1300 and 1400–2000 LT (July and August 0730–2200 LT)

Port-Joinville

This harbour, on the north side of the Ile d'Yeu, is exposed to N and E winds, swell enters in strong winds from these directions and there is sometimes a surge during gales from other directions. None of this, however, affects the berths in the yacht marina which are completely sheltered. It is the only safe harbour in the island.

APPROACH AND ENTRANCE

By day

The high water tower will be seen just behind the town; in the distance this is more conspicuous than the island's main lighthouse. The town and the breakwaters at the harbour entrance are easy to locate from seaward; an approach with the water tower bearing 224° will lead in.

On the E side of the entrance is the Passerelle de la Galiotte, a walkway on concrete columns with an elbow giving the outer half a lead of ENE, outside which are a 0·2m drying patch and a red can buoy 100m NE of the head.

Enter the harbour leaving the NW breakwater head 50m to starboard; on reaching the Passerelle elbow, bear to port (as the western side of the outer harbour dries 0·5m) and round the inner end of the breakwater to enter the marina.

By night

Approach in either of the white sectors of the NW breakwater light[5] and enter the harbour with the leading lights in line[6,7] bearing 219°.

BERTHS AND ANCHORAGE

There is an anchorage in 3 to 4m (sand and mud) ½M E of the port in Anse de Ker Châlon, a bay with rocky outcrops on either side, Rocher Ronde to the W (drying 2·3m) and some rocks in the sand close inshore. It is advisable to keep at least 600m offshore.

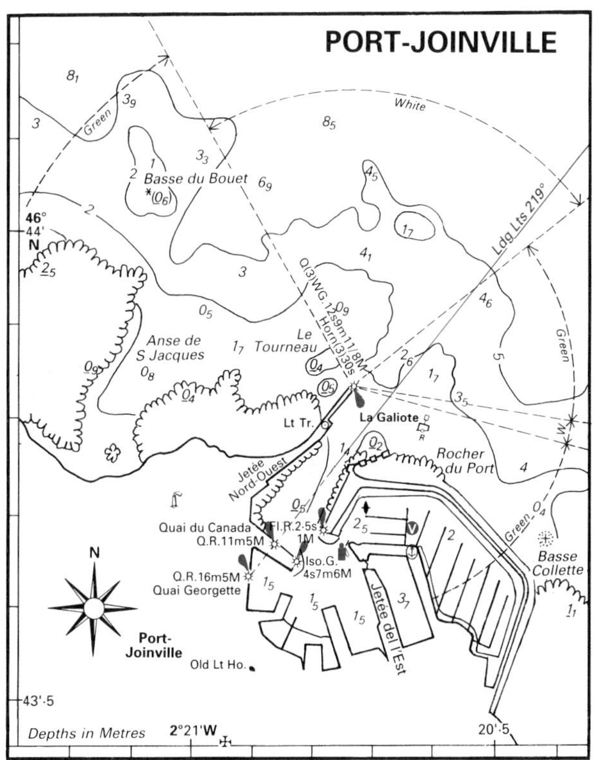

Plan 59

Port-Joinville, Ile d'Yeu

In the harbour visiting yachts no longer use the wet dock, but berth in the marina. The reception berth is the first N/S pontoon on entry, but at busy times marina staff in launches meet incoming yachts and direct them to a vacant berth.

FACILITIES

Fuel berth at entrance to marina. 18-tonne crane, slip, grid, shipyard, marine engineer, chandlery at fishermen's cooperative. In the town are banks, hotels, restaurants, all the usual shops, a good supermarket and, all-importantly, several bicycle-hire firms.

There is a regular ferry service to Fromentine, on the mainland; also, in summer, to St Gilles Croix de Vie, and less frequently to Les Sables d'Olonne.

Port de la Meule

46°41'·7N 2°20'·7W

GENERAL

A picturesque but tiny fishing harbour on the south side of Ile d'Yeu, which is rewarding to visit if one is lucky enough to get the right conditions of offshore wind, but is to be avoided in unsettled weather. The harbour is crowded with small fishing boats, with the occasional trawler at anchor in the entrance. The fishermen much prefer yachts to anchor outside and there is only room for a very small yacht to manoeuvre inside.

APPROACH AND ENTRANCE

By day

The entrance is not conspicuous, but lies between two fairly prominent headlands, Pointe du Châtelet (La Panrée), with a white stone cross, 1½M to the west, and Pointe de la Tranche, ¾M to the SE, behind which there are, on high ground, a conspicuous white semaphore tower and a red and white radio mast.

From seaward the entrance has little to distinguish it from the other inlets on this coast until it is opened up, when the white panel on the side of the lighthouse and the white chapel at the NE end of the inlet can be seen. The bay in which Port de la Meule is situated is clear of off-lying rocks, except for those off the headlands and in the immediate vicinity of the cliffs. Steer for the lighthouse, bearing 022°.

On near approach a headland on the west side of the entrance will lie to port. This has rocks off the S end, which are well off the line of approach, but there is also a reef projecting eastward almost facing the headland on the opposite side. These rocks can usually be seen as the swell breaks on them, but an incoming vessel should borrow to starboard to give them an offing.

The headland on the E side does not project seawards as far as the W headland does. There are rocks off its southern extremity, which form a short, underwater continuation of the headland.

In the near approach, first give reasonable clearance to the reef of rocks to port, then keep the inlet between the lighthouse and the cliff on the E side open, steering parallel with the eastern side of

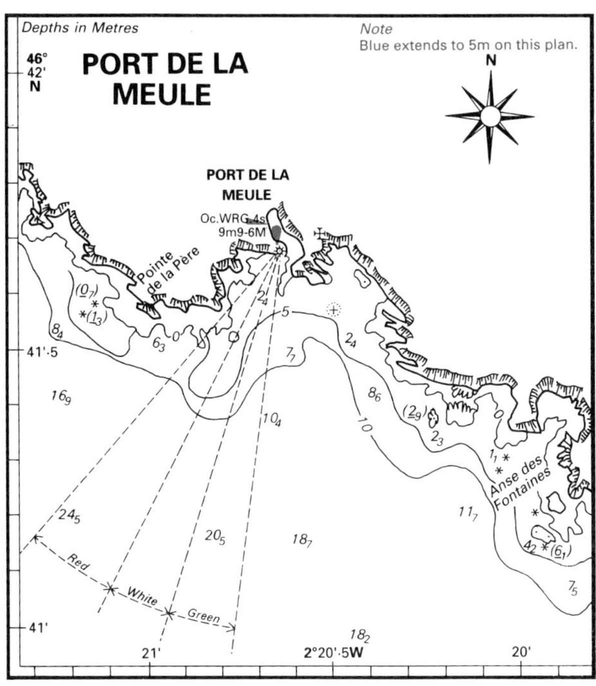

Plan 60

the inlet. When within the entrance, where there is 4m, lobster-pot buoys will be seen on the W side; these are an aid to navigation, as the outer ones are usually laid where they may be treated as port-hand marks, to be left close to port. On the opposite, E, side there are a few rocks at the foot of the cliffs, and one of them lies close to the channel. Hence, if proceeding to the quay, a vessel should now keep rather W of the centre and turn sharply to port round the point on which the lighthouse stands.

There is shelter at the quay in normal conditions with the wind from W through N to E, but if the wind goes into a southerly quarter the swell will surge right in and the harbour will be untenable. In southerly gales the harbour is a mass of breakers and the local boats move round to Port Joinville.

By night

Night entry should not be attempted.

ANCHORAGE AND MOORING

In settled offshore winds it is practicable to anchor in the entrance, though some swell comes in even in NE winds. The bottom is rocky and there is little swinging room, so two anchors are necessary.

The harbour dries; the fishermen are helpful, but say that there is really no room for a yacht. It would be wise to seek their advice before entering.

Port de la Meule is little more than a crack in the rocks, but in settled conditions visitors can anchor outside

FACILITIES

There are two restaurants, but almost no other facilities. There are paths over the hills and the cliffs to east and west. The ruined castle one mile to the W is interesting.

ANSE DES VIEILLES

This attractive bay with a sandy beach on the SE coast, 1¼M from Pointe des Corbeaux, can be entered from the SE. Avoid the line of rocks, the Ours des Vieilles (the outermost drying 3·5m), which runs out for 600m in a SE direction from the Pointe des Vieilles, on the W side of the bay. There is a small drying boat harbour on the W arm of the bay. The anchorage in 3m in the centre of the bay (in position 46°41'·7N 2°18'·5W) is sheltered from northerly winds.

ANSE DES BROCHES

There is a fair-weather anchorage, sheltered from SW through S to E, in this bay at the W end of the island. Approach with the Petit Foule lighthouse bearing 140°; there are drying and above-water rocks on both sides of the bay but this approach passes more than 300m from the nearest. When Les Chiens Perrins bear about 240° alter some 20° to port and go in as far as depth and draught allow to anchor on sand, with Petit Foule bearing 155° and Les Chiens Perrins on 250°.

50. Saint-Gilles-Croix-de-Vie

46°41'N 1°56'W

GENERAL

This harbour is formed by La Vie river; the entrance is protected by moles on either hand. The entrance faces southwest and is unsuitable for entry during strong onshore winds or if there is a swell. As the ebb tide can reach 6kts at springs, entry is impossible when a strong wind opposes this and it is safer to make both entry and exit before high water.

Within the river, there are two enclosed basins for the fishing fleet on the north side; above these lie the pontoons of the yacht marina. Croix-de-Vie is a substantial town with good facilities and communications; the fish quays near the railway station are very busy. There is much yachting activity in the port, with 800 permanent berths and 60 for visitors. There are also mooring trots along the river opposite the marina and on up to the bridge.

Charts

BA *2663, 3640*
Imray *C40*

Looking east over St-Gilles-Croix-de-Vie

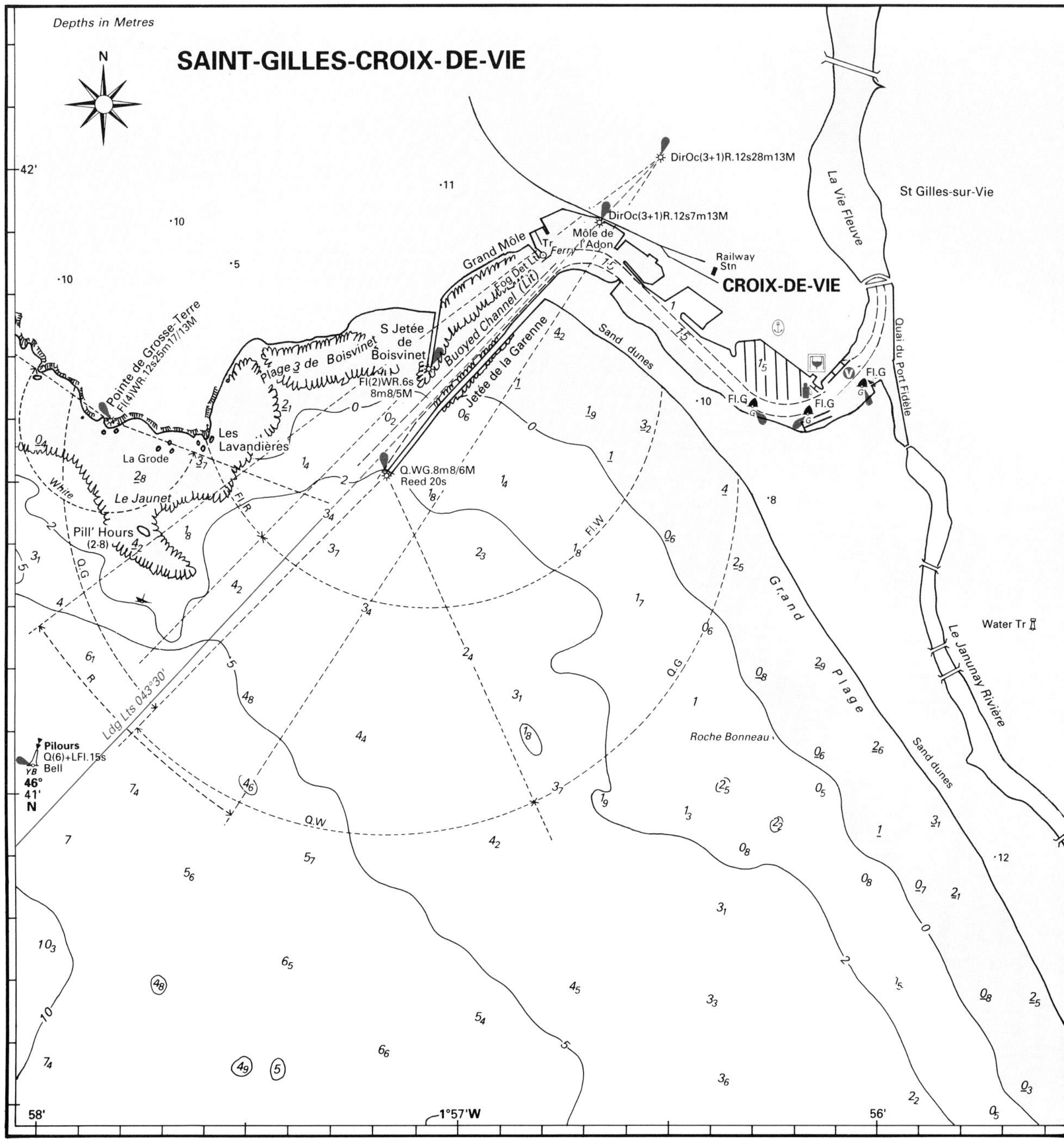

Plan 61

TIDAL DATA

Times and heights

Time differences				Height differences			
HW		LW		MHWS	MHWN	MLWN	MLWS
BREST							
0500 and 1700	1100 and 2300	0500 and 1700	1100 and 2300	6·9	5·4	2·6	1·0
Saint-Giles-Croix-de-Vie							
−0032	+0013	−0033	−0033	−1·8	−1·3	−0·6	−0·3

Tidal streams

The streams are weak in the offing, but strong in the harbour itself, the ebb can reach nearly 6kts in the narrow parts. It is best to approach the visitors pontoon, where there is not much space, just before HW to avoid being swept past the pontoon into very shallow water beyond it.

The ebb is increased and the flood reduced (it may even fail to occur) after heavy rain.

Depths

The channel is dredged to 1·5m, so both fishing harbours and the yacht marina should be accessible at all states of the tide. There is, however, a serious

The leading marks for the entrance to St Gilles

silting problem, with continuous dredging to prevent sand bars from forming. As there are shallows close to the channel it would be better to consider it as carrying 0·7m. In 1998 the visitors pontoon had 1·5 to 2·0m and the fuel berth about 0·5–1m.

LIGHTS

1. **Pointe de Grosse Terre** 46°41'·6N 1°57'·8W Fl(4)WR.12s25m17/13M 290°-W-125°-R-145° White truncated conical tower

Ldg Lts 043·5°

2. *Front* 46°41'·9N 1°56'·7W DirOc(3+1)R.12s7m13M 033·5°-intens-053·5° White square tower, red top
3. *Rear* 260m from front DirOc(3+1)12s28m13M 033·5°-intens-053·5° Synchronised with front White square tower, red top
4. **Pilours buoy** 46°41'·0N 1°58'·0W Q(6)+ LFl.15s S card pillar buoy Bell
5. **NW jetty head** 46°41'·6N 1°57'·2W Fl(2)WR.6s8m10/5M 045°-R-225°-W-045° Red column on white hut
6. **SE jetty head** 46°41'·5N 1°57'·2W Q.WG.8m8/6M Reed 20s 045°-G-335°-W-045° White structure, green top

RADIO

VHF Ch 9 0600–2200 LT

APPROACH AND ENTRANCE

By day

The entrance can be located by the low rocky headland of Grosse Terre on the N side and the high lighthouse of Croix-de-Vie. On nearer approach Pill'Hours – a low reef of rocks like a small island – will be seen with the entrance and the leading lighthouses beyond.

Approach should be made, preferably shortly before high water, with the leading lighthouses which are white towers with red tops, in transit bearing 043°. If coming from the S, the front leading mark is hidden behind the grassy dunes until nearly on the transit. This approach leaves Pilours S cardinal buoy 250m to port and, further in, the end of the Pilours reef 160m to port. The entrance lies between the two outer breakwater heads, and the transit leads on the SE side of the entrance following close to and parallel to the Jetée de la Garenne. This line is out of the dredged channel, so incoming vessels should borrow to port and keep in the buoyed channel after the mole head is passed.

Lit buoys lead up the channel and into the sharp curve to starboard. The stream runs very hard here and the buoys should be given a good berth as they are moored on the high ground beside the channel. After a 90° turn to starboard, the channel passes the fishing-boat basins to reach the marina. The reception berth lies at the far end, beyond the fuel berth and round the bend to port. There is not much room to manoeuvre off the pontoon and there are many moorings, but the shallow water on the

The visitors pontoon near low water. Whilst there is plenty of water on the berths, when turning the channel is narrow and the stream runs hard

east side is marked by green buoys. Beware of the strong stream.

Departure should be made before high water, as the strong ebb quickly raises a sea at the entrance.

By night

The entrance is well lit. Get the leading lights in line[2,3] before passing Pilours buoy[4] and once the SE breakwater head[6] is reached, use the lit buoys marking the channel as a guide. Unless conditions are ideal (slack water and little wind) it would be better for a stranger to borrow a vacant berth in the main part of the marina temporarily, rather than to attempt the constricted visitors' pontoon in the dark.

BERTHS AND ANCHORAGE

The visitors' pontoon is often crowded and marina staff may direct yachts, particularly those over 10m, to a vacant berth in the main part of the marina.

FACILITIES

Fuel berth, travel-lift. All repairs, engineers, chandlers. A popular beach resort with shops, banks, hotels and restaurants. Supermarket over the bridge in St-Giles. Croix-de-Vie is an important fishing port with all facilities for fishing vessels. Railway to Nantes.

51. Les Sables d'Olonne

46°30'N 1°48'W

GENERAL

Yachts bound south for La Rochelle often pass within sight of Les Sables d'Olonne, which is situated some 35M NW of their destination. It is a convenient staging point, although on a small-scale chart the entrance appears shallow, beset with rocks and a lee shore to the prevailing winds. In fact, the harbour is easy of access and the marina and town provide excellent facilities. The approach is rough in strong SE, S or SW winds, especially if there is a swell, owing to the shoals. In bad weather the southeast approach is the safer and, given plenty of rise of tide, fishing vessels approach and enter the harbour in really severe weather.

The town of Les Sables d'Olonne on the east side of the entrance is a large sophisticated holiday resort with a casino, many hotels and restaurants facing the sands. A narrow peninsula separates this from the fishing port with its market and cafés. Visiting yachts may not lie here, but Port Olona, a large marina, has been set up in the dredged scouring basin further inland. This is a long way from the town by the ring road but the facilities of the town of La Chaume on the west bank are readily accessible.

Les Sables d'Olonne from the east

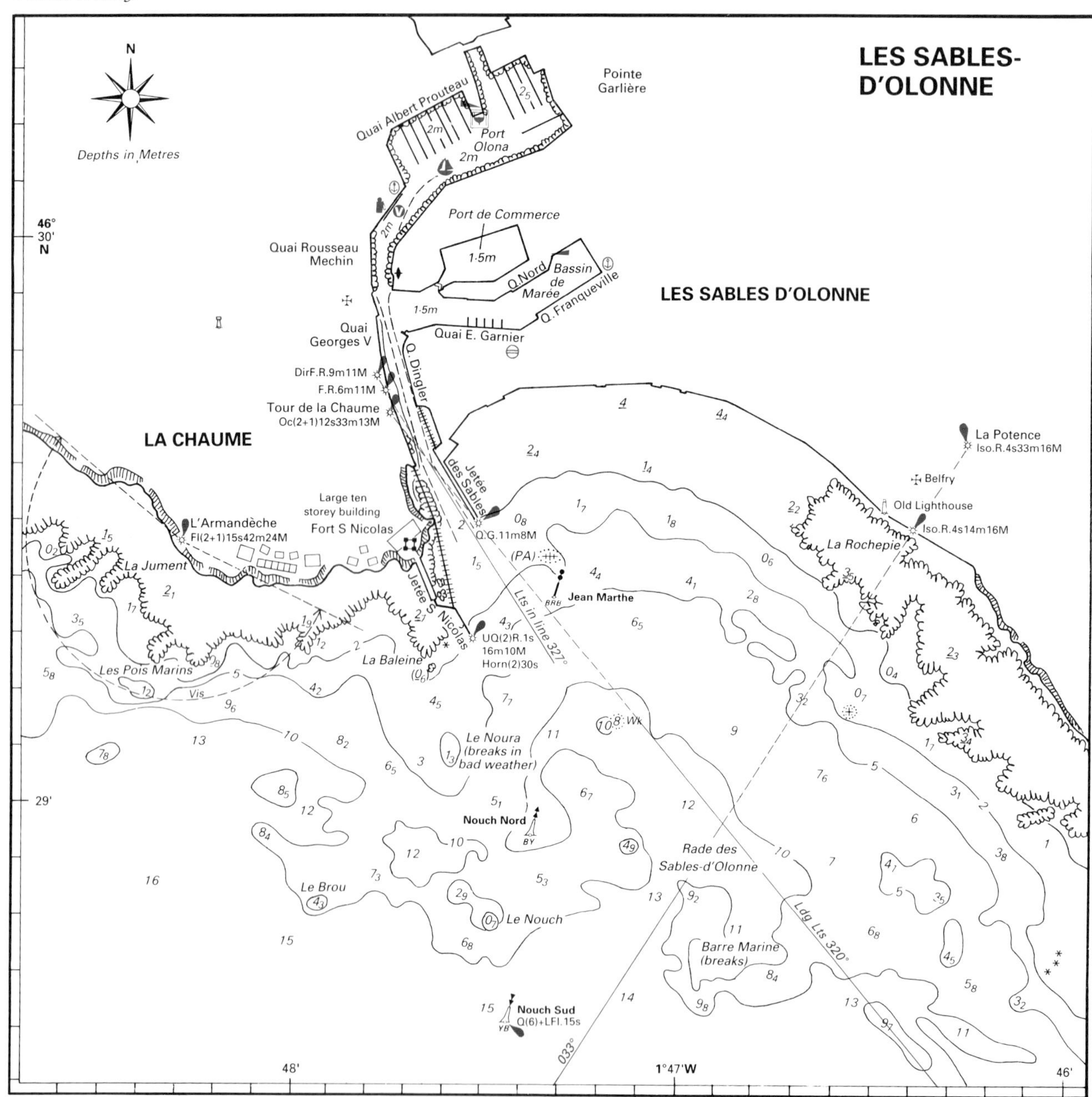

Plan 62

Charts

BA *3640, 2663*
Imray *C30*

TIDAL DATA

Times and heights

Time differences				Height differences			
HW		LW		MHWS	MHWN	MLWN	MLWS
BREST							
0500 and 1700	1100 and 2300	0500 and 1700	1100 and 2300	6·9	5·4	2·6	1·0
Les Sables d'Olonne							
–0030	+0015	–0035	–0035	–1·7	–1·3	–0·6	–0·3

Tidal streams

In the offing the streams are weak, rarely exceeding ½kt. In the Rade the streams are negligible but in the harbour itself they are stronger and on the reception pontoon the ebb may reach 2·5kts.

Depths

There is 1·1m just inside the west breakwater. The channel is dredged to 1·5m and the marina to 1·5m–3·5m with 2m in the main part.

The entrance to Les Sables d'Olonne is wide

LIGHTS

1. **L'Armandèche** 46°29'·4N 1°48'·3W
   Fl(2+1)15s42m24M 295°-vis-130°
   White 6-sided tower, red top
2. **Les Barges** 46°29'·7N 1°50'·4W
   Fl(2)R.10s25m13M 205°-obscd-265° Grey tower
3. **Petite Barge buoy** 46°28'·9N 1°50'·6W
   Q(6)+LFl.15s8m3M Whis **S** card HFPB

Passe du SW Ldg Lts 033°

4. *Front* 46°29'·5N 1°46'·3W Iso.R.4s14m16M
   Shown throughout 24hrs Metal mast
5. *Rear* 46°29'·6N 1°46'·1W 330m from front
   Iso.R.4s33m16M Shown throughout 24hrs
   White square masonry tower
6. **Nouch Sud buoy** 46°28'·6N 1°47'·3W
   Q(6)+LFl.15s S card pillar buoy
   (*Note* same light char as Petite Barge)

Passe du SE Ldg Lts 320°

7. *Front* **Jetée des Sables head** 46°29'·4N 1°47'·5W
   Q.G.11m8M White tower, green top
8. *Rear* **Tour de la Chaume** 46°29'·7N 1°47'·7W
   465m from front Oc(2+1)12s33m13M
   Large grey square tower surmounted by white turret
9. **Jetée Saint Nicolas head** 46°29'·2N 1°47'·5W
   UQ(2)R.1s16m10M Horn(2)30s 143°-vis-094°
   White tower, red top

Entrance Ldg Lts 327°

10. *Front* 46°29'·7N 1°47'·7W F.R.6m11M
    Red square on white hut
11. *Rear* 65m from front DirF.R.9m11M
    324°-intens-330° Red square on white hut

RADIO

VHF Ch 9, 16 0700–2100 LT

APPROACH AND ENTRANCE

The harbour lies about 1M to the SE of the Pointe de l'Aiguille, SE of which is the tall white lighthouse of L'Armandèche. On the E side of the harbour the hotels and other large buildings on the long curving front are also conspicuous when approaching from the S.

Entry under sail is prohibited.

By day

From the W or NW, round La Petite Barge S cardinal buoy then steer 095° to identify Nouch Sud buoy which is also left to port. Proceed eastwards until the entrance has been positively identified. The white lighthouse with red top on the head of the west breakwater should be conspicuous. Behind it the tall square crenellated tower of La Chaume is partially masked by an eight-storey building but can be located to the left of the church spire. Approach the entrance with La Chaume tower in transit with the light tower on the E mole (white with a green top) bearing 320°. If entering near low water, when the W breakwater head is abeam to port, alter to port to bring the red panels on the inner light structures into transit bearing 327°, and follow this transit into the channel.

Approaching at half tide or over, in ordinary weather, it is unnecessary to use the transits and yachts can cross over the rocks and shoals to the S and sail directly to the harbour entrance.

Approaching from the S, use the SE approach, sailing straight for the transit of the E mole head and La Chaume tower bearing 320°. This leaves all the shoals to port and the water is deep until within 400m of the harbour entrance; this approach should always be used in bad weather.

By night

The harbour is well lit. Follow the leading lights[7,8] on 320° until the E breakwater head light is abeam to port. At this point make a bold alteration to port to get the entrance leading lights[10,11] into line on 327°. Once inside the breakwaters there will be enough background light to follow the channel up past the fishing harbour to the marina.

BERTHS AND ANCHORAGE

The reception pontoon is on the port side just before the fuel berth and the marina basin. The ebb runs hard here. Secure and visit the *capitainerie* to be allocated a berth.

FACILITIES

All the facilities of one of France's premier yachting centres, including fuel, 28-tonne travel-lift, two slips, and all repair facilities. Some shops and café-bars and restaurants in the marina complex.

The nearest outside banks, shops and restaurants are those of La Chaume. Excellent communications from Les Sables d'Olonne by train, bus and air.

Bourgenay

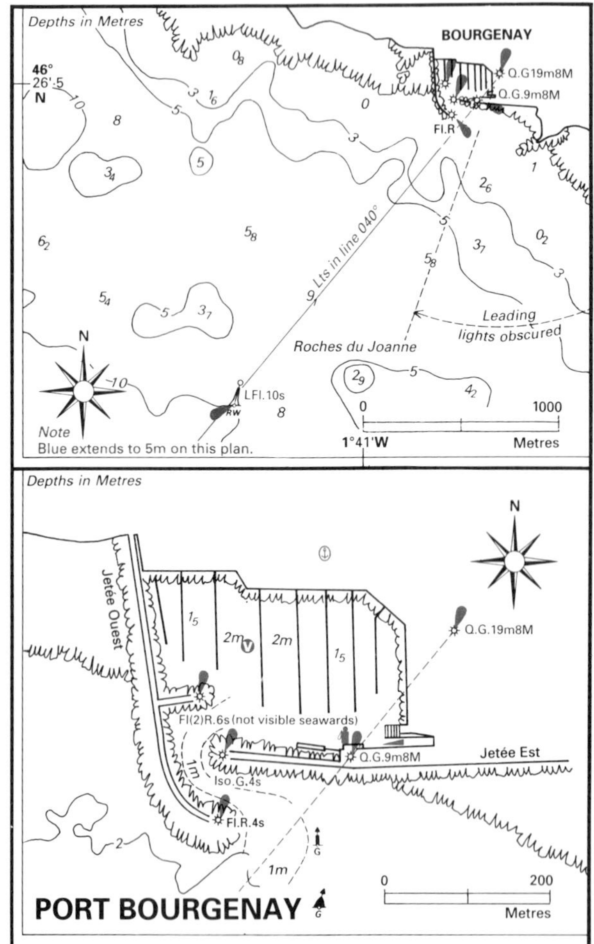

Plan 63

52. Bourgenay

46°26'N 1°41'W

GENERAL

This large marina is situated some 6M southeast of Les Sables-d'Olonne. Behind the marina is a large holiday complex and an old château with grey turrets which is now a convent; the conspicuous white topmark on the highest turret is in fact a statue of Notre Dame d'Esperance. The entrance lies between a low-lying, rocky and rather featureless coastline to the northwest and a sandy beach to the southeast, at the entrance to the river leading up to the town of Talmont. Entry should not be attempted in strong westerly winds, but there is complete shelter inside.

Although the marina is rather impersonal, it is conveniently placed for those heading for the Ile de Ré or La Rochelle and is less crowded and more peaceful than Les Sables-d'Olonne.

Charts

BA *2663*
Imray *C41*

TIDAL DATA

Times and heights

	Time differences				Height differences			
	HW		LW		MHWS	MHWN	MLWN	MLWS
BREST								
	0500 and 1700	1100 and 2300	0500 and 1700	1100 and 2300	6·9	5·4	2·6	1·0
Les Sables d'Olonne								
	−0030	+0015	−0035	−0035	−1·7	−1·3	−0·6	−0·3

Tidal streams

3M offshore the stream runs WNW from +0200 to +0500 Brest, ½ to 1½kts; SE from −0430 to −0000 Brest, ½ to 1kt.

Depths

1m in the entrance, 1–2m at the pontoons.

The entrance to Bourgenay is between overlapping breakwaters

LIGHTS

1. **Fairway buoy** 46°25'·3N 1°41'·8W LFl.10s
   Red and white striped pillar buoy

Ldg Lts 040°

2. *Front* 46°26'·4N 1°40'·5W Q.G.9m8M
   020°-vis-060° Green rectangle on white tower
3. *Rear* 190m from front Q.G.19m8M 010°-vis-070°
   Green rectangle on white tower
4. **W breakwater head** 46°26'·3N 1°40'·7W
   Fl.R.4s9M Red structure
5. **E mole head** 46°26'·4N 1°40'·7W Iso.G.4s5M
   Not visible to seaward
6. **W breakwater spur head** Fl(2)R.6s5M
   Not visible to seaward

RADIO

VHF Ch 16, 9 0800–2100LT

APPROACH AND ENTRANCE

By day

Locate the fairway buoy situated 1M SW of the marina. From the buoy the marina will be seen, bearing 040° and the leading marks, green panels on white columns, can be identified with binoculars.

Steer for the breakwaters, keeping the leading marks in line bearing 040°. On close approach leave a green buoy and a green beacon to starboard; then make a 90° turn to port to enter the marina, followed by a 90° turn to starboard. Fluorescent red and white chevrons indicate this latter turn. The water in the entrance can be confused and dangerous during strong SW winds.

By night

It is only necessary to keep on the leading lights[2,3] until the entrance is reached. The breakwater heads are lit[4,5].

BERTHING

The reception pontoon is marked E. Visitors should secure to it unless met by a marina launch and shown to a berth. There are 110 berths for visitors; maximum length 20m.

FACILITIES

Fuel berth, grid, slip, 15-tonne mobile crane, chandlery and engineers. Café-bars, chandlers, small food shop. Supermarket and post office up the hill past the convent, about 500m.

53. Jard-sur-Mer

46°24'N 1°35'W

GENERAL

This small drying harbour lies 10M north of the tip of Ile de Ré. It is seldom visited but is a pleasant spot for those who can take the ground. The village of Jard-sur-Mer has reasonable facilities and there are good beaches nearby.

In offshore weather at neaps a deeper draught yacht could find a pleasant day anchorage off the harbour.

Charts

BA *2641, 2663*
Imray *C41*

TIDAL DATA

Times and heights

Time differences				Height differences			
HW		LW		MHWS	MHWN	MLWN	MLWS
BREST							
0500 and 1700	1100 and 2300	0500 and 1700	1100 and 2300	6·9	5·4	2·6	1·0
Les Sables d'Olonne							
–0030	+0015	–0035	–0035	–1·7	–1·3	–0·6	–0·3

Tidal streams

Offshore the stream runs NW from +0220 to +0500 Brest, 1 to 2⅞kts; SE from −0430 to −0030 Brest, 1½–2kts.

Depths

Depths shelve during the approach from 5m at the first buoy to the breakwater head, which dries.

LIGHTS

There are no lights and night entry is not advised.

RADIO

VHF Ch 9 0800–1200 and 1400–1800 LT

APPROACH AND ENTRANCE

From an initial position 46°23'·5N 1°35'W identify the leading marks on the shore bearing about 035°. They consist of white beacons set amongst the sand dunes. Bring them into line, bearing 038° and maintain this heading towards the shore, passing between a red and a green buoy. The next transit, two red boards with white central stripe, which

Looking west into La Jard-sur-Mer near high water. From the beacons in, the harbour dries

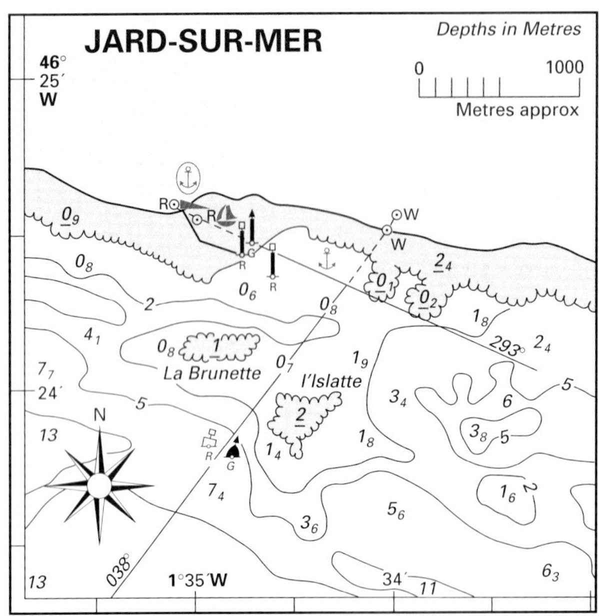

Plan 64

marks the course of 293° into the harbour is difficult to identify. It is sufficient to turn towards the harbour once past the line of the breakwater. Beacons mark the channel in.

BERTHS AND ANCHORAGE

The best anchorage is as shown on the plan, just west of the initial leading line and as close in as depth allows. Only yachts which can take the ground may use the harbour. They should use anchors out ahead and astern, clear of the moorings. Alternatively a mooring might be borrowed.

FACILITIES

There are showers and toilets at the *capitainerie*. Modest shops in the village which is a short walk away.

54. L'Aiguillon, La Faute-sur-Mer and Marans

L'Aiguillon Le Lay buoy 46°16'·15N 1°16'·4W
Marans Fairway buoy 46°15'·8N 1°11'·3W

GENERAL

Six miles north of La Pallice and to the NE of the Ile de Ré, two rivers flow between mud flats into the Pertuis Breton. The westernmost is Le Lay, leading to the town of L'Aiguillon. The E'most is La Sèvre Niortaise, which leads from the Anse de l'Aiguillon to a lock, from which a canal leads to Marans. It is perverse that the town of L'Aiguillon is on a river which does not flow into the Anse de l'Aiguillon.

The entrances to both rivers, though sheltered at a distance by the Ile de Ré, are exposed to the S and W and, being shallow, are rough in winds from that quarter. Entry should only be attempted in fine weather or with offshore winds. Neither river is much visited by yachts and they provide an

Le Lay river leads to the town of L'Aiguillon

interesting excursion off the beaten track in suitable conditions. The scenery is similar to that of Holland or the Fens. The land is low and the rivers wind between training banks. The bird life is considerable, and with every variety of hawk in action along the poplar-lined canal to Marans one wonders how the white egrets, duck and other birds can survive.

Marans is a pleasant inland market town, worth visiting, with reasonable, and improving, facilities for yachts and would be a good place to leave a boat. Visitors are made very welcome.

At L'Aiguillon and La Faute a yacht will almost certainly have to take the ground in very soft mud and she is likely to be a good way from any facilities.

Charts

BA *2641*
Imray *C41*

TIDAL DATA

Times and heights

Time differences				Height differences			
HW		LW		MHWS	MHWN	MLWN	MLWS
POINTE DE GRAVE							
0000 and 1200	0600 and 1800	0500 and 1700	1200 and 2400	5·4	4·4	2·1	1·0
St Martin, Ile de Ré							
+0007	−0032	−0030	−0025	+0·5	+0·3	+0·2	−0·1

Tidal streams

In the Pertuis Breton the flood runs ESE and the ebb WNW, spring rates 2kts. Off the Pointe du Grouin du Crou, they turn about half an hour after high low water. In Le Lay river, leading to L'Aiguillon, the currents are about 1·5kts springs. In La Sèvre Niortaise, leading to Marans, the streams are about 4kts springs.

Depths

Le Lay dries in parts. The approach channel to La Sèvre Niortaise dries 0·1m. The canal to Marans once had more than 3m, to accommodate the coaster which used the port. It is reported to have silted, but there are plenty of yachts of 2m draught at Marans that make the passage up and down the canal.

LIGHTS

Strangers should not attempt entry to either river at night.

L'Aiguillon and La Faute-sur-Mer

Cautions

The coast outside and the river banks are devoted to the culture of mussels. These are grown on substantial timber piles which cover at HW and are very dangerous. The areas are marked by a line of yellow buoys outside the river and withies with branching tops inside. However, the yellow buoys cannot be relied on and in 1998 many were missing. Withies with plain tops mark the oyster beds. Entering Le Lay river the channel is marked by beacons, but in places the timber piles for the mussels extend into the channel.

Lying SW of the Pointe d'Arçay is a rectangular shellfish-culture area, well marked by four (N, E, S and W) cardinal buoys and two yellow buoys. This area contains buoys connected by lines near the surface and should not be entered.

ENTRANCE

The entrance to Le Lay river is not easy to locate from seaward. The low Pointe d'Arçay merges with the low shore NW of Pointe de l'Aiguillon and it is not until an incoming vessel closes with the land that the course of the river opens up. Pointe de l'Aiguillon is a long finger of sand which may be seen from a considerable distance if the sun is on it. There is a large black beacon on the extremity.

Entry should only be made with the tide well up. From a position about 0·3M W of Le Lay buoy (S cardinal), the river is entered with the transformer on La Dive, adjacent to a conspicuous barn, bearing 035°. This course passes between No. 1 and No. 2 buoys.

Thence the channel swings steadily about 60° to port between oyster and mussel beds, until the river opens up and the distant town of L'Aiguillon, with the prominent water tower of Bel Air to the NW, is seen ahead. The channel is marked by beacons; keep closer to those on the SW side but at least 15m away from beacons and withies throughout.

A low stone jetty will be passed, and there are a few buildings on the starboard bank half a mile

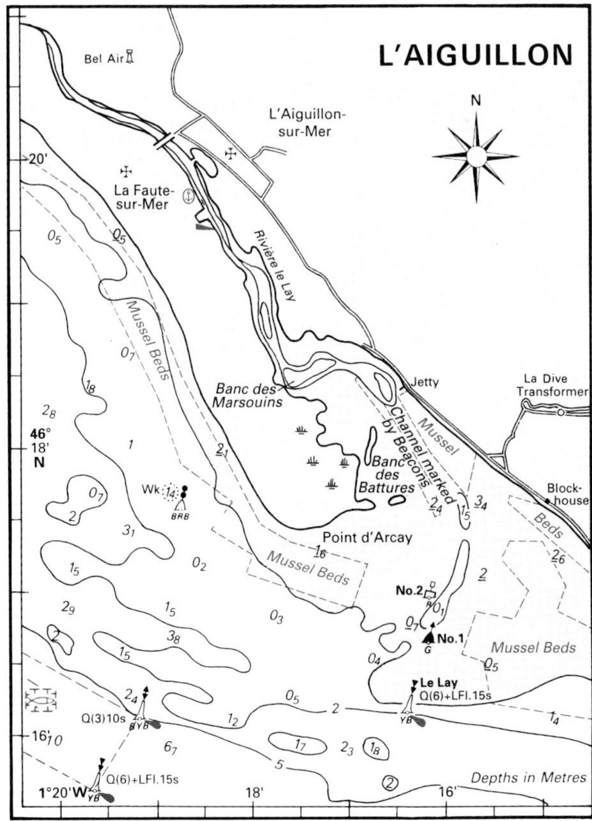

Plan 65

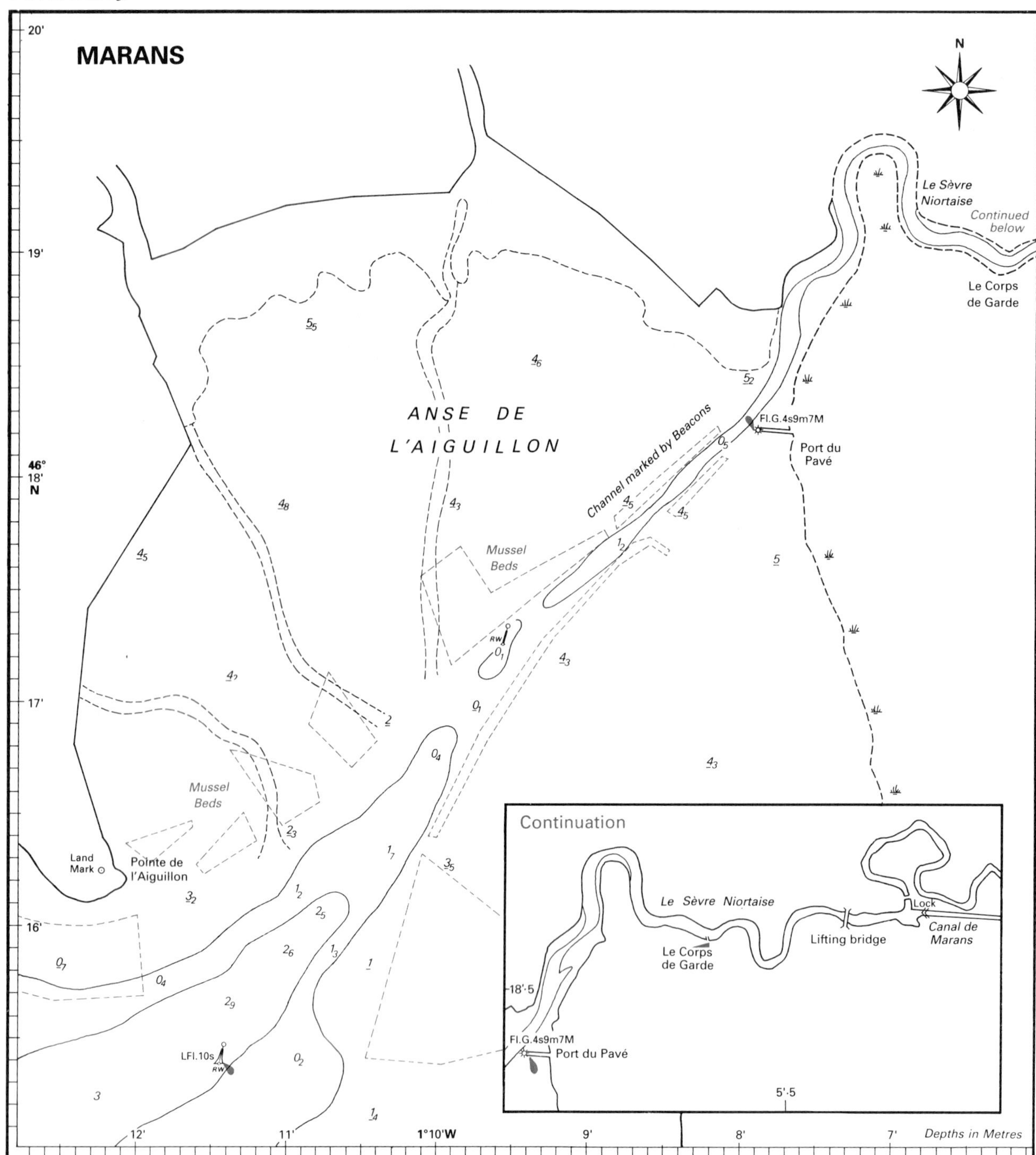

Plan 66

beyond the jetty. Here the channel swings round S of W and becomes very narrow. There is a middle ground, the Banc des Marsouins, marked by beacons. The S channel is narrow and, although it is deeper, the N one is to be preferred, though it is also narrow.

Past the Banc des Marsouins the river bends 90° to starboard into a reach running NW to the bridge at L'Aiguillon-sur-Mer. All along the bank to port are wooden jetties and mooring posts for small fishing boats and yachts, which dry out on a muddy bottom.

ANCHORAGE AND MOORING

On the west bank about two-thirds of the way up to the bridge, at the Port de la Faute, is a landing slip marked by two posts with orange tops. Just upstream of the slip is the 'yacht club' jetty (drying), where visitors may secure. Continuing up to L'Aiguillon, the river is full of fishing-boat moorings and wooden jetties line the starboard bank.

As an alternative to the La Faute jetty, it may be possible to anchor on soundings or arrange to borrow a mooring in the pool below the bridge at L'Aiguillon. Here depths are uncertain due to silting

At L'Aiguillon the river dries, except for a narrow channel in the centre

and the river can almost dry on any tide. Moorings are generally for shallow-draught fishing boats.

FACILITIES
Just below the bridge on the starboard side are a slipway and a boat yard. No fuel at L'Aiguillon. Hotel, restaurants, shops and bus service in the town. A short walk across the peninsula leads to good bathing at La Faute.

Marans

APPROACH AND ENTRANCE
The tides run very hard in La Sèvre Niortaise but it is desirable to enter well before high water to make sure of reaching the lock in time. On the Pointe de l'Aiguillon there is a large black beacon, with a topmark. A mile to the SE is L'Aiguillon fairway buoy. Leaving this buoy close to port, make good a course of 038° for the smaller RW spar buoy at the entrance to the buoyed channel leading into the river.

The Anse de l'Aiguillon is shallow, almost circular and about three miles wide. The mud flats on either side of the channel dry 4m or more and are covered with mussel beds, surrounded by piles. It is important to cross between the two RW buoys, which are nearly 2M apart, without deviating from the channel, and binoculars may be necessary to locate the second buoy. The channel dries 0·1m ½M before the second buoy and 0·0m just beyond, where the red and green channel buoys lead past the Port du Pavé slip marked by a green beacon and into the river.

In the river the plan shows where the channel lies in relation to the training banks. There are a few buoys marking shoals on the bends; otherwise keep in the middle. There is a landing on the starboard bank, at Le Corps de Garde, with fishing-boat moorings.

About three miles from the river entrance the yacht will reach the lifting bridge and the Brault lock giving access to the canal leading to Marans. There are two waiting buoys on the starboard side before the bridge. Do not lie to these on a falling tide with a strong westerly wind or you will be blown onto the bank.

The bridge is operated from the lock-keeper's cabin, with TV cameras to observe the road and river traffic. During working hours, if boats are waiting, the bridge will be opened to allow the lock to be entered at high water at the lock. Departure is possible one hour before high water. The lock-keeper can be telephoned in advance (☎ 46 01 53 77).

The lock is enormous (104m long and 45m wide), with gently sloping banks. There is a short pontoon on the port-hand side to which a yacht may secure while waiting for the lock to be operated. At the upper end of the lock is a swing road bridge.

The pretty tree-lined canal leads straight for about 3M to the port of Marans. Towards the end of the canal it appears to come to a dead end, but a channel opens up to starboard, through a pair of permanently open lock gates, into the port of Marans.

BERTHING
By far the best place is the port of Marans. Moor or raft alongside another yacht on the wall on the starboard side or secure to one of the pontoon berths further up.

FACILITIES
Water and electricity on the quay and on the pontoons. Fuel from the garage by the supermarket. Repairs; crane and slip. A number of yachts winter in Marans. Bank, hotels and a good choice of restaurants in the town, with all shops and an excellent supermarket on the main road out of town.

Marans has an attractive basin, with pontoons, close to the centre of the town

55. Ile de Ré

St-Martin-de-Ré 46°12'N 1°22'W

GENERAL

The island, over 13M long, projects to seaward west of La Rochelle, which can be approached either through the Pertuis d'Antioche on the south side of the island or by entering the Pertuis Breton on the north side and proceeding on under the road bridge connecting Ile de Ré with the mainland. This spectacular curving bridge, nearly two miles long, has ample clearance for most masts.

The three ports on the island, which are all tidal, lie in the Pertuis Breton. They are a popular destination for a weekend sail from the mainland as well as supporting substantial yachting activity of their own. Their approaches are all sheltered from the prevailing winds and it is often possible to anchor off whilst waiting to enter.

Ile de Ré is a sandy island fringed in many parts by rocks. It is low and the scenery similar to that in Holland, with windmills (now mostly converted into dwellings) and tall church spires rising high over the land. The island is a pleasant place in summer and since the bridge was opened ten years ago has become a popular holiday destination as well as seeing many day visitors. Bicycles can be hired and there are excellent cycle paths all over the island through the marshes, vineyards and salt pans where flowers and bird-life abound.

Peaceful as it is today, the Ile de Ré has been the scene of much fighting; it suffered greatly from the attacks of the English, and also during the religious wars. St-Martin, the capital, is a fortified town with Vauban ramparts and a citadel, which was considerably damaged during the bombardment by the Anglo-Dutch fleet in 1696.

There are three harbours: St-Martin, La Flotte, and Fier d'Ars. All the harbours are tidal but St-Martin and Ars en Ré have wet basins where yachts can lie afloat in complete shelter.

Charts

BA *2641, 2746, 2633*
Imray *C41*

TIDAL DATA

Times and heights

Time differences HW		Time differences LW		Height differences MHWS	MHWN	MLWN	MLWS
POINTE DE GRAVE							
0000 and 1200	0600 and 1800	0500 and 1700	1200 and 2400	5·4	4·4	2·1	1·0
St-Martin, Ile de Ré							
+0007	−0032	−0030	−0025	+0·5	+0·3	+0·2	−0·1

Tidal streams

The streams, which are weak offshore, increase as the island is approached. The streams S of the island, in the Pertuis d'Antioche, are given under La Rochelle on page 200. N of the island, in the Pertuis Breton where the harbours are, they are as follows:

Off Pointe de Lizay at the N of the island the flood runs ESE and the ebb WNW, spring rates 1½kts. Off the mainland opposite, near the Pointe du Grouin du Crou, the stream turns about half an hour after high water and low water and the rates are half a knot higher.

Near the E end of the island the flood meets the N-going flood through the Rade de la Pallice, and the ebb splits similarly, leaving a zone of relatively weak streams off the NE of the island. The streams in the Rade de Pallice do not exceed 1½kts springs.

Depths

These are given for individual ports.

LIGHTS

1. **Pointe du Grouin du Cou** (mainland)
   46°20'·7N 1°27'·8W Fl.WRG.5s29m20-16M
   034°-R-061°-W-117°-G-138°-W-034°
   White 8-sided tower, black lantern
2. **Les Baleineaux or Haut-Banc-du-Nord**
   46°15'·8N 1°35'·2W Oc(2)6s23m11M
   Pink tower, red top
3. **Les Baleines** 46°14'·7N 1°33'·7W
   Fl(4)15s53m27M Grey 8-sided tower, red lantern

Le Fier d'Ars Ldg Lts 265°

4. *Front* 46°14'·1N 1°28'·6W Iso.4s5m11M
   White rectangle on grey framework
5. *Rear* 46°14'·1N 1°28'·6W 370m from front
   DirIso.G.4s13m15M 264°-intens-266°
   Synchronised with front
   Green square tower on dwelling

Ars-en-Ré Ldg Lts 232°

6. *Front* 46°12'·8N 1°30'·5W Q.5m9M
   White rectangular hut, red lantern
7. *Rear* Q.13m11M 142°-vis-322°
   Black rectangle on white framework tower, green top

St-Martin de Ré

8. **Ramparts E of entrance** 46°12'·5N 1°21'·9W
   Oc(2)WR.6s18m10/7M
   shore-W-245°-R-281°-shore White tower, red top
9. **Mole head** 46°12'·6N 1°21'·9W Iso.G.4s10m 6M
   White tripod, green top
10. **W end of breakwater** Fl.R.2·5s7m2M
    White post, red top
11. **La Flotte-en-Ré** 46°11'·4N 1°19'·2W
    Fl.WG.4s10m12/9M 130°-G-205°-W-220°-G-257°
    Moiré effect Dir Lt 212·5°
    White round tower, green top
    Horn(3)30s sounded by day HW −2 to HW+2

RADIO

Ars-en-Ré VHF Ch 9 HW±2
St-Martin VHF Ch 9 0700–1900 LT

Fier d'Ars

46°14'N 1°29'W

GENERAL

The Mer du Fier is a lake-like expanse of water, most of which dries at low tide. It is entered from the Pertuis Breton through a narrow channel some 5M east of Les Baleines. Though shallow, it is well sheltered and is the principal yachting centre of the island. Deep-keel yachts may find space to lie afloat in the main anchorage off the Pointe du Fier, a

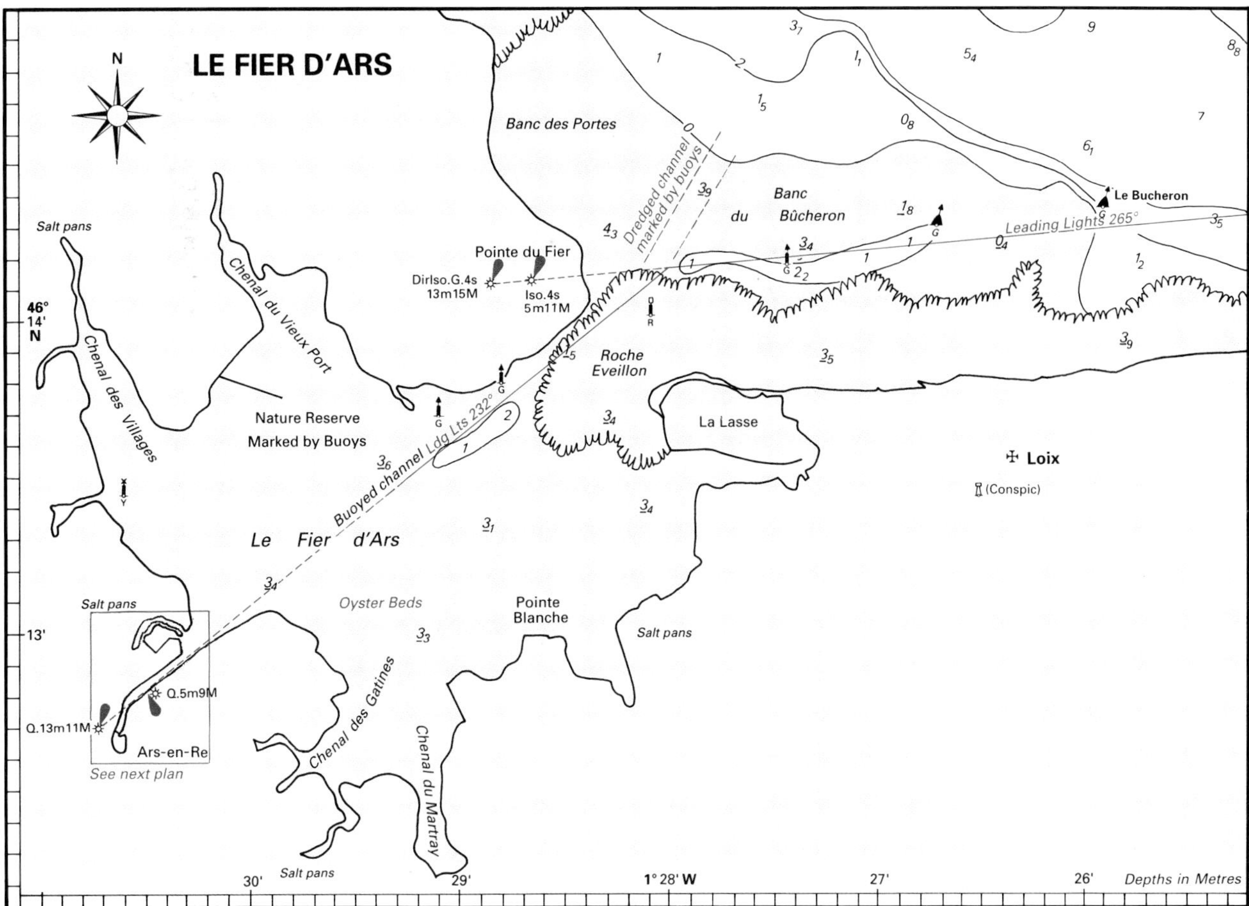

Plan 67

delightful spot, or further out in a more exposed anchorage.

At the head of the channel are two wet basins, the modern Port de la Criée and the older Bassin de la Prée in the centre of the village. Both can be accessed around HW.

Depths

The outer bar dries 0·4m. In the outer anchorage there is about 2m. The inner bar dries 1·5m and although the pool beyond it has 2m in places, it is silting and the best spots are taken by moorings; a yacht of over 1·5m draught will be pressed to find a space to anchor. The channel to the basins dries 3·4m. Port de la Criée has from 1·5 to 2m and the Bassin de la Prée has 1·8m.

APPROACH AND ENTRANCE

The approach is from the E. The channel lies between the ledges of rock extending from the island shore and the Banc du Bûcheron, a big sandbank extending 2M to the E of Pointe du Fer.

Close with the land ½M W of Pointe du Grouin. The water tower 1½M WSW of the point is conspicuous. To the E lies Les Islattes N cardinal tower, to the W the wooded Pointe du Fier and the shore north of it. The approach is with the two leading marks on the Pointe du Fier in transit, bearing 265°. These marks must not be confused with the high tower of Les Baleines lighthouse, which stands out more clearly over the trees and well to the right of the alignment. The leading marks appear in a gap in the trees. The rear mark is a green square tower on a dwelling and the front mark is square frame with glass panels and is usually easily visible.

Approaching on the transit, a buoy marking the end of the Banc de Bûcheron will be left to starboard. The Banc is tending to move southwards and a second starboard buoy close to the transit marks its present limit. This is followed by a green beacon which should be left 30–40m to starboard.

The channel shoals midway between the buoys, where it dries 0·4m; it then deepens again, and round the beacon is a long, narrow hole with up to 2·2m. This is the outer anchorage, but it is exposed and not recommended. Continuing on the transit for another ½M, Roche Eveillon port beacon will be seen. Just before the yacht reaches this beacon the leading lights/marks at Ars-en-Ré may be located (in transit on 232°). They are not easy to see by day, and the conspicuous slender black-topped church spire of Ars-en-Ré makes a better mark. When it bears 231° steer for it, leaving Roche Eveillon beacon 200m to port, over a rocky bottom which dries 1·5m. At this point the second deep pool forming the main anchorage begins; it has about 2m and is crowded with moorings. The tide runs strongly through the anchorage, especially near high water and continues to flood for up to ½hr after HW.

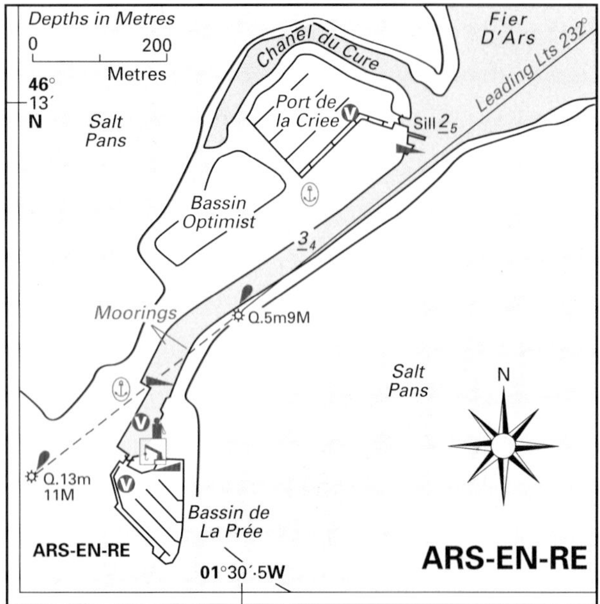

Plan 68

The entrance to the old basin, Bassin de la Prée, at Ars-en-Ré; the gate is open at tide time

If proceeding to the harbour, follow the buoyed channel which dries 3·4m.

A new channel has formed through the Banc du Bûcheron as shown on the plan. It is marked by small port and starboard-hand buoys, which do not always mark the deepest water. This channel carries the same depth as the main channel to the marinas – it is not recommended for a stranger until it has been inspected at low water, but on leaving provides a useful shortcut if heading north. It is possible that the formation of this channel will lead to increased silting in the main channel.

By night

Although both transits are lit, a night entry is not recommended for a stranger.

BERTHS AND ANCHORAGES

There are yacht moorings and an anchorage in 2m ½M E of Les Portes, which is N of Le Fier d'Ars. The outer anchorage in Le Fier is exposed and cannot be recommended.

The main anchorage has much better shelter, though it is somewhat exposed to the NE at high water. The tides also run hard here and the bottom is weedy. Land at the Pointe du Fier, which is a delightful strip of sand backed by woods.

The gate to Bassin de la Criée opens from 3hrs before to 3hrs after HW, sill 2·5m above the datum. At Bassin de La Priée the gate is open from 2½hrs before to 2½hrs after HW, sill 2·9m above the datum. Visitors secure to pontoons in both basins. There are drying berths immediately outside the gates to La Prée but these are mainly used by fishing vessels.

Le Chasse

Occasionally the channel is scoured by closing the gates to the basins at HW. At low water, the sluices are opened, allowing the water within the basins to fall to their normal level, a process which takes about 20 minutes. Access at these times is limited, but it is seldom done during the season.

The entrance to Port de la Criée at Ars-en-Ré

FACILITIES

From the anchorages by Pointe du Fier it is a 2M walk to Les Portes to reach the shops.

Bassin de la Criée has only marina facilities. At Bassin de la Prée, fuel, small crane, repairs, chandler. All shops, café-bars and restaurants in Ars-en-Ré.

St-Martin

46°12'N 1°22'W

GENERAL

St-Martin stands about halfway along the northeast side of the Ile de Ré. The harbour consists of an *avant-port*, sheltered by a mole, a wooden breakwater and a jetty; it is connected with the drying harbour by a narrow entrance channel. From the drying harbour a channel to starboard leads through dock gates to the wet dock. There is some fishing activity.

At one period Ile de Ré was independent for customs purposes and St-Martin was a prosperous port trading with America and distant parts; salt and wine were the principle exports. The wet dock is now used by yachts, for which it is ideal, being clean and having every convenience at hand. The town is pleasant and attractive and the Vaubin fortifications which surround it make an interesting visit, with an enjoyable walk around the ramparts. It was from the prison here that convicts were shipped to the penal settlements in French Guiana.

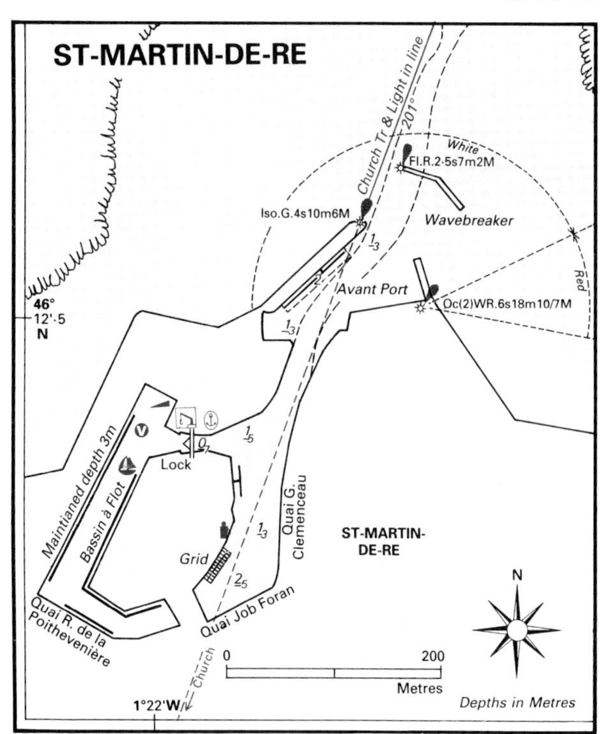

Plan 69

St-Martin de-Ré

St-Martin becomes almost impossibly crowded with coaches and day trippers during the holiday season and the basin becomes similarly crowded with yachts, particularly at the weekends.

Depths
The near approach dries 1·6m, the inner harbour dries 1·5m. Berths at the pontoon along the NW mole in the *avant-port* have been dredged to 2·0m, but they silt up quickly – however the bottom is soft mud in which a yacht will remain upright. In the wet dock there is 3m at neaps, more at springs.

APPROACH AND ENTRANCE

By day
There are extensive ledges of rock in and especially E and W of the approach to St-Martin, extending over ½M out from the shore. They are not so formidable as they appear at first glance on a chart, as the ones to the W farther offshore do not dry as much as the entrance channel and the ones to the E are marked by a N cardinal beacon.

The approach should be timed according to the draught of the yacht; between 2hrs before and 1½hrs after HW should give 2·2m of water at the entrance at neaps, and more at springs. A convenient leading line is with the square church tower in transit with St-Martin mole head light column on 201°. Leaving the wooden wavebreaker close to port, enter leaving the mole head very close to starboard. Then steer straight for the centre of the channel leading into the drying harbour. The channel to the dock gates will open up to starboard.

Approaching from the E, do not confuse the citadel and its small, walled boat harbour, 600m E of the port, with St-Martin itself; keep well to the N of the beacon on the Couronneau rocks, E of the town, as rocks drying up to 1m lie to the N of it.

By night
Make an initial position of about 46°15'N 1°21'W and approach with St-Martin light[8] bearing 200°. Note that the white sector of this light extends from 090° to 245° and crosses part of the outer ledges; it is not safe simply to keep in the white sector. On close approach alter to starboard to bring the mole light[9] to bear 195° and enter leaving the light[10], marking the NW end of the wooden wavebreaker, close to port and the mole light close to starboard.

MOORING

There are a number of white mooring buoys off the entrance and the Rade de St-Martin provides an anchorage, sheltered from winds from W through S to SE, in from 1·8 to 4m, inshore of La Rocha N cardinal buoy. This is a recognised anchorage for big ships; in offshore winds yachts can get closer in to anchor outside the yacht moorings, rather less than half a mile off the entrance in 2m sand and mud.

In the summer months a long pontoon is arranged along the Grand Môle with a section dredged to 2m along its length. This is said to be 16m broad to allow yachts to raft alongside the pontoon, but it quickly silts up with soft mud, into which the keels of deep-draught yachts sink. In northerly winds a swell enters round the wavebreaker, causing the pontoon to pitch.

There are quays in the drying harbour which dry 1·5m; vessels should not berth along the inner half of the W quay, where there is a large grid. However yachts normally use the wet dock. To be sure of a place inside during summer weekends it is essential to arrive early. To wait for the dock to open one can secure to the pontoon along the Grand Môle.

The gates are operated during the day from about 3hrs before to 2½hrs after HW, the exact time depending on the height of tide, with a shorter period at neaps. During the summer the 'day' runs from 0630–2200 and in July and August from 0500–2300. In the winter, hours are 0800–1800. Predicted times are posted at the *capitainerie* and are normally available at other harbours in the area.

In the wet basin, berth as directed by the harbour staff. There is not much room, visitors are likely to be rafted and plenty of fenders will be needed.

FACILITIES

Water on the pontoons and electricity on the quay, showers and toilets in the *capitainerie*. Fuel berth on the E wall of the drying basin. Shipyard, chandler and engineers. Slipway, grid and 9-tonne crane.

Bank, hotels, restaurants and all shops close by. Bicycle hire.

La Flotte-en-Ré

46°11'N 1°19'W

GENERAL

The drying harbour of La Flotte lies about 2M southeast of St-Martin; it is easily identified and the tall square church tower is conspicuous. The harbour is formed by two jetties, protected by a long curved outer mole. The narrow entrance faces east across the shallow bay. Although there is no wet basin as at St-Martin, the harbour is well sheltered, and is uncomfortable only in strong onshore winds.

A fishing port famous for lobsters, shrimps and sole, La Flotte is a compact town of short narrow streets and whitewashed houses, with a beautiful church.

Depths
The approach and harbour dry 2m.

APPROACH AND ENTRANCE

By day
La Flotte is easy to locate in the bay ½M W of Pointe des Barres. It is approached by a channel with mud and sand bottom which dries 2m and lies between ledges of rock, extending up to ½M seaward, covered with oyster beds marked by yellow beacons with diagonal cross topmarks.

Approach with the lighthouse bearing about 215°. A N cardinal beacon on the rocks off Pointe des Barres will be left about 600m to port. If

La Flotte-en-Ré

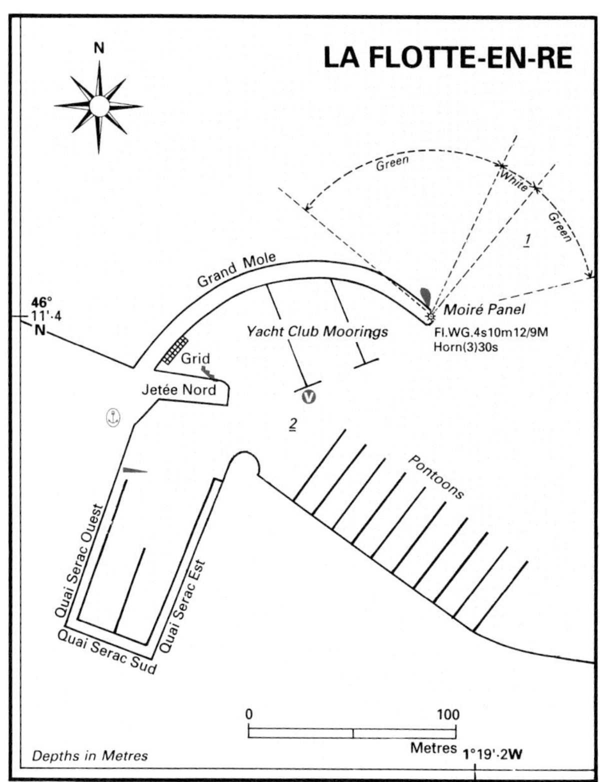

Plan 70

approaching from the E give a good berth to the beacon, as the rocks extend outside it.

Within 500m of the lighthouse, an illuminated panel with vertical black and orange stripes will be visible day and night, defining the close approach on 215·5°. This ingenious Moiré fringe system changes to an arrowhead pointing to the right if you are off course to port and to the left if you are off to starboard. If your error is great the arrowhead doubles or even triples! Change course in the direction indicated by the arrowhead and the vertical stripes will return when you are in the channel. Leave the breakwater head to starboard and steer for the narrow entrance between the jetty heads.

By night

The Moiré panel makes the approach easy.

MOORING

Deep-draught yachts can anchor or use the white mooring buoys some ¾M offshore in 2m.

The inner harbour is rectangular and dries 2m. Pontoons for local boats are installed in the inner half of the basin. Space for visitors is limited and it is more usual for them to secure to the ends of the pontoons on the inside of the outer breakwater where they sit in the mud. Alternatively they may dry out against the inner side of the Jetée Nord.

FACILITIES

Water and electricity on the pontoons. Water taps on the quay. Hotels, banks, restaurants and shops in the town.

Anse du Martray

46°11'N 1°28'W

GENERAL

This is an open anchorage on the south coast of Ile de Ré, off a sandy tourist beach, suitable in light NW to E winds.

APPROACH AND ENTRANCE

From a position ½M E of Chanchardon tower (octagonal, black with white base), steer north to a white iron mooring buoy and thence a further ½M on 018° to a second white buoy. Use the church spires of Ars-en-Ré and La Couarde-sur-Mer for fixing.

ANCHORAGE

From the second buoy, run in on about 340° towards the E end of the sea wall and anchor as tide and depth permit. The bottom is largely sandy, with a gentle gradient, but it is difficult for a deep draught yacht to get close to the beach.

FACILITIES

Land at the E end of the sea wall, where there is a ramp. 100m to the E there is a camp site with small supermarket, café, showers, toilets and launderette. The coast road leads W to Martray, where there are seafood shops and a cycle track through the saltpans and a road to Ars-en-Ré.

56. La Rochelle and Minimes

46°09'N 1°10'W

GENERAL

La Rochelle, halfway down the coastline of the Bay of Biscay, is often visited by yachts on passage to or from Spain or bound for the Mediterranean via the Midi canal. For others, it marks the farthest port in a cruise from England. There are few yachting centres south of it until the Gironde is entered. Beyond the Gironde, Arachon is the only port in a long, sandy, featureless coastline and it is not accessible in strong onshore weather.

The geographical position of La Rochelle therefore makes it important to yachtsmen. The shallow entrance to the Vieux Port, where yachts often berth in the heart of the city, passes between the impressive ancient towers of St Nicolas and La Chaine, between which a chain was once stretched to keep out marauding English privateers. Now, visiting yachts are welcomed and, except at big spring tides, most can lie afloat on the pontoons; there are also two wet basins.

The marina at Port des Minimes has pontoon berths for 3,000 yachts, which must make it amongst the largest yacht harbours in the world. It

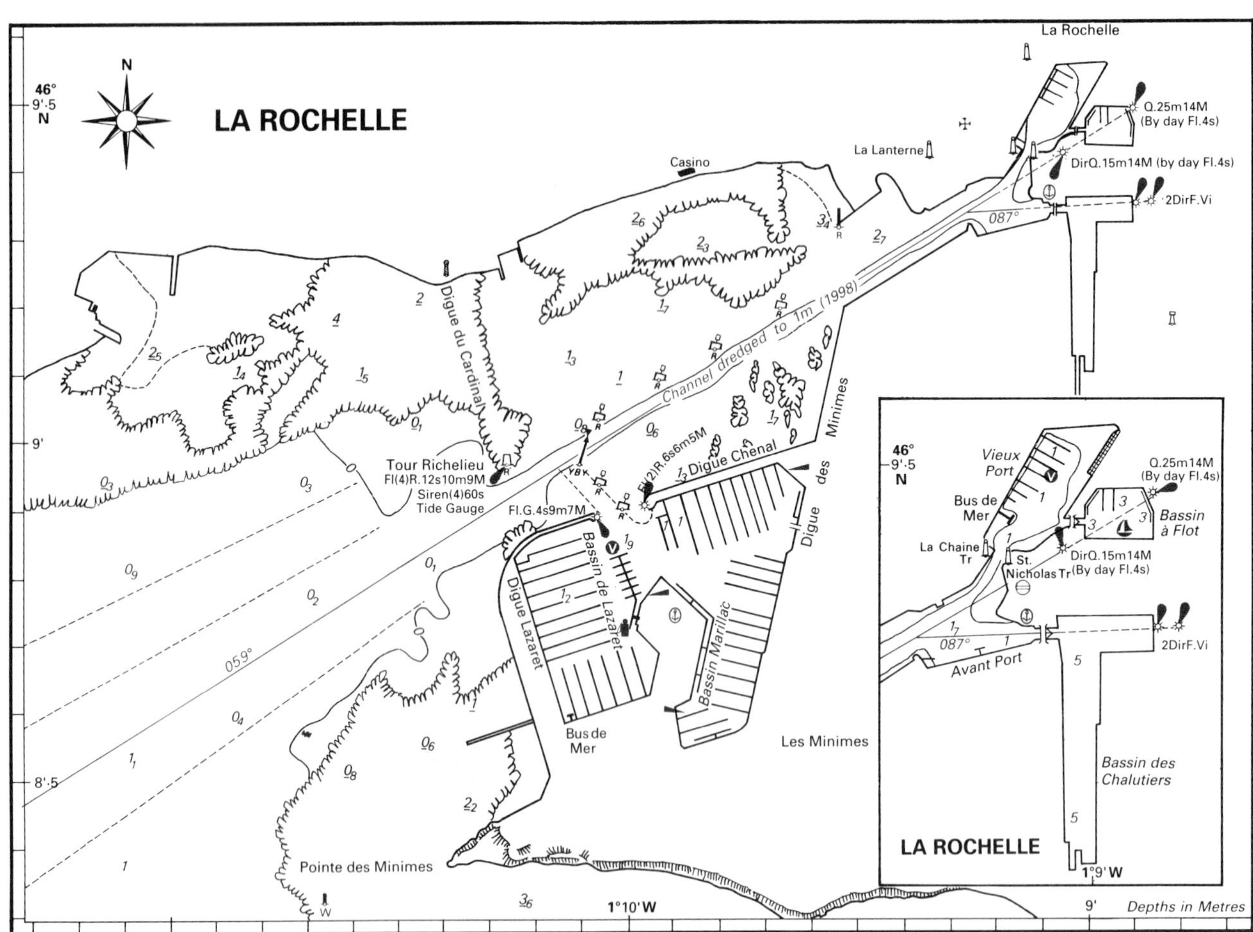

Plan 71

Minimes marina and La Rochelle

is a good place to leave a yacht and there is a frequent water taxi into the Vieux Port. It is, however, a long way from the shops and sights and, whilst practical, cannot be described as attractive.

La Rochelle has all the facilities a yachtsman, or holiday-maker, could wish for with excellent communications. Although it suffered in the Second World War, much of historic interest remains and it is a fine base from which to explore Iles d'Oléron and Ré, either by yacht or by road.

The Bassin à Flot in the centre of La Rochelle, suitable for a longer stay or for larger yachts

Yachts are not permitted to use either the commercial port of La Pallice or the fishing harbour, both of which lie west of the city.

Charts

BA *2743, 2746, 2641, 2663*
Imray *C41*

TIDAL DATA

Times and heights

Time differences				Height differences			
HW		LW		MHWS	MHWN	MLWN	MLWS
POINTE DE GRAVE							
0000 and 1200	0600 and 1800	0500 and 1700	1200 and 2400	5·4	4·4	2·1	1·0
La Rochelle							
+0015	–0030	–0025	–0020	+0·6	+0·5	+0·3	–0·1

Tidal streams

For the Pertuis Breton, see under Ile de Ré, page 194. In the narrows off La Pallice the flood runs N the ebb S, spring rates 1½kts. In the entrance to the Pertuis d'Antioche, N of Pointe de Chassiron, the flood runs E, the ebb W, spring rates 2kts; S of the Ile de Ré the streams turn about ½hr after HW and LW and are slightly weaker. The streams are weak in the harbour and its near approaches.

Depths

The approach carries 0·5m as far as Tour Richelieu; the buoyed channel beyond that was dredged to 1m in 1998 as far as the towers, but will silt. 1·0m can be found at some of the pontoons in the Vieux Port,

The entrance to Minimes marina

the bottom is so soft as to be almost liquid. The sill to the Bassin à Flot dries 1·2m with 3m maintained inside. There is 5m in Bassin des Chalutiers and 2m at Minimes marina.

LIGHTS

1. **Le Lavardin** 46°08'·1N 1°14'·5W
   Fl(2)WG.6s14m11/8M 160°-G-169°-W-160° two black balls on black tower, red band
2. **Tour Richelieu** 46°08'·9N 1°10'·4W
   Fl(4)R.12s10m9M Siren(4)60s Red 8-sided tower

Ldg Lts 059°

3. *Front* 46°09'·4N 1°09'·1W DirQ.15m13M 056°-intens-062°
   Red round tower, white bands (By day Fl.4s)
4. *Rear* 46°09'·5N 1°08'·9W 235m from front Q.25m14M 044°-vis-061°-obscd-065°-vis-074°
   Synchronised with front
   White 8-sided tower, green top (By day Fl.4s)
5. **Port de Minimes W mole head** 46°08'·9N 1°10'·1W Fl.G.4s9m7M White tower, green top
6. **Port de Minimes E mole head** 46°08'·9N 1°10'·0W Fl(2)R.6s6m5M White tower, red top

RADIO

Port des Minimes VHF Ch 9 24hr
La Rochelle VHF Ch 9 0600–2100 LT

APPROACH AND ENTRANCE

Caution

A firing danger area exists to the south of the entrance, marked by yellow buoys. This area is prohibited during working hours on weekdays, except public holidays.

By day

The distant approach is either through the Pertuis Breton, on the N side of Ile de Ré, and thence through the Rade de Pallice, or through the Pertuis d'Antioche on the S side.

The near approach is from a position about 1M S of Le Lavardin isolated danger beacon tower. In most conditions the red Tour Richelieu stands out against the background of the port buildings. Coming from the S of Ile de Ré, leave Le Lavardin at least ½M to port, as spoil ground of varying depth lies to the SE of the tower; its extremity is marked by a slender unlit S cardinal beacon. Coming from the Rade de Pallice, after passing under the Ile de Ré bridge, the outer breakwaters of La Pallice commercial harbour and the fishing harbour are left to port and the coastline followed at a distance of 500m until the Tour Richelieu has been sighted.

Steer for the red Tour Richelieu and identify the church and two towers of La Rochelle. Keep the towers bearing about 060° until the leading lighthouses are identified. These are just to the right of the larger, right-hand Tour St Nicolas. The front leading lighthouse is red with white bands and the rear lighthouse white with a green top – they show bright white lights by day, flashing every 4 seconds. With the 2 lighthouses in transit bearing 059° steer up the channel, leaving Tour Richelieu close to port.

If bound for Minimes Marina, the dredged entrance channel is marked by a W cardinal buoy and two red port-hand buoys. Do not cut the corner but rather get close to the W cardinal buoy before turning in.

If bound for the old port, follow the transit leaving four red channel buoys well to port. When close to the towers, bear to port and enter the harbour.

By night

Entry by night is easy with the leading lights[3,4] in transit bearing 059°. N of the line the leading lights can be obscured by the Tour St Nicolas. To enter Minimes marina, make the turn to starboard (course 140°) 200m past Tour Richelieu. The W cardinal buoy and two port-hand buoys marking the channel are unlit, but there is normally plenty of background light.

BERTHS AND ANCHORAGE

It is possible to anchor in Anse l'Oubye on the E end of Ile de Ré, in 2m sand and mud. There is good shelter from the W, but it is difficult to get ashore and there are no facilities.

In Port des Minimes, secure to the reception pontoon opposite the entrance and obtain a berth from the *capitainerie*.

In the Vieux Port there are visitors pontoons. If a deep draught yacht takes the ground at spring tides, she will remain upright in the soft mud. The basin is in the very centre of the liveliest part of the city and, whilst vibrant, may not be peaceful every night. It is possible to lock into the Bassin à Flot, and for a yacht over 12m, or one remaining for more than a couple of nights, this may be preferable. Access is from 2hrs before to ½hr after HW, but only by prior arrangement at night. Bassin de Chalutiers is for very large yachts which should discuss their requirements with the harbourmaster before arrival.

FACILITIES

Every imaginable facility is available. Banks, all kinds of shops, hotels and restaurants of every grade, yacht builders, chandlers, engineers and sailmakers. Most major marine manufacturers have agencies.

In the Vieux Port, the pontoons have water and electricity and there are showers and toilets by the Bassin à Flot.

Port des Minimes has a fuel berth at the *capitainerie*. There are showers and toilets, cranes and a travel-lift. Restaurants, cafés, food shops, chandlers, sailmakers and engineers are available on site, making a visit to the town for supplies unnecessary. Except at lowest tides, a ferry runs approximately hourly to the Vieux Port from the SW corner of the marina.

57. Ile d'Aix

46°01'N 1°11'W

GENERAL

Ile d'Aix lies about 8M south of La Rochelle and is a popular objective for a day sail; the anchorage is sufficiently sheltered for a night stop in fine weather. It is pleasanter in the evening, after the day-trippers have gone. The island is horseshoe-shaped and measures about a mile at its maximum. Within this area is a walled and moated village where Napoleon was imprisoned before he was taken to St Helena in HMS *Bellerophon*.

A few fishermen live on Ile d'Aix, together with people who seek the peace of an island free of convention and so small that all parts are within earshot of the sea.

The island is a pleasant place to stop whilst waiting for the tide to go up La Charente river.

Charts

BA *2748, 2746*
Imray *C41*

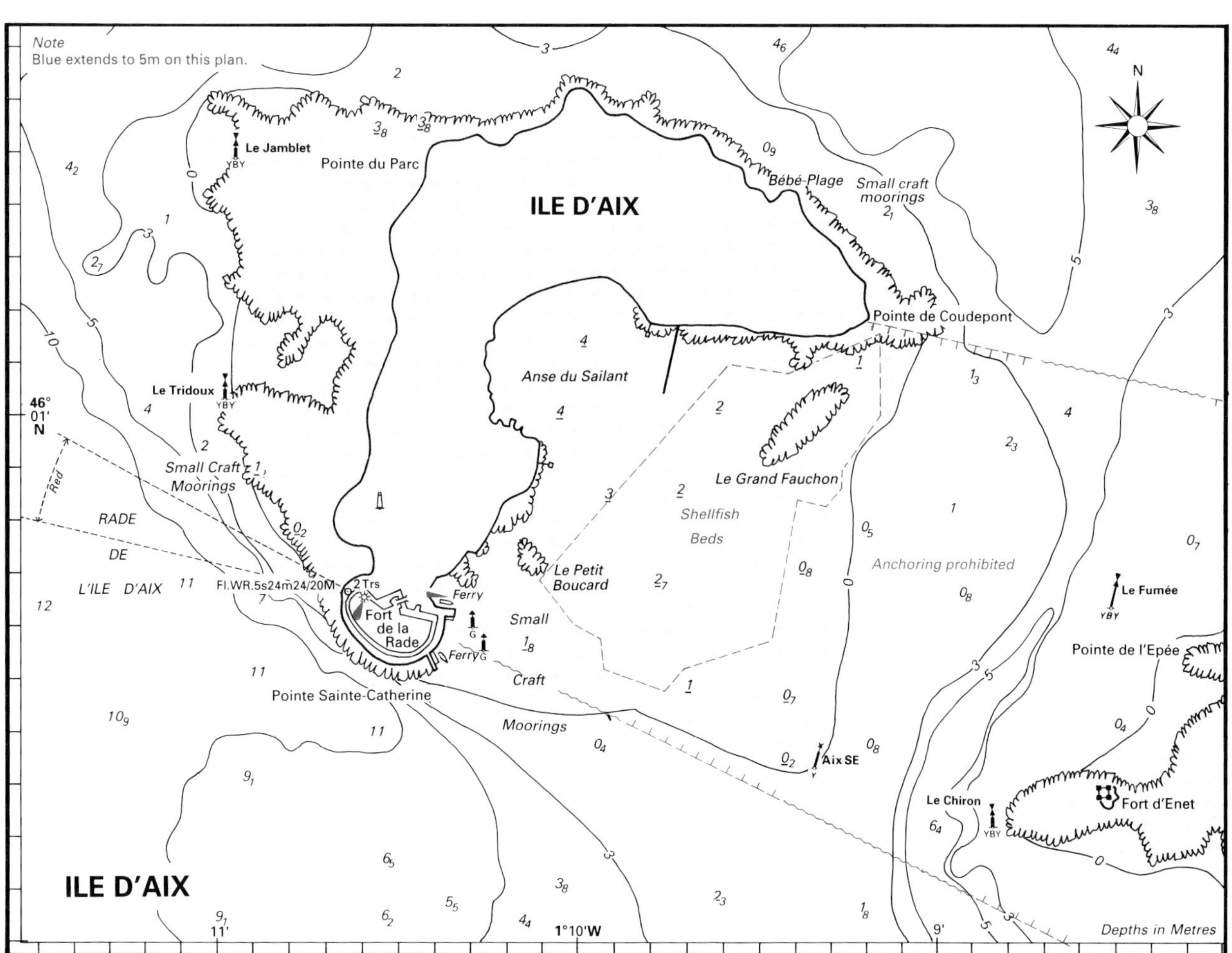

Plan 72

TIDAL DATA

Times and heights

Time differences				Height differences			
HW		LW		MHWS	MHWN	MLWN	MLWS
POINTE DE GRAVE							
0000	0600	0500	1200				
and	and	and	and	5·4	4·4	2·1	1·0
1200	1800	1700	2400				
Ile d'Aix							
+0015	−0040	−0030	−0025	+0·7	+0·5	+0·3	−0·1

Tidal streams

3M NW of the island the SE stream begins −0600 Pte de Grave and the NW begins −0030 Pte de Grave, spring rates 1kt. 1M SW of the island the SE stream begins −0530 Pte de Grave and the NW begins HW Pte de Grave, spring rates 2kts.

Depths

An open roadstead or drying beach; depths as required.

LIGHTS

1. **Chauveau** (SE of Ile de Ré) 46°08'·1N 1°16'·3W Oc(2+1)WR.27m15/11M 057°-W-094°-R-104°-W-342°-R-057° White round tower, red top
2. **Fort Boyard** 46°00'·0N 1°12'·8W Q(9)15s27m Fort
3. **Ile d'Aix** 46°00'·6N 1°10'·7W Fl.WR.5s24m24/20M 103°-R-118°-W-103° Two white round towers, red tops, one for the light, the other supporting the red sector screen

Looking NW over Ile d'Aix towards La Pallice. The twin light towers stand out well on Pte St Catherine

Fort Boyard

The twin light towers on Ile d'Aix are conspicuous

Shellfish beds are a real hazard in this area. These substantial posts are all just covered at high water

La Charente river entrance Ldg Lts 115°
4. *Front* 45°58'·0N 1°04'·3W
DirQ.R.8m19M 113°-intens-117°
White square tower, red top
5. *Rear* 45°57'·9N 1°03'·8W 600m from front
DirQ.R.21m20M 113°-intens-117°
White square tower, red top

APPROACH

By day

The approach is straightforward from any direction but probably easiest from the NW. Two W cardinal beacons mark the outlying rocks on the W side. The N one should be given a berth of at least 500m and the S one 200m. The SW side of the island is fairly clean and can be passed at a distance of 200m.

There is a narrow, deep channel to the E of the island. From the N, leave the E point of the island at least 500m to starboard to avoid a rocky spur and steer 195° to leave a W cardinal buoy and the conspicuous Fort d'Enet to port, passing between a W cardinal beacon to port and a yellow buoy, marking the SE corner of the Aix oyster beds, to starboard.

By night

From the NW, keep in the white sector of the Ile d'Aix light[3] until Chauveau light[1] turns from red to white, bearing 342°; steer 162° down this boundary, passing through the red sector of Ile d'Aix light. When this turns white again, steer on the leading lights for the Charante[4] bearing 115°. When Ile d'Aix light bears N steer 020° and anchor in 3m, or pick up a free mooring. There are liable to be yachts on moorings in this area.

ANCHORAGE

Anchor 100 to 200m off the jetty and landing slip at Pointe Sainte Catherine, the S point of the island, going in as far as draught allows. There are many moorings in this area. This anchorage is really sheltered only from the N and NE, but is partially sheltered from other directions by the mainland and Ile d'Oléron, so that it can be used in fine summer weather. The approaches are so well lit that there would be no difficulty in running for shelter to La Rochelle or elsewhere. The mud is very soft and the holding poor.

It is also possible to anchor off the N or SW side of the island on a calm day; there are moorings for visitors off Bebé-Plage. The Anse du Saillant, a sandy bay on the east side of the island, is a delightful place in which to dry out. It is essential to observe the obstructions at low water before venturing in from the south between the oyster beds and the rocky patches off the SE side of the island.

FACILITIES

Those of a village with modest shops, PO, restaurants, hotel, café-bars.

58. La Charente, Rochefort

Entrance 46°00'N 1°10'W
Rochefort 45°57'N 0°57'W

GENERAL

La Charante is an interesting river, away from the crowds, with a lot of bird life and some commercial traffic. The river winds through green fields between reedy banks, which have been reported to harbour mosquitoes on occasion. Rochefort is an historic town; it is a former naval base, well up the river for security from the British fleets. The wet basins have been converted into a flourishing marina close to the centre of the city, accessible at HW. The new road bridge gives a clearance of 30m and the old lifting bridge, still marked on the charts has been removed. Masted vessels can go up to Tonnay; the river is navigable for motor yachts, and said to be very attractive, for a considerable distance upstream to Saintes.

The transits at the river entrance are lit and at night a yacht can find her way far enough in to anchor in shelter. Night passage above Port-des-Barques is not permitted for small craft.

Most visitors find that Rochefort is a highlight of their cruise. The old rope-walk has been restored, and museums have been established in other buildings in the base. Upstream of the wet basin is what is claimed to be the oldest hydraulically-operated dry dock in the world, constructed in 1669. The original pumping apparatus has been repaired. In 1998, a full size replica of the frigate *Hermione* was under construction on the site where the original was built. This ship sailed from Rochefort to America in 1779 to assist the colonists during the American War of Independence. Below the town is one of the last working transporter bridges in Europe.

Rochefort has all the facilities of a regional centre and good facilities for yachtsmen as well. It has excellent communications. For all of these reasons, a growing number of British yachtsmen visit and

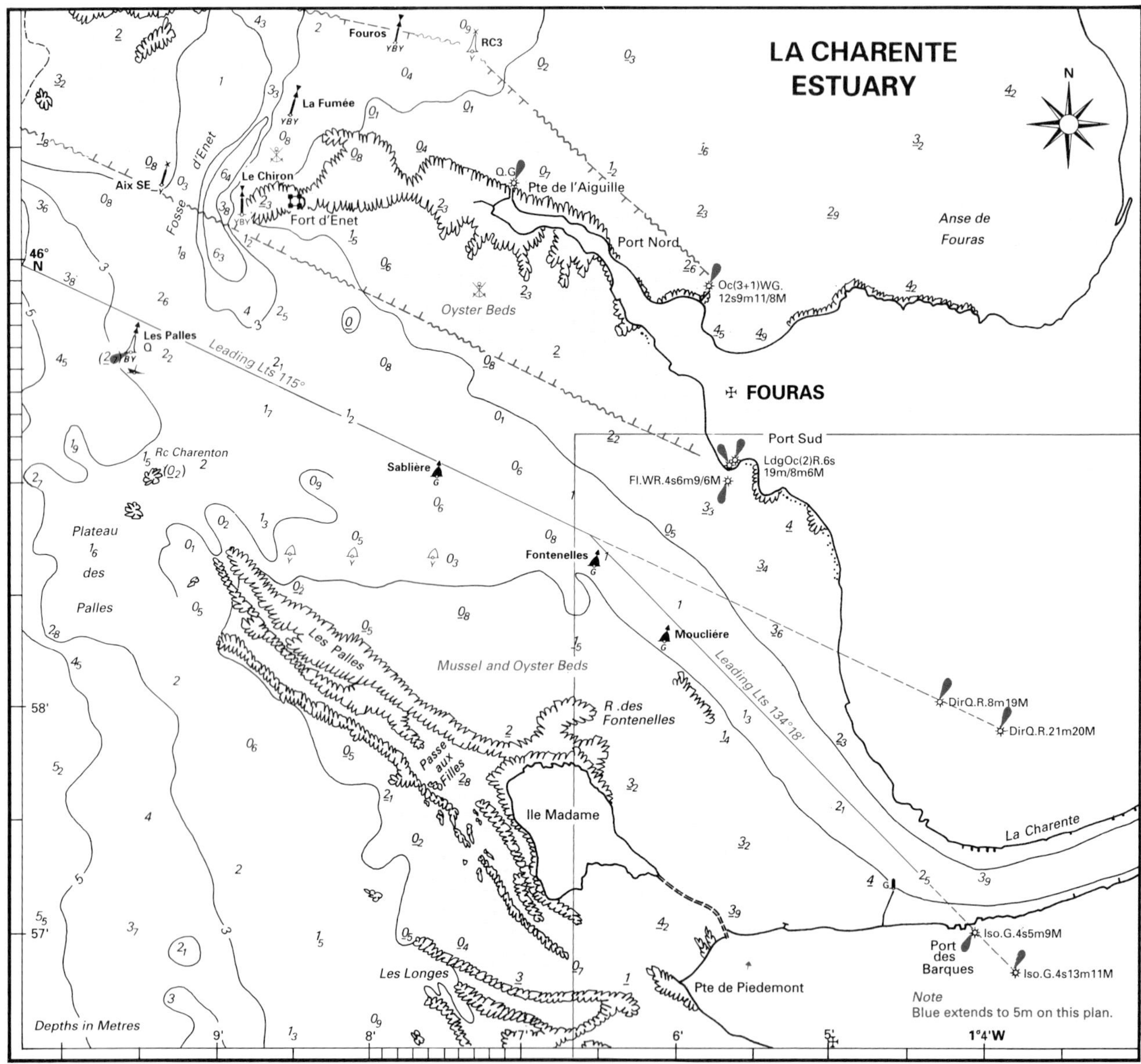

Plan 73

some base their yachts here, encouraged by the very reasonable prices in the marina and the helpful staff.

All in all, if time can be found for the passages up and down the river during a cruise, Rochefort is highly recommended.

Charts

BA *2748, 2746*
Imray *C41*

TIDAL DATA

Times and heights

Time differences				Height differences			
HW		LW		MHWS	MHWN	MLWN	MLWS
POINTE DE GRAVE							
0000 and 1200	0600 and 1800	0500 and 1700	1200 and 2400	5·4	4·4	2·1	1·0
Ile d'Aix							
+0015	−0040	−0030	−0025	+0·7	+0·5	+0·3	−0·1
Rochefort							
+0035	−0010	+0030	+0125	+1·1	+0·9	+0·1	−0·2

Tidal streams

Off the entrance the SE stream starts −0530 Brest and the NW starts +0130 Brest, spring rates 2kts. In general streams in the river are about 2kts, but where the river narrows they run up to 4kts; they are affected by flood water. Above Rochefort, there is a bore on big spring tides which can attain 1·5m; at such times the river should be avoided. At Rochefort the streams turn about 1hr after HW and LW.

Depths

The approach is shallow (0·8m), but there is more water in the river. Without the large-scale chart, it should be treated as having 1m. Off Soubise there is 4m or more. There is some commercial traffic in the river, and vessels of 5,000 tons with a draught of 5m navigate the river at HW neaps.

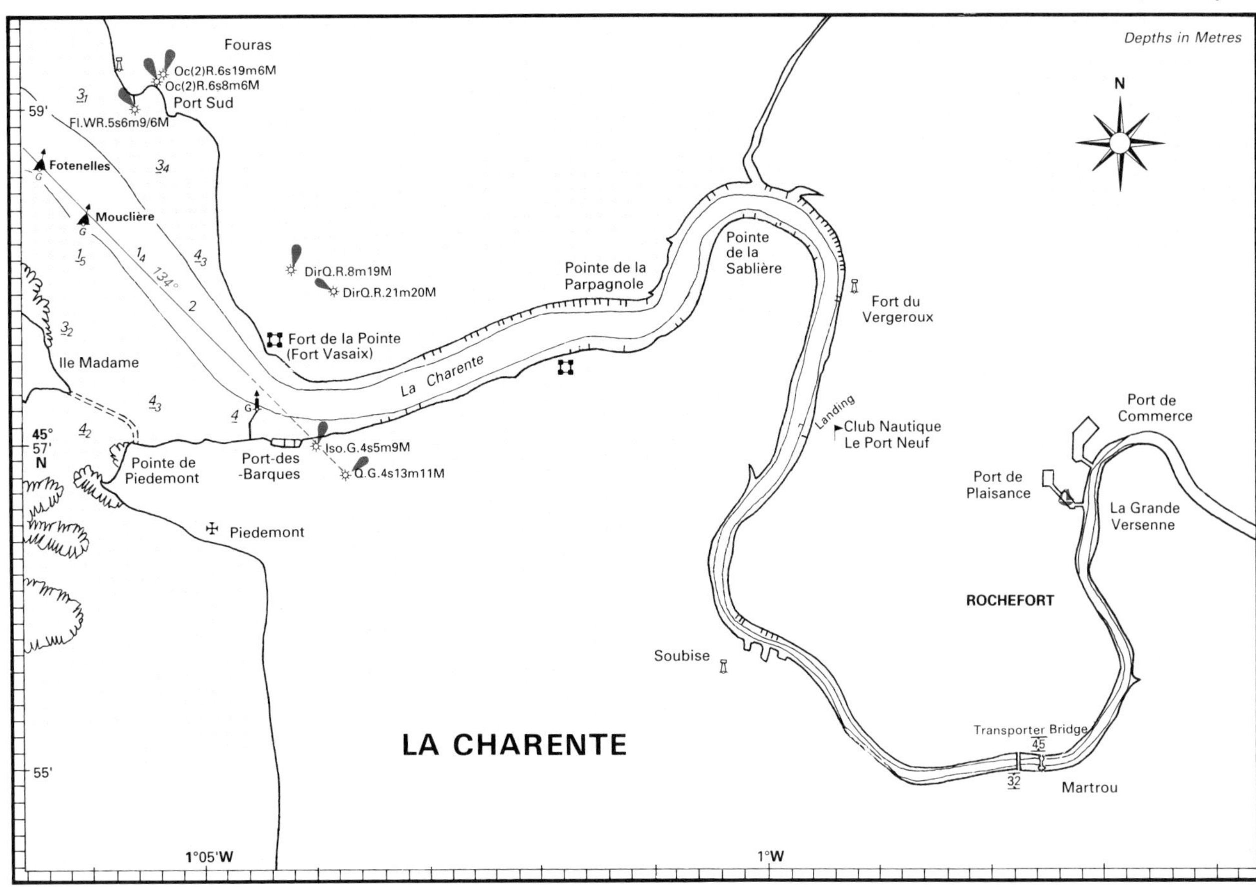

Plan 74

LIGHTS

Ldg Lts 115°

1. *Front* 45°58'·0N 1°04'·3W
   DirQ.R.8m19M 113°-intens-117°
   White square tower, red top
2. *Rear* 45°57'·9N 1°03'·8W 600m from front
   DirQ.R.21m20M 113°-intens-117°
   White square tower, red top

Ldg Lts 134·5°

3. *Front* 45°56'·9N 1°04'·2W Iso.G.4s5m9M
   125°-intens-145° White square tower
4. *Rear* 45°56'·7N 1°03'·9W Iso.G.4s13m11M
   125°-intens-145° Synchronised with front
   White square tower with black band on W side

RADIO

VHF Ch 9 office hours and HW±1

APPROACH AND PASSAGE UP RIVER

By day

Entrance and exit should be made on the flood as on the ebb any sea outside produces breakers on the bar. The approach is straightforward with sufficient rise of tide. There are two pairs of leading marks to follow through the outer shoals, and a line of starboard-hand buoys. The first set of marks are white towers with red tops and are easy to see. The second pair are less conspicuous. Oyster beds are extensive outside the channel.

Once the river has been entered it is generally sufficient to keep in midstream. There are beacons on the shore, defining a succession of transits. The posts for each line carry conspicuous letters running from T at Port-des-Barques to A, just below Rochefort. It is not necessary to adhere precisely to the lines which are maintained for the benefit of coasters.

It is seventeen miles from Ile d'Aix to the lock at Rochefort, and whilst making the passage one may wonder how it was achieved in an 18th-century ship of the line.

There is a waiting pontoon outside the gate to the basins. The fuel pumps are non-operational

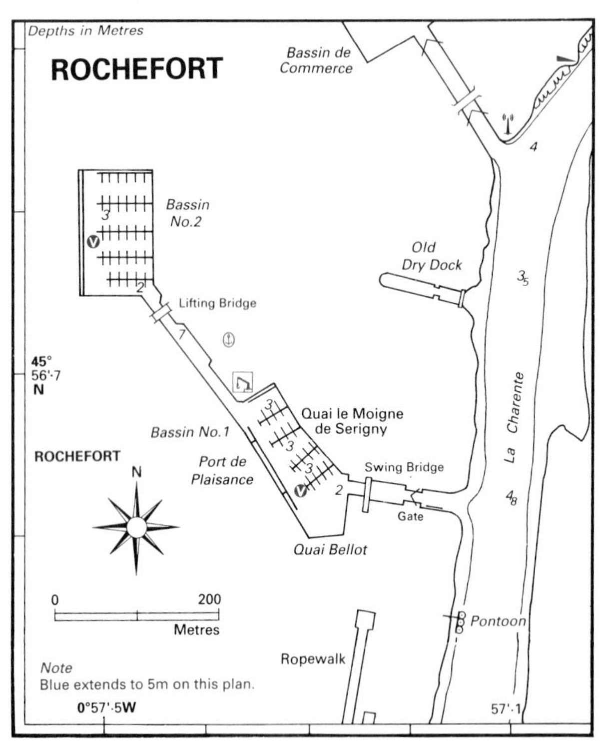

Plan 75

Access to the inner basin is via a bridge which opens at the same time as the gate

By night

Using the leading lights it is possible to enter the river and proceed as far as Port-des-Barques.

ANCHORAGES AND MOORINGS

Anchorage can be found at Port-des-Barques, just upstream from the village on the left side in 2–3m.

At Soubise, anchor on the S side of the river as near to the bank as possible, or arrange to borrow a mooring. The Yacht Club de Rochefort is on the north bank downstream of Soubise has landing facilities and a number of moorings along the south bank.

Upstream of Soubise there are sections where anchoring in the river is forbidden. Elsewhere it is not recommended, as the bottom is foul with old cables.

At Rochefort, the gate to the wet dock is on the left-hand side directly after the rope-walk. It is a right-angle turn into the channel to the lock and it is easy to be swept past by the flood. There is a waiting pontoon immediately to port after turning in.

The gate is opened from HW for 30 minutes, between 0600 and 2200 LT from May to September and from 0700–2000 for the rest of the year. The two bridges operate at the same time. Visitors will be directed to a berth, those staying longer than a night or two normally going into No. 2 basin.

It is possible to berth for up to 24 hours at the pontoon by the rope-walk. This dries, but the bottom is soft mud.

Downstream from Rochefort is one of the last working transporter bridges in Europe. The crossing is made on a platform suspended from the bridge by cables

FACILITIES

At Soubise all shops and hotel in the village, 5 minutes' walk.

At Rochefort all the facilities of a marina, apart from fuel. Chandlers, engineers and repairs. Small crane suitable for masting. Mobile cranes are used for lift out. Storage afloat or ashore. All the resources of a substantial town, good communications.

A bicycle tour over the old suspension bridge, upstream at Tonnay Charente, returning via the transporter bridge is recommended.

59. Ile d'Oléron

GENERAL

This island, formerly something of a backwater, has been connected to the mainland with a bridge and is now a busy summer holiday resort. It is low and sandy with pine trees and many spectacular beaches and a profusion of camp sights. The east side of the island is well sheltered and at the south end is fringed with extensive shallows. The west coast has a bad reputation and yachts should stand well off except in calm conditions.

Ile d'Oléron has an interesting history and was once part of the realm of the kings of England. It has a very ancient seafaring tradition and much maritime law can be traced back to the Laws of Oléron enacted in 1152.

The island has five harbours. The fishing harbour of La Cotinière is on the west side of the island and is closed to yachts except in an emergency. The remaining four, described below, are accessible only at tide time. St-Denis, Port du Douhet and Port Boyardville have basins in which yachts remain afloat but Le Chateau dries. North of Boyardville there are many places to anchor in settled weather.

Le Coureau d'Oléron, the shallow passage between the southern part of the island and the mainland, is an interesting place, rather off the beaten track. The English chart BA *2663* is of too small a scale for exploration and *2746* and *2748* each covers only part of the island. French charts are comprehensive and are recommended for those going south of Boyardville.

South of Ile d'Oléron, Pertuis Maumusson leads to the sea. This passage is dangerous in anything other than ideal conditions as breakers form in the entrance. Although the passage was described in previous editions of this book, the channel is constantly changing and local advice is that it should not be attempted by yachts.

Charts

BA *2746, 2663, 2748*
Imray *C41*

TIDAL DATA

Times and heights

Time differences				Height differences			
HW		LW		MHWS	MHWN	MLWN	MLWS
POINTE DE GRAVE							
0000 and 1200	0600 and 1800	0500 and 1700	1200 and 2400	5·4	4·4	2·1	1·0
Ile d'Aix							
+0015	−0040	−0030	−0025	+0·7	+0·5	+0·3	−0·1
Le Chapus							
+0015	−0040	−0025	−0015	+0·6	+0·6	+0·4	+0·2

Tidal streams

Off St-Denis, the SE stream begins −0600 Pte de Grave and NW begins −0100 Pte de Grave, spring rates 1·5kts; off Boyardville the streams change 30 minutes earlier.

North of Le Château the streams reach 2kts, SSE on the flood and NNW on the ebb. S of the road bridge, under which the streams can reach 4kts, they reach up to 3kts NE of the Pertuis de Maumusson, the flood running N and the ebb S. Off the entrance to Le Château the streams are weak. The SSE stream begins −0330 Pte de Grave, the NNW at +0030 Pte de Grave.

Depths

See under individual harbours.

LIGHTS

1. **Pointe de Chassiron** 46°02'·9N 1°24'·5W
   Fl.10s50m28M White round tower, black bands
   Semaphore station close to NW
2. **Rocher d'Antioche** 46°04'N 1°23'·6W Q.20m11M
   N card beacon tower, surrounded by above-water wrecks.

St-Denis

3. **Dir Ldg Lt 205°** 46°01'·7N 1°21'·8W
   DirIso.WRG.4s14m11-8M
   190°-G-204°-W-206°-R-220° White concrete mast
4. **East breakwater head** 46°02'·1N 1°21'·9W
   Fl(2)WG.6s6m9/6M 205°-G-277°-W-292°-G-165°
   Square masonry hut with pole
5. **South breakwater head** 46°02'·2N 1°22'·1W
   Fl(2)R.6s3m6M Square masonry hut

Boyardville

6. **La Perrotine mole head** 45°58'·2N 1°13'·8W
   Fl(2)R.6s8m5M
   White metal framework tower, red top
7. **Tourelle Juliar** 45°54'·1N 1°09'·5W
   Q(3)WG.10s12m11/8M 147°-W-336°-G-147°
   E card beacon tower

Le Château
Ldg Lts 319°

8. *Front* 45°53'·1N 1°11'·4W Q.R.11m7M
   191°-vis-087° Red rectangle on low white tower
9. *Rear* 240m from front Q.R.24m7M
   Synchronised with front White tower, red top

RADIO

St-Denis VHF Ch 9 for a period at HW between 0700–2200 LT
Port du Douhet VHF Ch 9 0730–2130 LT
Port de Boyardville VHF Ch 9 0800–2100 LT

St-Denis d'Oléron

46°02'N 1°22'W

GENERAL

This fairly modern, purpose-built marina lies 2M from the north tip of the island. It is entered over a sill. Once inside the shelter is good. There are the usual marina facilities.

Depths

The entrance channel dries 1·3m and the sill is 1·5m above the datum. At half tide there is about 1·9m over the sill. Inside, the marina is dredged to 1·5–2·5m.

APPROACH AND ENTRANCE

By day

The marina is on a point NE of the town. Approach with the church spire bearing 260°, when

St Denis, at the north end of Ile d'Oléron

it should be in transit with a green beacon pole. Leaving the green beacon 100m to starboard, alter to starboard and leave a red beacon well to port. In the season the channel is marked with small red and green buoys.

By night

From a position 2M NNE of the harbour approach in the narrow white sector of the directional light[3] on 205°. On entering the white sector of the E breakwater head light[4], alter to starboard to enter the marina, leaving the E breakwater 40m to starboard to avoid an outcrop of sand and stones encroaching on the channel.

BERTHS AND MOORING

There are three waiting buoys 1m ENE of the entrance. In the marina, secure to the visitors' pontoon which is immediately beyond the fuel berth.

FACILITIES

Fuel, café-bar, bicycle hire. Bread van calls 0930–0945. In the town, 15 minutes walk, all shops, PO and well-stocked supermarket.

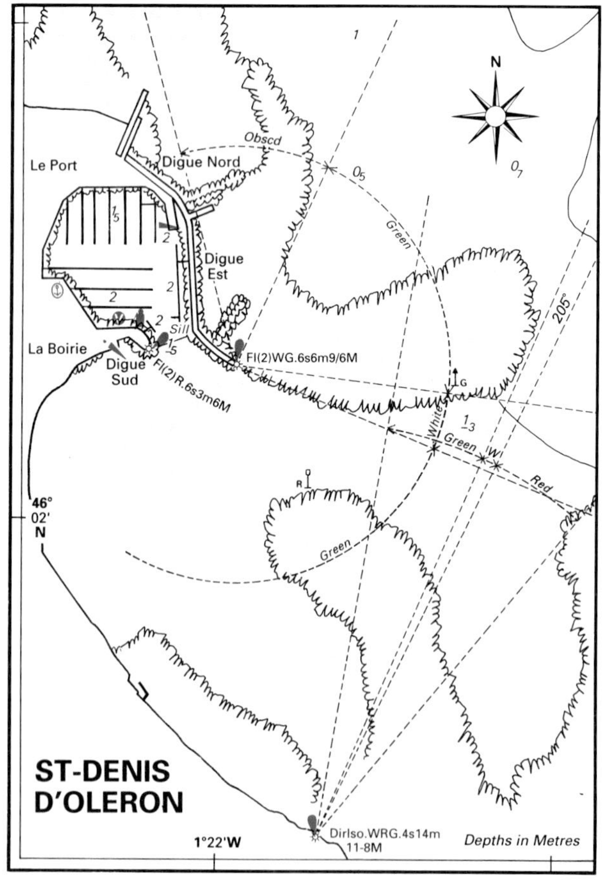

Plan 76

Port du Douhet

46°00'N 1°19'W

GENERAL

The Port du Douhet lies midway between the Pointe de Chassiron and Boyardville. It has a dredged and marked approached channel and pontoons for 350 boats, with berths for some 30 visitors. Entrance is made across ½M of drying sand, with rocky shoals drying 2·5m or more on either side and a shifting sand bank to the south. The channel is disturbed in northerly and easterly winds and the marina must be positively identified before attempting an entrance.

Once inside there is good shelter with modest facilities but it is a long way from town. The port is in an attractive setting amongst the pine trees.

Depths

A new channel was cut through the sand and rock in 1998 and is reported to have 1m. The sill into the SE basin, where visitors berth, dries 1·8m. Once inside there is 1·5m in the basin.

APPROACH AND ENTRANCE

By day

Coming from the N it is advisable to keep at least 2M offshore. Make an initial position 46°00'·5N 1°17'·5W close to a W cardinal buoy. From here the marina bears 250°. Head towards the marina and locate the red and green buoys which mark the channel through the sands and rocks to the marina entrance.

The ends of the submerged loose-rock breakwaters are marked by a green starboard and a red port beacon. There is a second green beacon 300m N of the entrance beacon, marking Le Gros Roc, which dries 3·7m.

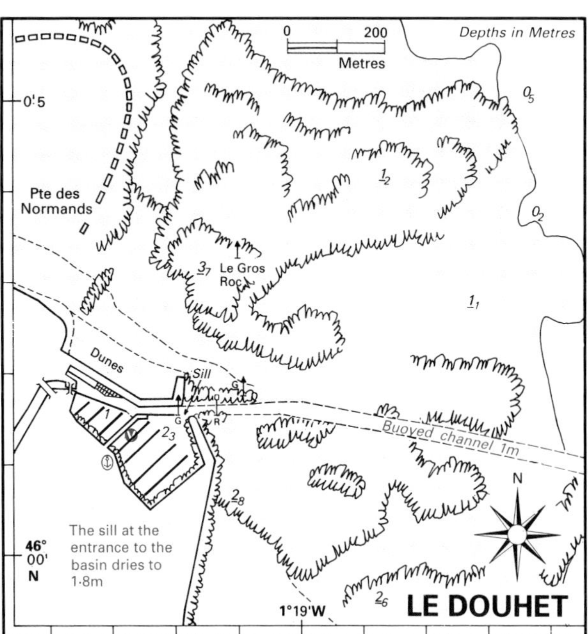

Plan 77

After entering the channel, a turn to port just inside the entrance will lead over the sill to the visitors' pontoon. Visitors berth on the most northwesterly pontoon.

By night

The harbour is not lit and night entry is not advised.

FACILITIES

Boatyard, laying up for small yachts. Launderette, café-bar. Scrubbing platform. Bicycle hire. Small shops, including baker, close by. Nearest other shops at La Brée les Bains (3km) or St Georges d'Oléron (4km).

Le Douhet is a small marina; the approach channel is shallow, but there is plenty of water inside the sill which is crossed immediately after passing the southern breakwater.

Port du Boyardville

45°58'N 1°14'W

GENERAL

The small port of Boyardville is on a tidal river, La Perrotine, with a bar at the entrance, which dries. There is a long stone mole on the southeast side of the entrance. A basin is entered through gates and once inside there is complete shelter. The marina is close to the centre of the village, which has adequate facilities. The ambience is pleasant, but the village becomes busy in the season.

On the weekend after 14 July a spectacular firework display takes place at Fort Boyard, 2M off the port. This can be watched from the beach, north of the town or from a yacht at anchor off the beach.

Depths

The bar dries 2m. Yachts take the ground inside, but the channel does not completely dry. The wet basin has 2m.

Boyardville

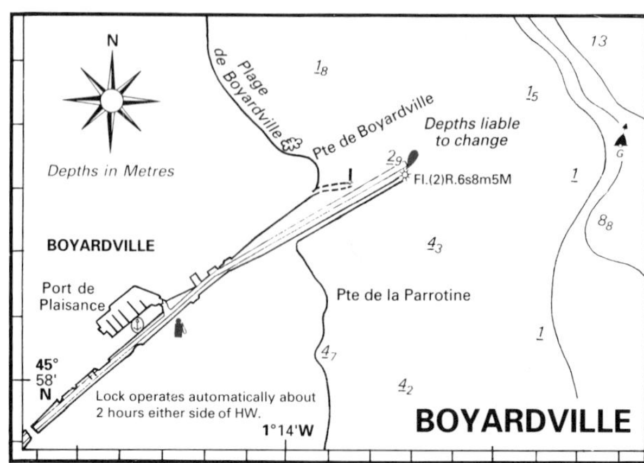

Plan 78

At Boyardville there is a gate to the wet basin which opens automatically with the tide

APPROACH AND ENTRANCE

By day

The entrance lies about 2M from the conspicuous Fort Boyard. A green buoy lies in 11m, 700m NE of the mole head. 150m inside the buoy the bottom shoals almost vertically to the sand bank, which dries 2m. Between the mole head and the buoy the direction of the channel is unpredictable as the sands shift. In 1998 the channel was directly from the buoy to the mole head, but it was necessary to pass the mole head very close to. Thence keep close to the mole, say 10m off, until the side begins to slope as the river is entered. From here steer midchannel and be prepared for a sharp turn to starboard to enter the wet basin.

The gate to the wet basin operates automatically depending on the actual water level 1½ hours either side of HW at neaps and up to 2¾ hours either side of HW at springs.

By night

Although the mole head is lit night entry is not advised unless the port is well known.

MOORING

There is little room to manoeuvre in the basin. Visitors must be prepared to berth against the NE wall, which is piled so that a plank is useful.

Yachts can lie in the river against quays above the marina entrance, the second from the sea end being recommended, or they can take the ground between the last quay and the bridge. The harbourmaster's office is on the wet dock quay. He is most obliging and his help should be sought. Yachts take the ground but do not dry out completely. The bottom is not level everywhere, so care is needed.

¾M north of the mole is a line of visitors' moorings, and one can anchor nearby in from 8 to 12m, with due regard to the rapidly shoaling bottom.

FACILITIES

Fuel berth on the port hand entering the river. Repairs, chandlery, 10-tonne crane. Shops, supermarket, café-bars, restaurants, bank.

Le Château d'Oléron

46°53'N 1°11'W

GENERAL

Le Château d'Oléron is a small port wholly occupied with oysters, a place of historical interest whose many fishing boats, backed by the walls of the old fortifications overlooking the harbour, make a picturesque scene. Yachts are not particularly welcome in the port as they are expected to use the facilities provided for them elsewhere on the island. However, entrance to Le Château is described in this edition, since a short visit on the tide is interesting, provided that the fishermen suffer no interference.

Le Château has the facilities of a holiday town.

Depths

The approach has a depth of 0·6m; the harbour dries 1·6m.

APPROACH

The approach is made in the Coureau d'Oléron. French chart SHOM *6335* is recommended.

From the north

The shallows in the southern half of the Coureau are entirely covered by oyster beds. The channels are narrow and winding. Buoy-hopping is the order of the day, with a careful lookout for withies and the beacons which are often located well into the shallows. Read the name on the buoy to confirm your position before proceeding.

From a position midway between Ile d'Aix and Fort Boyard, a course of 155° should lead nearly 5M to the W cardinal buoy Chenal EN (the northern buoy at the entrance to the east channel) and will clear the dangers off the mouth of the Charente. Leaving Chenal EN close to port, continue on 155° for 1½M to leave the E cardinal Chenal ES buoy to starboard and Brouage red buoy close to port. From here on port-hand marks should be left to starboard, as the channel is marked for entry from the S. A course of 210° leads clear of Banc Lamouroux. The Banc de Charret beacon, well into the mud flats to port, and a red beacon and the green Agnas buoy to starboard should be located.

Steer for Agnas, leaving it close to port, then leave two red beacons on the Grande Mortanne to starboard and make for the Mortanne Sud S cardinal beacon, marking the entrance of the channel to Le Château d'Oléron.

Looking out of Le Château

From the south

The channels look rather intricate and are subject to change. At low water an up-to-date chart is the best guide. If the rise of tide is sufficient to enter the harbour, it will be possible to pass safely over the shoals in midstream; note that the Banc d'Agnas dries up to 2m.

By night

A stranger would not be able to navigate the Coureau d'Oléron by night. If he has reached the entrance channel by nightfall, the leading lights[1] will take him up to the harbour.

ENTRANCE

Keep the Mortanne Sud S cardinal beacon close-to to starboard. Steer straight for the leading light structures. The front mark is a tubby white cylindrical tank with a red board above it, the rear mark is an ordinary white light tower with a red top. The starboard side of the entrance channel is marked by a line of withies; leave these about 10m to starboard. The channel is 10m wide. Do not obstruct the passage of the fishing boats and oyster barges, which are working to beat the tide.

The best water is at the quay on the port side of the outer harbour, drying 1·6m. The bottom is soft mud. Here a yacht will be very much in the way of fishing vessels and must take advice. The quay on the starboard side dries about 3m (bottom soft mud) near the seaward end, getting shallower near the shore. Here the yacht will be out of the way, so this is the place to go. There are plenty of ladders and mooring rings.

There is an inner harbour. It has a serviceable dock gate, but this is not used. The inner harbour is therefore shallower, and it is absolutely packed with fishing boats.

FACILITIES

Fuel on the quay, but may not be available to pleasure craft. Chandlers near the harbour. All shops in the town, about 10 minutes' walk.

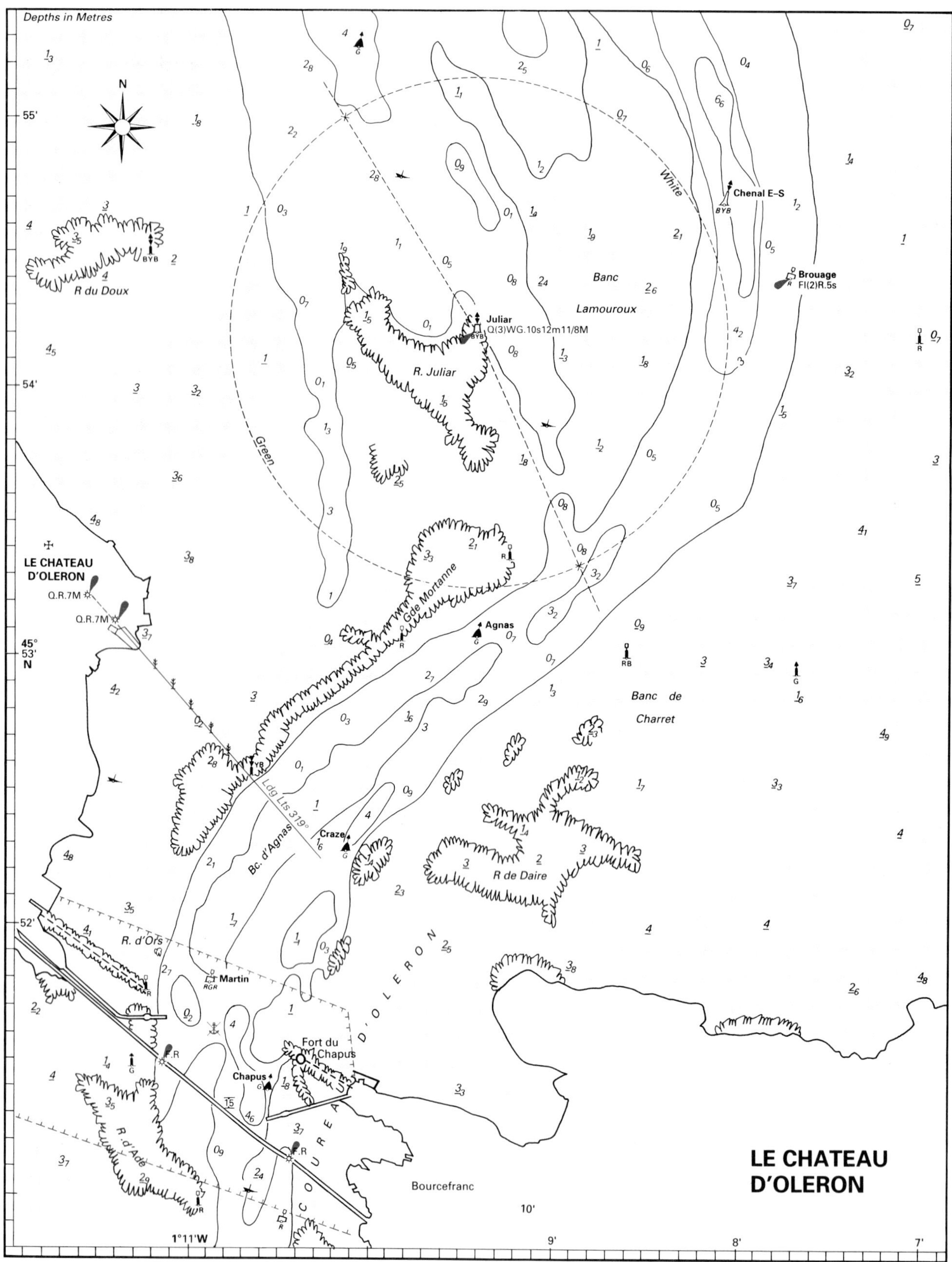
Depths in Metres
N
55'
54'
45°
53'
N
52'
R du Doux
LE CHATEAU
D'OLERON
Q.R.7M
Q.R.7M
Green
White
Banc
Lamouroux
Chenal E-S
BYB
Brouage
Fl(2)R.5s
Juliar
Q(3)WG.10s12m11/8M
R. Juliar
Gde Mortanne
Agnas
Banc de
Charret
Ldg Lts 319°
Bc. d'Agnas
Craze
R de Daire
R. d'Ors
Martin
Fort du
Chapus
Chapus
F.R
R. d'Ade
COUREAU D'OLERON
Bourcefranc
LE CHATEAU
D'OLERON
1°11'W
10'
9'
8'
7'

Plan 79

60. La Seudre

45°49'N 1°10'W

GENERAL

La Seudre offers an anchorage in fair conditions near the south end of the Coureau d'Oléron. It is little visited by yachts but is interesting to explore in suitable conditions.

The entrance to the river is shallow and should not be taken near low water, but once inside the river is deep. The scenery is not exciting, as old saltpans lie for some distance behind either bank; in these an extensive and intensive oyster culture is carried on. Both La Tremblade and Marennes are pleasant towns in the season; the latter is farther from both the river and the inner end of its canal.

Charts

BA charts are not sufficiently detailed to navigate La Seudre.
Imray *C41*
French SHOM *6335*

TIDAL DATA

Times and heights

Time differences				Height differences			
HW		LW		MHWS	MHWN	MLWN	MLWS
POINTE DE GRAVE							
0000 and 1200	0600 and 1800	0500 and 1700	1200 and 2400	5·4	4·4	2·1	1·0
La Cayenne							
+0030	–0015	–0010	–0005	+0·2	+0·2	+0·3	0·0

Tidal streams

In the Coureau d'Oléron the tides vary considerably from point to point but typically run at up to 2kts springs, except under the Oléron-to-mainland road bridge and in La Seudre river, where they can reach 4kts.

Depths

The approach channel described is shallow, drying 1m. The river is deep, typically about 7m. The canals to Marennes and Tremblade can be assumed to dry 2·5m. In the basin at Marennes there is 2·5m.

LIGHTS

There are lights on the bridges and a few other lights but the area is not well enough lit for night navigation by a stranger.

APPROACH AND ENTRANCE

There are two entrance channels, La Soumaille to the N and La Garrigue to the S, but only the former is described here. The channel is narrow but the echo sounder will help the stranger to keep in the deepest water. The configuration of the banks and positions of the buoys is subject to change.

The simplest way to enter La Soumaille is across part of the Banc Bourgeois, drying 1m. Coming from the N pass under the road bridge joining Oléron to the mainland which has a clearance of 15m. 400m S of the bridge in midchannel is a wreck, which may be marked by a red beacon. The channel is buoyed for entry from the S and it is advisable to check the buoys' names as they are passed. The preferred arches for passage under the bridge are S of the old ferry piers on either side of the channel and are marked by white squares with a red square or a green triangle. Local fishing boats ignore these and pass under the central arches.

To make use of the SE preferred arch, leave a green buoy to port and round the head of the old ferry pier on the mainland bank. Leave a red buoy (if it is in position) to starboard and pass under the marked arch of the bridge to leave the next red buoy close to starboard. The next buoy to steer for, bearing 198°, is the green Meule NW, to be left close to port. Meule SE is the next green buoy to leave to port, followed by a red buoy, Trompe de Sot. Leave this and La Palette to starboard and approach Bry NE green buoy closely enough to read its name without passing it, as it will be left to starboard.

From Bry NE buoy, the red buoy, Soumaille NW, marking the beginning of the Soumaille channel bears 113°. Steer to leave this buoy to port, as you will now be passing up the channel. The S end of Banc Bourgeois, drying 1m, will be crossed. After Soumaille NW, the channel, which is narrow and steep-to on its N side, deepens to 2m and shortly after to 4·5m. Leave Soumaille SE buoy and Le Jéac beacon to port, and Saut de Barat E cardinal buoy to starboard, before passing under the marked arch of the Seudre road bridge (clearance 18m).

ANCHORAGE AND MOORING

The best anchorages are near the disused ferry slips for Marennes (north bank) and La Tremblade (south bank). The former is called La Cayenne and

The canal to La Tremblade. The ponds are used for oyster cultivation

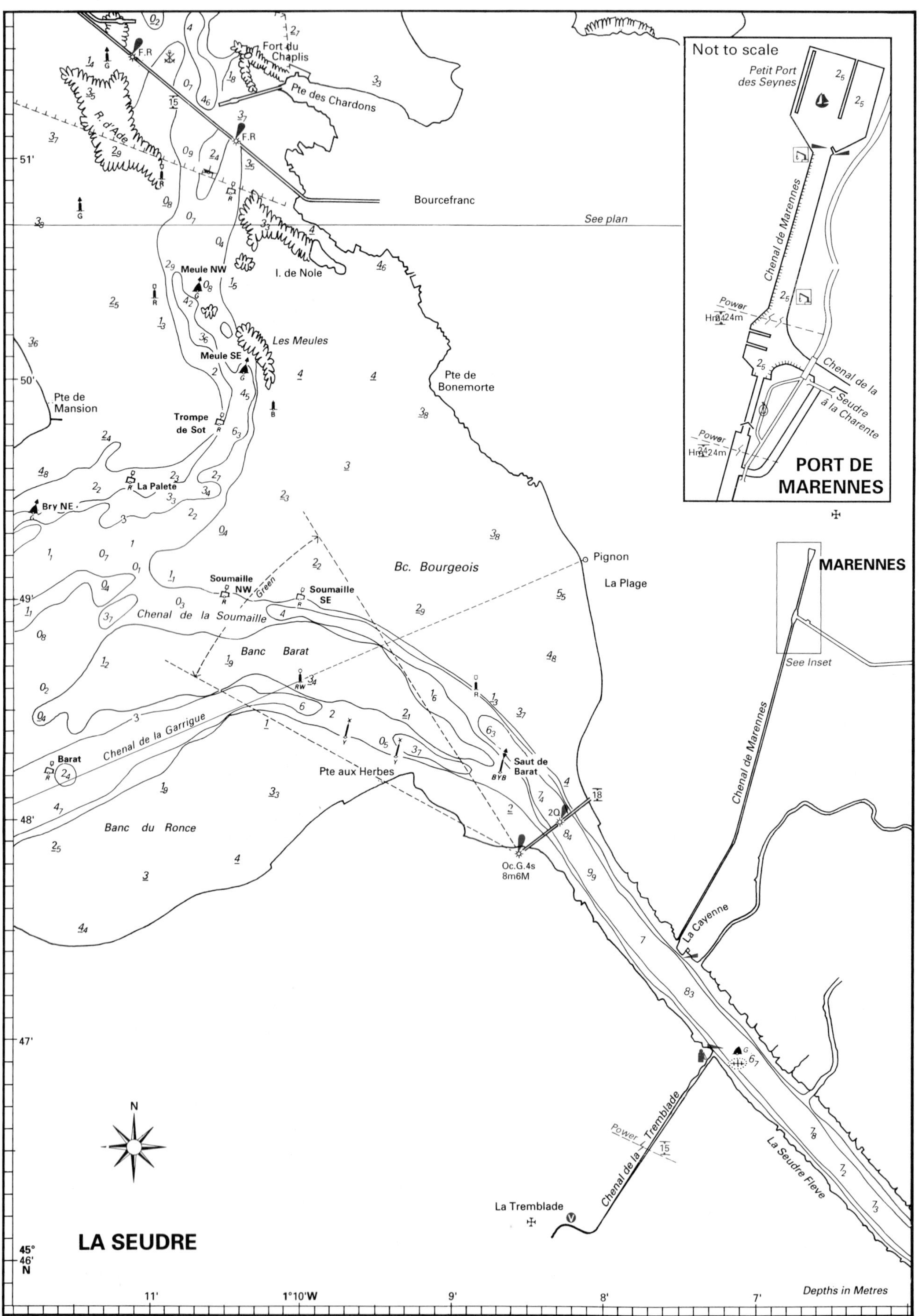

LA SEUDRE
PORT DE MARENNES
Not to scale
Petit Port des Seynes
Chenal de Marennes
Chenal de la Seudre à la Charente
MARENNES
See Inset
See plan
Bourcefranc
Fort du Chaplis
Pte des Chardons
R. d'Ade
I. de Nole
Meule NW
Meule SE
Les Meules
Pte de Bonemorte
Pte de Mansion
Trompe de Sot
La Palete
Bry NE
Bc. Bourgeois
Pignon
La Plage
Soumaille NW
Soumaille SE
Chenal de la Soumaille
Banc Barat
Chenal de la Garrigue
Barat
Saut de Barat
Pte aux Herbes
Banc du Ronce
Oc.G.4s 8m6M
La Cayenne
Chenal de la Tremblade
La Tremblade
La Seudre Fleve
Depths in Metres

Plan 80

is about ½M downstream of the latter. Anchor near the side of the river and land on the ferry slip. Above the entrance to the canal to La Tremblade there is a wreck, marked by a green buoy.

There are drying canals leading to the villages of Marennes and La Tremblade. To get this depth it is essential to keep exactly in the middle of the channel. The canals are lined on each side by the boats and other apparatus for oyster culture.

At La Tremblade the canal is crossed by cables with a clearance of 15m. It is possible to berth alongside the stone quay to starboard just round the bend at the top end of the canal. Once round the bend the best water is on the starboard side; the bottom is soft mud. The water shoals rapidly once the far end of the quay is reached. There is not much room, but visitors may find a berth. Although some yachts are based at the top of the canal, it is really better for a dinghy excursion, which is worth while if only to have it brought home how many oysters there are.

At the entrance to the Marennes canal, which lies just downstream of the ferry pier, there is a slight bend to starboard. The perches are high on the mud, but the best water lies roughly halfway between them. At the upper end of the canal is the wet basin, the gates of which open automatically about one hour each side of high water. A power line with 16m clearance crosses the canal below the gate and another with 24m clearance crosses the dock. The dock is used by some 70 yachts and provides a convenient and pleasant berth.

FACILITIES

At La Tremblade which is a small market town, there are all shops, banks, restaurants. Marine engineer, outboard specialist, boatyard.

At Marennes there are modest shops, cafés and a large hypermarket at the rear of the post office, reached by a few minutes' walk through pretty municipal gardens. Yacht builder at the wet dock, 6-tonne crane. Very basic toilets and shower.

61. La Gironde to Bordeaux

BXA light buoy 45°37'·6N 1°28'·6W

Note

La Gironde is fully described in the companion volume *Biscay Spain.* In the present book only an abridged version of that description is given, sufficient to enable the yachtsman bound for the canals to reach Bordeaux, the upper limit of navigation for masted yachts, or to visit the ports of Royan and Port Bloc at the river entrance.

GENERAL

This wide and long estuary leads to the city of Bordeaux and to the Canal Lateral a la Garonne, entered from the river above Bordeaux. Details, in English, of the canal (and of the Midi to which it connects) and the passage to the Mediterranean are contained in *Guides Vagnon: Guide des Canaux du Midi* which can be obtained from Imray, Laurie, Norie & Wilson Ltd.

There are two harbours just inside the entrance to the estuary, Royan on the east bank and Port Bloc on the west. There is a yacht harbour at Pauillac halfway to Bordeaux together with a number of minor harbours, some with facilities for yachts. There are quays, basins and a marina at Bordeaux. It is possible for a yacht capable of maintaining 5kts to carry a single tide up to Bordeaux.

In the mouth of the estuary the tidal streams and river currents are very strong and do not always follow the expected direction. A recently corrected chart is essential; the banks shift, and this entails frequent movement not only of the buoys, but also of the leading lights. In strong winds from the SW through W to N do not attempt to enter the estuary, if there is any swell or on the ebb tide, as the overfalls can reach 5m in height. The Banc de la Mauvaise/Banc de la Coubre has an evil reputation which is well merited. Coming from the north, keep at least 5M offshore.

Charts

BA *2663, 2910, 2916*
Imray *C42*

TIDAL DATA

Times and heights

Time differences				Height differences			
HW		LW		MHWS	MHWN	MLWN	MLWS
POINTE DE GRAVE							
0000 and 1200	0600 and 1800	0500 and 1700	1200 and 2400	5·4	4·4	2·1	1·0
Royan							
+0000	–0005	–0005	–0005	-0·3	–0·2	0·0	0·0
Pauillac							
+0100	+0100	+0135	+0205	+0·1	0·0	–1·0	–0·5
Bordeaux							
+0200	+0225	+0330	+0405	-0·1	–0·2	–1·7	–1·0

Winds between S and NNW can raise the water level up to 1m whilst winds from the N through E to S can decrease the level by up to 0·3m.

Tidal streams

The streams run as follows, times referenced to Pte de Grave and rates at springs: in the main entrance channel the flood begins at about −0430, 3½kts, and the ebb at about +0100, 4kts; at Pauillac the flood begins at −0315, 3kts and the ebb at +0215, 4kts; at Bordeaux the flood begins at −0115, 3kts and the ebb at +0315, 4kts.

The streams are very much altered if the river is in spate and ebb currents of over 10kts have been known at Bordeaux.

Depths

The channel is deep. The outer side of the marina at Pauillac is deep, but the inner side dries. The pontoons at Point du Jour, Bordeaux shoal from deep on the outside to less than 1m near the bank.

LIGHTS

1. **BXA light buoy** 45°37'·6N 1°28'·6W
   Iso.4s8m7M Whis
   Red HFPB, white stripes
2. **La Coubre** 45°41'·8N 1°14'·0W Fl(2)10s64m28M
   White tower, red top
   Auxiliary light F.RG.42m12/10M
   030°-R-043°-G-060°-R-110°
   Same structure
3. **Cordouan** 43°35'·2N 1°10'·4W
   Oc(2+1)WRG.12s60m22-18M
   014°-W-126°-G-178·5°-W-250°-W(unintens)-267°-R(unintens)-294·5°-R-014°
   White conical tower, dark grey band and top, dark grey base

Ldg Lts 081·5°

4. *Front* 45°39'·6N 1°08'·7W DirIso.4s21m22M
   080·5°-intens-082·5° White pylon on dolphin
   Auxiliary Q(2)5s10m3M Same structure
5. *Rear* **La Palmyre** 45°39'·8N 1°07'·2W 1·1M from front DirQ.57m27M 080·5°-intens-082·5°
   White radar tower
   Auxiliary DirF.R.57m17M 325·5°-intens-328·5°
   Same structure

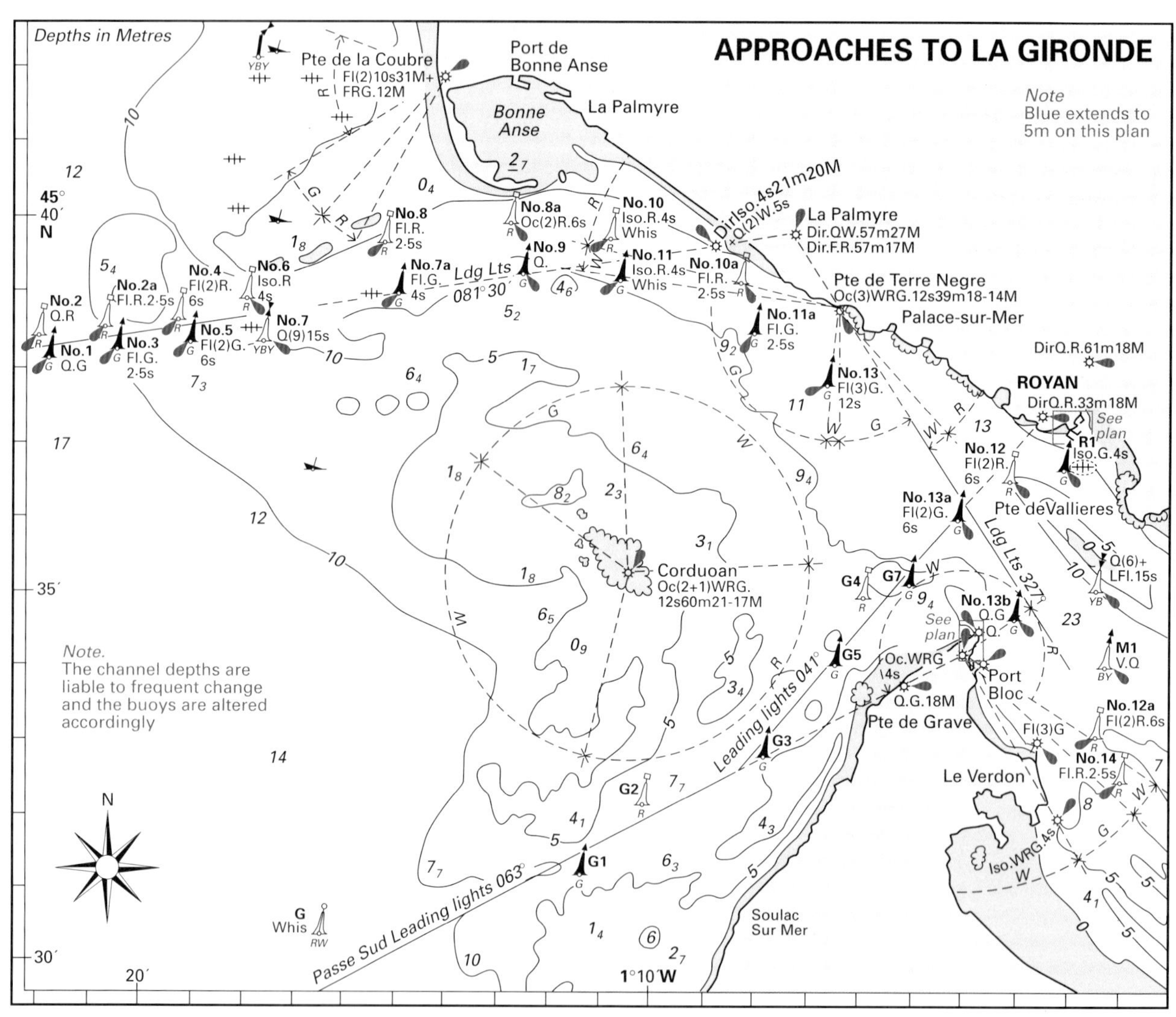

Plan 81

Ldg Lts 327°
6. *Front* **Terre Nègre** 45°38'·8N 1°06'·3W Oc(3)WRG.12s39m18-14M 304°-R-319°-W-327°-G-000°-W-004°-G-097°-W-104°-R-116° White tower, red top on W side
7. *Rear* Light No. 5 above (La Palmyre) 1·1M from front

Passe Sud Ldg Lts 063°
8. *Front* **St Nicholas** 45°33'·8N 1°04'·9W DirQ.G.22m16M 061·5°-intens-064·5° White square tower
9. *Rear* **Pointe de Grave** 45°34'·2N 1°03'·9W 0·84M from front Oc.WRG.4s26m19-15M 033°-W-233·5°-R-303°-W-312°-G-330°-W-025° White square tower, black corners and top

Leading Lights 041°
10. *Front* **Le Chay** 45°37·3N 1°02'·4W DirQ.R.33m18M 039·5°-intens-042·5° White tower, red top
11. *Rear* **Saint Pierre** 45°38'·1N 1°01'·4W 0·97M from front DirQ.R.61m18M 039·5°-intens-043·5° Red water tower

Royan entrance
12. **South jetty head** 45°37'·1N 1°01'·7W VQ(2)R.1s11m12M White tower, red brick base Horn (2)20s by day from HW–2½ to HW+2
13. **New jetty** 45°37'·2N 1°01'·5W Oc(2)R.6s8m6M White mast, red top
14. **North mole spur** 45°37'·2N 1°01'·6W Iso.4s Strip light
15. **East jetty head** 45°37'·2N 1°01'·5W Fl.G.4s2m6M 311°-vis-151° White post, green top

Port Bloc
16. **Pointe de Grave north jetty head** 45°34'·5N 1°03'·6W Q.6m2M N card beacon
17. **Pointe de Grave north jetty spur** 45°34'·4N 1°03'·6W Iso.G.4s8m2M Green triangle on green mast
18. **Entrance, N side** 45°34'·2N 1°03'·7W Fl.G.4s9m3M White metal framework tower, green top lit by day in fog
19. **Entrance, S side** 45°34'·2N 1°03'·6W Iso.R.4s8m4M White tower, red top lit by day in fog

Pauillac
20. **Breakwater elbow** 45°12'·0N 0°44'·6W Fl.G.4s5M Green mast
21. **Breakwater head** 45°11'·8N 0°44'·6W Q.G.7m4M Green mast
22. **Mole head** 45°11'·9N 0°44'·5W Q.R.4m 320°-vis-050° Large red wine bottle

RADIO

Whilst in the Gironde yachts should, if possible, monitor VHF Ch 16 and 12 to be aware of ship movements.
Royan VHF Ch 9 0800–2000 LT
Pauillac Marina VHF Ch 9 0800–1800 LT
Bordeaux Marina VHF Ch 9 office hours

APPROACH AND ENTRANCE

Only the approach from the north is given here. Yachts bound south may wish to use Passe Sud, described in *Biscay Spain.*

The approach and entrance is navigationally simple, provided that the weather is good. During the ebb, an onshore wind or swell generates very steep seas between No. 3 and No. 9 buoys which may break on the banks on either side of the channel. In strong winds the seas become dangerous and may break right across the channel. With a westerly gale blowing against a spring ebb the whole entrance becomes a lethal expanse of broken water.

In light weather reliable auxiliary power is necessary to prevent a yacht being set into the breakers on the banks. The best time for a yacht to enter is during the first of the flood. Outward bound, Royan should be left well before HW so as to be well clear of the channel before the ebb sets in.

Pte de la Coubre light, with the coastguard tower behind

La Palmyre leading marks

By day

The coast immediately N of the entrance has few conspicuous features. It is essential to keep at least 5M off the land in the later approach to the entrance to avoid the dangerous shoal of Banc de la Mauvaise. The corner must not be cut and landfall should be made on BXA buoy.

From the buoy, make good a track of 081° until the buoys or the leading marks are identified; it is not necessary to follow the transit precisely but a yacht should keep in the buoyed channel. When No. 9 buoy is reached course may be altered to the SE to No. 11a, and 13 buoys. If going to Royan leave the main channel here and steer for R1 buoy off the harbour, turning short of it to the entrance. If proceeding up river, turn down the back leading line of Terre-Negre and Palmyre of 327° until the subsequent channel buoys can be seen and followed. If bound for Port Bloc, leave the channel at No. 13b buoy and pass 200m off Pointe de Grave.

By night

On a clear dark night the profusion of lights can be confusing.

Make a position in the vicinity of BXA buoy[1] and identify the first pair of leading lights[4,5] on 081°. Follow this transit, passing between the lit red and green channel buoys. BXA buoy lies in the green sector of Pte de La Coubre light[2], but as the channel buoys are reached it will show red. When it turns to green again (0·8M after No. 7 W cardinal buoy has been left to starboard) alter to 065° to remain in the channel and to get into the white sector of Terre Nègre light[6]. Steer towards the light, remaining in the white sector, until the main transit front light[4] is abeam to port. Alter to about 120°, keeping parallel to the shore, and continue thus past No. 11a and 13 buoys until the second transit[6,7] is reached. Maintain this transit on a heading of 147° to enter the river.

Bound for Royan, do not alter onto this second transit, but rather maintain the 120° course, parallel to the shore toward R1 buoy off Royan.

For port Bloc, leave the second transit when No. 13B Q.G buoy is abeam to starboard. At this point the buoy will be roughly in transit with Port Bloc entrance, bearing about 235°, and the way is clear towards the harbour.

Royan

45°37'N 1°02'W

GENERAL

A modern town with a marina of 1,000 berths, 100 of which are for visitors, offering a good staging post on the way to or from Bordeaux. The harbour can be entered without danger provided weather and sea conditions permit entry to La Gironde estuary.

In the 1939–45 war Royan was badly bombed, with heavy loss of life to the inhabitants. The buildings are all new and the asymmetrical spire of the church stands up above the town as a landmark. Royan is now a holiday centre with a yacht harbour; it is twinned with Gosport. The harbourmaster is

Royan

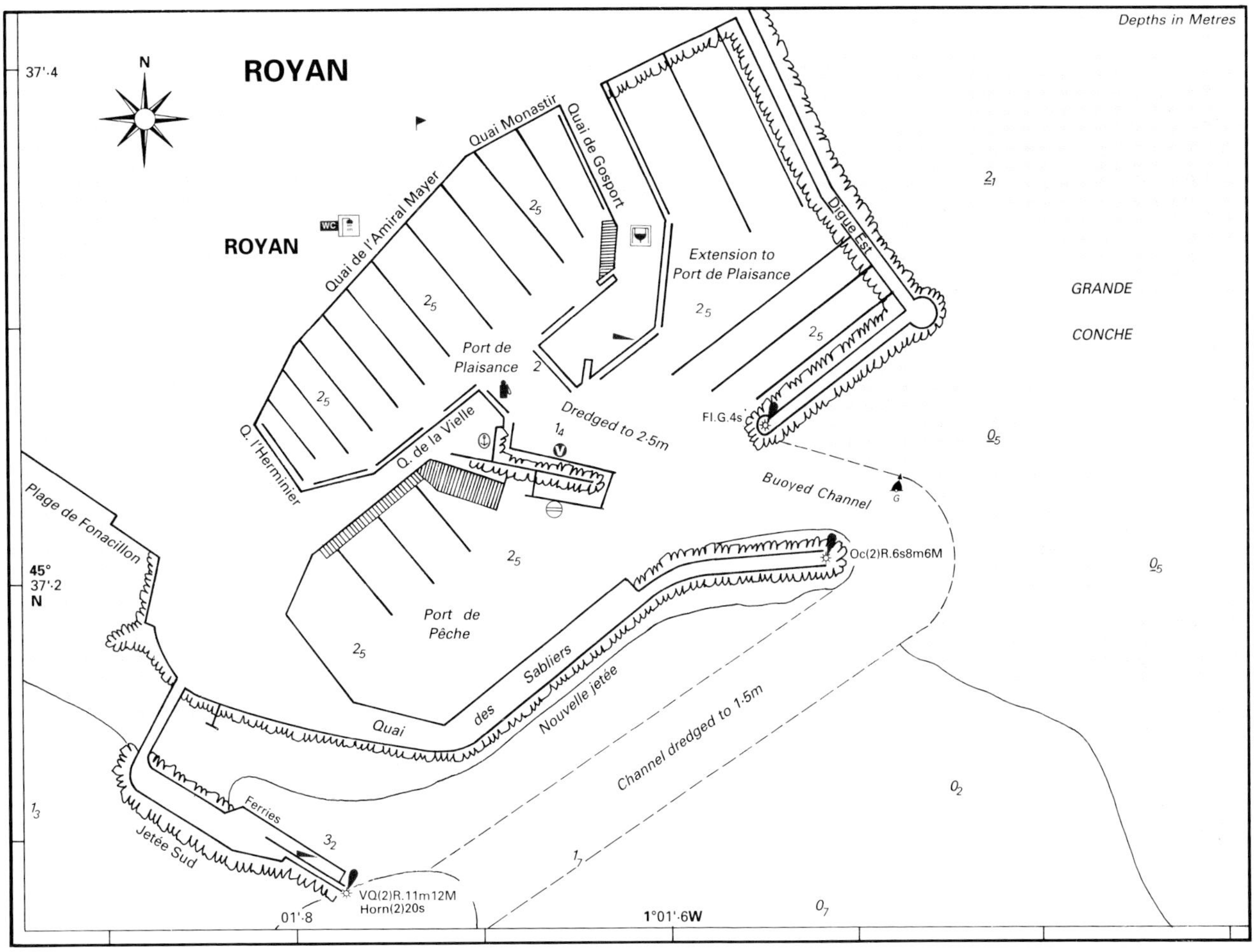

Plan 82

most helpful and will do his best to find a berth for a short stay even in the busiest part of the season.

There are good shops and facilities and Royan is a suitable place to step or unstep masts, although it becomes crowded in the season There are excellent train services to Paris and a ferry service to Port Bloc.

Depths

There is 1·7m in the entrance and the marina is dredged to 2·5m.

APPROACH AND ENTRANCE

By day

Coming from seaward, at No. 13 buoy steer for R1 buoy, passing Pointe du Chay at least 200m off; alter to port to bring Jetée Sud head on to 020° and leave this 100m to port to round Nouvelle Jetée head. If coming from the river there are dangerous wrecks off Pte de Valliers and a yacht should pass outside the bank off the point and alter towards the harbour entrance when Jetée Sud head bears 025°, leaving R1 buoy to starboard.

Enter the harbour by rounding Nouvelle Jetée head at no more than 50m leaving an unlit green buoy to starboard which is not always in position.

At Royan, the reception pontoon is immediately in front of the *capitainerie*

By night

R1 buoy is lit and so are the breakwater heads at Royan, making a night approach by the daytime routes simple.

BERTHS

The reception berth is on the N side of the central spur to the left of the inner harbour entrance directly below the *capitainerie*. Secure here unless met by the harbour launch in the entrance.

FACILITIES

Fuel, slipway, 26-tonne travel-lift, 1·5-tonne crane for masting. Chandlers, all repairs, sailmaker. Shops, banks, hotels and restaurants in this large town.

Port Bloc

45°3'N 1°04'W

GENERAL

Port Bloc, a small harbour just behind Pointe de Grave, is a convenient passage harbour. It is used by the ferries to Royan and by the buoy-maintenance vessels.

Space is limited and there are no moorings or berths available specifically for visitors within the harbour. Masting is possible if bound to or from the canals. Pleasantly situated among the pine trees, the harbour is reasonably sheltered, though some swell is said to enter in bad weather. It is a long way from any shops.

Depths

The approach is deep. There is 2·5m in the harbour.

APPROACH AND ENTRANCE

Entrance by day or night is straightforward as the deep water runs right up to the harbour. The entrance can be difficult to distinguish from the background land by day. If ferries are entering or leaving, stand off until they are clear as there is not much room in the harbour. There is only about 50m width in the entrance – keep in the centre as the walls slope outwards underwater.

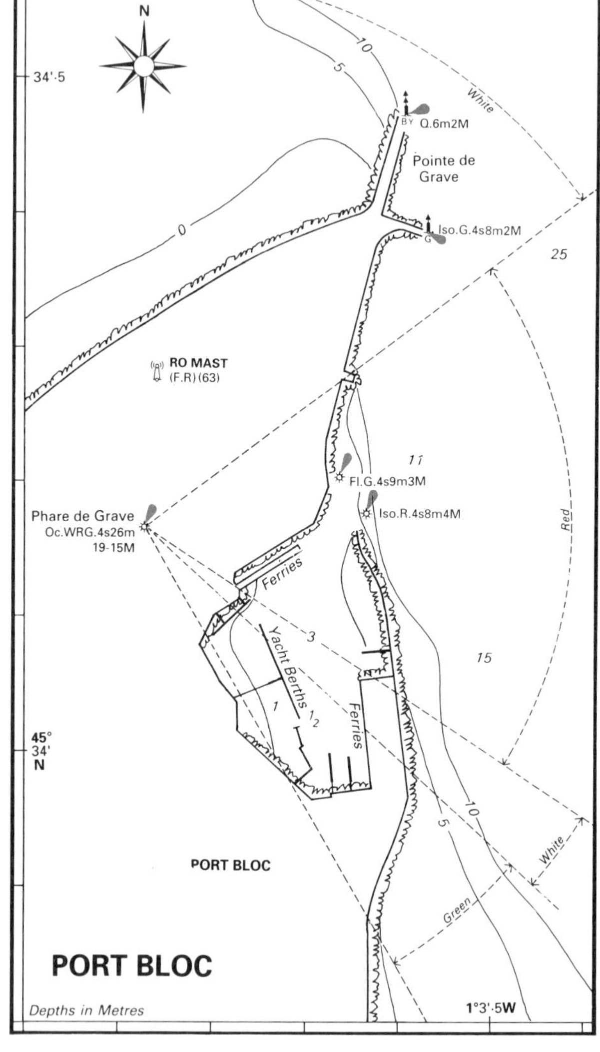

Plan 84

BERTHS

There are pontoons in the W part of the harbour. The ones in the NW corner are for fishing boats, the one in the middle for local boats but there may be a space on the pontoon in the SW corner.

FACILITIES

A mobile crane can be arranged. Water on the pontoons. Nearest shops 1M. A new marina has, for some time, been planned in the bay S of the harbour.

Port Bloc

The River to Bordeaux

GENERAL

Although Bordeaux is one of the largest cities in France and a pleasant place to visit, the estuary is not particularly attractive and becomes increasingly industrialised as one approaches the city. Unless entering the canal system, the 55M journey is hardly worth the effort. It is possible with a yacht capable of maintaining 5kts and starting at low water to carry a single tide up to Bordeaux; also by leaving Bordeaux well before high water to carry the ebb down to the mouth.

There are several places to stop at between Port Bloc and Bordeaux, but only Pauillac, 27M from Port Bloc and 25M from Bordeaux is described here. For the other harbours in the estuary see *Biscay Spain*.

NAVIGATION

The passage presents no problems as it is comprehensively marked by buoys and beacons, the vast majority of which are lit. It can be rough, particularly downstream of Pauillac, and if a mast is being carried on deck it needs to be very well secured.

With the large-scale chart a yacht will not need to keep within the channel, but as the river is fairly straight there is little to be gained by leaving it. The streams run strongly and should be worked to advantage. When the river is in spate considerable amounts of debris, including whole trees, may be encountered.

Power cables cross the river with a safe vertical clearance of 48m. The Pont d'Aquitaine at Bordeaux has 51m.

Pauillac, taken near low water

Pauillac

45°12'N 0°44'W

GENERAL

A useful yacht and fishing harbour on the west bank halfway between Bordeaux and the sea. An excellent staging port when either ascending or descending, Pauillac is a useful place to unstep or step masts. There are adequate facilities ashore. The town is in the centre of the Medoc wine region and visits may be arranged for wine lovers through the tourist office.

WARNINGS

The strong stream flows through the harbour as the breakwaters do not reach the bottom. It is best to enter, leave or manoeuvre inside only at local slack water. If early or late, yachts are advised to anchor outside and wait.

APPROACH AND ENTRY

Heading upstream, after passing the Shell Refinery at Trompeloup and No. 43 buoy, the black shuttering of the breakwater will be conspicuous. Heading downstream, after passing No. 45 buoy, identify the entrance before shaping a course to allow for the stream. Approach the S end of the harbour on a W course, allowing for the stream, and round the head of the outer breakwater close to starboard into the harbour. Because of the strong streams, a night entry is not recommended without a previous visit.

BERTHS AND ANCHORAGE

There is a prohibited anchorage, because of cables, 200m S of the entrance. While it is possible to find an anchorage between this and the harbour entrance, it would be safer to the N of the harbour in a suitable depth until daylight and/or slack water. Berths for visitors are on the first two pontoons to starboard inside the entrance.

FACILITIES

1-tonne crane for masting, only usable 3hrs either side of HW. Fuel. Supermarket, shops, chandlery, hotel, restaurants and café-bars nearby.

Point du Jour, Bordeaux

44°53'N 0°32'W

GENERAL

Bordeaux is a very pleasant city and port in the centre of the famous wine-producing area. There are usually berths available at the yacht pontoons by Pont d'Aquitaine. It is not recommended to secure alongside the wharves on the W bank in the city which are high, rough and subject to very strong currents. All needs of yachtsmen can be met in the city. Pont de Pierre is the limit of masted navigation.

It is possible to lock into the basins in the city and if planning more than a short stay this will offer the most peace. A full description of the procedure is in *Biscay Spain*.

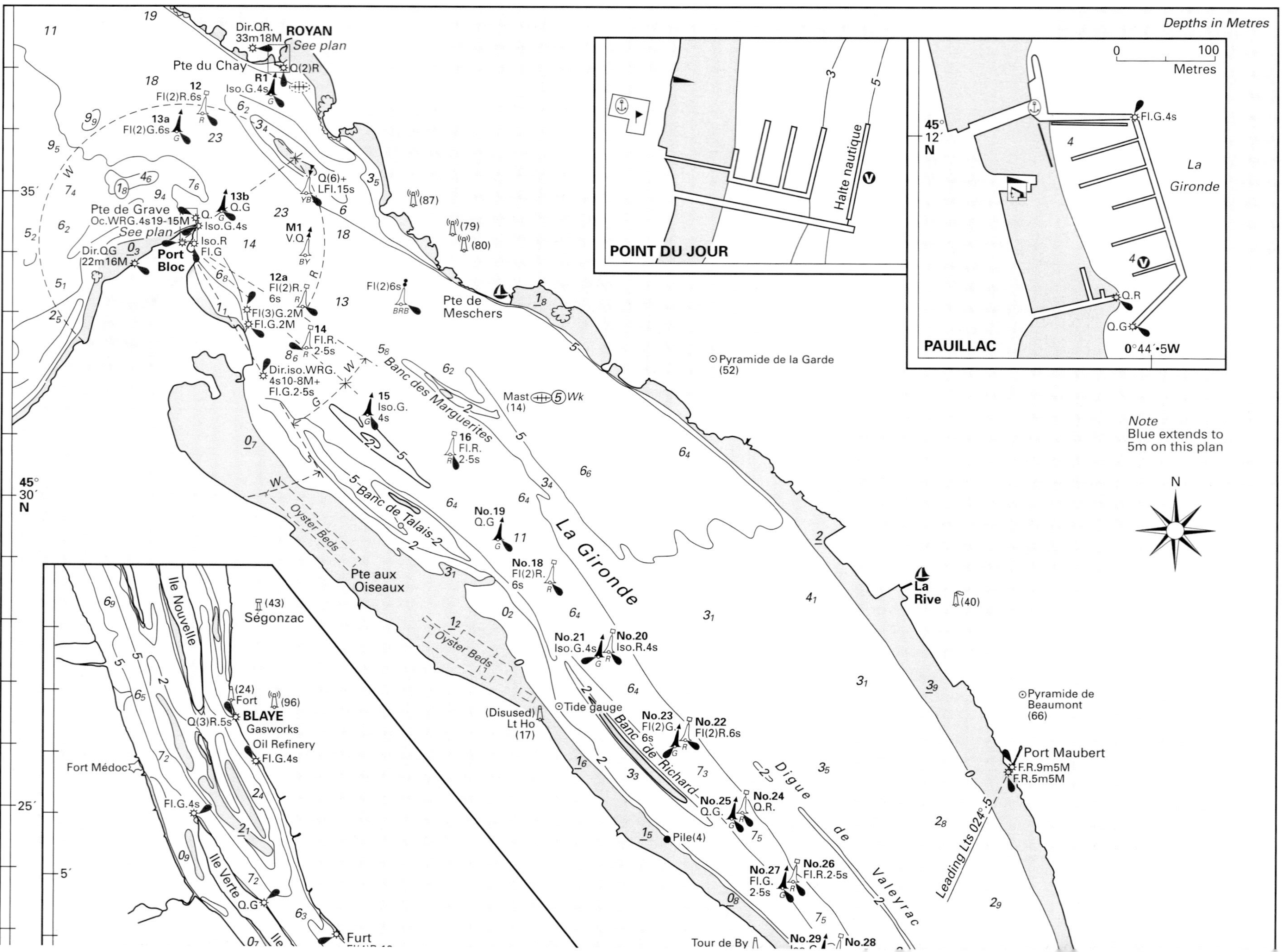
Depths in Metres
Note
Blue extends to
5m on this plan
La Gironde
PAUILLAC
0°44′·5W
POINT DU JOUR
Halte nautique
ROYAN
See plan
Pte du Chay
Pte de Grave
Oc.WRG.4s19-15M
Port Bloc
Pte de Meschers
Banc des Marguerites
Banc de Talais
Pte aux Oiseaux
Oyster Beds
Tide gauge
Banc de Richard
Digue de Valeyrac
Port Maubert
Pyramide de Beaumont
Pyramide de la Garde
La Rive
BLAYE
Gasworks
Oil Refinery
Ile Nouvelle
Ile Verte
Fort Médoc
Ségonzac
Tour de By
Leading Lts 024°·5

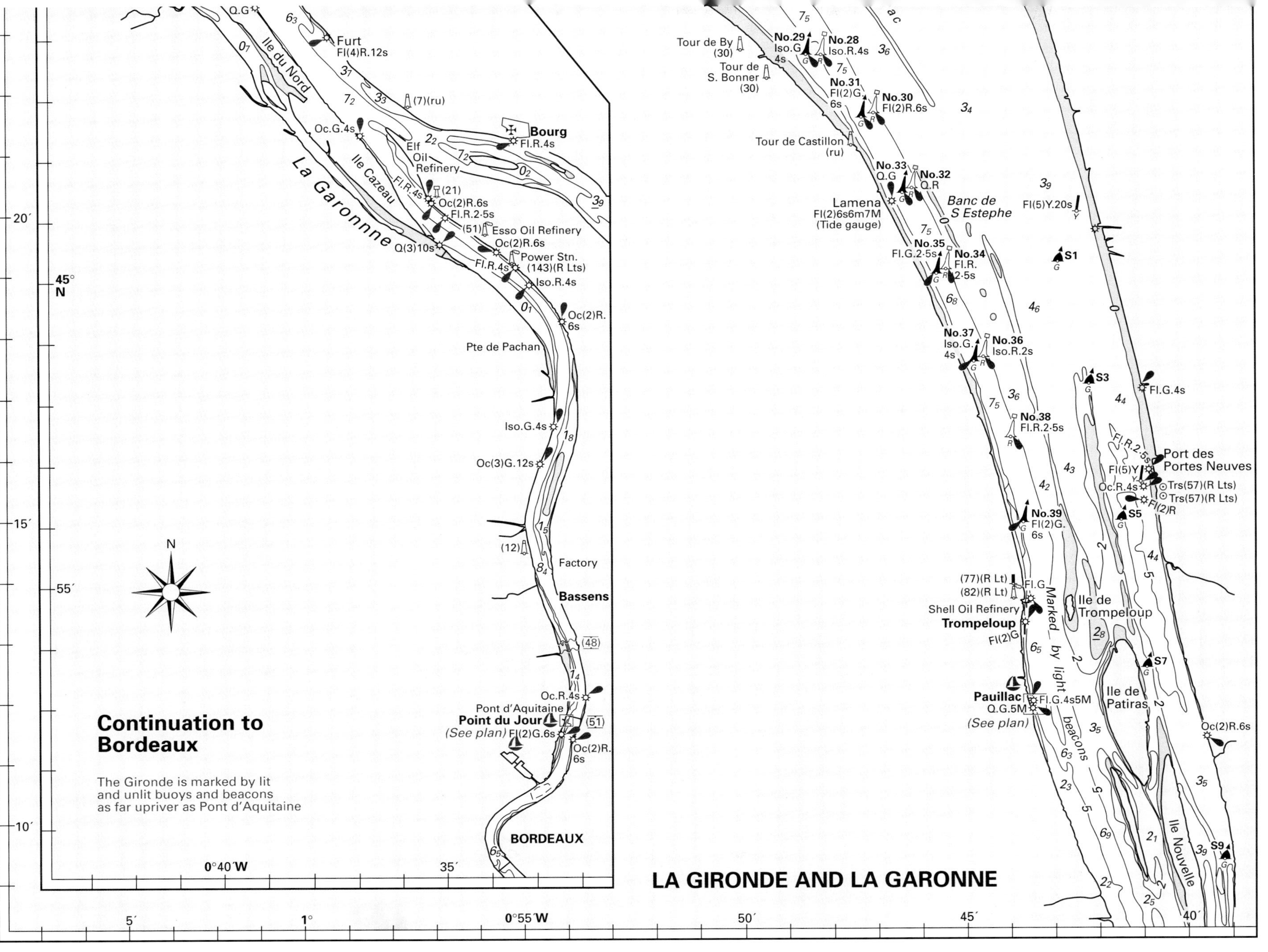
LA GIRONDE AND LA GARONNE
Continuation to Bordeaux
The Gironde is marked by lit and unlit buoys and beacons as far upriver as Pont d'Aquitaine
Tour de By (30)
Tour de S. Bonner (30)
No.29 Iso.G 4s
No.28 Iso.R.4s
No.31 Fl(2)G 6s
No.30 Fl(2)R.6s
Tour de Castillon (ru)
No.33 Q.G
No.32 Q.R
Lamena Fl(2)6s6m7M (Tide gauge)
Banc de S Estephe
Fl(5)Y.20s
S1
No.35 Fl.G.2·5s
No.34 Fl.R. 2·5s
No.37 Iso.G. 4s
No.36 Iso.R.2s
S3
Fl.G.4s
No.38 Fl.R.2·5s
Fl.R.2·5s
Port des Portes Neuves
Fl(5)Y
Oc.R.4s
Trs(57)(R Lts)
Trs(57)(R Lts)
Fl(2)R
S5
No.39 Fl(2)G. 6s
(77)(R Lt)
(82)(R Lt)
Fl.G
Shell Oil Refinery
Trompeloup
Fl(2)G
Marked by light beacons
Ile de Trompeloup
S7
Pauillac
Fl.G.4s5M
Q.G.5M
(See plan)
Ile de Patiras
Oc(2)R.6s
Ile Nouvelle
S9
Q.G
Furt Fl(4)R.12s
Ile du Nord
(7)(ru)
Bourg Fl.R.4s
Oc.G.4s
Elf Oil Refinery
La Garonnne
Ile Cazeau
Fl.R.4s
(21)
Oc(2)R.6s
Fl.R.2·5s
(51) Esso Oil Refinery
Q(3)10s
Oc(2)R.6s
Power Stn. (143)(R Lts)
Fl.R.4s
Iso.R.4s
Oc(2)R. 6s
Pte de Pachan
Iso.G.4s
Oc(3)G.12s
(12)
Factory
Bassens
(48)
Oc.R.4s
Pont d'Aquitaine
Point du Jour
(51)
(See plan) Fl(2)G.6s
Oc(2)R. 6s
BORDEAUX
45° N
0°40'W
0°55'W

Plan 83

BERTHS
Berth alongside the outer pontoon in 3m and report to the Yacht Club. There are special berthing arms to hold yachts off the pontoon as there is considerable wash from passing vessels.

FACILITIES
Fuel. A small crane is available for masts up to 12m long but it is not a very happy arrangement except at slack water. Larger, or through-deck stepped, masts must be shifted in the basins or in one of the ports downstream. All facilities in the city. Should parts of the Midi be unexpectedly closed, the Club Sport Nautique de la Gironde may be able to arrange overland transport for yachts.

The small marina at Le Point du Jour, Bordeaux just above Pont d'Aquitaine

Pont de Pierre marks the upper limit of the Gironde for masted yachts. The strength of the stream can be clearly seen

Appendix

A. TIDES - MEAN SPRING AND NEAP CURVES

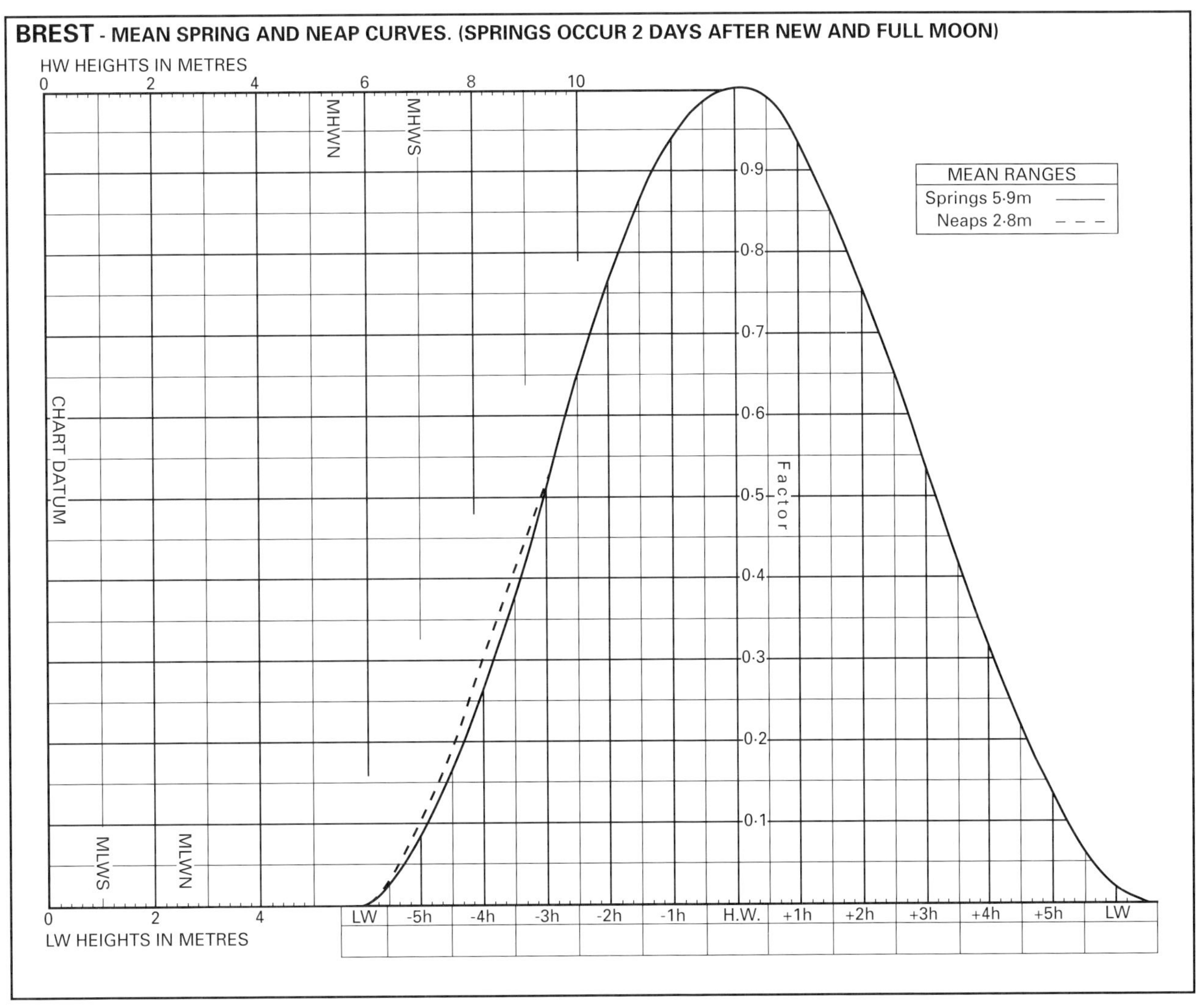

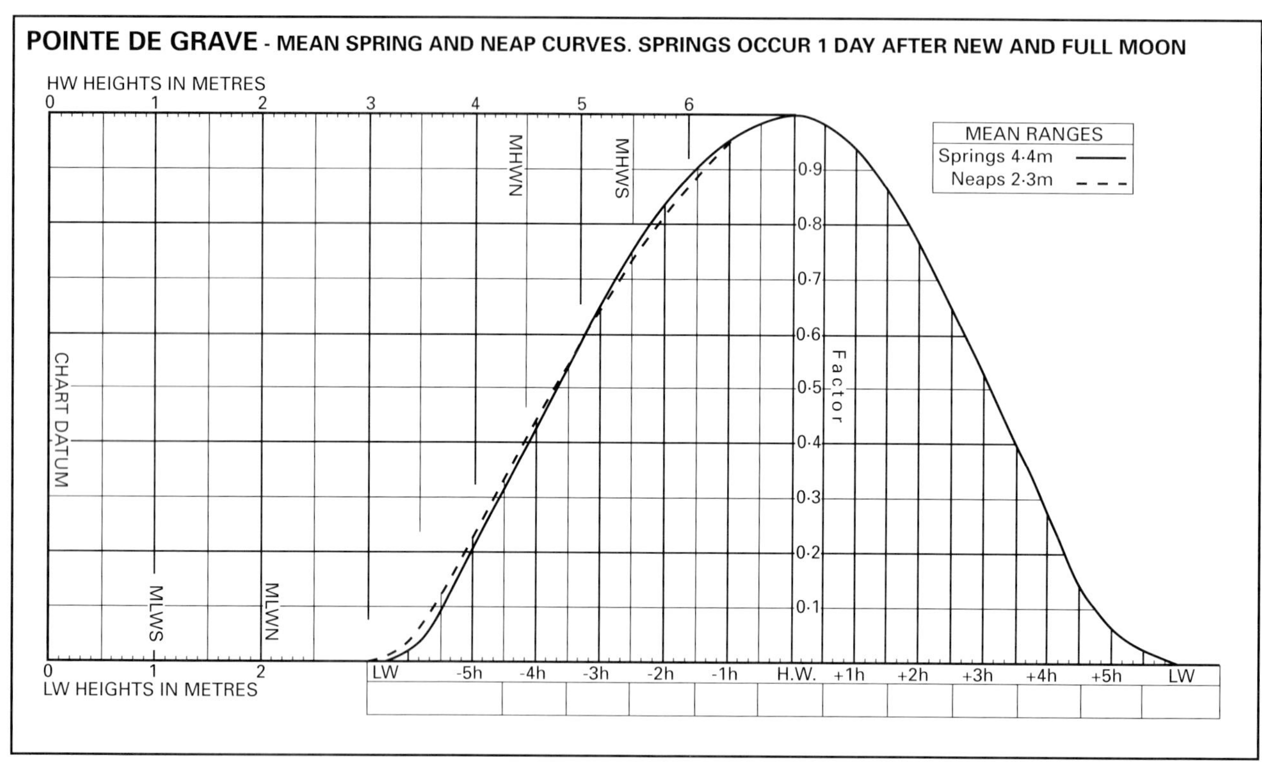

B. FRENCH COEFFICIENTS AND HEIGHTS OF HIGH AND LOW WATER

Brest			Pte de Grave	
HW	*LW*	*Coefficient*	*HW*	*LW*
(metres)			*(metres)*	
7.7	0.2	120	5.9	0.5
7.4	0.5	110	5.7	0.7
7.2	0.8	100	5.5	0.9
6.9	1.0	95	5.4	1.0
		Mean springs		
6.8	1.2	90	5.3	1.1
6.6	1.3	85	5.2	1.2
6.5	1.5	80	5.1	1.3
6.3	1.6	75	5.0	1.5
6.2	1.8	70	4.9	1.6
6.0	2.0	65	4.8	1.7
5.9	2.1	60	4.7	1.8
5.7	2.3	55	4.6	1.9
5.6	2.4	50	4.5	2.0
5.4	2.6	45	4.4	2.1
		Mean Neaps		
5.3	2.8	40	4.3	2.2
5.0	3.1	30	4.1	2.4
4.7	3.4	20	3.9	2.6

Index